STREE

Carmarthenshire
Pembrokeshire
Swansea

ATLAS STRYDOEDD
Abertawe, Sir Benfro, Sir Gaerfyrddin

First published in 2005 by

Philip's, a division of
Octopus Publishing Group Ltd
2-4 Heron Quays, London E14 4JP

First edition 2005
First impression 2005

ISBN-10 0-540-08662-2 (pocket)
ISBN-13 978-0-540-08662-7 (pocket)

© Philip's 2005

Ordnance Survey®

Printed and bound in Spain
by Cayfosa-Quebecor

Contents

III   **Administrative and Postcode boundaries**

IV   **Key to map pages**

VI   **Route planning**

X   **Key to map symbols**

2   **Street maps** at 1⅓ inches to 1 mile

118   **Street maps** at 2⅔ inches to 1 mile

174   **Street map of Swansea city centre**
at 5⅓ inches to 1 mile

175   **Index** of towns and villages

178   **Index** of streets, hospitals, industrial estates, railway
stations, schools, shopping centres, universities
and places of interest

Digital Data

The exceptionally high-quality mapping found in this atlas is available as digital data in TIFF format, which is
easily convertible to other bitmapped (raster) image formats.

The index is also available in digital form as a standard database table. It contains all the details found in
the printed index together with the National Grid reference for the map square in which each entry is named.

For further information and to discuss your requirements, please contact Philip's on 020 7644 6932 or
james.mann@philips-maps.co.uk

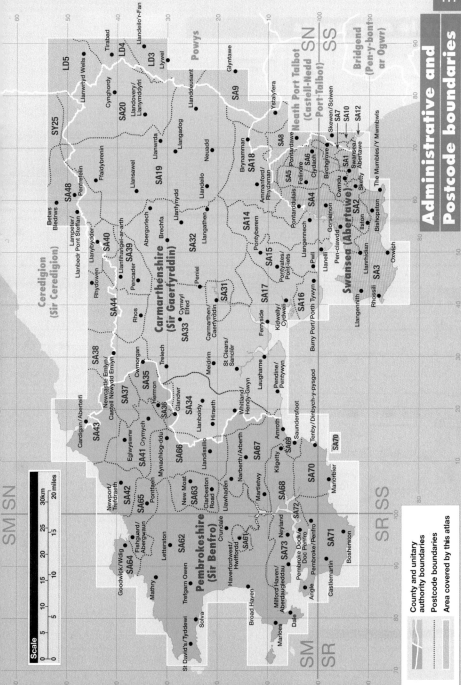

Administrative and Postcode boundaries

Scale

0   5   10   15   20   25   30km
0   5   10   15   20 miles

County and unitary authority boundaries

Postcode boundaries

Area covered by this atlas

SM | SN

SN
SS

SR | SS

SM
SR

Ceredigion (Sir Ceredigion)

Powys

Carmarthenshire (Sir Gaerfyrddin)

Pembrokeshire (Sir Benfro)

Swansea (Abertawe)

Neath Port Talbot (Castell-Nedd Port Talbot)

Bridgend (Pen-y-bont ar Ogwr)

IV

Key to map pages

174 **Map pages at** 5⅓ inches to 1 mile

139 **Map pages at** 2⅔ inches to 1 mile

41 **Map pages at** 1⅓ inches to 1 mile

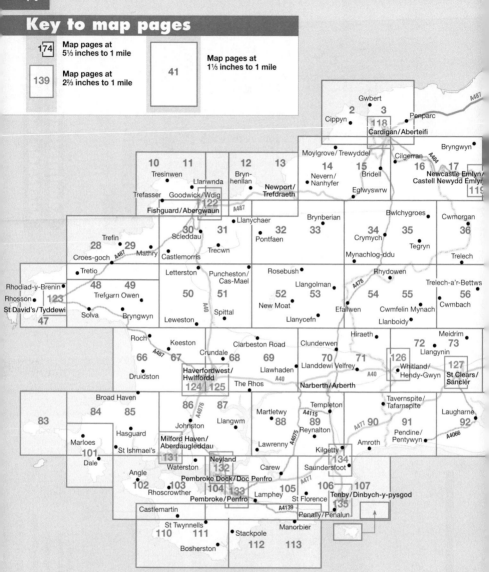

Gwbert

2 2 **3** Penparc

Cippyn

118
Cardigan/Aberteifi

Bryngwyn

Moylgrove/Trewyddel Cilgerran

10 **11** **12** **13** **14** **15** **16** **17**
Tresinwen Bryn- Nevern/ Bridell Newcastle Emlyn/
Llanwnda henllan Nanhyfer Castell Newydd Emlyn
Trefasser Goodwick/Wdig **Newport/** Eglwyswrw **119**
Trefdraeth
122
Fishguard/Abergwaun Brynberian Bwlchygroes Cwmorgan
Llanychaer
30 **31** **32** **33** **34** **35** **36**
Scleddau Pontfaen Crymych Tegryn
28 **29** Trecwn Trelech
Trefin Mynachlog-ddu
Croes-goch Mathry Castlemorris
Tretio Letterston Puncheston/ Rosebush Rhydowen Trelech-a'r-Bettws
Cas-Mael
Rhodiad-y-Brenin **48** **49** **50** **51** Llangolman **54** **55** **56**
Rhosson Trefgarn Owen **52** **53** Cwmfelin Mynach Cwmbach
St David's/Tyddewi Spittal New Moat Efailwen Llanboidy
47 Solva Bryngwyn Llanycefn
Leweston
Roch Keeston Clarbeston Road Clunderwen Hiraeth Meidrim
66 **67** Crundale **68** **69** **70** **71** **72** **73**
Druidston Llanddewi Velfrey **126** Llangynin
Haverfordwest/ Llawhaden Whitland/ **127**
Hwlffordd The Rhos Hendy-Gwyn St Clears/
124 **125** **Narberth/Arberth** Sancler
Broad Haven Tavernspite/
84 **85** **86** **87** Templeton Tafarnspite Laugharne
Martletwy **88** **89** **90** **91** **92**
83 Johnston Llangwm Reynalton Pendine/
Hasguard Lawrenny Amroth Pentywyn
Marloes St Ishmael's Milford Haven/ Kilgetty **134**
101 Aberdaugleddau **131** Neyland **132** **106** **107**
Dale Angle Waterston Carew Saundersfoot Tenby/Dinbych-y-pysgod
102 Pembroke Dock/Doc Penfro **104** **133** **105** **135**
Rhoscrowther Pembroke/Penfro Lamphey St Florence
Castlemartin Penally/Penalun
110 St Twynnells **111** Stackpole Manorbier
Bosherston **112** **113**

Scale

0   5   10   15 km

0   5   10 miles

Route Planning

Scale

| 0 | | 1 | 2 | 3 | 4 | 5 | | 6 miles |

| 0 | | 5 | | 10 km |

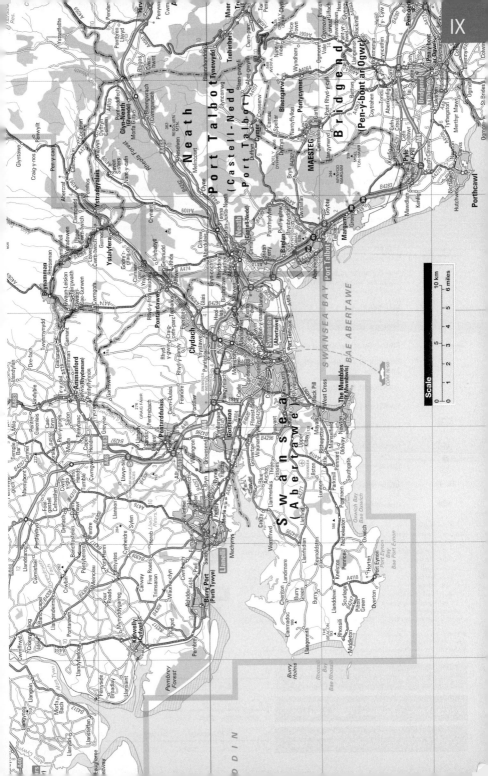

X   Allwedd i symbolau'r map

	Traffordd gyda rhif y gyffordd		**Gorsaf ambiwlans**
	Prif dramwyfeydd – ffordd ddeuol/un lôn		**Gorsaf gwylwyr y glannau**
	Ffordd A – ffordd ddeuol/un lôn		**Gorsaf Dân**
	Ffordd B – ffordd ddeuol/un lôn		**Swyddfa'r heddlu**
	Ffyrdd bychan – ffordd ddeuol/un lôn		**Mynedfa damwain ac argyfwng i'r ysbyty**
	Ffyrdd bychan eraill – ffordd ddeuol/un lôn	**H**	**Ysbyty**
	Ffordd yn cael ei hadeiladu		**Lle o addoliad**
	Twnnel, ffordd dan orchudd	**i**	**Canolfan gwybodaeth** (a'r agor drwy'r flwyddyn)
	Trac gwledig, ffordd breifat, neu ffordd mewn ardal ddinesig		**Canolfan siopa**
	Llidiart neu rhwystr i draffig (gall fod cyfyngiadau ddim yn ddilys ar gyfer bob amser neu i bob drafnidiaeth)	**P** **P&R**	**Parcio, Parcio a chludo**
	Llwybr, llwybr march, cilffordd yn agored i bob trafnidiaeth, ffordd a ddefnyddir yn lwybr cyhoeddus	**PO**	**Swyddfa'r post**
	Mân cerddwyr	Ӽ	**Safle gwersylla, Safle carafan**
DY7	**Ffiniau codau-post**		**Cwrs golff**
	Ffiniau Sir ac awdurdod unedol		**Safle picnic**
	Rheilffordd, twnnel, rheilffordd yn cael ei hadeiladu		**Adeiladau pwysig, ysgolion, colegau, prifysgolion ac ysbytai**
	Tramffordd, tramffordd yn cael ei hadeiladu	Prim Sch	**Ardal adeiledig**
	Rheilffordd ar raddfa fychan		**Coed**
Walsall	**Gorsaf rheilffordd**	River Ouse	**Dŵr llanw, Enw dŵr**
South Shields	**Gorsaf rheilffordd breifat**		**Dim dŵr llanw** – llyn, afon, camlas neu nant
	Gorsaf metro	⟨ ⟩ ⟩ (	**Loc, cored, twnnel**
	Atalfa tram, atalfa tram yn cael ei hadeiladu	Church	**Hynafiaeth anrhufeinig**
	Gorsaf fysiau	ROMAN FORT	**Hynafiaeth rhufeinig**

Acad	**Academi**	Inst	**Institiwt**	PH	**Tŷ tafarn**
Allot Gdns	**Gerddi ar osod**	Ct	**Llys cyfraith**	Recn Gd	**Maes chwaraeon**
Cemy	**Mynwent**	L Ctr	**Canolfan hamdden**	Resr	**Cronfa ddŵr**
C Ctr	**Canolfan ddinesig**			Ret Pk	**Parc adwerthu**
CH	**Tŷ Clwb**	LC	**Croesfan wastad**	Sch	**Ysgol**
Coll	**Coleg**	Liby	**Llyfrgell**	Sh Ctr	**Canolfan Siopa**
Crem	**Amlosgfa**	Mkt	**Marchnad**	TH	**Neuadd y dref**
Ent	**Menter**	Meml	**Coffa**	Trad Est	**Ystad Fasnachol**
Ex H	**Neuadd Arddangos**	Mon	**Cofgolofn**	Univ	**Prifysgol**
Ind Est	**Ystad ddiwydiannol**	Mus	**Amgueddfa**	W Twr	**Twrdŵr**
IRB Sta	**Gorsaf bad achub y glannau**	Obsy	**Arsyllfa**	Wks	**Gwaith**
		Pal	**Palas brenhinol**	YH	**Hostel ieuenctid**

■ Y mae'r rhifau bach o gwmpas ochrau'r mapiau yn dynodi llinelli grid cenedlaethol 1 cilomedr
■ Mae'r ffin llwyd tywyll ar ochr fewn rhai tudalennau yn dynodi nad yw'r mapio yn canlyn ymlaen i'r tudalen gyffiniol

87	**Arwyddion dalennau cyfagos a bandiau gorymylon** Y mae lliw y saeth â'r band yn dynodi gradd y ddalen cyfagos â'r ddalen gorymyl (gwelwch y graddau islaw)
228	

Mapio wedi ei fwyhau yn unig

	Rheilffordd neu gorsaf bws adeilad
	Man o ddiddordeb
	Parcdir

Gradd y mapiau ar y dalennau gyda rhifau glas yw 4.2 cm i 1 km • 2⅔ modfedd i 1 filltir • 1: 23810

0	¼	½	¾	1 milltir
0	250m	500m	750m	1 km

Gradd y mapiau ar y dalennau gyda rhifau gwyrdd yw is 2.1 i 1 km • 1⅓ modfedd i 1 filltir • 1: 47620

0	¼	½	¾	1 milltir
0	250m	500m	750m	1 km

Gradd y mapiau ar y dalennau gyda rhifau coch yw is 8.4 i 1 km • 5⅓ modfedd i 1 filltir • 1: 11900

0	220 llathenni	440 llathenni	660 llathenni	½ milltir
0	125m	250m	375m	½ km

Symbol	Description
Motorway with junction number	Motorway with junction number
Primary route – dual/single carriageway	Primary route – dual/single carriageway
A road – dual/single carriageway	A road – dual/single carriageway
B road – dual/single carriageway	B road – dual/single carriageway
Minor road – dual/single carriageway	Minor road – dual/single carriageway
Other minor road – dual/single carriageway	Other minor road – dual/single carriageway
Road under construction	Road under construction
Tunnel, covered road	Tunnel, covered road
Rural track, private road or narrow road in urban area	Rural track, private road or narrow road in urban area
Gate or obstruction to traffic (restrictions may not apply at all times or to all vehicles)	Gate or obstruction to traffic (restrictions may not apply at all times or to all vehicles)
Path, bridleway, byway open to all traffic, road used as a public path	Path, bridleway, byway open to all traffic, road used as a public path
Pedestrianised area	Pedestrianised area
DY7 — Postcode boundaries	DY7 — Postcode boundaries
County and unitary authority boundaries	County and unitary authority boundaries
Railway, tunnel, railway under construction	Railway, tunnel, railway under construction
Tramway, tramway under construction	Tramway, tramway under construction
Miniature railway	Miniature railway
Walsall — Railway station	Walsall — Railway station
Private railway station	Private railway station
South Shields — Metro station	South Shields — Metro station
Tram stop, tram stop under construction	Tram stop, tram stop under construction
Bus, coach station	Bus, coach station

Ambulance station
Coastguard station
Fire station
Police station
Accident and Emergency entrance to hospital
H Hospital
+ Place of worship
i Information Centre (open all year)
Shopping Centre
P **P&R** Parking, Park and Ride
PO Post Office
Å 🚐 Camping site, caravan site
Golf course
Picnic site
Prim Sch — Important buildings, schools, colleges, universities and hospitals
Built up area
Woods
River Ouse — Tidal water, water name
Non-tidal water – lake, river, canal or stream
Lock, weir, tunnel
Church Non-Roman antiquity
ROMAN FORT Roman antiquity

87 Adjoining page indicators and overlap bands
228 The colour of the arrow and the band indicates the scale of the adjoining or overlapping page (see scales below)

Enlarged mapping only

Railway or bus station building
Place of interest
Parkland

Acad	Academy	Inst	Institute	Recn Gd	Recreation Ground
Allot Gdns	Allotments	Ct	Law Court		
Cemy	Cemetery	L Ctr	Leisure Centre	Resr	Reservoir
C Ctr	Civic Centre	LC	Level Crossing	Ret Pk	Retail Park
CH	Club House	Liby	Library	Sch	School
Coll	College	Mkt	Market	Sh Ctr	Shopping Centre
Crem	Crematorium	Meml	Memorial	TH	Town Hall/House
Ent	Enterprise	Mon	Monument	Trad Est	Trading Estate
Ex H	Exhibition Hall	Mus	Museum	Univ	University
Ind Est	Industrial Estate	Obsy	Observatory	W Twr	Water Tower
IRB Sta	Inshore Rescue Boat Station	Pal	Royal Palace	Wks	Works
		PH	Public House	YH	Youth Hostel

■ The small numbers around the edges of the maps identify the 1 kilometre National Grid lines
■ The dark grey border on the inside edge of some pages indicates that the mapping does not continue onto the adjacent page

The scale of the maps on the pages numbered in blue is 4.2 cm to 1 km • 2⅔ inches to 1 mile • 1: 23810	0 — ¼ — ½ — ¾ — 1 mile 0 — 250m — 500m — 750m — 1 kilometre
The scale of the maps on pages numbered in green is 2.1 cm to 1 km • 1⅓ inches to 1 mile • 1: 47620	0 — ¼ — ½ — ¾ — 1 mile 0 — 250m — 500m — 750m — 1kilometre
The scale of the maps on pages numbered in red is 8.4 cm to 1 km • 5⅓ inches to 1 mile • 1: 11900	0 — 220 yards — 440 yards — 660 yards — ½ mile 0 — 125m — 250m — 375m — ½ kilometre

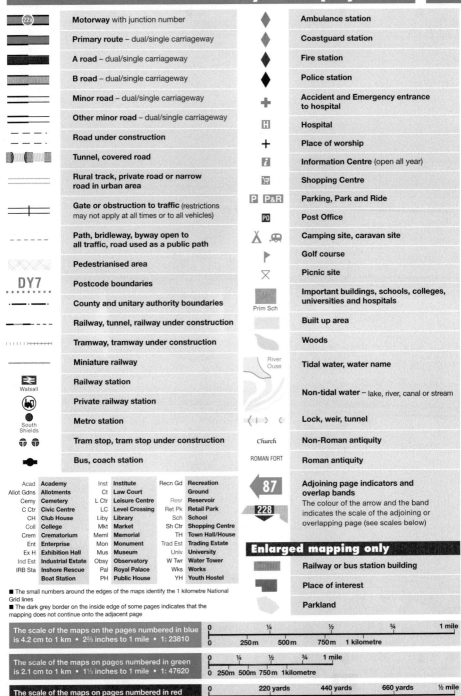

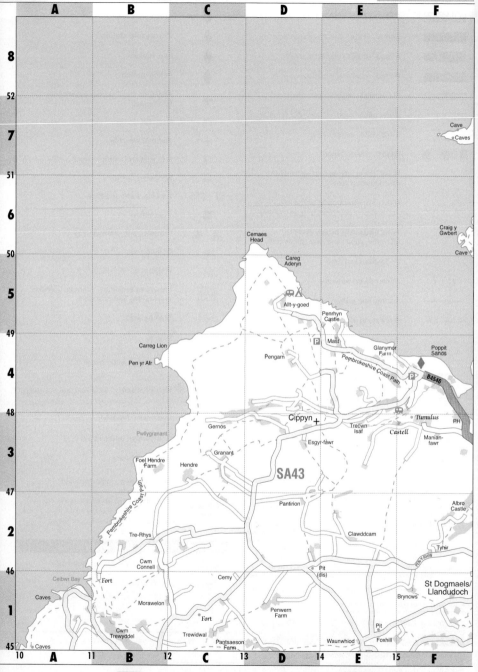

Cave
Caves

Craig y
Gwbert

Cave

Cemaes
Head

Careg
Aderyn

Allt-y-goed

Penrhyn
Castle

Carreg Lion

Pen yr Afr

Pengarn

Mast

Glanymor
Farm

Poppit
Sands

Pembrokeshire Coast Path

B4546

Cippyn

Gernos

Pwllygranant

Trecwn
Isaf

Castell

Tumulus

PH

Manian-
fawr

Esgyr-fàwr

Granant

SA43

Foel Hendre
Farm

Hendre

Pantirion

Pembrokeshire Coast Path

Clawddcam

Albro
Castle

Tre-Rhys

Tyhir

FFORDD Y RHIW

Cwm
Connell

Ceibwr Bay

Fort

Cemy

Pit
(dis)

St Dogmaels/
Llandudoch

Caves

Morawelon

Bryncws

Cwm
Trewyddel

Fort

Trewidwal

Penwern
Farm

Pit

Foxhill

Caves

Pantsaeson
Farm

Waunwhiod

Scale: 1⅓ inches to 1 mile
0 ¼ ½ mile
0 250m 500m 750m 1 km

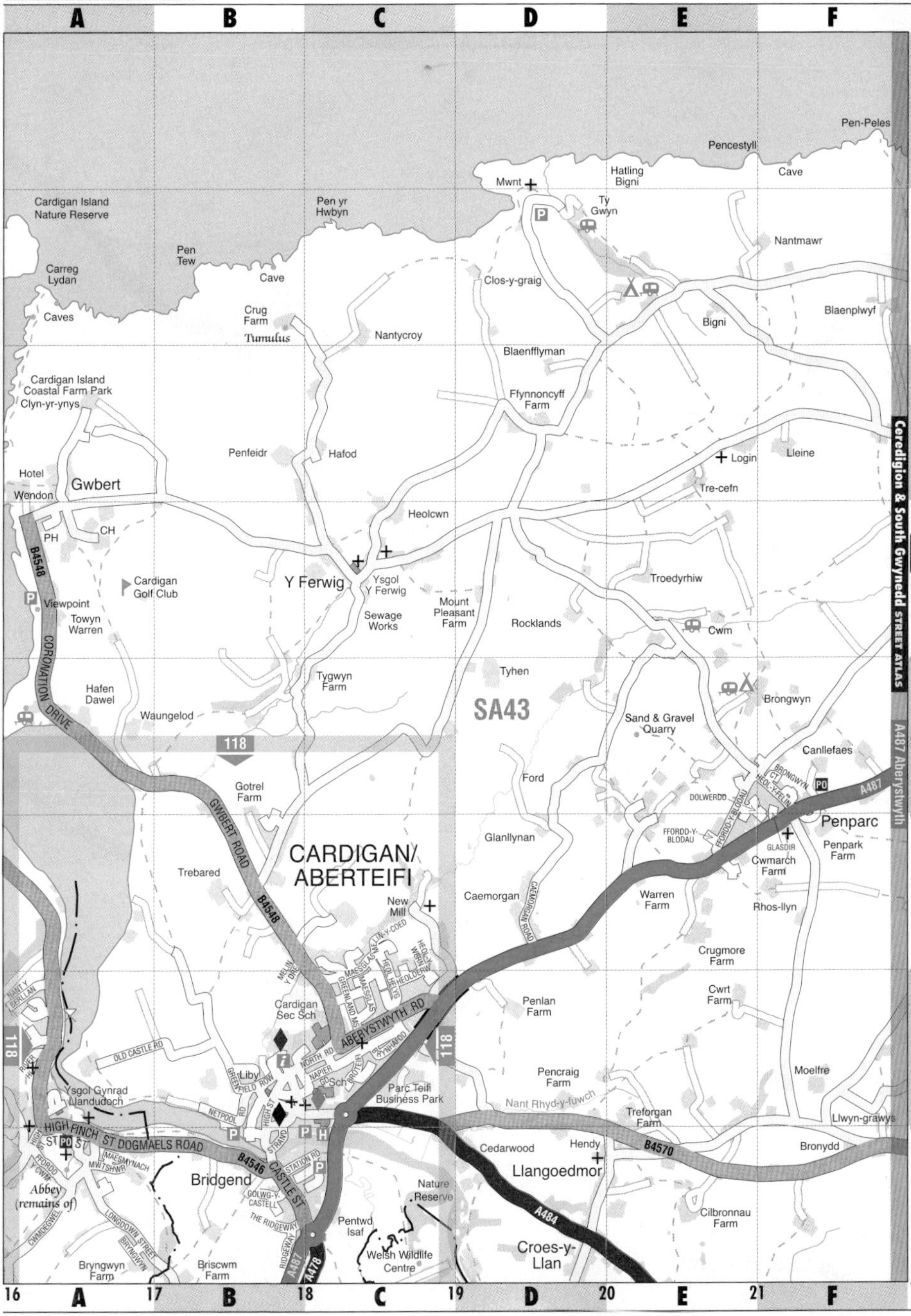
A
B
C
D
E
F
8
7
6
5
4
3
2
1
52
51
50
49
48
47
46
45
16
17
18
19
20
21
Pen-Peles
Pencestyll
Cave
Hatling Bigni
Mwnt
Ty Gwyn
Cardigan Island Nature Reserve
Pen yr Hwbyn
Nantmawr
Pen Tew
Carreg Lydan
Cave
Clos-y-graig
Blaenplwyf
Caves
Crug Farm
Tumulus
Nantycroy
Bigni
Blaenfflyman
Cardigan Island Coastal Farm Park
Clyn-yr-ynys
Ffynnoncyff Farm
Penfeidr
Hafod
Login
Lleine
Hotel Wendon
Gwbert
Tre-cefn
Heolcwn
PH
CH
B4548
Cardigan Golf Club
Y Ferwig
Ysgol Y Ferwig
Troedyrhiw
Viewpoint
Towyn Warren
Sewage Works
Mount Pleasant Farm
Rocklands
Cwm
CORONATION DRIVE
Tygwyn Farm
Tyhen
Hafen Dawel
Brongwyn
Waungelod
SA43
Sand & Gravel Quarry
118
Canllefaes
Ford
Gotrel Farm
BRONGWYN CT
HEOL-Y-FELIN
DOLWERDD
A487
Penparc
FFORDD-Y-BLODAU
GLASDIR
GWBERT ROAD
Glanllynan
Penpark Farm
CARDIGAN/ ABERTEIFI
Cwmarch Farm
Trebared
Caemorgan
Warren Farm
Rhos-llyn
New Mill
CAEMORGAN ROAD
LLYN-Y-COED
Crugmore Farm
MAESGLAS
HEOL HELYG
HEOLDERW
GREENLAND MS
Cwrt Farm
NANT Y BERLLAN
Cardigan Sec Sch
Penlan Farm
ABERYSTWYTH RD
OLD CASTLE RD
Moelfre
Liby
NORTH RD
NAPIER
Sch
BRUTEIFI
PYNHAFOD
Pencraig Farm
GREENFIELD ROW
Parc Teifi Business Park
Ysgol Gynradd Llandudoch
NETPOOL RD
Nant Rhyd-y-fuwch
Treforgan Farm
Llwyn-grawys
HIGH ST
FINCH ST
ST DOGMAELS ROAD
B4570
Bronydd
STRAND
Cedarwood
Hendy
MWTSHWR
MAESMYNACH
B4546
CASTLE ST
STATION RD
Llangoedmor
Abbey (remains of)
Bridgend
Nature Reserve
GOLWG-Y-CASTELL
THE RIDGEWAY
A484
Cilbronnau Farm
CWMDEGWEL
LONGDOWN STREET
BRYNGWYN
Pentwd Isaf
Welsh Wildlife Centre
Croes-y-Llan
Bryngwyn Farm
Briscwm Farm
RIDGEWAY
A487
A478
Ceredigion & South Gwynedd STREET ATLAS
A487 Aberystwyth

118 15 16

For full street detail of the highlighted area see page 118.

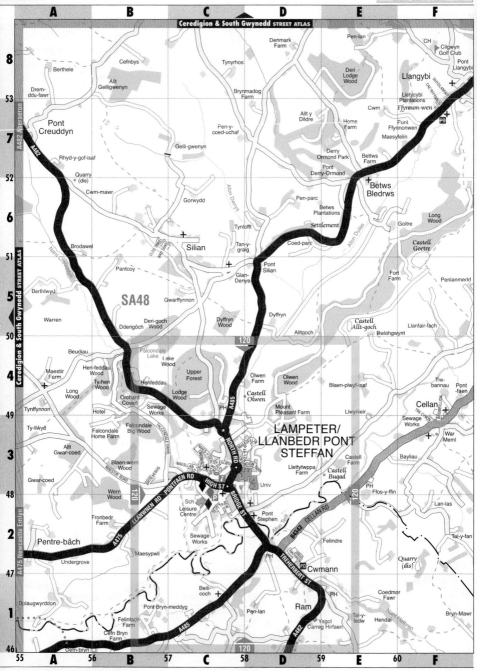

Scale: 1⅓ inches to 1 mile

0   ¼   ½ mile
0   250m 500m 750m 1 km

Ceredigion & South Gwynedd STREET ATLAS

CH
Cilgwyn
Golf Club
Pen-lan   Pont
Denmark   Llangybi
Farm   +
Deri   Llangybi
Lodge   Lletycybi
Wood   Plantations
Tynyrhos   Cwm   Ffynnon-wen
Brynmadog   PO
Farm   Allt y   Pont
            Dildre   Home   Flynnonwen
Pen-y-   Farm   Maesyfelin
coed-uchaf   Derry
                           Ormond Park Bettws
Gelli-gwenyn   Pont   Farm
                           Derry-Ormond
                                         + Betws
                           Pen-parc   Bledrws
Gorwydd   Betws
                           Plantations   Goitre
                    Tynlofft   Long
            +   Settlement   Wood
            Silian   Tan-y-   Castell
                     graig Coed-parc   Goetre
            Glan-   Pont
            Denys   Silian   Fort
Pantcoy   Farm   Penlanmedd
Gwarffynnon Dyffryn
             Wood   Dyffryn   Llanfair-fach
SA48   Castell
        Deri-goch   Allt-goch   Bwlohgwynt
Dderigôch Wood   Alltgoch
                                        120
Beudiau   Falcondale   Olwen   Olwen   Tre-
          Lake   Lake   Wood   Wood   bannau Pont
Hen-feddau Wood   -faen
Ty-hen   Upper   Castell
Wood   Henfeddau   Forest   Olwen   Cellan
Orchard   Lodge   Mount
Covert   Wood   PH   A485 Pleasant Farm
Hotel   Llwynieir   Sewage
         Falcondale   War   Works
Falcondale Big Wood   LAMPETER/   Meml
Home Farm   LLANBEDR PONT
Ty-llwyd   STEFFAN   +
                      Univ Castell Castell
          Blaen-wern   Bugad   Llettytwppa
          Wood   Farm   Bayliau   Lan-las
Gwar-coed   Wern   HIGH ST   PH Ffos-y-ffin
               Wood   PH
                         Sch   Tal-y-
Fronbedr   Leisure   Pont   fedw
Farm   Centre   Stephen   Felindre
Pentre-bâch   Quarry
         Sewage   (dis)
Maesypwll Works   Cwmann
Undergrove   PH   Ram
Dolaugwyrddon   Pen-lan Coedmor
            Pont Bryn-meddyg   Fawr
Beili-   Bryn-Mawr
coch   Ysgol Tal-y-
Felinfach   Carreg Hirfaen fedw Hendai
Farm Cefn Bryn
      Farm
Cefn-bryn   120

For full street detail of the
highlighted area see page 120.

22

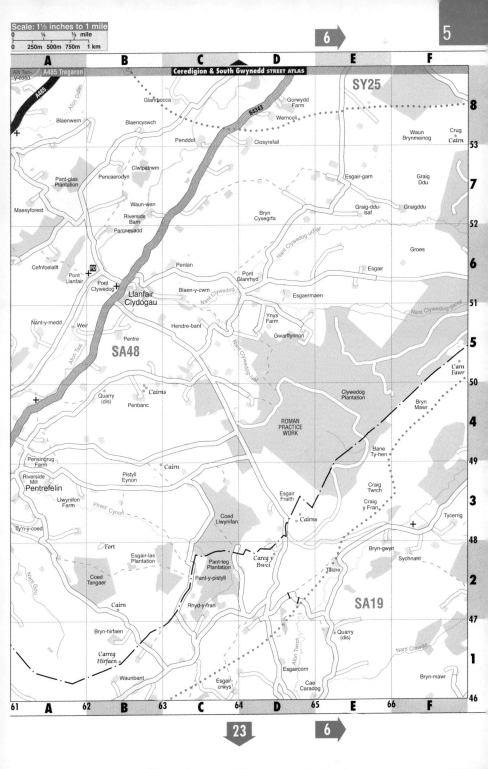

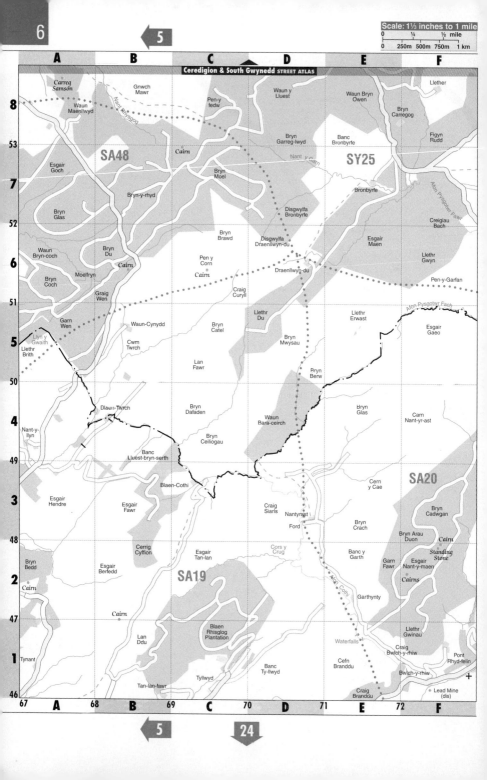

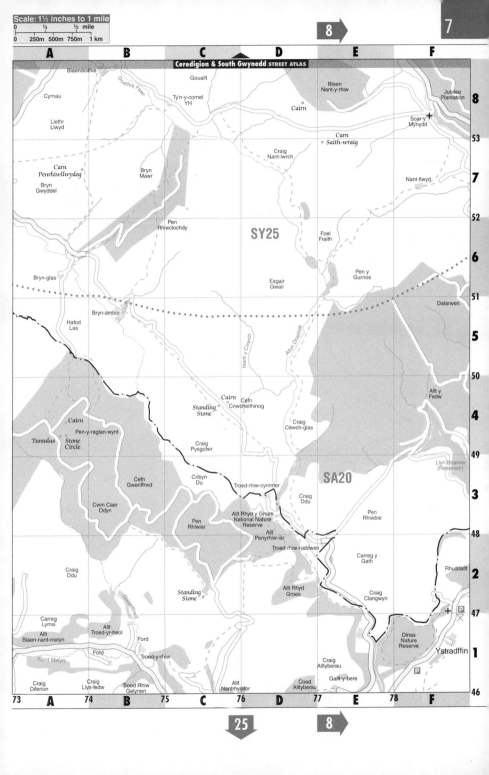

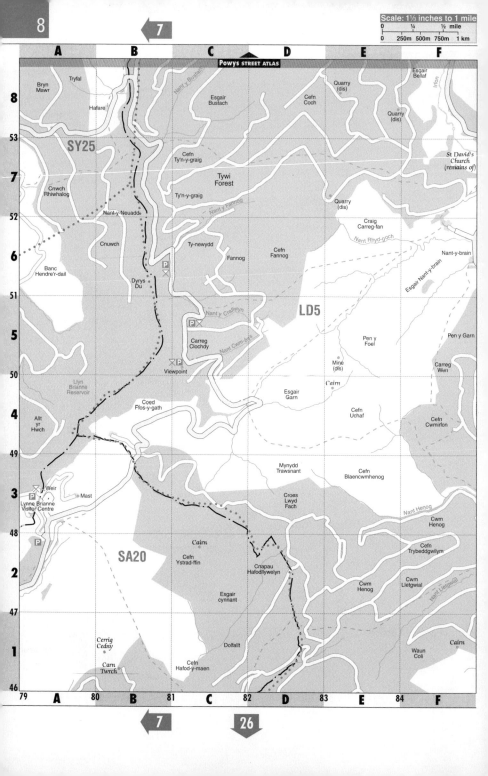

Scale: 1⅓ inches to 1 mile

0   ¼   ½   mile
0   250m 500m 750m 1 km

Powys STREET ATLAS

A   **B**   **C**   **D**   **E**   **F**

8

Bryn
Mawr

Tryfal

Hafare

Esgair
Bustach

Cefn
Coch

Quarry
(dis)

Esgair
Bellaf

Irfon

Quarry
(dis)

53

SY25

Cnwch
Rhiwhalog

Cefn
Ty'n-y-graig

Tywi
Forest

St David's
Church
(remains of)

7

Nant-y-Neuadd

Ty'n-y-graig

Nant y Fannog

Quarry
(dis)

Craig
Carreg-fan

52

Cnuwch

Ty-newydd

Fannog

Cefn
Fannog

Nant Rhyd-goch

Nant-y-brain

6

Banc
Hendre'r-dail

Dyrys
Du

Esgair Nant-y-brain

51

Nant y Crafiwyn

LD5

Pen y Garn

5

Carreg
Clochdy

Nant Cwm-brif

Pen y
Foel

Carreg
Wen

50

Viewpoint

Mine
(dis)

Cairn

Llyn
Brianne
Reservoir

Coed
Ffos-y-gath

Esgair
Garn

Cefn
Uchaf

Cefn
Cwmirfon

4

Allt
yr
Hwch

49

Weir

Mast

Mynydd
Trawsnant

Cefn
Blaencwmhenog

Nant Henog

Cwm
Henog

3

Lynne Brianne
Visitor Centre

Croes
Lwyd
Fach

48

Cairn

SA20

Cefn
Ystrad-ffin

Cnapau
Hafodllywelyn

Cwm
Henog

Cefn
Trybeddgwilym

2

Esgair
cynnant

Cwm
Henog

Cwm
Lletgwial

Nant Llennwint

47

Cerrig
Cedny

Dolfallt

Cairn

1

Carn
Twrch

Cefn
Hafod-y-maen

Waun
Coli

46

79   **A**   **80**   **B**   **81**   **C**   **82**   **D**   **83**   **E**   **84**   **F**

Scale: 1⅓ inches to 1 mile

0 ¼ ½ mile
0 250m 500m 750m 1 km

A **B** **C** **D** **E** **F**

Shaft

Bryn Clun
Quarry (dis)
Glangwesyn
Bryn Mawr
Cefn-cendu-isaf
Lan Uchaf
Quarry (dis)

Tŷ-mawr
Llethr Melyn
Cairn
Garn Wen

Cefn-cendu-uchaf
Llofft-y-bardd

Pentwyn Farm
Carn Rhys-Rowland
Banc Paderau
Bryn
Graig y Cwm

Abergwesyn
Llethr Dal-iar
Cefn Waun-lwyd
Cairn
Esgair-las
Allt-y-gest
Llwyn Madoc
Cynfiad

Ffynnon Ffos-yr-haidd (Spring)
Cribyn Bedw
Coed y Felin
Llyn Cwmamell
Cairn

Crug Farm
Cefn Crug
Crugwydd
Cwm Siâms
Cefn Cynllaith
Nant yr Annell
Cwm Annell

Cefn Pen-y-bont
Cwm Cerdin
Esgair Fraith
Cefn Blaeneinon

Pwllbo
Irfon Forest
Craig Disgwylfa
Pen Disgwylfa
LD5
Bwlchmawr
Tir-gorw
Nant Eirion

Craig Dinas Fach
Penybont Uchaf
Pen Beddowen
Nant-y-cerdin
Carcwm
Llwynmeurig Farm
Brynarth

Llethr Penygarreg
Waterfall
Esgair Foel
Pen y Garn-goch
Penfedw
Troedrhiw-goch

Mine (dis)
Standing Stone
Waterfall
Coed Alltwinau
Mynydd Gwyn
Pistyllgwyn
Ffosyrhyddod
Coed Llawes-heli

Cwmirfon Farm
Cwm Irfon
Cefn Alltwinau
Llawes-heli

Craig Cwmirfon
Waterfall
Nant Cerdin

Craig Cwm-bach
Alltwineu
Pen-y-banc
Garn Dwad
Ty-gwyn
Tynypant

Craig Cwmhenog
Irfon
Nant-Gwyn
Gilfach
LD4

Cwm-Henog
Cairns
Geufron
Y Foel
Bronffynnon

Pen Ddinas
Kilsby
Penhenwernfach

Cerny
Pont Newydd
Pont Maes-y-gwaelod

Llanwrtyd
Quarry (dis)
Cambrian Mill Heritage Centre
Tweedside
Standing Stone

Nant Gynman
Dinas Mill
Cerny
LLANWRTYD WELLS

Banc y Ddinas
Victoria Wells
Ysgol Dolafon
Ffos Farm

Banc Blyngyrnant
Hen Fron Farm
Maesydre Ind Est
Sewage Works
Irfon

Penmaenllwyd
Hotel
Llanwrtyd
Abernant Lake

A483 Builth Wells
Powys STREET ATLAS

85 86 87 88 89 90

C1
1 ZION ST
2 FFOSS RD

D1
1 ERW HAF
2 BRYNAWELON
3 BERTHLLWYD
4 IRFON TERR
5 LAYTON CL

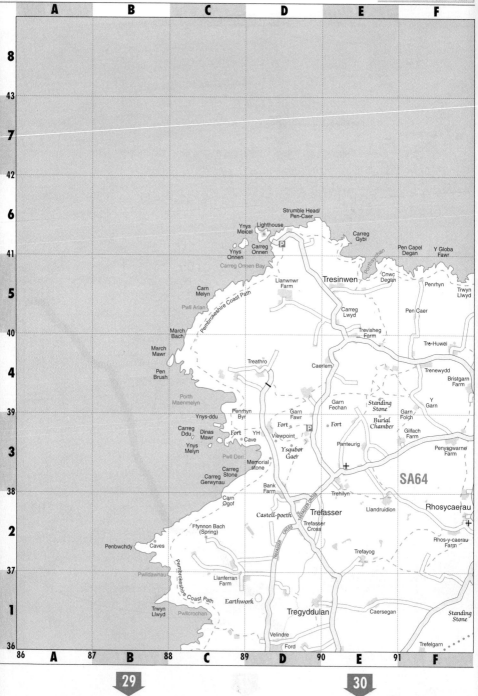

A **B** **C** **D** **E** **F**

8

43

7

42

6

Strumble Head/
Pen-Caer

Ynys
Meicel   Lighthouse

41   Ynys
Onnen   Carreg
Onnen

Carreg Onnen Bay

Carreg
Gybi

Porthsychan

Pen Capel
Degan   Y Globa
Fawr

Llanwnwr
Farm   Tresinwen   Cnwc
Degan   Penrhyn   Trwyn
Llwyd

5

Carn
Melyn

Pwll Arian

Pembrokeshire Coast Path

Carreg
Lwyd

Pen Caer

40

March
Bach

Trevisheg
Farm   Tre-Huwel

4

March
Mawr

Pen
Brush   Treathro   Caerlem   Trenewydd   Bristgarn
Farm

39

Porth
Maenmelyn   Ynys-ddu   Penrhyn
Byr   Garn
Fawr   Garn
Fechan   Standing
Stone   Garn
Folch   Y
Garn

3   Carreg
Ddu   Dinas
Mawr   Fort   YH
Cave   Fort   Viewpoint   Fort   Burial
Chamber   Gilfach
Farm

Ynys
Melyn   Pwll Deri   Panteurig   Penysgwarne
Farm

Memorial
stone   Ysgubor
Gaer

38   Carreg
Gerwynau   Carreg
Stone   Trehilyn   SA64   Rhosycaerau

Carn
Ogof   Bank
Farm   Trefasser

2   Castell-poeth   Trefasser
Cross   Llandruidion   Rhos-y-caerau
Farm

Ffynnon Bach
(Spring)   Trefayog

Penbwchdy   Caves   TREFASSER CROSS

37   Pwlldawnau

Pembrokeshire
Coast Path   Llanferran
Farm

1   Trwyn
Llwyd   Pwllcrochan   Earthwork   Tregyddulan   Caersegan   Standing
Stone

36   Velindre   Trefelgarn
Ford

A   87   **B**   88   **C**   89   **D**   90   **E**   91   **F**
86

29   30

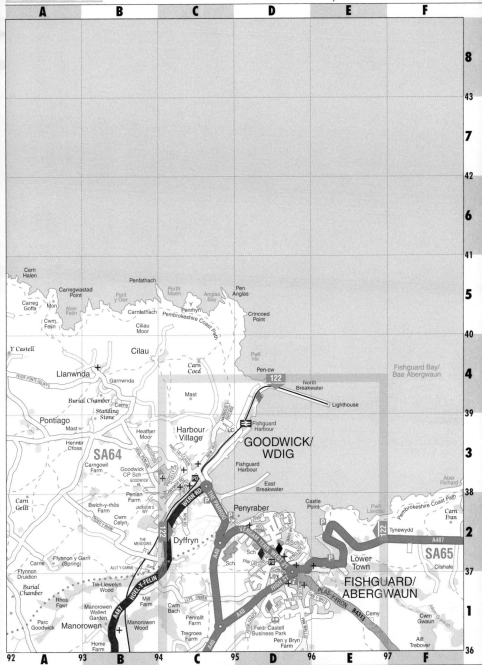

A B C D E F

8
43
7
42
6
41
5
40
4
39
3
38
2
37
1
36

Carn Halen
Carregwastad Point
Penfathach
Carreg Goffa
Mon
Aber Felin
Cwm Felin
Pant y Owr
Porth Maen
Carnfathach
Y Penrhyn
Pembrokeshire Coast Path
Anglas Bay
Pen Anglas
Crincoed Point
Ciliau Moor

Y Castell
Cilau
Carn Coed
Pwll Hir
Pen-cw

Fishguard Bay/ Bae Abergwaun

Llanwnda
Garnwnda

122
North Breakwater
Lighthouse

Feidr Ponte Gwlwys
Burial Chamber
Cefn Standing Stone
Mast

Pontiago
Mast
Heather Moor
Harbour Village
LC
Fishguard Harbour

GOODWICK/ WDIG

Henner Cross
SA64
Fishguard Harbour

Carngowil Farm
Goodwick CP Sch
GOODWICK HILL
PO
East Breakwater

Aber Richard

Penlan Farm
Penyraber
Castle Point
Pwll Landdu
Pembrokeshire Coast Path
Carn Fran

Carn Gelli
Bwlch-y-rhôs Farm
JACKSON'S WY
Cwm Celyn
P
122
Tynewydd
A487
SA65

THE MEADOWS
Dyffryn
Sch
Sch
Lower Town
Cilsafe

Carne
Flynnon y Garn (Spring)
ALLT Y CARNE
Sch
Sch
Liby
FISHGUARD/ ABERGWAUN

Flynnon Druidion
Tre-Llewelyn Wood
HIGH ST
Cerny
Cwm Gwaun

Burial Chamber
Rhos Fawr
Mill Farm
LLYS ONNEN
Cwm Bach
Penrallt Farm
B4313
Allt Trebover

Parc Goodwick
Manorowen Walled Garden
Manorowen Wood
Manorowen
Tregroes Farm
Feidr Castell Business Park
Pen y Bryn Farm

Home Farm

92 A 93 B 94 C 95 D 96 E 97 F

For full street detail of the highlighted area see page 122.

Scale: 1⅓ inches to 1 mile

0   ¼   ½   mile
0   250m 500m 750m 1 km

A   B   C   D   E   F

8
43
7
42
6
41
5
40
4
39
3
38
2
37
1
36

95 **A** 96 **B** 97 **C** 98 **D** 99 **E** 00 **F**

Dinas
Head

Caves

Aber
Pen-clawdd
Viewpoint
Pen y Fan

Cafnau
Cave
Pen-clawdd

Aber Pensidan
Dinas
Island

Aber
Careg-y-Fran

Careg-y-Fran

Pen
Castell

Crincoed
Point

Pwllgwaelod
PH
P

Pwll
Hir
Pwll
Cwm
Bryn-henllan

Pen-cw
Liwyn
Hendy
122
Cerrig
Duon
Cwm
Gwylog
Aber
Bach
North
Breakwater
Pwll
Gwylog
SA42

Fishguard Bay/
Bae Abergwaun
Lighthouse

Dinas
CP Sch

Carreg
Pen-las
Y DDERWEN
MAES

Fishguard
Harbour
LC
Penrhyn
Erw-goch
Dinas
Cross

Penrhyn
Mawr

**GOODWICK/
WDIG**
Viewpoint

Penrhyn
Ychen
Pont y Meddyg

Aber
Grugog

Fishguard
Harbour
FEIDR
CEFN
Pen y
Foel

East
Breakwater
Aber
Richard
Penrhyn
Trewrach
Farm
Glendower
Bwlch-
mawr

Castle
Point
Castell
Farm

Penyraber
Pwll
Landdu
Rhos
Isaf

122
Carn
Fran
Cwm
Mawr

P
Tynewydd
A487
Carn
Gelli

P
Bryn-Awelon
Mynydd
Dinas

Lower
Town
SA65
Cilshafe
Carn
Slani
Haulwen
Garn
Fawr

Sch
PO
Liby
Sch
**FISHGUARD/
ABERGWAUN**
Crug
Cilshafe
Pen-y-mynydd
Brigwarn

Cemy
Cwm
Gwaun
Cwm
Gwyn
Trenewydd
Myndd
Llanllawer

Feidr Castell
Business Park
Pen y Bryn
Farm
Allt
Trebover
Cilshafe
Wood
Trellan
Farm

For full street detail of the
highlighted area see page 122.

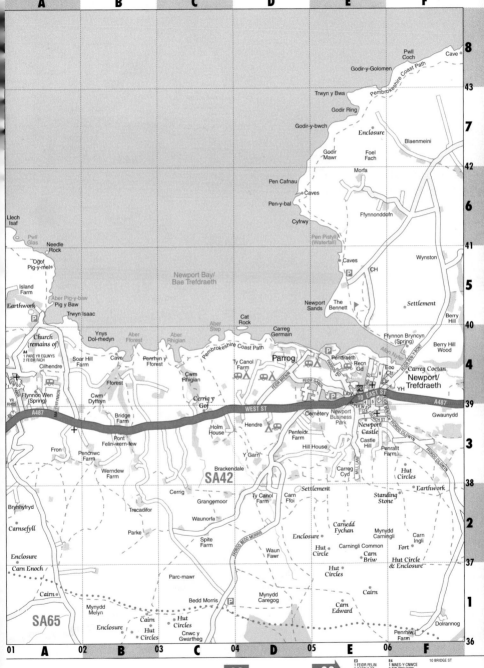

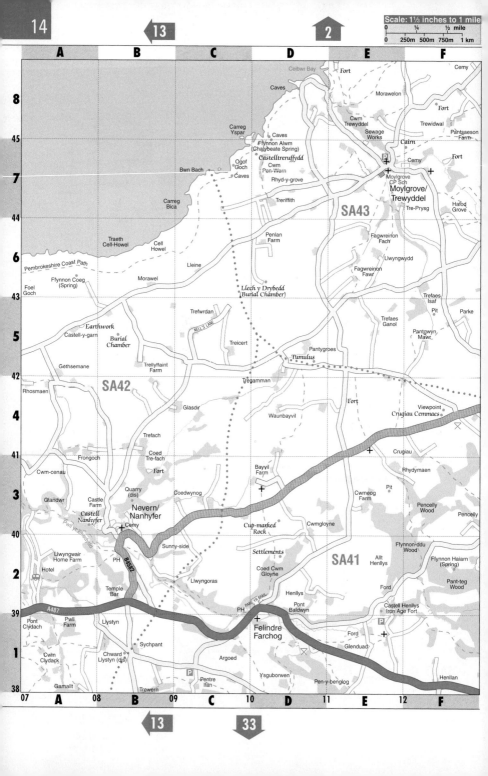

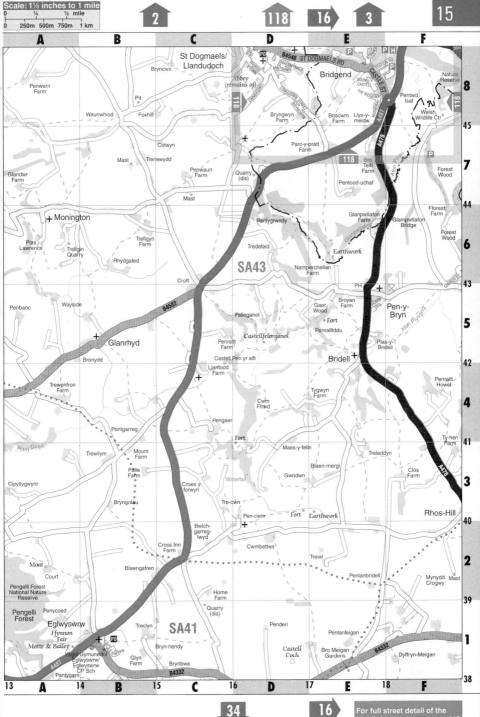

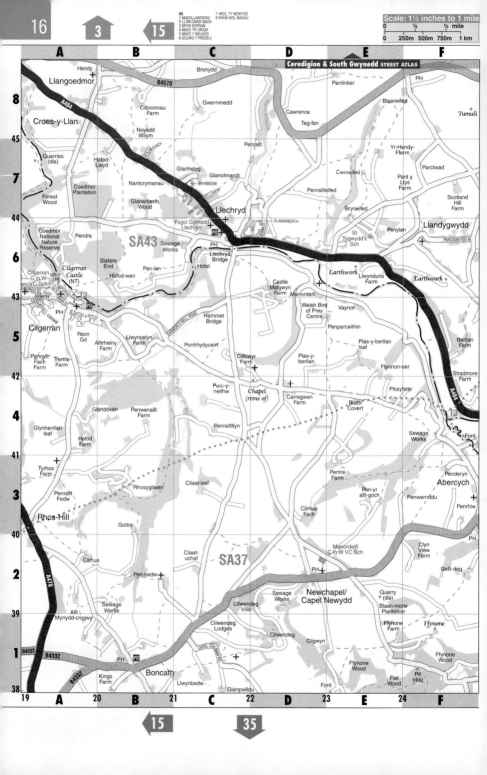

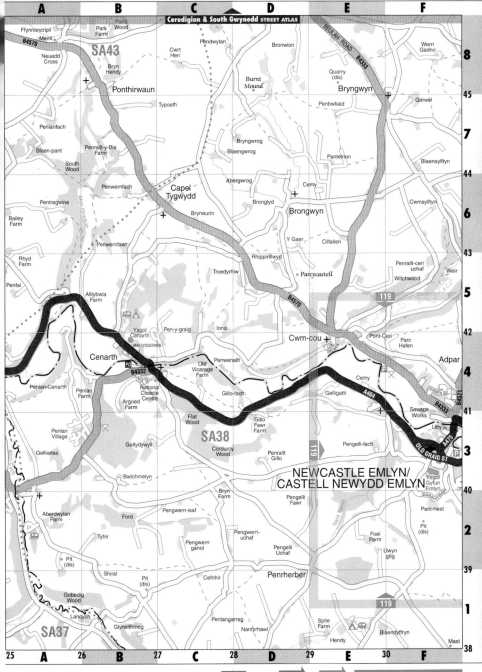

Scale: 1⅓ inches to 1 mile

| 0 | ¼ | ½ | mile |
| 0 | 250m | 500m | 750m | 1 km |

Ceredigion & South Gwynedd STREET ATLAS

Ffynnoncripil
Meml
B4570

SA43

Park Farm
Pond Wood

Pendwylan

Cwrt Hen

Bronwion

BEULAH ROAD
B4333

Wern Gadno

Neuadd Cross

Bryn Hendy

Burnt Mound

Quarry (dis)

8

Bryngwyn

45

Ponthirwaun

Typoeth

Penbwliaid

Gorwel

Penlanfach

Bryngwrog

Blaengwrog

7

Blaen-pant

Penrallt-y-Bie Farm

Abergwrog

Cemy

Panteinon

Blaensylltyn

South Wood

Pentregwine

Penwernfach

Capel Tygwydd

Bryneurin

Bronglyd

Brongwyn

44

Bailey Farm

Afon Hirwaun

Penwernfawr

Y Gaer

Cilfallen

Cwmsylltyn

6

Rhyd Farm

Rhippinllwyd

Penrallt-ceri uchaf

Weir

Penfai

Troedyrhiw

Parcycastell

Witchwood

43

Alltybwla Farm

B4570

119

Pont-Ceri

Parc Hafen

5

42

Ysgol Cenarth

Pen-y-graig

Iona

Cwm-cou

Adpar

MAESYDDERWEN

Cenarth

Old Vicarage Farm

Penwenallt

Afon Teifi

Cemy

P

DERWEN RD

B4571

4

Penian-Cenarth

B4332

National Coracle Centre

Penlan Farm

Gillo-fach

Gelligatti

A484

B4333

Sewage Works

Liby

41

Argoed Farm

Flat Wood

Gillo Fawr Farm

OLD GRAIG ST

P

Penlan Village

Gelliorlas

Gellydywyll

Corduroy Wood

Penrallt Gillo

Pengelli-fach

Ysgol Gyfun Emlyn

3

A475

SA38

NEWCASTLE EMLYN/
CASTELL NEWYDD EMLYN

Parc-nest

40

Bwlchmelyn

Bryn Farm

Pengelli Fawr

Nant Swch

Foel Farm

Pit (dis)

2

Aberdwylan Farm

Ford

Pengwern-isaf

Pengwern-uchaf

Pengelli Uchaf

Llwyn gôg

Tyhir

Pengwern ganol

39

Pit (dis)

Shiral

Cefnhir

Penrherber

119

1

Gobedig Wood

Pit (dis)

Penlangarreg

Nantyrhawl

Spite Farm

Blaendyffryn

Lancych

Glyneithinog

Hendy

Mast

SA37

38

18

36 18 119

For full street detail of the highlighted area see page 119.

Ceredigion & South Gwynedd STREET ATLAS

A B C D E F

Penrhiw-pâl

8

Cefnmaes
Calderbrook
Pantyrpdyn
Troedyraur
Brongest PO
Crug y Balog
Coed-y-bryn
Quarry (dis) Tumuli
Nantgwylan
Gernos Farm

45

Pantyronen
Crymant
Brynhawen
Coedybryn CP Sch
Garden Wood

7

Pant-y-bwla
Ford
Dolgian
Ffynnon-Fair
Motte
Blaenllan
Maes llyn

44

Blaengwenllan Cross
Llangynllo Farm
Glebe Farm
Ford

6

Dinas Ceri
Pwllyrheirn
Pengelli
Quarries (dis)
Quarry (dis)
Quarry (dis)
Roughwood
Pantygwenith Farm
Bronwydd
Penbeili-mawr
Ffynnon-wen

43

Cafan Farm
Blaen-Cil-Llech
Llwch-yr-hâl
Llwyncadfor Farm
Pengallt

5 119 B4571

Blaenant
Sychpant Farm
SA38
Bronrwen Farm
Llain Farm
Castell Nant-y-garau
Parke PO

42

Old Cilgwyn
Sychpant
Alltyresgob
Pit (dis)
Wernfach Farm
Quarry (dis)
Cwrws Fawr

4

Bryndioddef
Cilgwyn
A475
Danc Farm
Llandyfriog
Plasnewydd
Berthyfedwen
Felin Cwrws Farm
Ford
Aberbanc CP Sch
Aber-banc

41

Castle (rems of)
STATION RD A484
Gilwen Farm
Aberhalen
Quarry (dis)
Penddol
Moat
Teifi Valley Railway
SA44
Trebedw
Henllan

3 119

Teifi Valley Business Park
PH
Dolhaidd
Henllan Ind Est
HEOL Y BEDW PO
Henllan
Fort

40

Penlon
Ford
Blaenhalen
Pentrecagal
Quarries (dis)
Llyshewydd
Pen-ffynnon

2

Allt Boeth
Rhyddgoed-fawr
Aberlleinau
Penllwyn
Cryngae
National Woollen Mus

39

Quarry (dis)
Waungilwen
Settlement
Penllwyncoch-fawr
PH Drefach
Cefny

1 119 B4333

Sychnant
Clifforest Farm
Tyrlon Hendon
PO
Ysgol Penboyr
Cefn-isaf

38

Blaenffos
Ford
Felindre

31 A 32 B 33 C 34 D 35 E 36 F

For full street detail of the highlighted area see page 119.
119 17 37

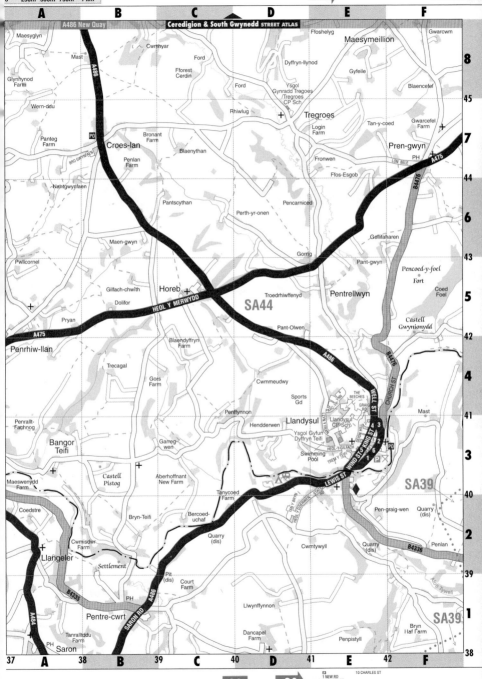

A486 New Quay

A B C D E F

Maesyglyn

Mast

Ffosheylg

Maesymeillion

Gwarcwm

Cwnhyar

Ford

Dyffryn-llynod

Gyfeile

Glynhynod Farm

Fforest Cerdin

Ford

Ysgol Gynradd Tregroes /Tregroes CP Sch

Blaencefel

Wern-ddu

Rhiwlug

Tregroes

Tan-y-coed

Gwarcefel Farm

Panteg Farm

Croes-lan

Bronant Farm

Login Farm

Pren-gwyn

PH

LON BELE

A475

Penlan Farm

Blaenythan

Fronwen

B4476

Nahtgwynpfaen

Pantscythan

Ffos-Esgob

Maen-gwyn

Perth-yr-onen

Pencarniced

Pwllcornel

Gorrig

Geflifaharen

Pant-gwyn

Pencoed-y-foel Fort

Gilfach-chwith

Horeb

Troedrhiwffenyd

Pentrellwyn

Coed Foel

Dolifor

HEOL Y MERWYDD

SA44

Castell Gwynionydd

Pryan

Pant-Olwen

A475

Penrhiw-llan

Blaendyffryn Farm

A486

B4476

Trecagal

Gors Farm

Cwmmeudwy

Sports Gd

THE BEECHES

Mast

Penrallt-Fachnog

Pentfynnon

GRAIG

Llandysul CP Sch

Bangor Teifi

Garreg-wen

Hendderwen

Llandysul

SA39

Ysgol Gyfun Dyffryn Teifi

Maeswenydd Farm

Castell Pistog

Aberhoffnant New Farm

Swimming Pool

LEWIS ST

Pen-graig-wen

Quarry (dis)

Coedstre

Bryn-Teifi

Tanycoed Farm

Bercoed-uchaf

Quarry (dis)

Penlan

Cwmisdwr Farm

Cwmtywyll

Quarry (dis)

B4336

Llangeler

Settlement

Pit (dis)

Court Farm

B4535

PH

SARON RD

A486

Llwynffynnon

SA39

Pentre-cwrt

Tanralltddu Farm

Dancapel Farm

Penpistyll

Bryn Haf farm

A484

PH

Saron

37 38 39 40 41 42

A B C D E F

38

20

10 CHARLES ST

1 NEW RD
2 CHURCH ST
3 LON LETTY
4 HIGH ST
5 LINCOLN ST
6 HEOL-Y-NEUADD
7 LON CHANNING
8 LON FEDWEN
9 LON WESLEY

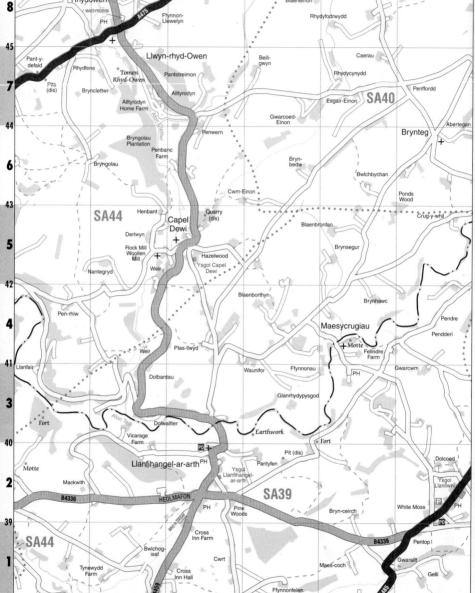

Scale: 1½ inches to 1 mile

0   ¼   ½ mile
0   250m 500m 750m 1 km

Ceredigion & South Gwynedd STREET ATLAS

Pantmoch

Rhydowen
Camnant Farm

MAESYRODYN
PH

Pant-y-defaid

Pits (dis)

Rhydfene

Brynclettwr

Alltyrodyn Home Farm

Tomen Rhyd-Owen

Llwyn-rhyd-Owen

Pantstreimon

Alltyrodyn

Pyllau'r-bryn

Flynnon-Llewelyn

Blaeneinon

Rhydyfodrwydd

Beili-gwyn

Caerau

Rhydycynydd

Esgair-Einon

SA40

Penffordd

Bryngolau Plantation

Penbanc Farm

Bryngolau

Penwern

Gwarcoed-Einon

Bryn-bedw

Bwlchbychan

Bryn-teg

Abertegan

Ponds Wood

SA44

Henbant

Derlwyn

Capel Dewi

Quarry (dis)

Cwm-Einon

Blaenbronfan

Crug-y-whil

Rock Mill Woollen Mill

Nantegryd

Weir

Hazelwood

Ysgol Capel Dewi

Blaenborthyn

Brynsegur

Brynhawc

Pendre

Pendderi

Pen-rhiw

Weir

Plas-llwyd

Maesycrugiau

Motte

Felindre Farm

Gwarcwm

Llanfair

Dolbantau

Waunifor

Ffynnonau

PH

Fort

Glanrhydypysgod

Dolwallter

Vicarage Farm

Earthwork

Fort

Motte

Mackwith

Llanfihangel-ar-arth

PO
PH

Ysgol Llanfihangel-ar-arth

Pit (dis)

Pantyfen

Dolcoed

Ysgol Llanllwni

B4336

HEOLMAFON

SA39

White Moss

P

PH

PO

SA44

Tynewydd Farm

Bwlchog-isaf

Cross Inn Farm

PH

Pine Woods

Cross Inn Hall

Cwrt

Bryn-ceirch

Maes-coch

B4336

Pentop I

Gwarallt

Gelli

Ffynnonfelen

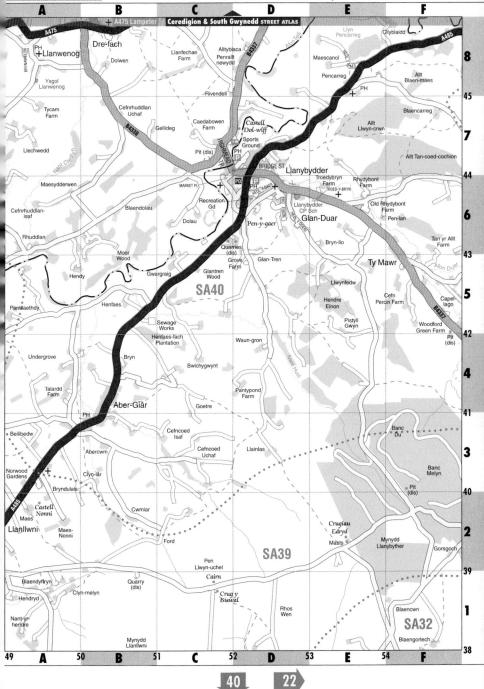

Scale: 1½ inches to 1 mile

0 ¼ ½ mile
0 250m 500m 750m 1 km

A475 Lampeter

A475

PH
Llanwenog
Dre-fach
Dolwen
BRYNAMLWG

Ysgol
Llanwenog

Tycam
Farm

Llechwedd

Cefnrhuddlan
Uchaf
Gellideg

B4336

Llanfechan
Farm

Alltyblaca
Penrallt
newydd

Rivendell

Caedabowen
Farm

Castell
Dol-wlff

Sports
Ground
PH

BRIDGE ST

Llanddewi

Llyn
Pencarreg

Ollyblaidd

Maescanol

Pencarreg

Allt Blaen-maes

Blaencarreg

Allt
Llwyn-crwn

Allt Tan-coed-cochion

A485

PH

8

45

7

Maesydderwen

Cefnrhuddlan-
isaf

Blaendolau

Pit (dis)

MARKET PL

Rhuddlan

Dolau

Recreation
Gd

PO
P
PH

Llanybydder

Troedybryn
Farm
TROED-Y-BRYN

Llanybydder
CP Sch

Glan-Duar

Rhydybont
Farm

Old Rhydybont
Farm

Pen-lan

44

6

Moor
Wood

Hendy

Gwargraig

Quarries
(dis)

Grove
Farm

Pen-y-gaer

Glan-Tren

Bryn-llo

Tan yr Allt
Farm

Ty Mawr

43

Glantren
Wood

SA40

Llwynfedw

Cefn
Percin Farm

Afon Duar

Capel-
lago

B4337

5

Panllaethdy

Henfaes

Henfaes-fach
Plantation

Sewage
Works

Bryn

Waun-gron

Hendre
Einon

Pistyll
Gwyn

Woodford
Green Farm

Pit
(dis)

42

Undergrove

Talardd
Farm

Aber-Giâr
PH

Goetre

Bwlchygwynt

Pantypond
Farm

4

Beilibedw

Norwood
Gardens

Abercwm

Cefncoed
Isaf

Clŷn-iâr

Cefncoed
Uchaf

Llainlas

Banc
Du

Banc
Melyn

41

3

Bryndulais

Castell
Nonni

Cwmiar

Pit
(dis)

40

Llanllwni

Maes

Maes-
Nonni

Ford

Crugiau
Edryd
Masts

Mynydd
Llanybyther

Gorsgoch

2

A485

Pen
Llwyn-uchel

Cairn

SA39

39

Blaendyffryn

Hendryd

Clyn-melyn

Quarry
(dis)

Crug y
Biswal

Rhos
Wen

Blaencwn

1

Nant-yr-
heidre

Mynydd
Llanllwni

Blaengorlech

SA32

38

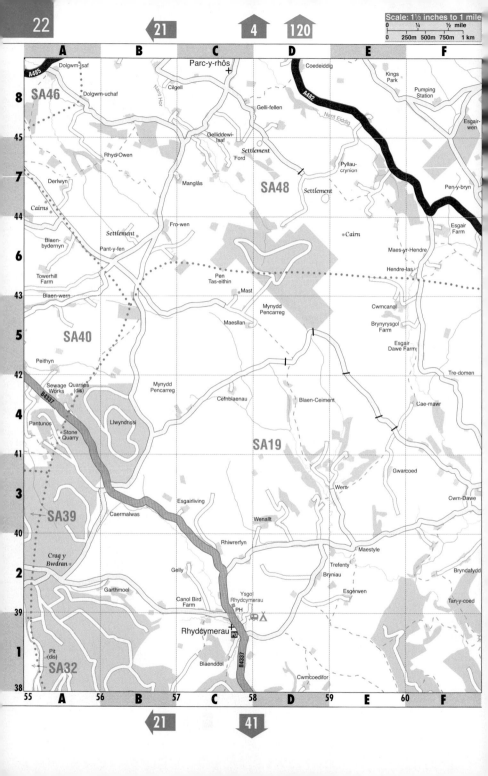

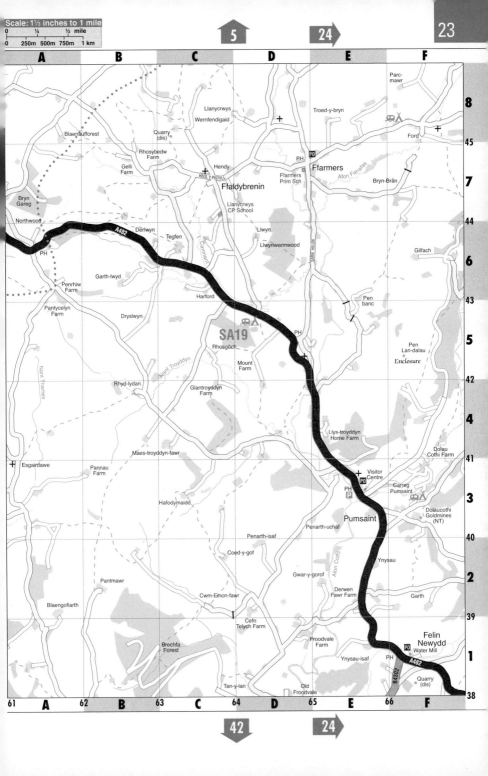

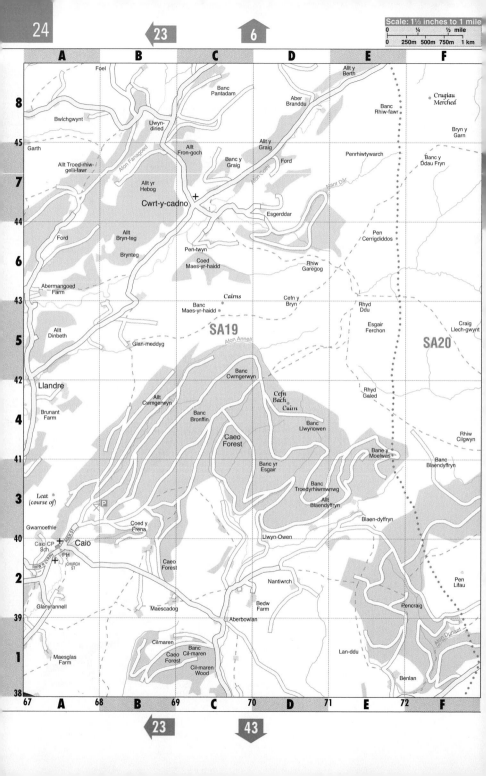

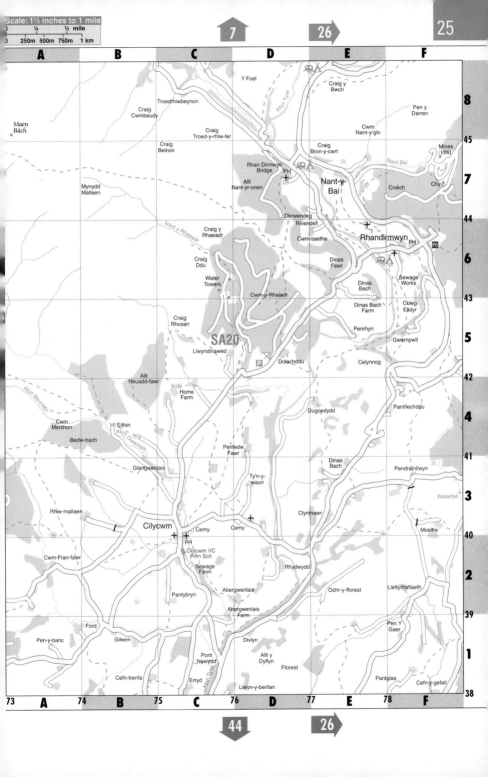

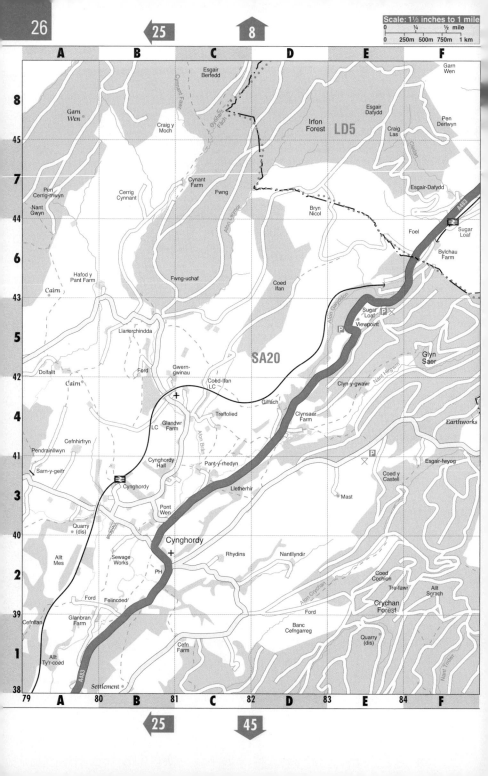

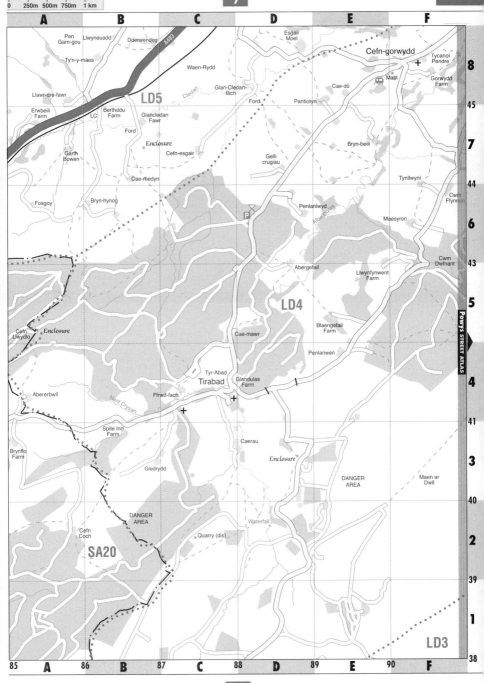

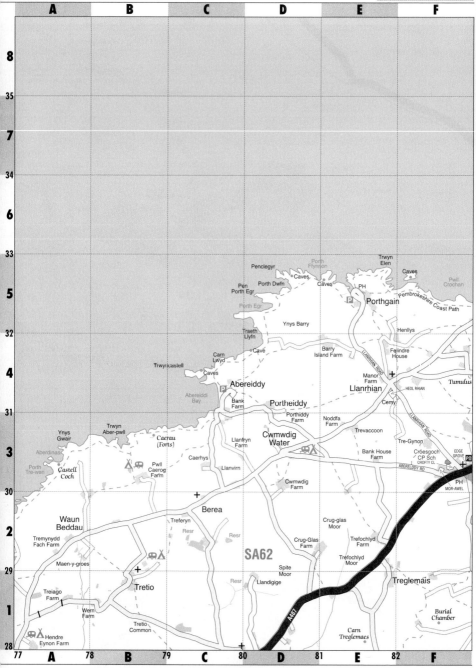

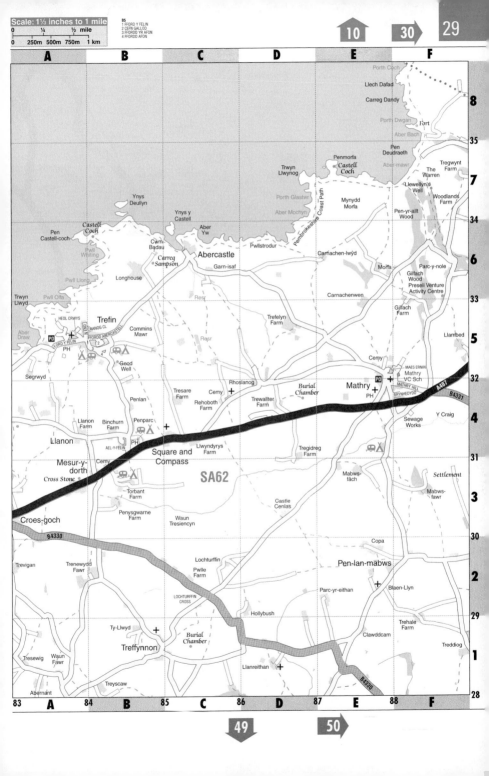

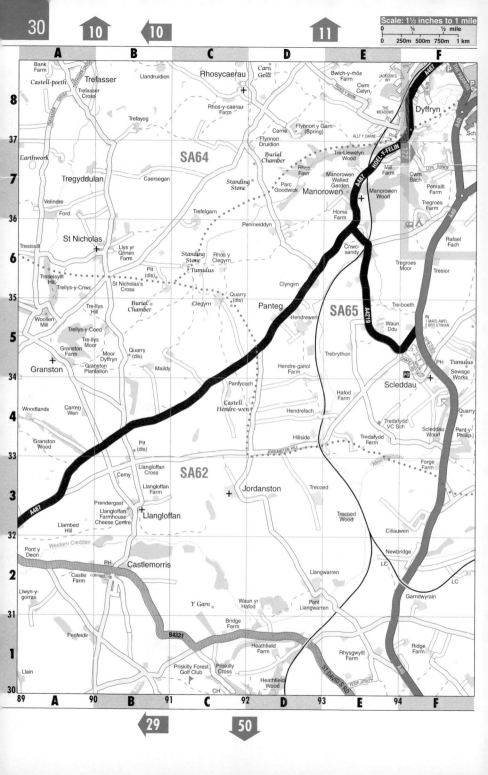

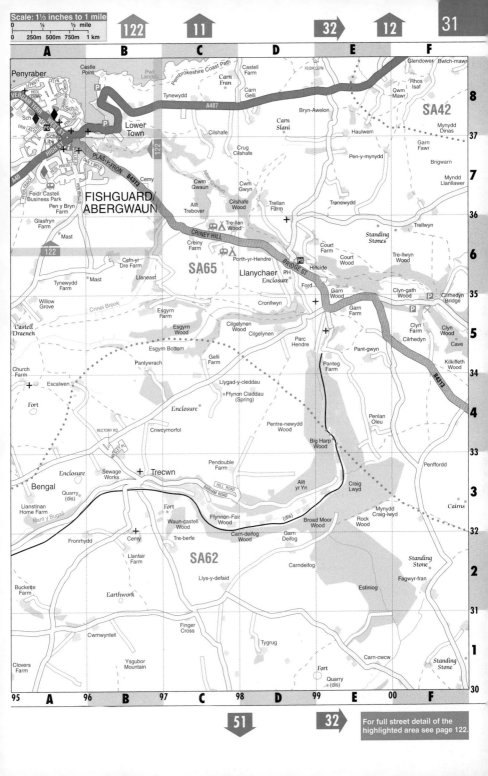

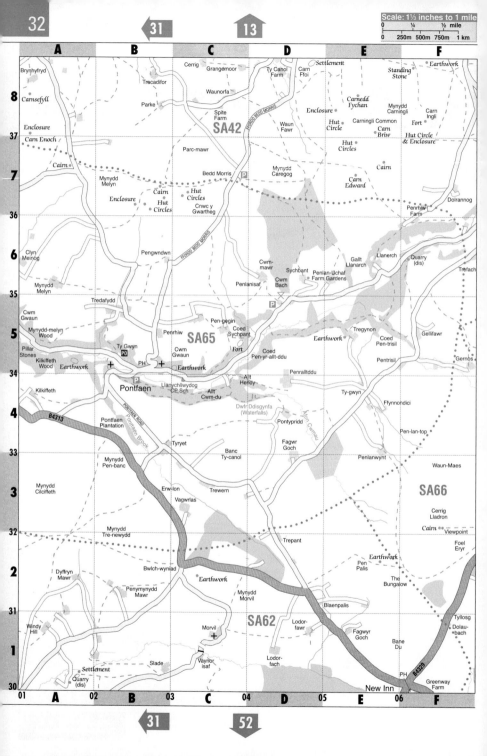

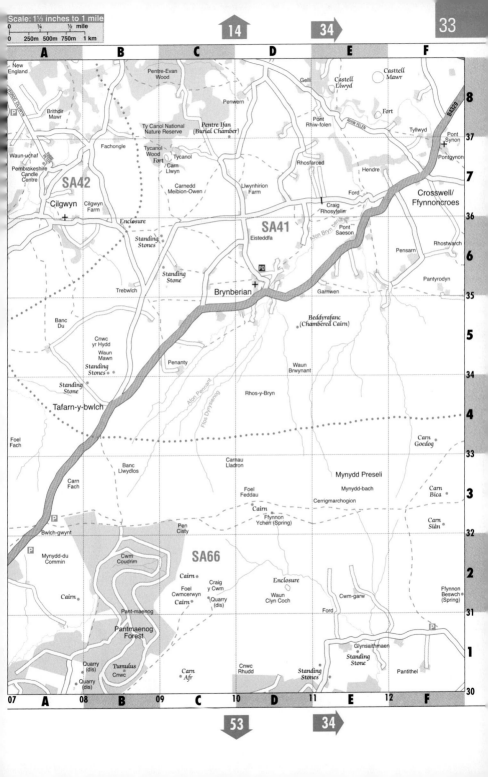

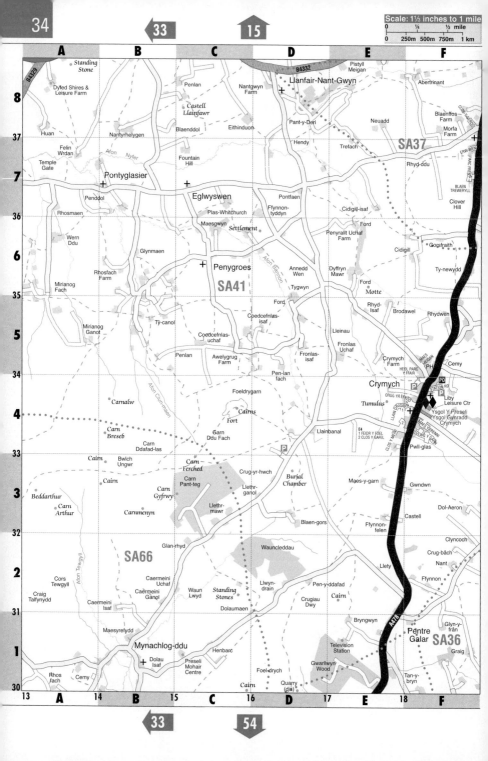

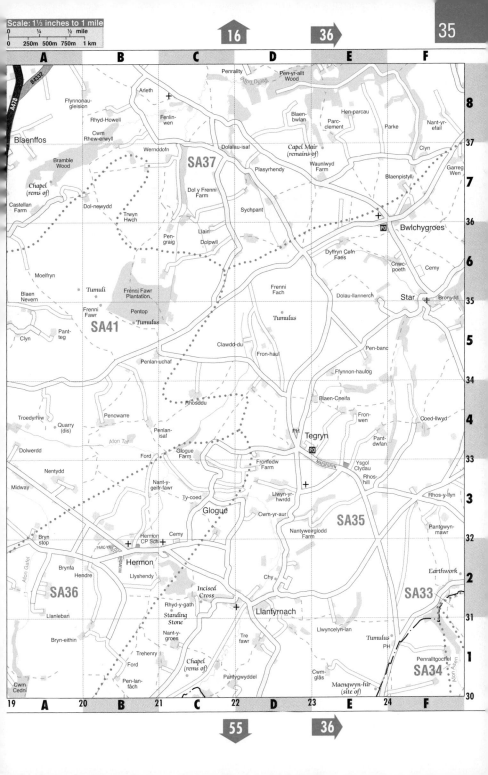

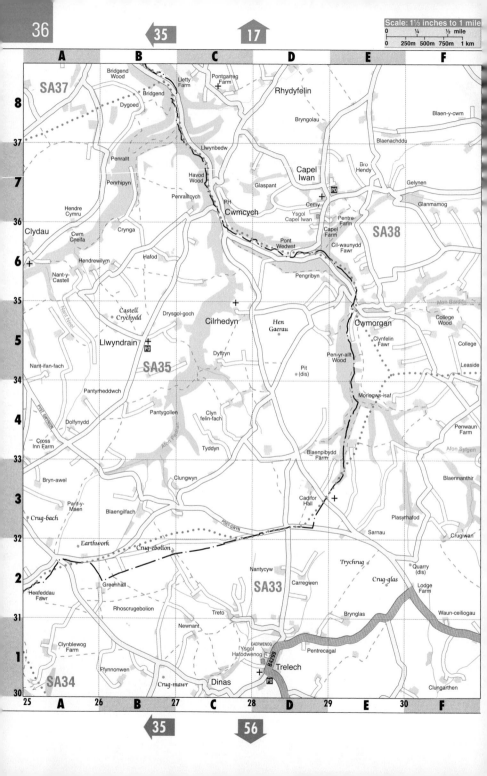

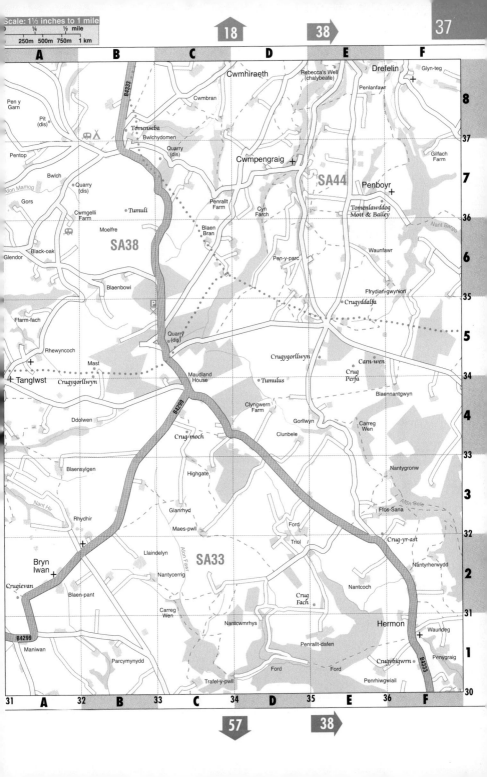

37 19

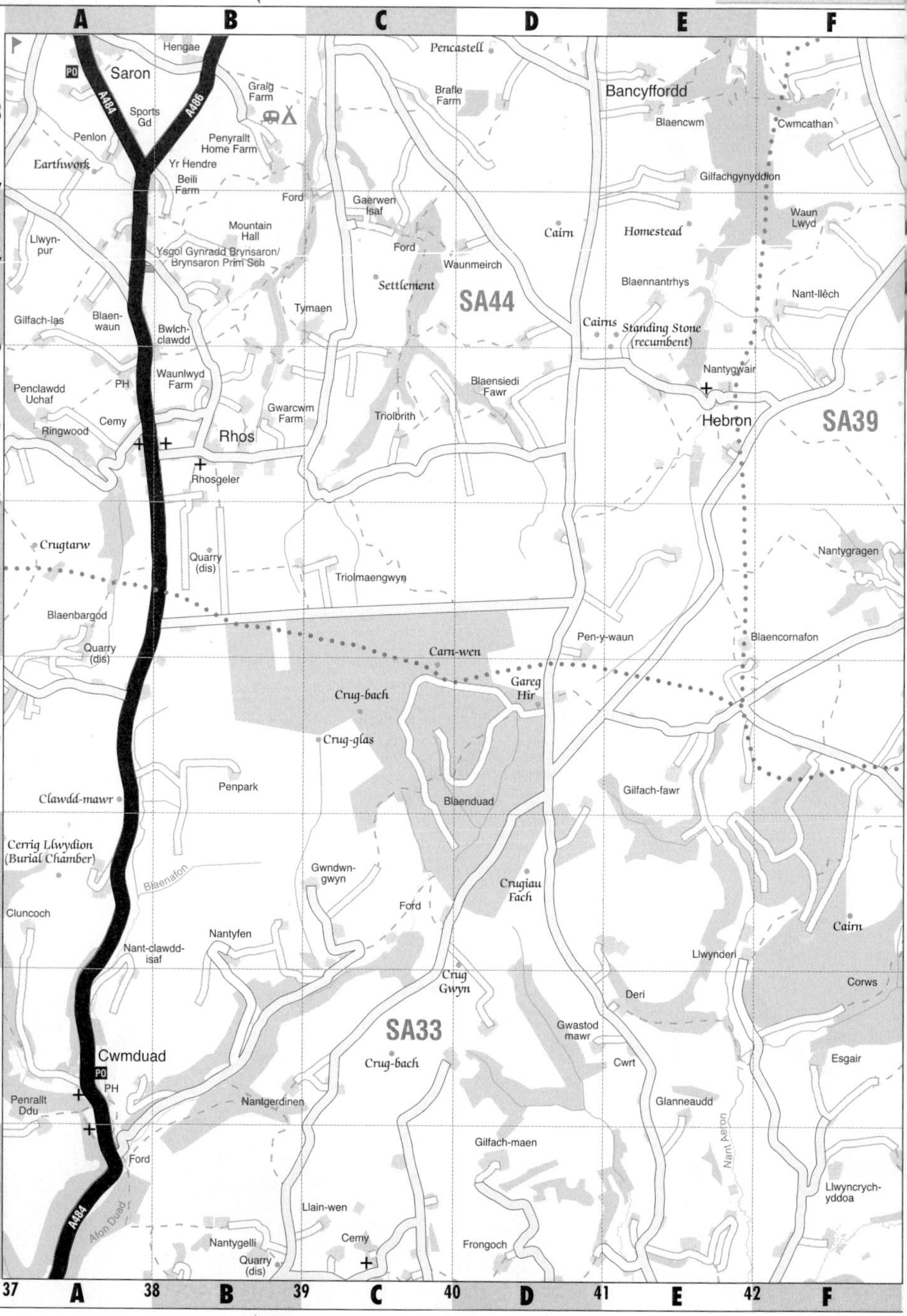

Scale: 1½ inches to 1 mile

0 ¼ ½ mile
0 250m 500m 750m 1 km

8
Hengae
Saron
PO
A484 A486
Sports Gd
Graig Farm
Penllon
Penyrallt Home Farm
Earthwork
Yr Hendre
Beili Farm
Pencastell
Brafle Farm
Bancyffordd
Blaencwm
Cwmcathan
Gilfachgynyddton
Waun Lwyd

37
Mountain Hall
Ford
Gaerwen Isaf
Ford
Cairn
Homestead
Blaennantrhys
Nant-llêch

7
Llwyn-pur
Ysgol Gynradd Brynsaron/ Brynsaron Prim Sch
Waunmeirch
Settlement
SA44

36
Gilfach-las
Blaen-waun
Bwlch-clawdd
Tymaen
Cairns
Standing Stone (recumbent)
Nantygwair

6
Penclawdd Uchaf
PH
Waunlwyd Farm
Gwarcwm Farm
Blaensiedi Fawr
Hebron
SA39
Ringwood
Cemy
Rhos
Triolbrith
Nantygragen

35
Rhosgeler
Crugtarw
Quarry (dis)
Triolmaengwyn
Blaencornafon

5
Blaenbargod
Quarry (dis)
Carn-wen
Pen-y-waun
Gareg Hir

34
Crug-bach
Gilfach-fawr

4
Clawdd-mawr
Crug-glas
Penpark
Blaenduad

33
Cerrig Llwydion (Burial Chamber)
Gwndwn-gwyn
Crugiau Fach
Cairn

3
Cluncoch
Blaenaton
Ford
Llwynderi
Corws

32
Nant-clawdd-isaf
Nantyfen
Crug Gwyn
Deri
Gwastod mawr
Esgair

2
Cwmduad
PO
PH
SA33
Crug-bach
Cwrt
Glanneaudd
A484
Penrallt Ddu
Nantgerdinen
Gilfach-maen
Nant Aeron

31
Ford
Llwyncrych-yddoa

1
Llain-wen
Cemy
Frongoch
Nantygelli
Quarry (dis)

30

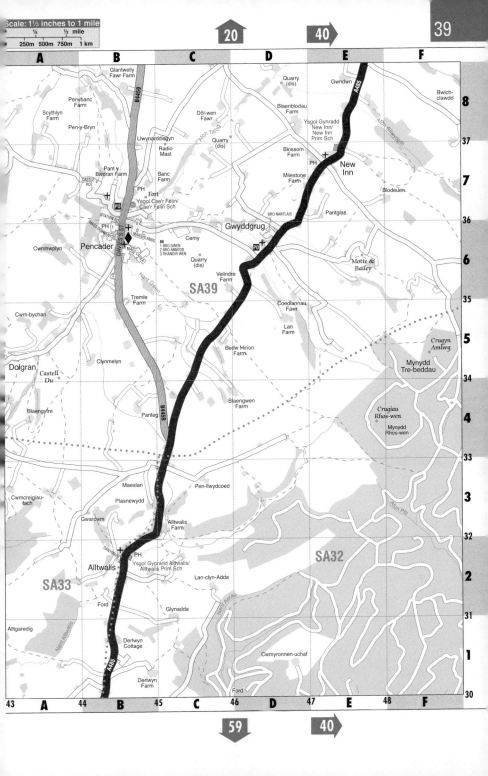

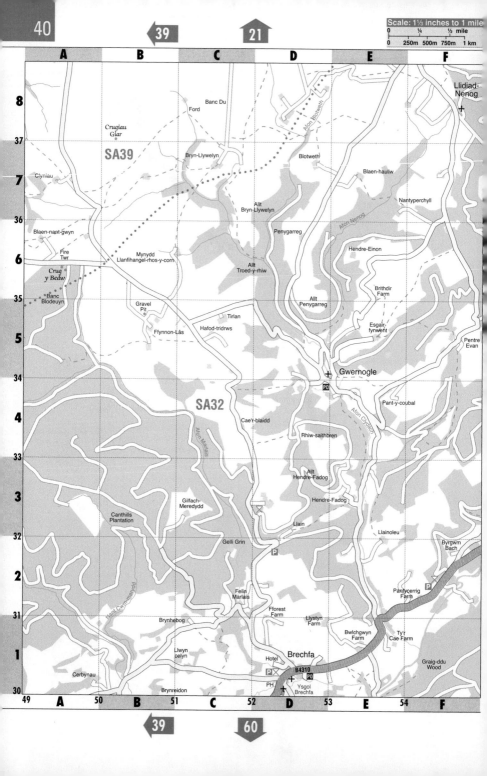

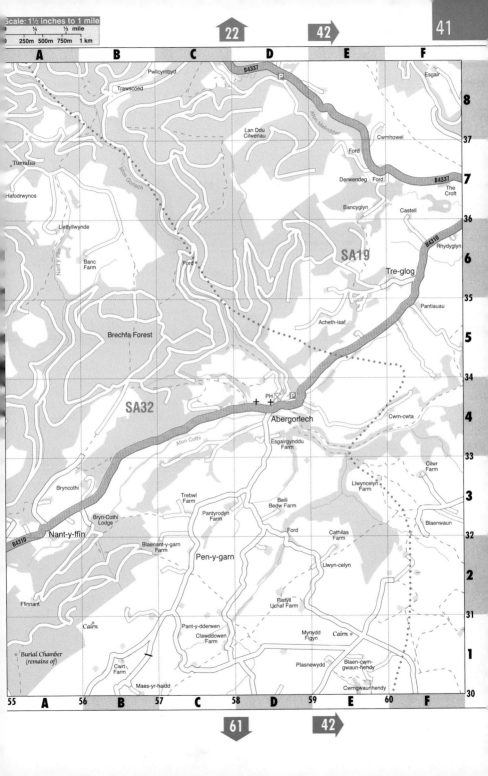

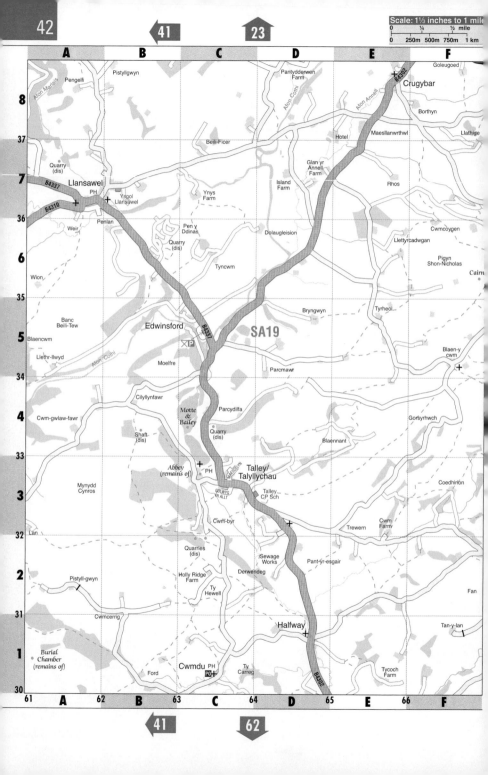

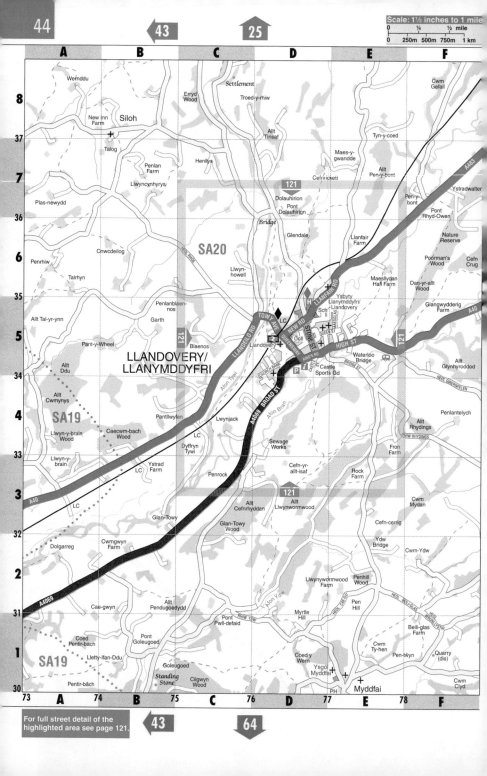

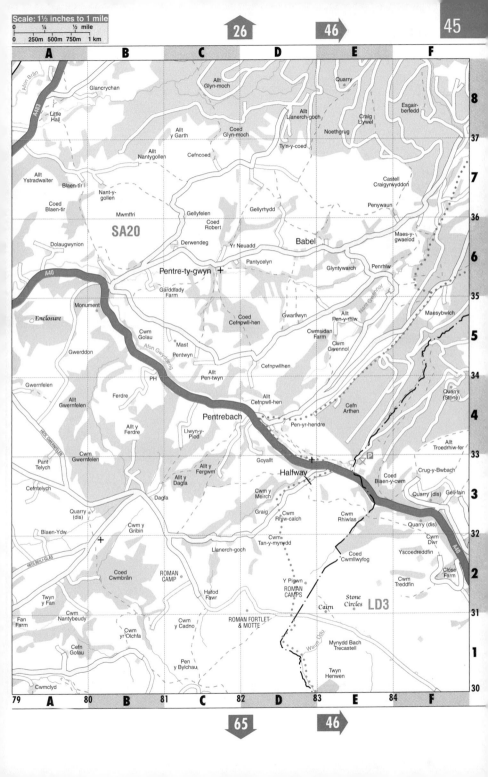

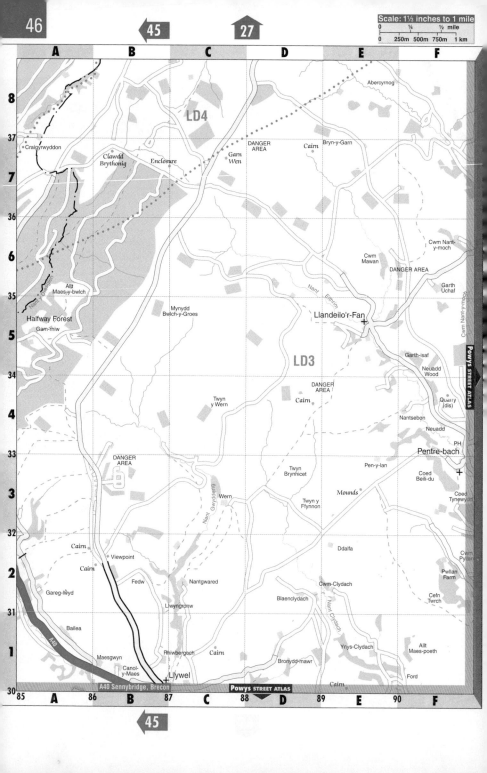

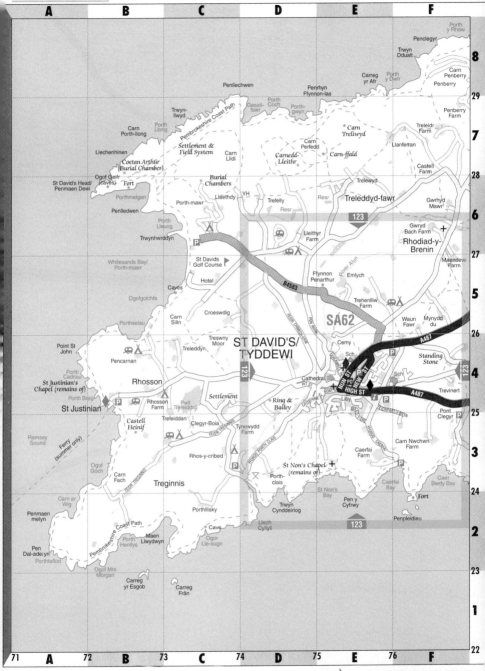

48

For full street detail of the highlighted area see page 123.

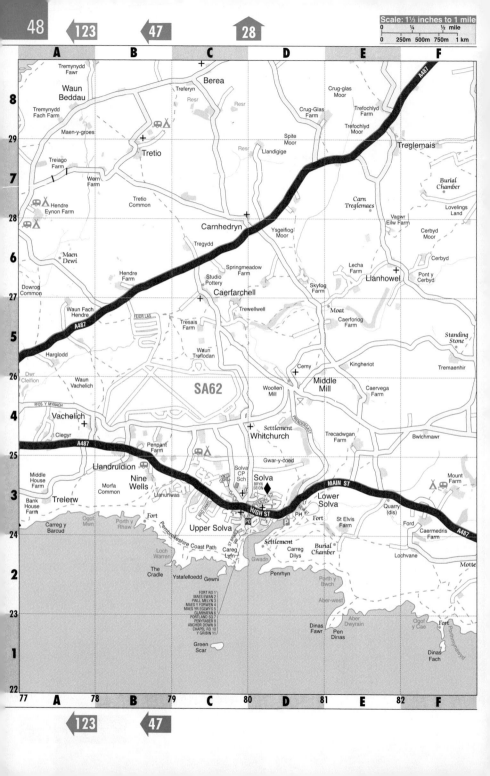

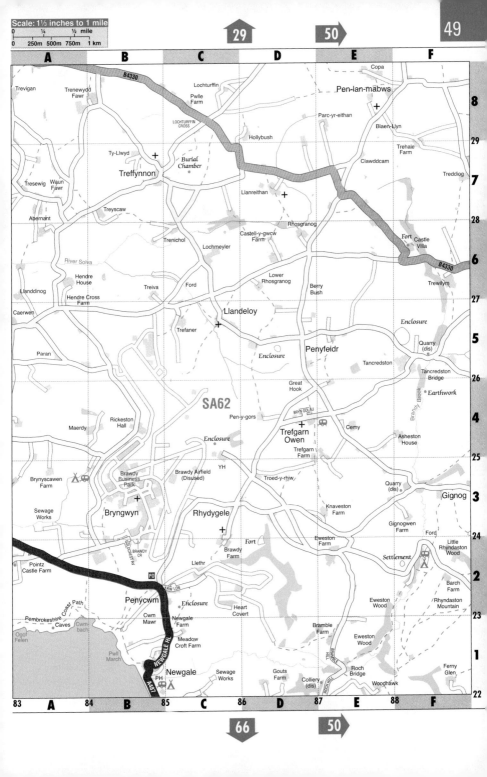

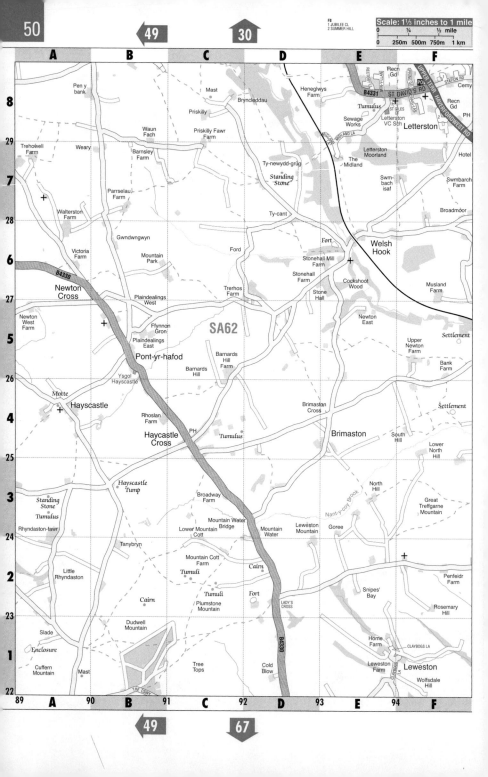

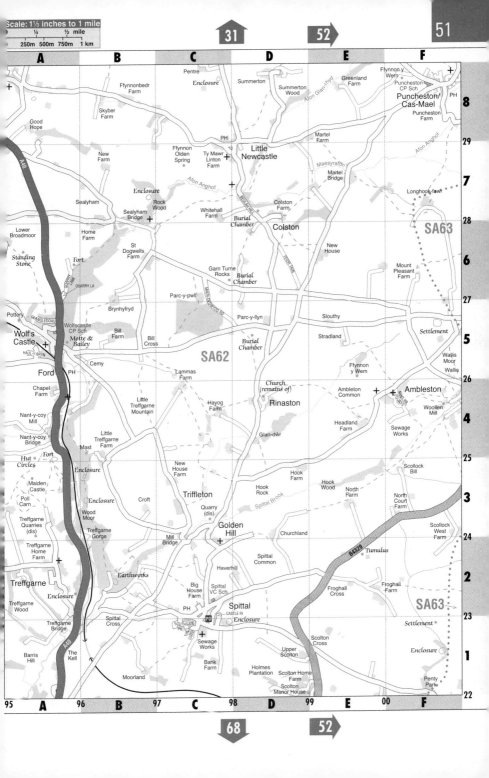

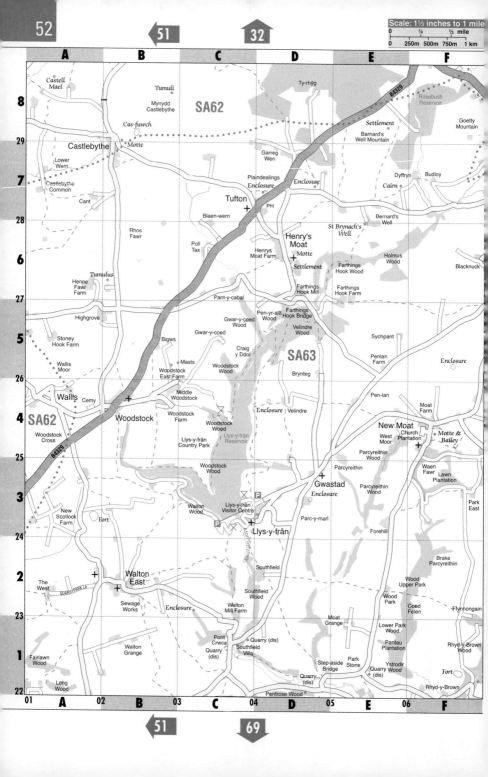

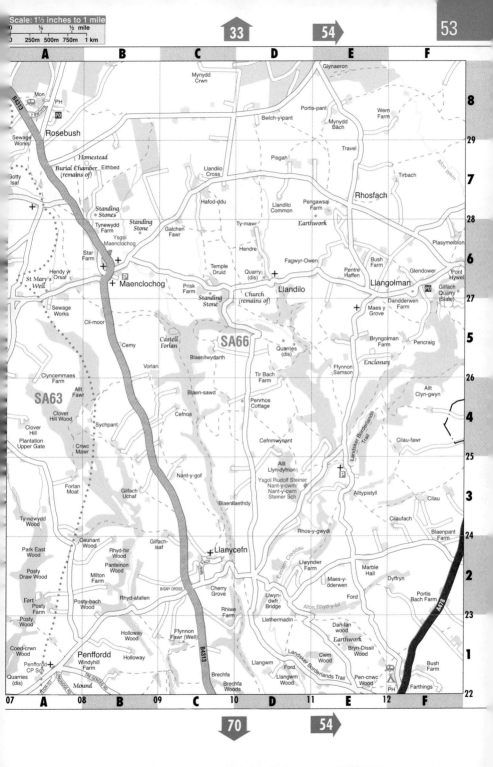

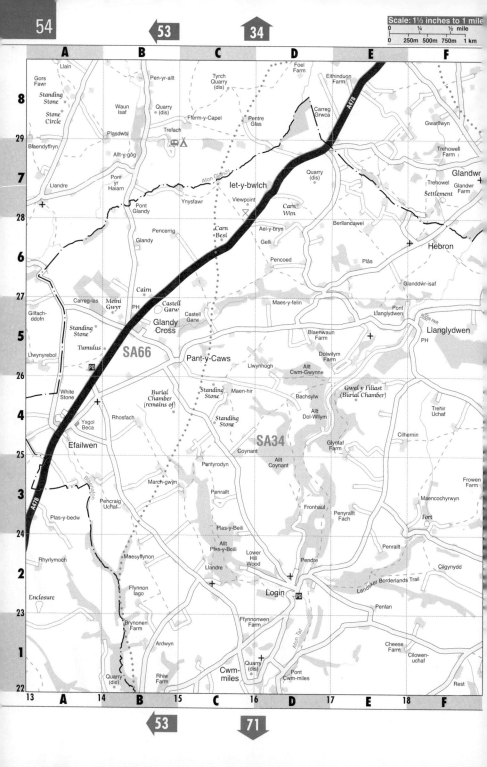

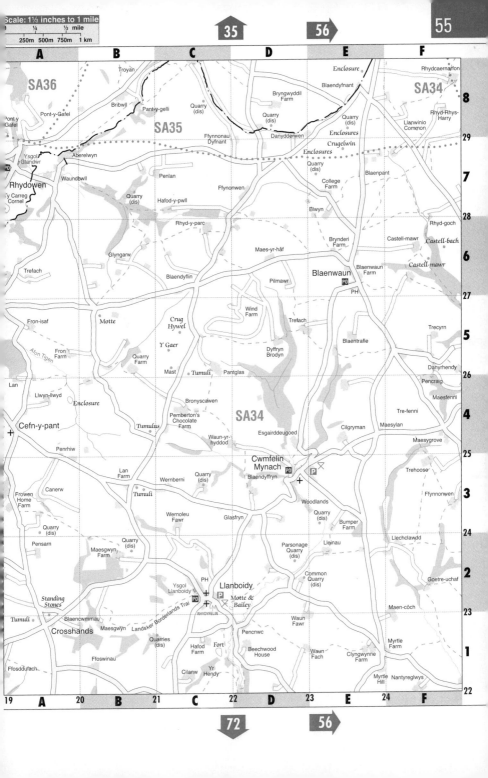

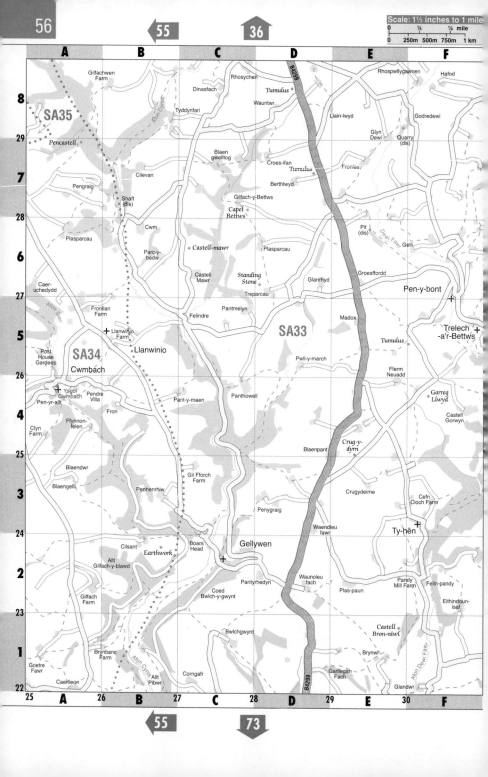

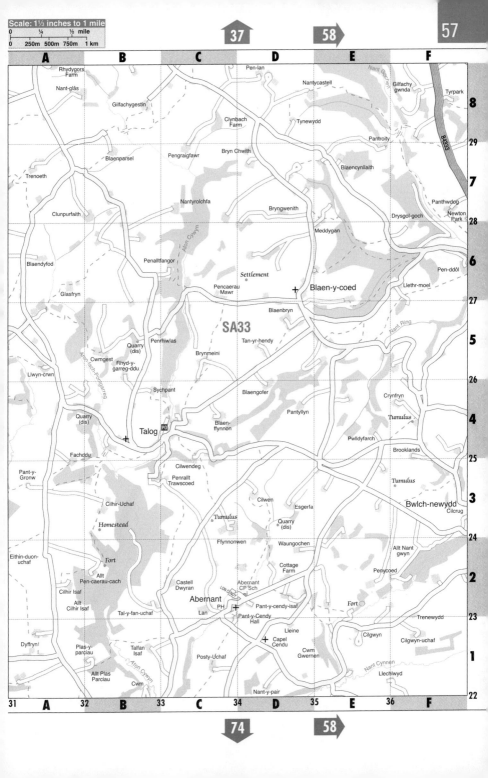

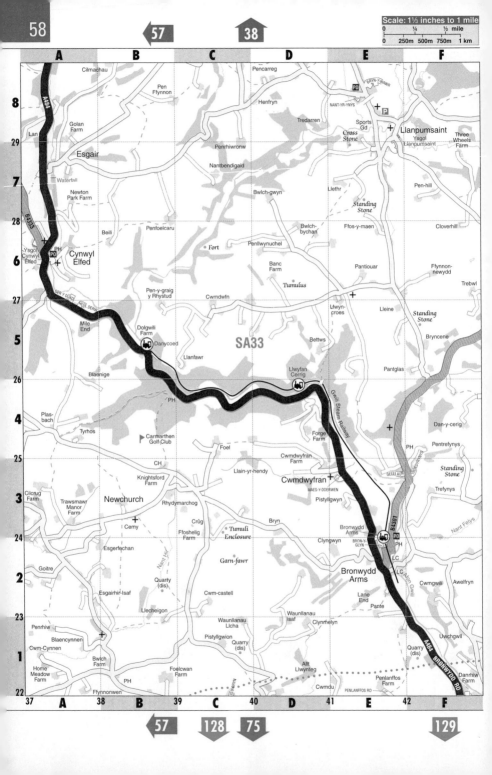

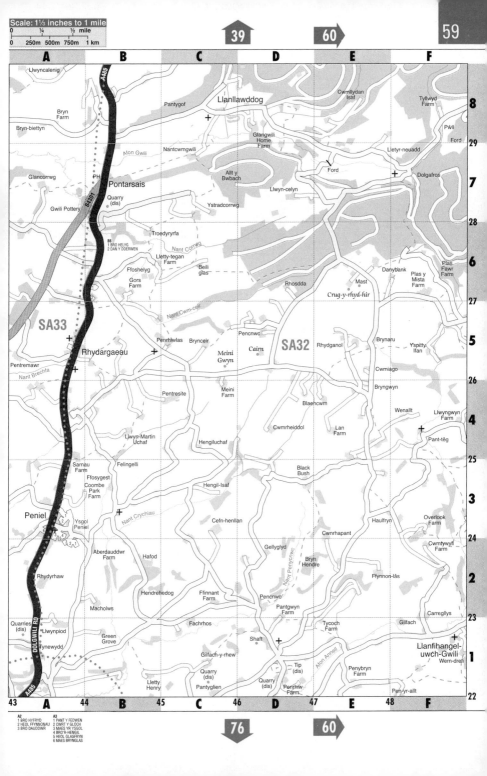

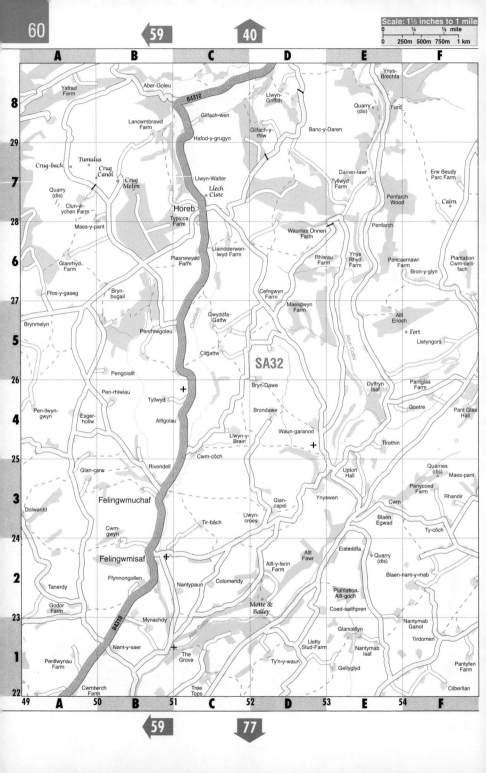

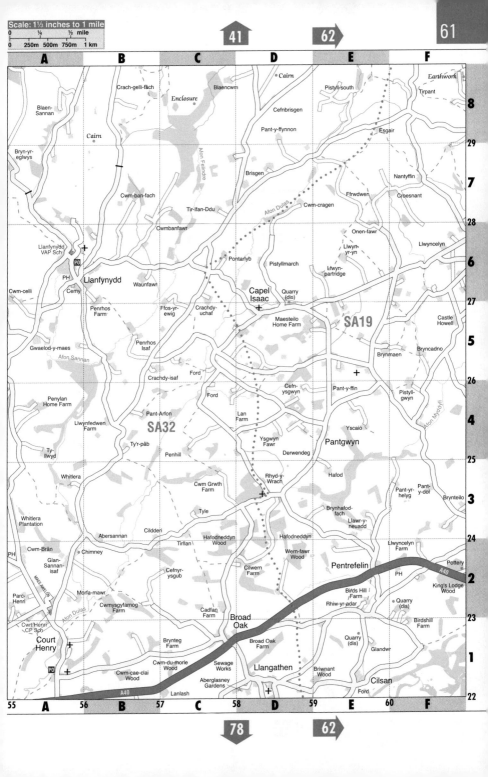

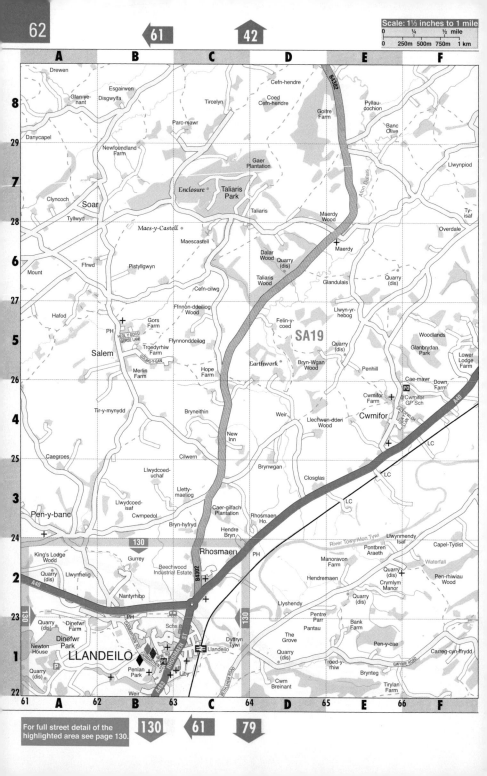

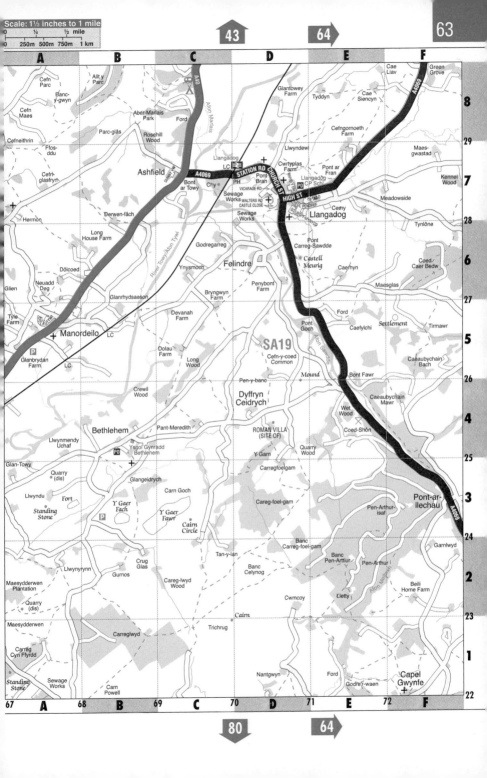

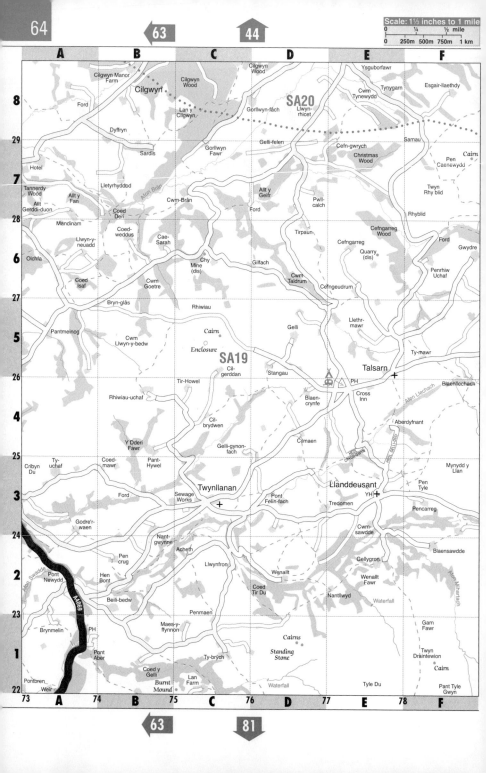

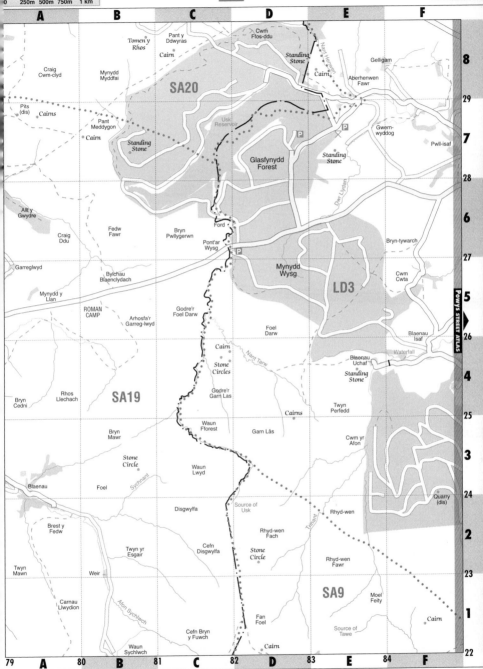

Scale: 1⅓ inches to 1 mile

0   ¼   ½ mile
0 250m 500m 750m 1 km

A **B** **C** **D** **E** **F**

Craig
Cwm-clyd

Tomen y
Rhos

Pant y
Ddwyras

Cwm
Ffos-ddu

Standing
Stone

Gelligam

Cairn

Mynydd
Myddfai

Cairn

SA20

Cairn

Aberhenwen
Fawr

8

Pits
(dis)

Cairns

Pant
Meddygon

Usk
Reservoir

P

P

Gwern-
wyddog

29

Cairn

Standing
Stone

Pwll-isaf

7

Allt y
Gwydre

Fedw
Fawr

Bryn
Pwllygerwn

Glasfynydd
Forest

Standing
Stone

28

Craig
Ddu

Ford

Bryn-tywarch

6

Garreglwyd

Bylchau
Blaenclydach

Pont'ar
Wysg

P

Mynydd
Wysg

Cwm
Cwta

27

Mynydd y
Llan

ROMAN
CAMP

Arhosfa'r
Garreg-lwyd

Godre'r
Foel Darw

LD3

Blaenau
Isaf

Waterfall

5

26

Bryn
Cedni

Rhos
Llechach

SA19

Cairn

Stone
Circles

Foel
Darw

Nant Tarw

Blaenau
Uchaf

Standing
Stone

4

Godre'r
Garn Las

Cairns

Twyn
Perfedd

25

Bryn
Mawr

Waun
Fforest

Garn Lâs

Cwm yr
Afon

3

Stone
Circle

Foel

Sychnant

Waun
Lwyd

24

Blaenau

Quarry
(dis)

Disgwylfa

Source of
Usk

Rhyd-wen

Brest y
Fedw

Twyn yr
Esgair

Cefn
Disgwylfa

Rhyd-wen
Fach

Tirmaur

2

Twyn
Mawr

Weir

Stone
Circle

Rhyd-wen
Fawr

23

Carnau
Llwydion

Afon Sychlwch

Fan
Foel

SA9

Moel
Feity

Source of
Tawe

Cairn

1

Cefn Bryn
y Fuwch

Waun
Sychlwch

Cairn

22

79 **A** 80 **B** 81 **C** 82 **D** 83 **E** 84 **F**

49

Scale: 1⅓ inches to 1 mile

A B C D E F

8
21
7
20
6
19
5
18
4
17
3
16
2
15
1
14

Wood
WOOD HILL
A487
Southwood
Porter's Well
Hill Side
GRASS HOLM CL
Newgale Sands
Sibbernock Point
Midway Farm
PH
Roch CP Sch
Roch
Castle
Church Hill
Bathesland Water
CHURCH RD
PO
CASTLE LEY
CASTLE CL
Chapel Farm
Motel
Bathesland Wood
Caves
Maidenhall Point
Folkeston Moor
Rainbolts Hill Farm
Little Hilton
Hilton Court Gardens
Trefrane Farm
WELSH ROAD
Hilton Home Farm
A487
Folly
Shaft (dis)
Folkeston Hill Farm
Folkeston Farm
FOLKESTON ROAD
SUMMERHILL CL 1
KEEP HILL END 2
Black Cliff
Folkeston Hill
Greenacre Farm
Rickets Head
Nolton Haven Farm
Simpson
Nolton Haven
SA62
Simpson Hill
Nolton Haven
Nolton Haven
Cemy
WEST LANE
Nolton
East Nolton Farm
Trapps Farm
Pembrokeshire Coast Path
North Nolton Farm
Hill Side
Madoc's Haven
Longlands Farm
South Nolton Farm
Druidston Haven
Marlsborough Farm
Quarry (dis)
Rogeston Farm
Hotel
Shortlands Farm
South Rogeston Farm
Druidston
New House Farm
LEYS LANE
Rogeston Cross Farm
Haroldston Chins
Haroldston Hall Farm
Quarry
Settling Nose
Haroldston Tonges Farm
Haroldston Farm
Haroldston West
Black Point
Fort
HAROLDSTON HILL
Timber Hill Farm
Folly Farm
Broomsgrove Farm
LONG LANE
Bellmoor Farm
Timber Hill
Harold Stone
Williamston Farm
ASKERS LANE
Sieck Stone
Headlands
Belmont Farm
Millmoor
Quarry (dis)
MILLMOOR WY
B4341
B4341

83 A 84 B 85 C 86 D 87 E 88 F

85

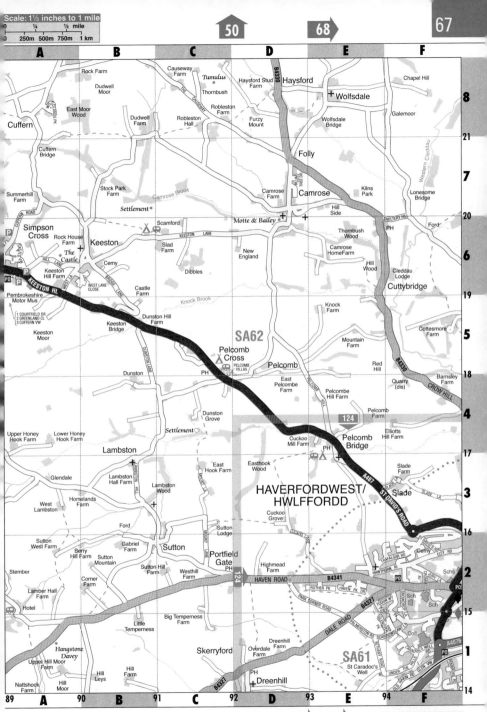

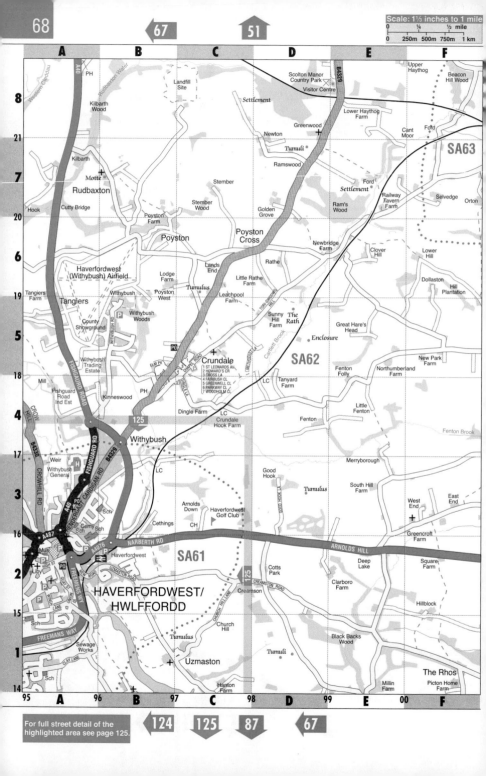

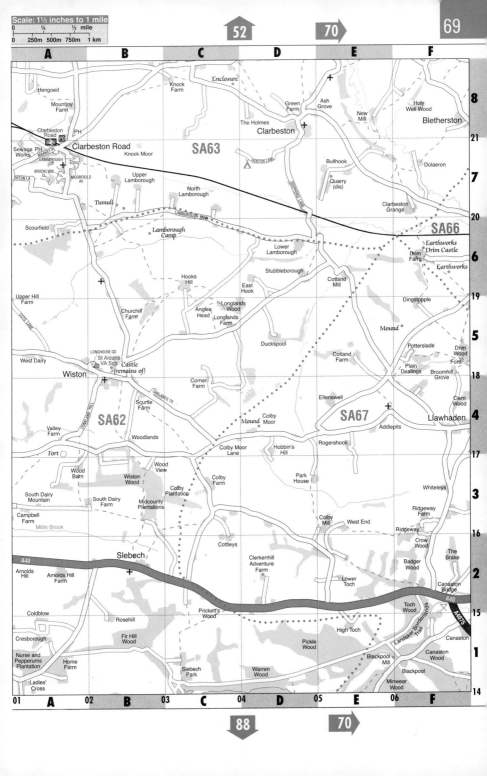

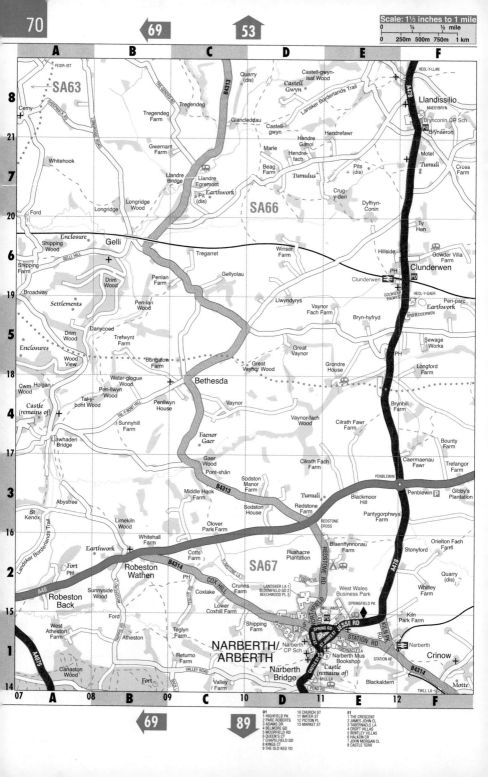

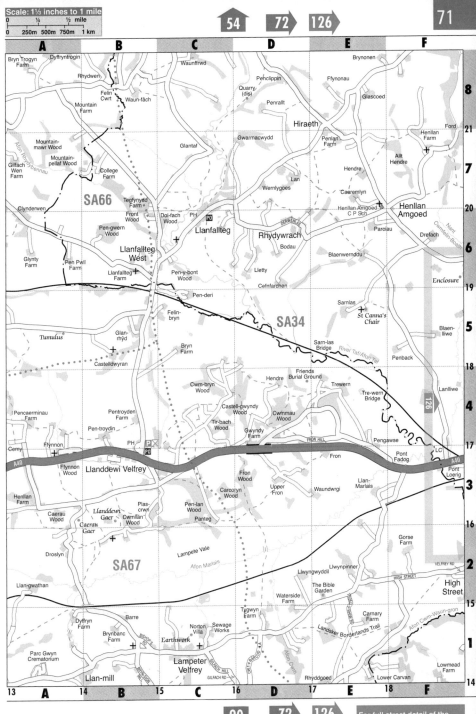

54 72 126

0 ¼ ½ mile
0 250m 500m 750m 1 km

A **B** **C** **D** **E** **F**

Bryn Trogyn Farm
Dyffryntrogin
Rhydwen
Felin Cwrt
Waun-fâch
Mountain Farm
Waunffrwd
Quarry (dis)
Pehclippin
Penclippin
Penrallt
Ffynonau
Glascoed
Brynonen
Henllan Farm
Ford

8
21

Mountain-mawr Wood
Mountain-pellaf Wood
Gilfach Wen Farm
Llochtybennau
College Farm
Glantaf
Gwarmacwydd
Penlan Farm
Hendre
Allt Hendre

Hiraeth

7
20

SA66

Tegfynydd Farm
Front Wood
Dol-fach Wood
PH
PO
Llanfallteg
Lan
Wernlygoes
Caeremlyn
Henllan Amgoed C P Sch
Parciau
Henllan Amgoed
Drefach

Clynderwen
Pen-gwern Wood
Rhydywrach
Bodau
Blaenwernddu
Nant Cwmfelin-Boeth

6
19

Glynty Farm
Pen Pwll Farm
Llanfallteg West
Llanfallteg Farm
Pen-y-bont Wood
Lletty
Cefnfarchen
Enclosure

Pen-deri
Felin-bryn
Sarnlas
St Canna's Chair
Blaen-lliwe

5
18

Tumulus
Glan-rhyd
Castelldwyran
Bryn Farm
Sarn-las Bridge
River Taf/Afon Taf
Penback
Lanlliwe

SA34

Cwm-bryn Wood
Hendre
Friends Burial Ground
Trewern
Tre-wern Bridge
Pengawse

4
17

Pencaerminau Farm
Pentroyden Farm
Pen-troydin
PH
PX
PO
Castell-gwyndy Wood
Tir-bach Wood
Cwmmau Wood
Gwyndy Farm
FRON HILL
Fron
Pont Fadog
LC
Pont Loerig

126

Cemy
Ffynnon
Ffynnon Wood
Llanddewi Velfrey
Fron Wood
Upper Fron
Waundwrgi
Llan-Marlais

A40
A40

3
16

Henllan Farm
Caerau Wood
Llanddewi Gaer
Plas-crwn
Cwmllan Wood
Pen-lan Wood
Panteg
Carcoryn Wood

Caeran Gaer
Droslyn

2

Gorse Farm

Llan-gwathan
SA67
Lampete Vale
Afon Marlais
Llwyngwyddil
Llwynpinner
The Bible Garden
HIGH STREET
VELFREY RD
High Street

15

Dyfryn Farm
Brynbanc Farm
Barre
Norton Villa
Earthwork
Sewage Works
Tygwyn Farm
Waterside Farm
Landsker Borderlands Trail
Carnary Farm
Lowmead Farm

1
14

Parc Gwyn Crematorium
Lampeter Velfrey
Lower Carvan
Rhyddgoed
Lowmead Farm

Llan-mill

13 A 14 B 15 C 16 D 17 E 18 F

90 72 126

For full street detail of the highlighted area see page 126.

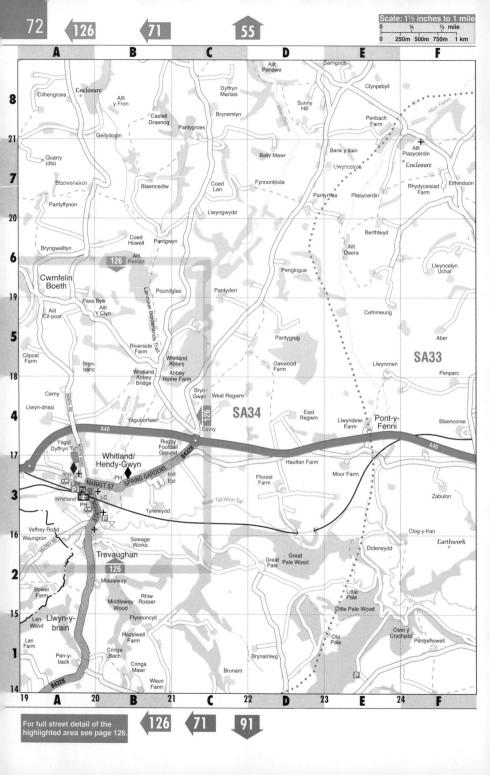

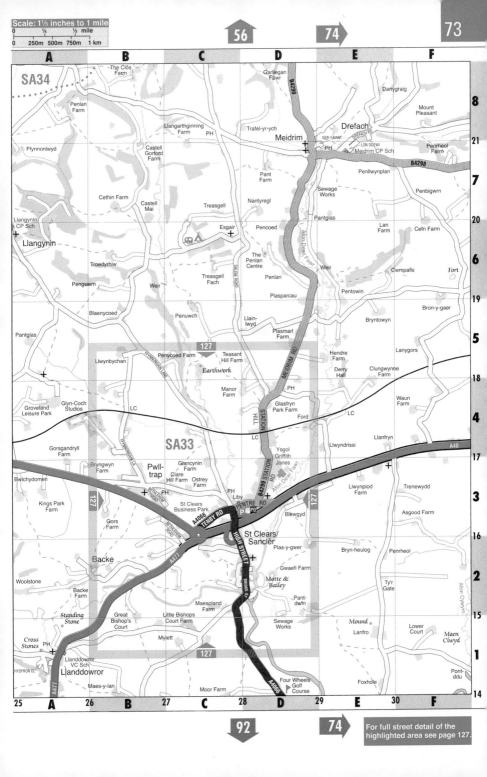

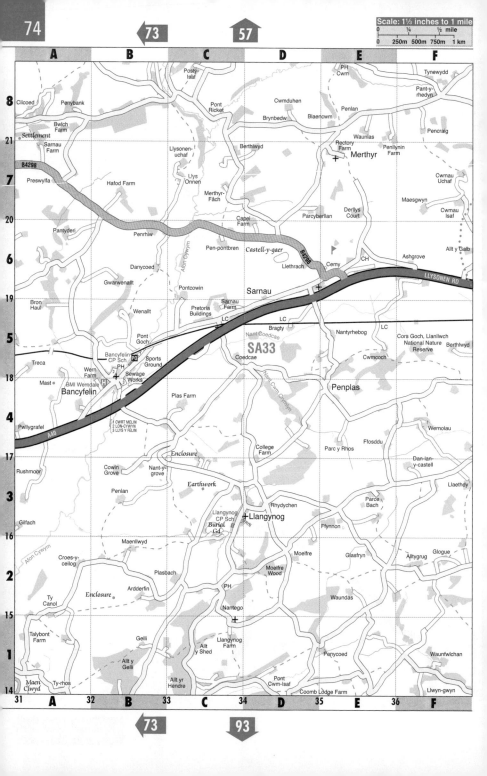

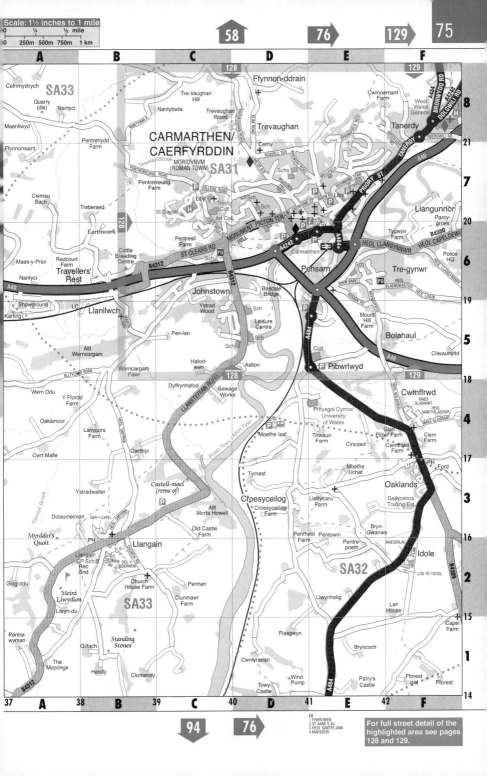

128   129

8

Cefnmystrych
SA33
Quarry (dis)
Nantyci
Maenllwyd
Ffynnonsaint
Pentrehydd Farm

Ffynnon-ddrain

Tre-Vaughan Hill
Nantybwla
Trevaughan Wood
Trevaughan

Cwmoernant Farm
West Wales General
Tanerdy

21

CARMARTHEN/ CAERFYRDDIN
MORIDVNVM (ROMAN TOWN)
SA31

Cwmau Bach
Trebersed
Pentremeurig Farm
St Davids

Cefny
Schs
Russell Ter

7

Llangunnor
Parcy-groes
B4300
Tygwyn Farm

20

Maes-y-Prior
Redcourt Farm
Nantyci
Travellers' Rest
Earthwork
Cattle Breeding Centre

Pentresil Farm
Art Coll
Trinity Coll
Liby
Sch

Pensarn

Tre-gynwr
Police HQ

6

ST CLEARS RD
B4312

Johnstown
Bascule Bridge
Ystrad Wood

Mount Hill Farm

19

Showground
Karting
Llanllwch
LC

Pen-lan
Leisure Centre
Sch
Sch

Bolahaul
Cilwaunydd

5

Allt Werncorgam
Hafod-wen
Werncargam Fawr

Aslton

Coll
Pibwrlwyd

18

Wern Ddu
Y Ffordd Farm
Oakamoor

Dyffrynhafod
Sewage Works

Cwmffrwd
MAES GLASNANT
HEOL NANTYGLASDWR
MAES GLASNANT

4

Lanygors Farm
Cwrthyr
Cwrt Malle

Moelfre Isaf

Prifysgol Cymru/ University of Wales
Tirwaun Farm
Cincoed

Glan Pibwr Farm
Cwmffrwd Farm
Cwm Farm
PH
Ford

17

Ystradwalter

Castell-moel (rems of)

Tyrnest

Moelfre Uchaf

Oaklands
Gellyceiros Trading Est

3

Dolaumeinion
Myrddin's Quoit
PH

Croesyceilog
Croesyceilog Farm

Llettycaru Farm

Bryn-Gwanws

16

Glog-ddu
Llangain
Llangain CP Sch Rec Gnd
Church House Farm
Penhen
Old Castle Farm
Allt Morfa Howell

Penrheol Farm
Pentowin
Pentre-poeth

Idole

SA32

2

Rentrewyman
Meini Llwydion
Llwyn-du
SA33
Gilfach
Standing Stones
Clunmawr Farm

Llwynhelig
Llan House

15

The Moorings
Hendy
Clomendy

Plasgwyn
Cwmyrarian
Towy Castle
Wind Pump
Bryncoch
Parry's Castle
Fforest isaf
Capel Farm
Fforest

1

37   38   39   40   41   42   14

F3
1 FFWROWEN
2 ST ANNE'S AV
3 HEOL SANTES ANN
4 MAESDERI

For full street detail of the highlighted area see pages 128 and 129.

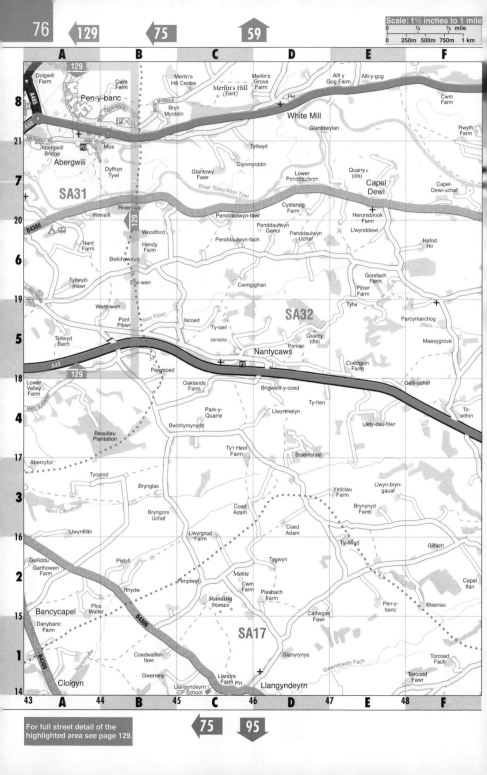

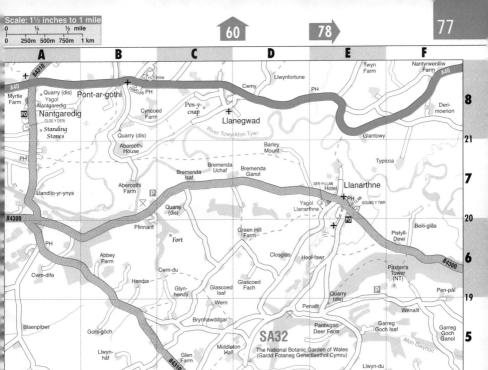

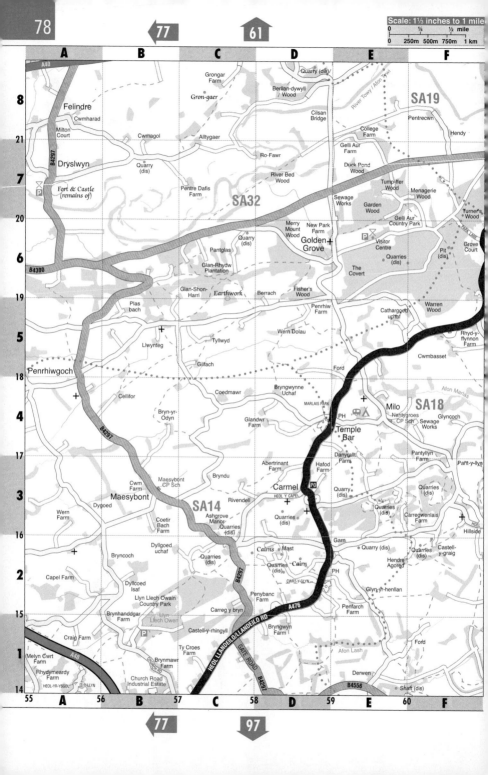

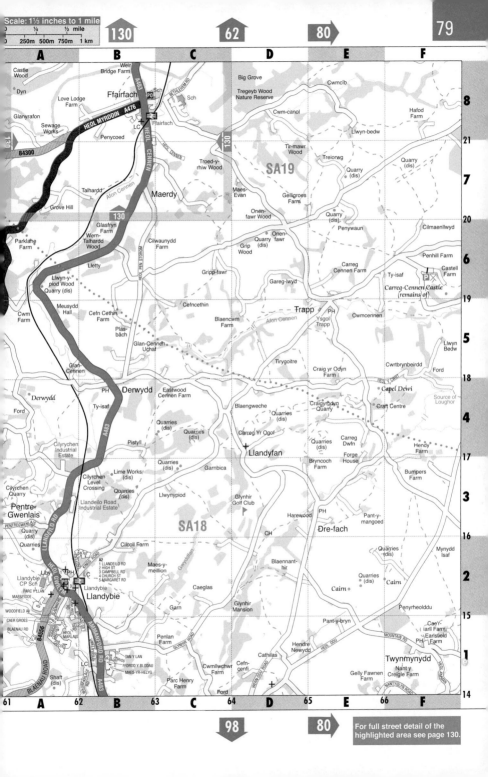

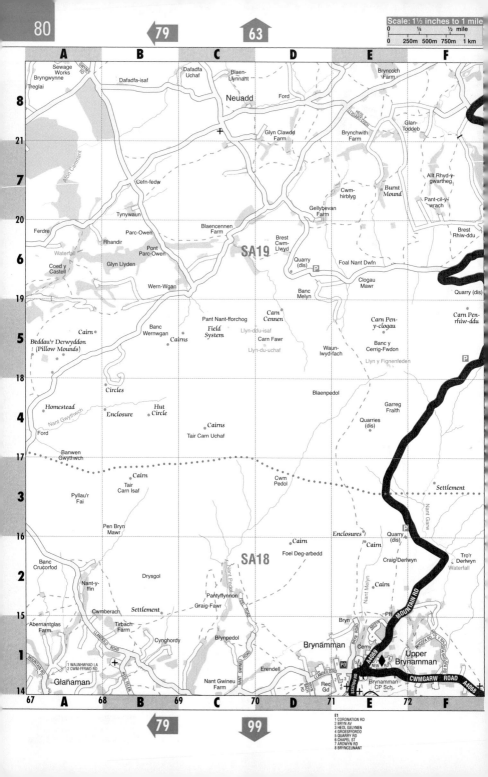

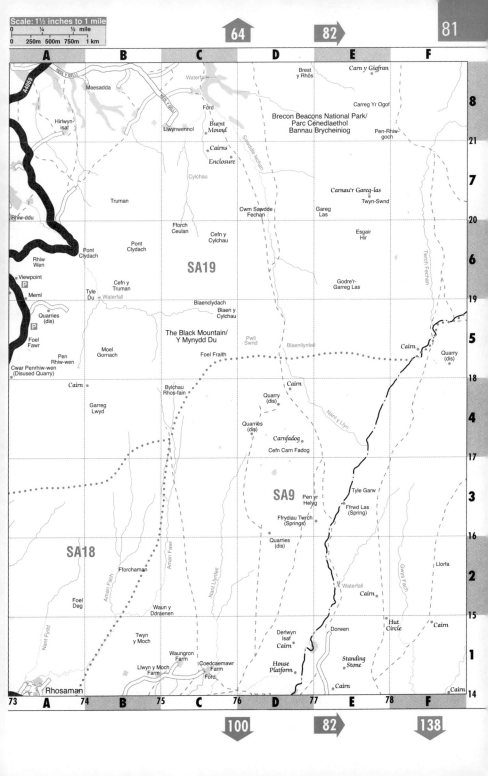

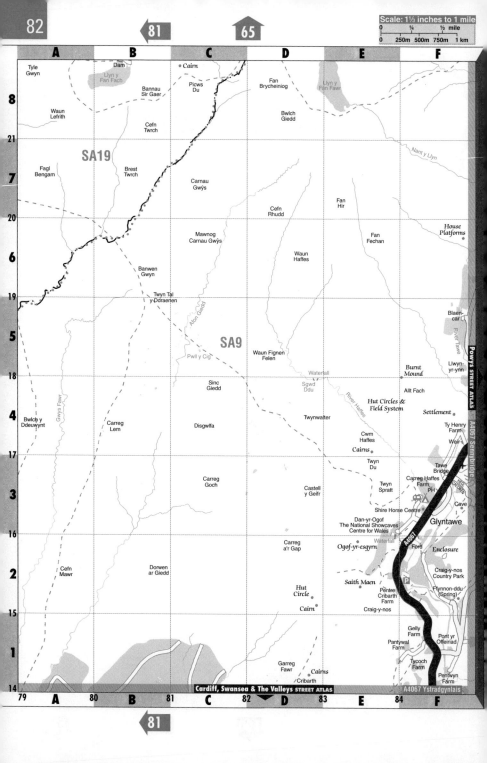

A   B   C   D   E   F

Tyle Gwyn

Dam
Llyn y Fan Fach

Cairn

Picws Du

Fan Brycheiniog

Llyn y Fan Fawr

8

Bannau Sir Gaer

Waun Lefrith

Cefn Twrch

Bwlch Giedd

21

SA19

Fagl Bengam

Brest Twrch

Carnau Gwŷs

Nant y Llyn

7

Cefn Rhudd

Fan Hir

20

Mawnog Carnau Gwŷs

House Platforms

6

Banwen Gwyn

Waun Haffes

Fan Fechan

Twyn Tal y-Ddraenen

Afon Giedd

Blaen-car

19

Pwll y Cig

SA9

Waun Fignen Felen

River Tawe

Llwyn-yr-ynn

5

Waterfall

Burnt Mound

18

Sinc Giedd

Sgwd Ddu

Allt Fach

Powys STREET ATLAS

Gwys Fawr

Hut Circles & Field System

Settlement

A4067 Sennybridge

4

Bwlch y Ddeuwynt

Carreg Lem

Disgwlfa

Twynwalter

River Haffes

Ty Henry Farm

17

Cwm Haffes

Weir

Cairns

Tawe Bridge

3

Carreg Goch

Castell y Geifr

Twyn Du

Carreg Haffes Farm

PH

Cave

Twyn Spratt

Shire Horse Centre

Glyntawe

Dan-yr-Ogof The National Showcaves Centre for Wales

16

Carreg a'r Gap

Ogof-yr-esgyrn

Waterfall

Ford

Enclosure

2

Cefn Mawr

Dorwen ar Giedd

Saith Maen

Pentre Cribarth Farm

Craig-y-nos Country Park

Ffynnon-ddu (Spring)

Hut Circle

Craig-y-nos

Gelly Farm

Pont yr Offeiriad

15

Cairn

Pantywal Farm

Tycoch Farm

1

Garreg Fawr

Cairns

Cribarth

Pentwyn Farm

14

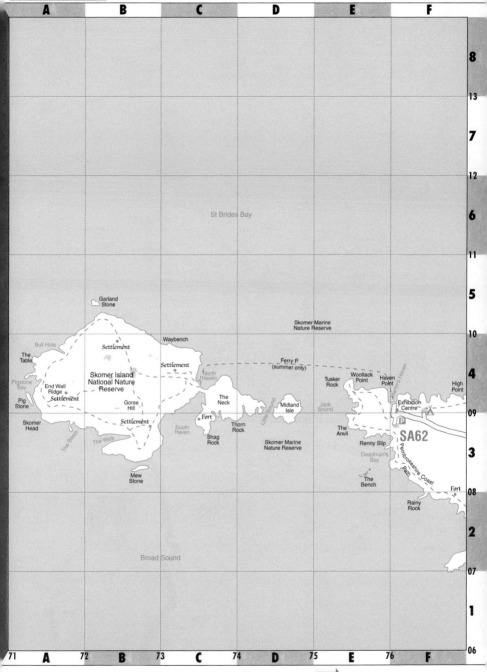

A B C D E F

8

13

7

12

6

St Brides Bay

11

5

10

Garland
Stone

Skomer Marine
Nature Reserve

Bull Hole   Waybench

The
Table   *Settlement*

Settlement

Skomer Island
National Nature   North
Reserve   Haven   Ferry P   Wooltack   4
(summer only)   Tusker   Point   Haven
Pigstone   Rock   Point
Bay   High
End Wall   The   Exhibition   Point
Pig   Ridge   Gorse   Neck   Jack   Centre
Stone   *Settlement*   Hill   Midland   Sound
Skomer   *Fort*   Isle   09
Head   *Settlement*   The
The Basin   The Wick   South   Thorn   Anvil   SA62
Haven   Shag   Rock   Skomer Marine   Renny Slip
Rock   Nature Reserve   3

Mew   Deadman's
Stone   Bay
The
Bench   Fort
08

Broad Sound   Rainy
Rock

2

07

1

06

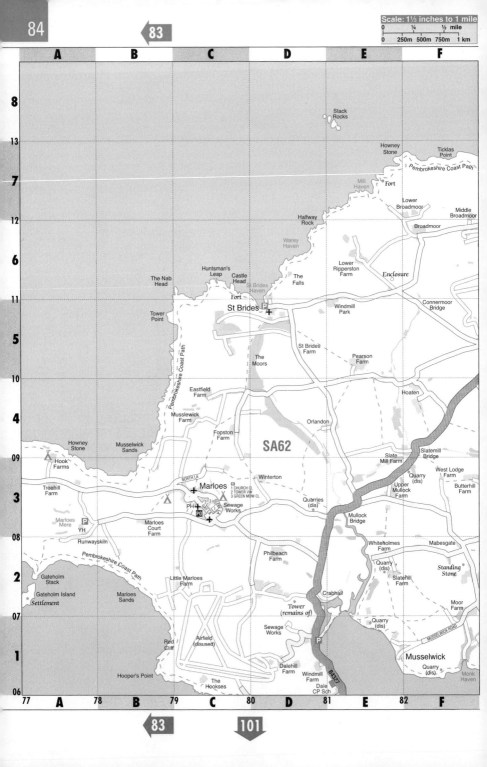

Scale: 1⅓ inches to 1 mile

0   ¼   ½   mile
0   250m 500m 750m 1 km

A **B** **C** **D** **E** **F**

8

13

7

12

6

11

5

10

4

09

3

08

2

07

1

06

Stack Rocks

Howney Stone

Ticklas Point

Pembrokeshire Coast Path

Mill Haven

Fort

Lower Broadmoor

Middle Broadmoor

Broadmoor

Halfway Rock

Warey Haven

Lower Ripperston Farm

Enclosure

The Nab Head

Huntsman's Leap

Castle Head

St Brides Haven

The Falls

Fort

St Brides

Connermoor Bridge

Tower Point

Windmill Park

Pembrokeshire Coast Path

The Moors

St Brides Farm

Pearson Farm

Hoaten

Eastfield Farm

Musslewick Farm

Fopston Farm

Orlandon

SA62

Slatemill Bridge

Howney Stone

Hook Farms

Musselwick Sands

Winterton

Slate Mill Farm

Quarry (dis)

West Lodge Farm

Butterhill Farm

Treehill Farm

Marloes

C1
1 CHURCH CL
2 TOWER VW
3 GREEN MDW CL

Upper Mullock Farm

NORTH LA

PH

PO

Sewage Works

Quarries (dis)

Mullock Bridge

Marloes Mere

YH

Marloes Court Farm

Whiteholmes Farm

Mabesgate

Runwayskiln

Philbeach Farm

Quarry (dis)

Slatehill Farm

Standing Stone

Pembrokeshire Coast Path

Gateholm Stack

Gateholm Island
Settlement

Marloes Sands

Little Marloes Farm

Crabhall

Tower (remains of)

Quarry (dis)

Moor Farm

Red Cliff

Airfield (disused)

Sewage Works

MUSSELWICK ROAD

Hooper's Point

The Hookses

Dalehill Farm

Windmill Farm

Dale CP Sch

Quarry (dis)

Musselwick

Monk Haven

B4327

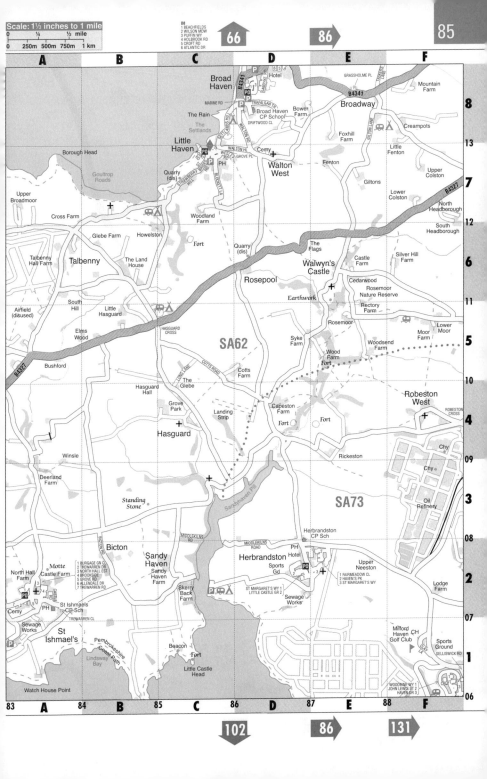

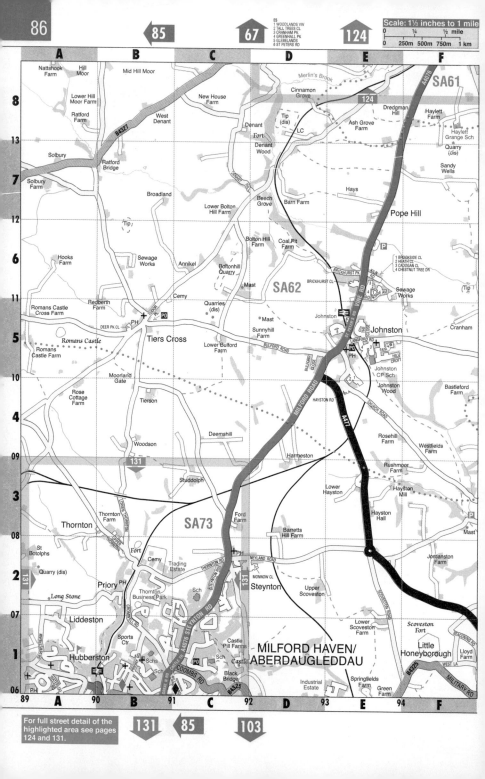

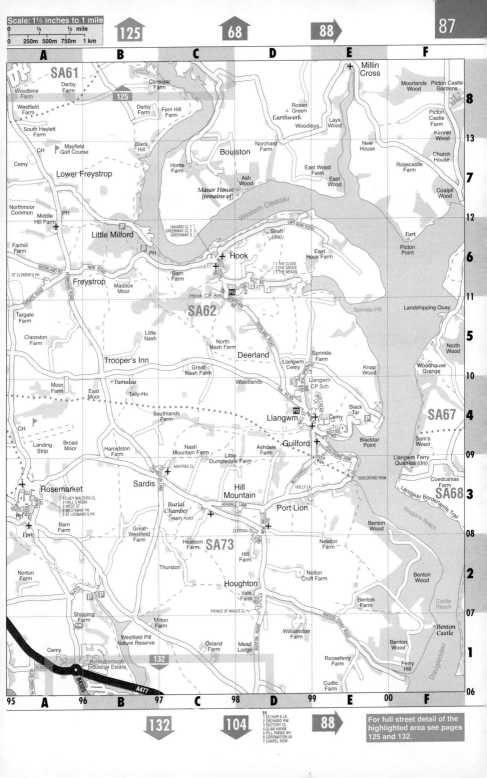

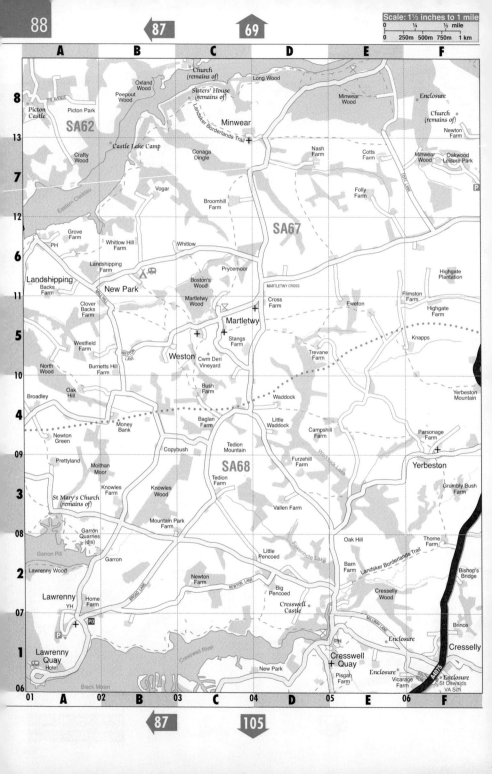

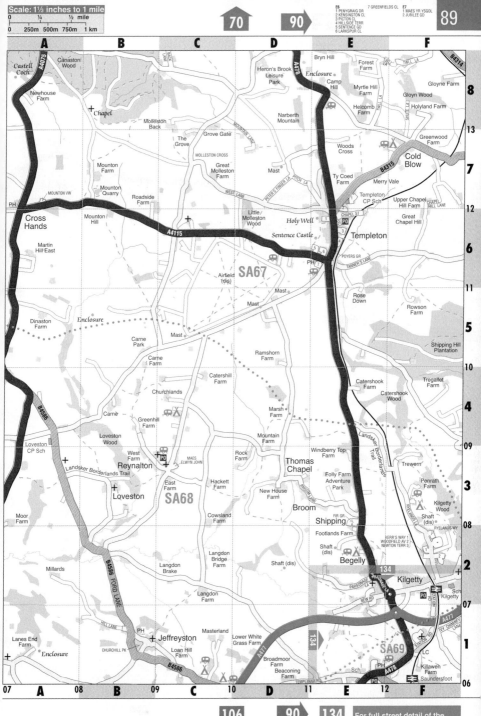

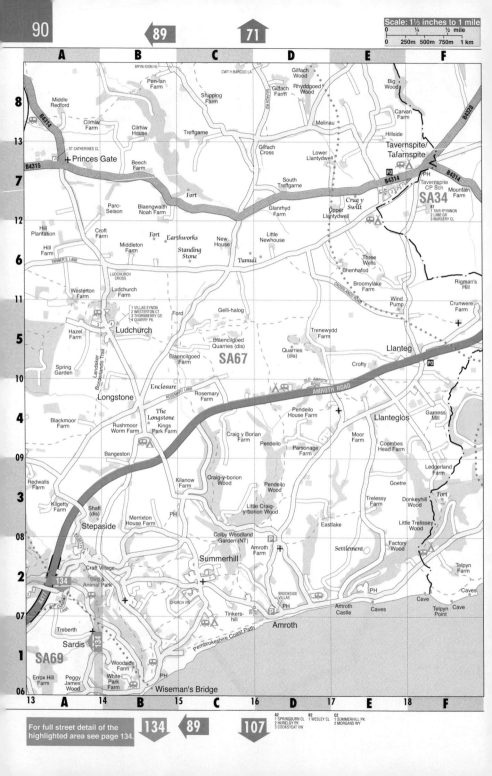

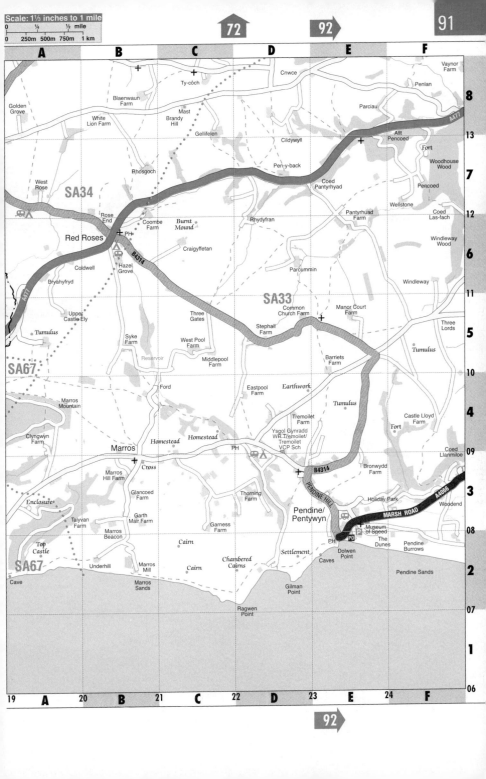

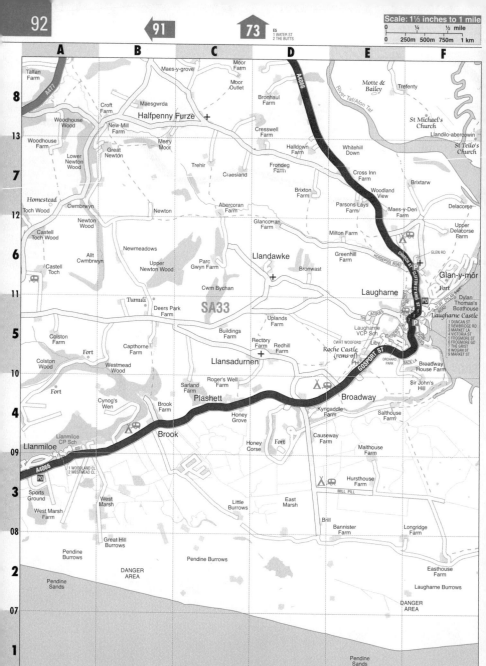

A **B** **C** **D** **E** **F**

8

13

7

12

6

11

5

10

4

09

3

08

2

07

1

06

Talfan
Farm

Woodhouse
Wood

Woodhouse
Farm

Homestead

Toch Wood

Castell
Toch Wood

Castell
Toch

Colston
Farm

Fort

Colston
Wood

Fort

Llanmiloe
CP Sch

Llanmiloe

Sports
Ground

West Marsh
Farm

Pendine
Sands

Pendine
Burrows

Croft
Farm

New Mill
Farm

Great
Newton

Lower
Newton
Wood

Cwmbrwyn

Newton
Wood

Allt
Cwmbrwyn

Newmeadows

Tumuli

Deers Park
Farm

Capthorne
Farm

Westmead
Wood

Cynog's
Wen

Brook
Farm

1 WOODLAND CL
2 WESTMEAD CL

West
Marsh

Great Hill
Burrows

Maes-y-grove

Maesgwrda

Halfpenny Furze

Merry
Moor

Trehir

Newton

Upper
Newton Wood

Parc
Gwyn Farm

Cwm Bychan

Buildings
Farm

Brook

Plashett

Honey
Grove

Little
Burrows

DANGER
AREA

Pendine Burrows

Moor
Farm

Moor
Outlet

Cresswell
Farm

Craesiand

Abercoran
Farm

Llandawke

Roger's Well
Farm

Sarland
Farm

Honey
Corse

Bronhaul
Farm

Halldown
Farm

Frondeg
Farm

Brixton
Farm

Glancorran
Farm

Bronwast

Uplands
Farm

Rectory
Farm

Redhill
Farm

Llansadurnen

Fort

East
Marsh

Brill

Bannister
Farm

River Taf/Afon Taf

Motte &
Bailey

Whitehill
Down

Cross Inn
Farm

Woodland
View

Parsons Lays
Farm

Milton Farm

Greenhill
Farm

Laugharne
VCP Sch

Roche Castle
(rems of)

CWRT WOOFORD

Liby

ORCHARD
PARK

Kyngaddle
Farm

Causeway
Farm

Malthouse
Farm

Hursthouse
Farm

MILL PILL

Trefenty

St Michael's
Church

Llandilo-abercowin

St Teilo's
Church

Brixtarw

Maes-y-Deri
Farm

Delacorse

Upper
Delacorse
Farm

GLEN RD

Glan-y-môr
Fort

Laugharne

Dylan
Thomas's
Boathouse

Laugharne Castle

1 DUNCAN ST
2 NEWBRIDGE RD
3 MARKET LA
4 VICTORIA ST
5 FROGMORE ST
6 FROGMORE GD
7 THE GRIST
8 WOGAN ST
9 MARKET ST

Broadway

Sir John's
Hill

Broadway
House Farm

Salthouse
Farm

Longridge
Farm

Easthouse
Farm

Laugharne Burrows

DANGER
AREA

Pendine
Sands

SA33

A4066

A477

A4066

HORSEPOOL ROAD

CHURCH ST

CLIFTON ST

CLIFTON ST

KING ST

GOSPORT ST

BACK LA

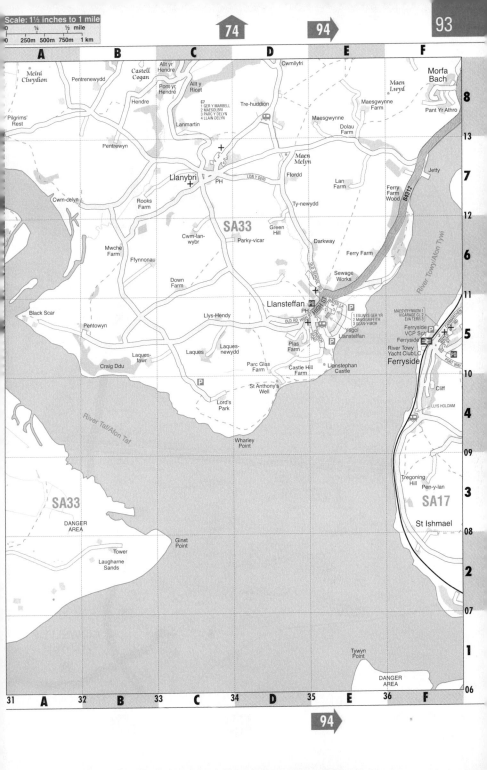

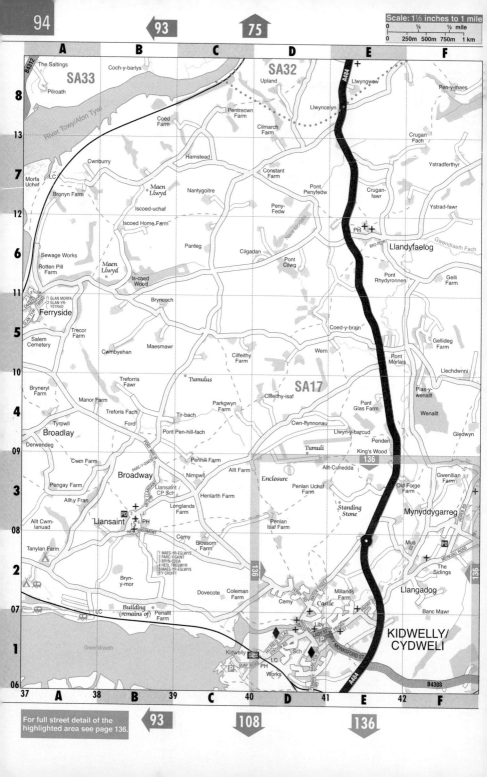

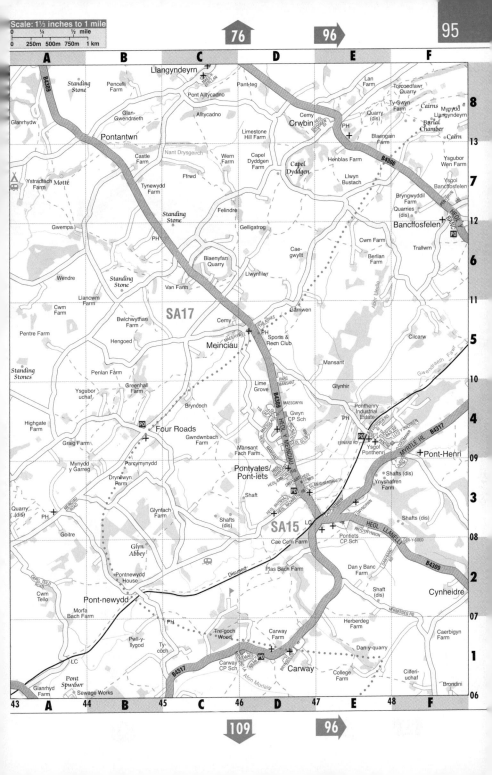

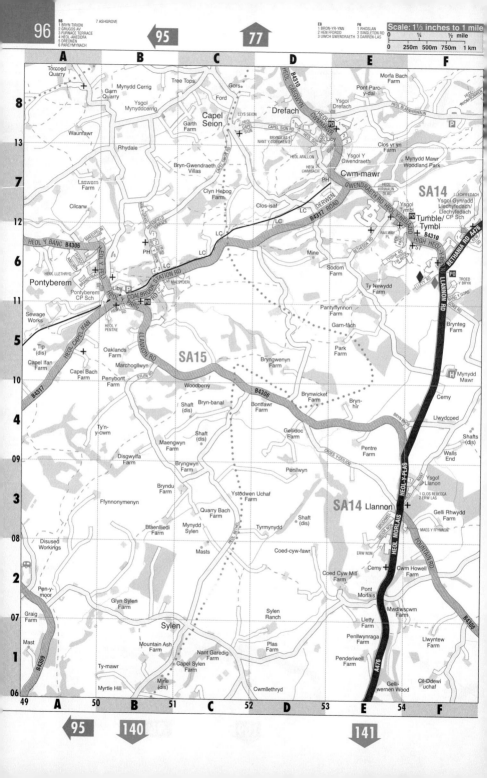

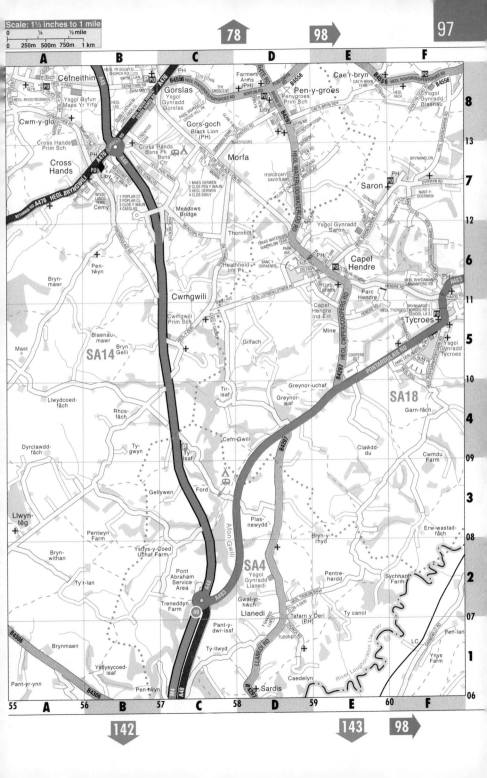

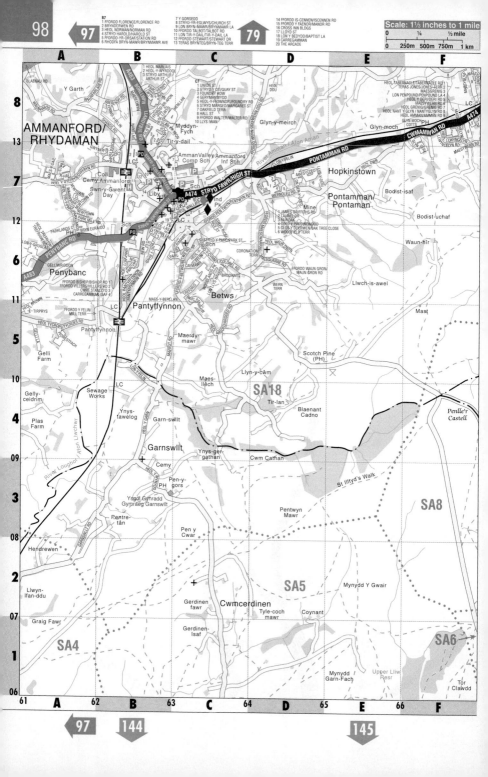

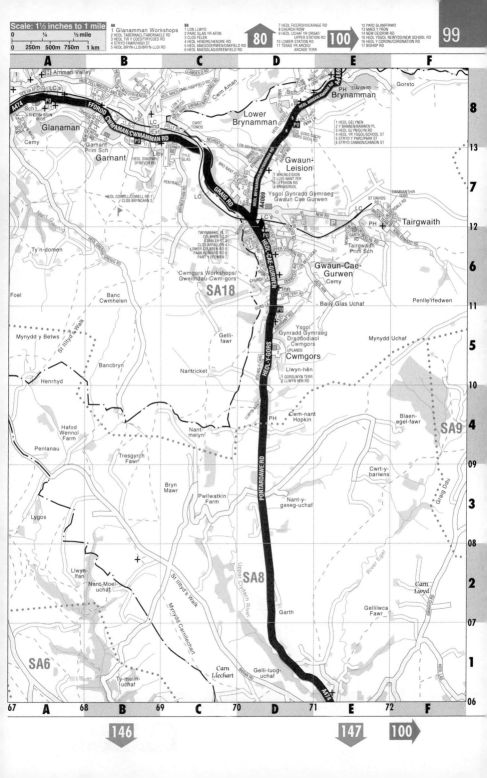

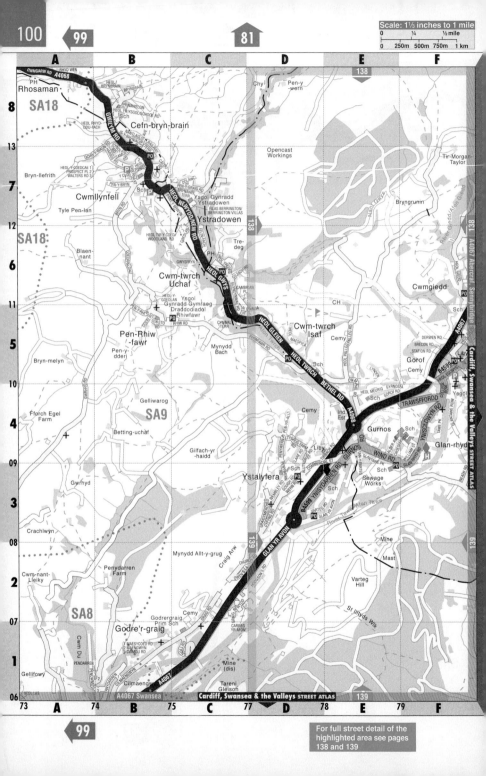

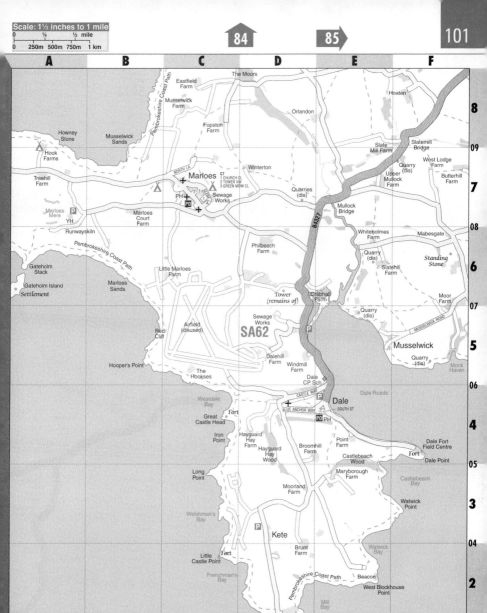

The Moors

Hoaten

Eastfield
Farm

Musselwick
Farm

Orlandon

Slate
Mill Farm

Slatemill
Bridge

Fopston
Farm

West Lodge
Farm

Pembrokeshire Coast Path

Howney
Stone

Musselwick
Sands

Winterton

Quarry
(dis)

Upper
Mullock
Farm

Butterhill
Farm

Hook
Farms

NORTH LA

Marloes

C7
1 CHURCH CL
2 TOWER VW
3 GREEN MDW CL

Quarries
(dis)

B4327

Treehill
Farm

PH
PO

Sewage
Works

Mullock
Bridge

Marloes
Mere

P

Marloes
Court
Farm

Whiteholmes
Wood

Mabesgate

YH

Runwayskin

Philbeach
Farm

Quarry
(dis)

Standing
Stone

Pembrokeshire Coast Path

Little Marloes
Farm

Slatehill
Farm

Gateholm
Stack

Marloes
Sands

Tower
(remains of)

Crabhall
Farm

Moor
Farm

Gateholm Island
Settlement

Quarry
(dis)

MUSSELWICK ROAD

Airfield
(disused)

Sewage
Works

SA62

P

Musselwick

Red
Cliff

Dalehill
Farm

Windmill
Farm

Quarry
(dis)

Monk
Haven

Hooper's Point

The
Hookses

Dale
CP Sch

P

Dale Roads

Westdale
Bay

CASTLE WAY

P

Dale

Fort

BLUE ANCHOR WAY

SOUTH ST

Great
Castle Head

PO PH

Iron
Point

Hayguard
Hay
Farm

Point
Farm

Dale Fort
Field Centre

Broomhill
Farm

Fort

Hayguard
Hay
Wood

Castlebeach
Wood

Dale Point

Long
Point

Maryborough
Farm

Castlebeach
Bay

Welshman's
Bay

Moorland
Farm

Watwick
Point

P

Kete

Watwick
Bay

Little
Castle Point

Fort

Brunt
Farm

Frenchman's
Bay

West Blockhouse
Point

Pembrokeshire Coast Path

Beacon

Mill
Bay

Radio Mast

Lighthouse

St Ann's
Head

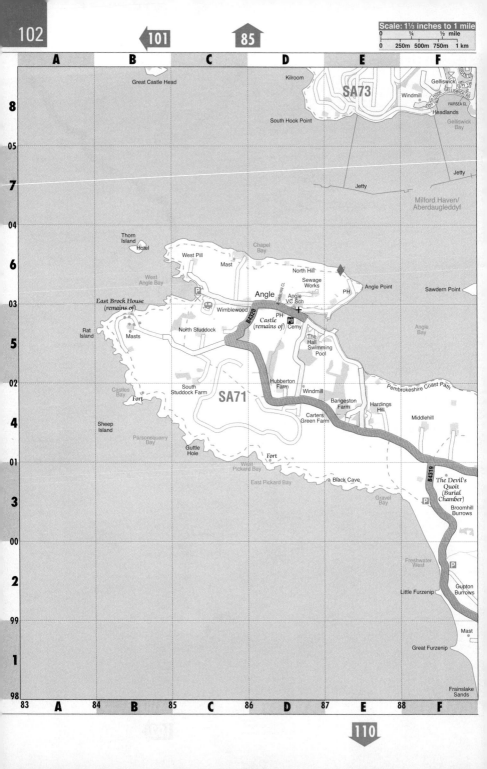

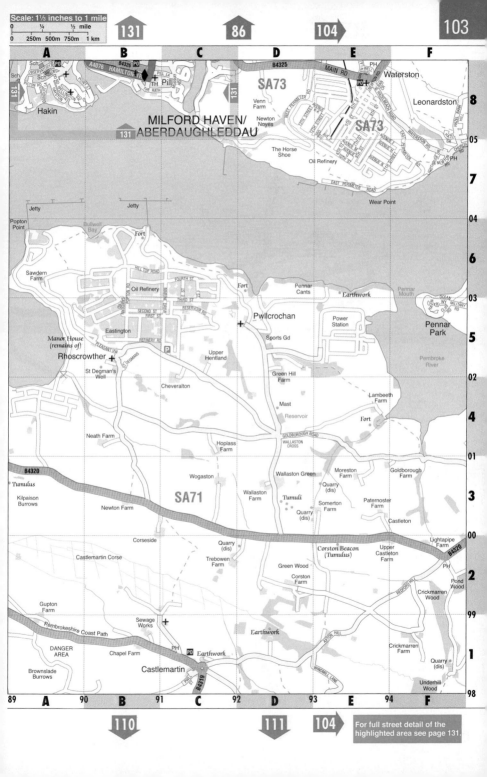

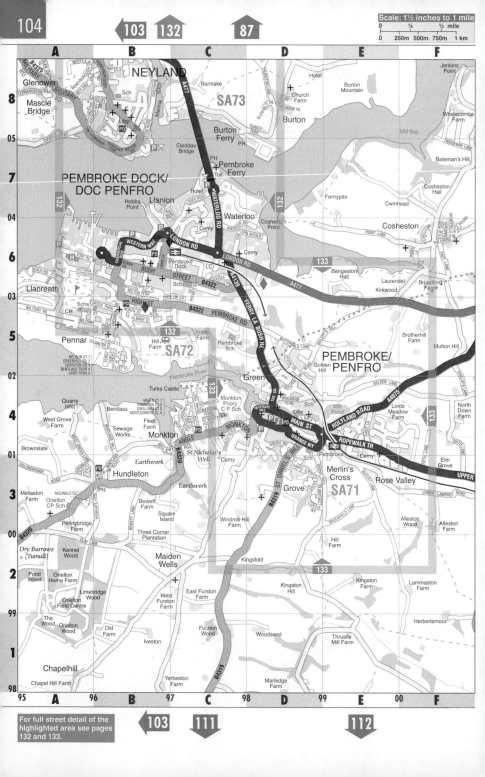

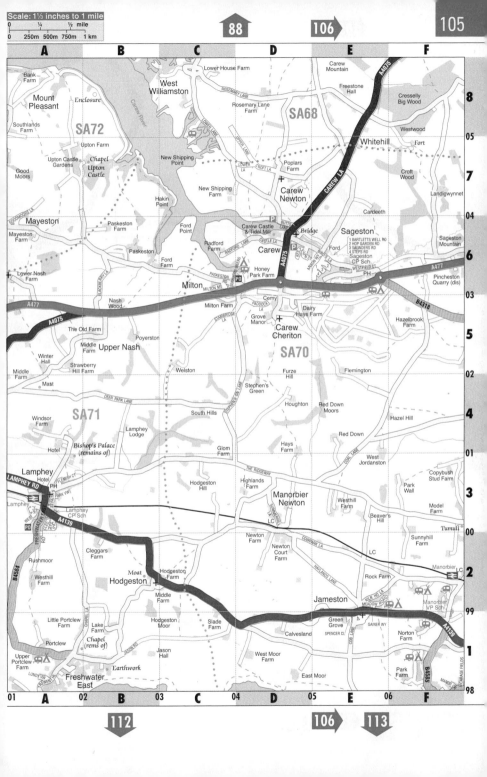

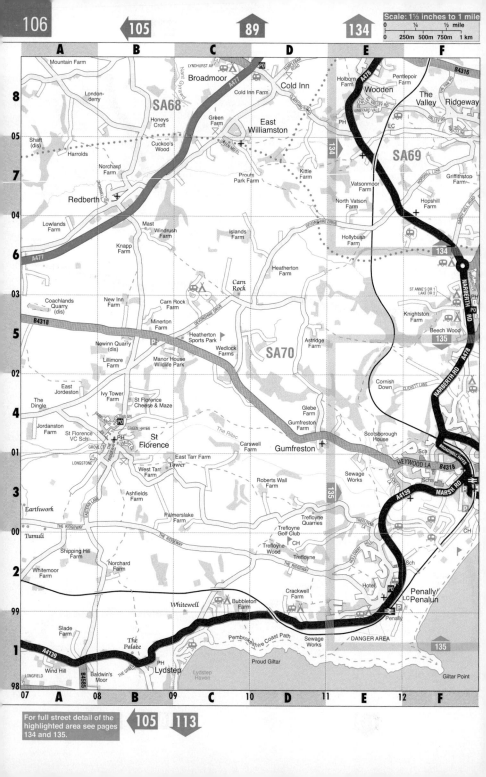

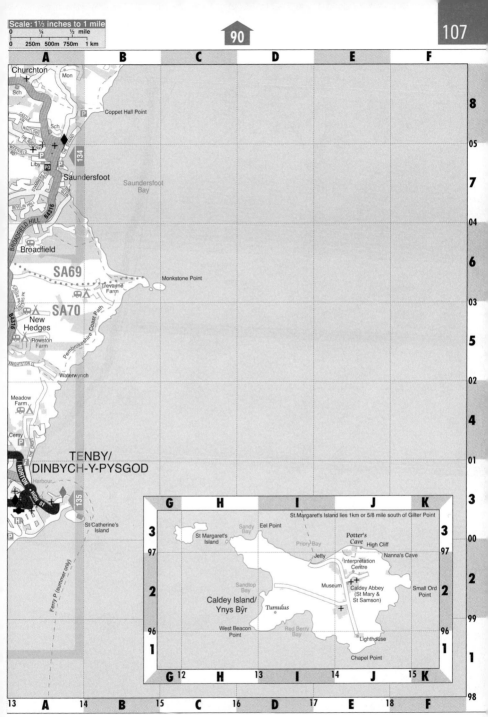

Scale: 1½ inches to 1 mile

0 ¼ ½ mile
0 250m 500m 750m 1 km

90

Churchton
Mon
Sch
Coppet Hall Point
P
CASTLE DR
WHITLOW
THE ROAD WAY
WESTFIELD
THE INCLINE
Liby
P
PO
P
Saundersfoot
134
BEVELIN HALL
BROADFIELD HILL
B4316
Saundersfoot Bay
Broadfield

SA69
Trevayne Farm
Monkstone Point

CROSS PK
SA70
New Hedges
Pembrokeshire Coast Path
B4316
Rowston Farm

KNIGHTSTON CL
Waterwynch

Meadow Farm
Cemy
P

TENBY/
DINBYCH-Y-PYSGOD
Harbour
NORTON
HIGH ST
135
St Catherine's Island
P

Ferry P (summer only)

St.Margaret's Island lies 1km or 5/8 mile south of Gilter Point

G   H   I   J   K

3
97
St Margaret's Island
Sandy Bay
Eel Point
Priory Bay
Potter's Cave
High Cliff
Jetty
Nanna's Cave
Interpretation Centre
3
97

2
Sandtop Bay
Museum
Caldey Abbey
(St Mary & St Samson)
Small Ord Point
2
99

Caldey Island/
Ynys Bŷr
Tumulus

96
West Beacon Point
Red Berry Bay
Lighthouse
96

1
Chapel Point
1

G 12   H   13   I   14   J   15   K

98

8
05
7
04
6
03
5
02
4
01
3
00
2
99
1
98

13 A 14 B 15 C 16 D 17 E 18 F

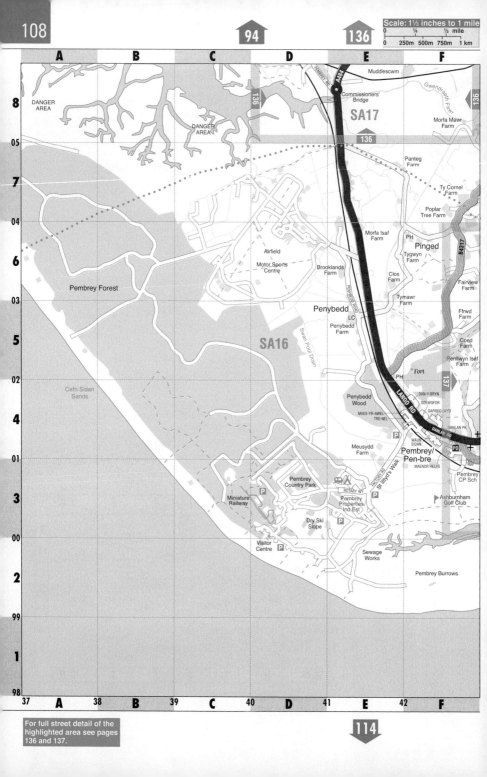

Scale: 1⅓ inches to 1 mile

0 ¼ ½ mile
0 250m 500m 750m 1 km

94

136

A   B   C   D   E   F

8

DANGER
AREA

Muddlescwm

Commissioners'
Bridge

Gwendraeth Fawr

SA17

Morfa Mawr
Farm

136

05

DANGER
AREA

Panteg
Farm

Ty Cornel
Farm

7

Poplar
Tree Farm

04

PH

Morfa Isaf
Farm

Pinged

B4317

6

Pembrey Forest

Airfield

Motor Sports
Centre

Brooklands
Farm

Tygwyn
Farm

Clos
Farm

Fairview
Farm

03

Penybedd

Tymawr
Farm

Ffrwd
Farm

LC

Penybedd
Farm

Coed
Farm

5

SA16

Swan Pool Drain

Penllwyn Isaf
Farm

02

PH

Fort

137

Penybedd
Wood

DAN-Y-BRYN
GOLWGFOR

4

Cefn Sidan
Sands

MAES-YR-AWEL
TRE-NEL

GARREGLWYD

DANLAN PK

P

WAUN
SIDAN

PO

01

Meusydd
Farm

Pembrey/
Pen-bre

MAENOR HELYG

Pembrey
CP Sch

3

Miniature
Railway

P

Pembrey
Country Park

ROTARY WY

Pembrey
Properties
Ind Est

P

St Illtyd's Walk

FACTORY RD

Ashburnham
Golf Club

00

Dry Ski
Slope

P

Visitor
Centre

P

Sewage
Works

2

Pembrey Burrows

99

1

98

37   A   38   B   39   C   40   D   41   E   42   F

For full street detail of the
highlighted area see pages
136 and 137.

114

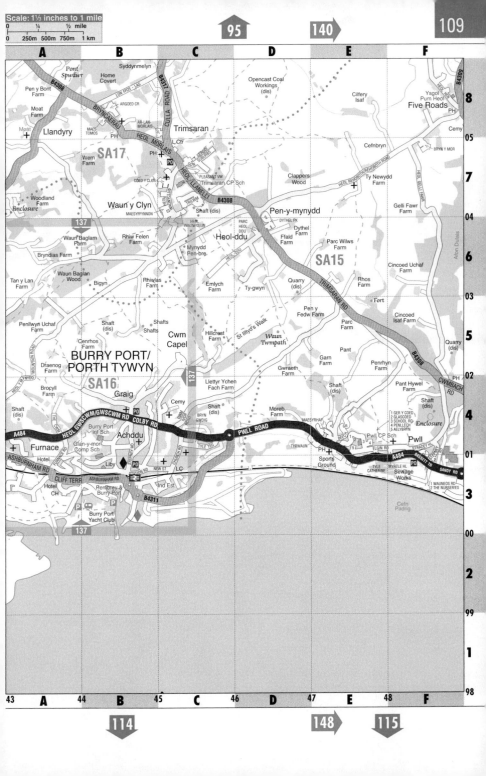

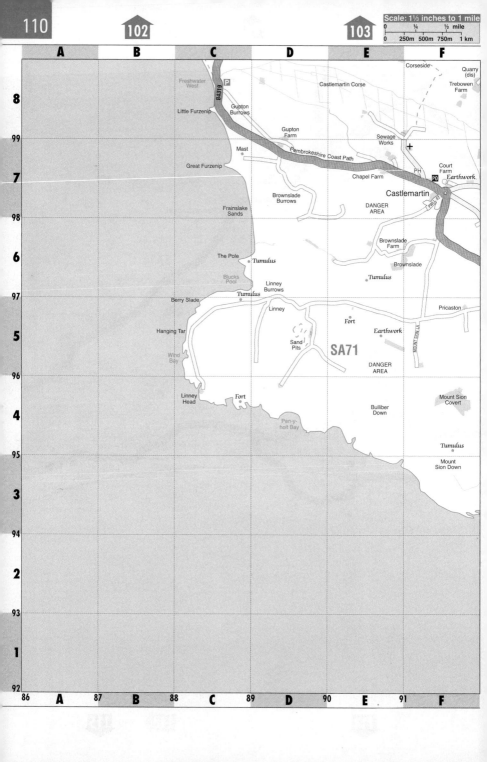

Scale: 1½ inches to 1 mile
0   ¼   ½ mile
0   250m 500m 750m 1 km

8

99

7

98

6

97

5

96

4

95

3

94

2

93

1

92

A   B   C   D   E   F

Corseside
Quarry (dis)
Trebowen Farm
Castlemartin Corse
Freshwater West
P
B4319
Little Furzenip
Gupton Burrows
Gupton Farm
Sewage Works
Mast
Pembrokeshire Coast Path
Great Furzenip
Chapel Farm
PH
Court Farm
Earthwork
PO
Castlemartin
Brownslade Burrows
Frainslake Sands
DANGER AREA
Brownslade Farm
The Pole
Tumulus
Brownslade
Blucks Pool
Linney Burrows
Tumulus
Tumulus
Berry Slade
Linney
Pricaston
Hanging Tar
Fort
Earthwork
MOUNT SION LA
Sand Pits
SA71
Wind Bay
DANGER AREA
Linney Head
Fort
Mount Sion Covert
Pen-y-holt Bay
Bulliber Down
Tumulus
Mount Sion Down

86   A   87   B   88   C   89   D   90   E   91   F

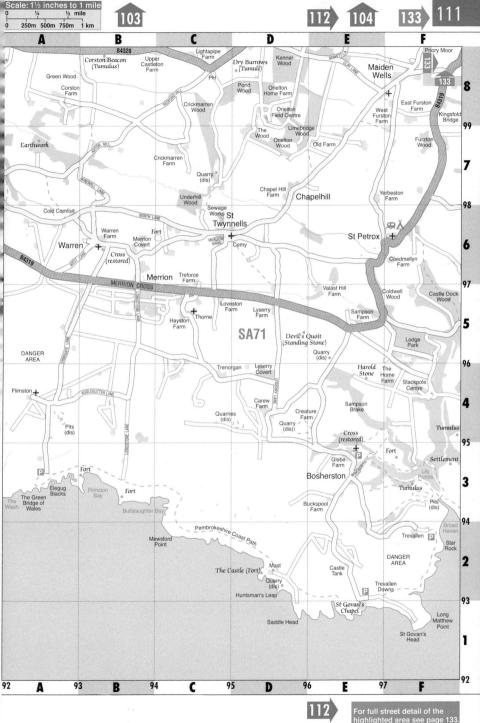

A   B   C   D   E   F

B4320

8

Green Wood

Corston Beacon (Tumulus)

Upper Castleton Farm

Lightapipe Farm

Dry Burrows (Tumuli)

Kennel Wood

Maiden Wells

Corston Farm

PH

Pond Wood

Orielton Home Farm

West Furston Farm

East Furston Farm

Kingsfold Bridge

133

Crickmarren Wood

Orielton Field Centre

99

Earthwork

Crickmarren Farm

The Wood

Limebridge Wood

Furzton Wood

7

Quarry (dis)

Chapel Hill Farm

Orielton Wood

Old Farm

Yerbeston Farm

Underhill Wood

Chapel Hill Farm

Chapelhill

Cold Comfort

NORTH LANE

Sewage Works

St Twynnells

St Petrox

98

Warren Farm

Merrion Covert

Fort

MEADOW BANK

Cemy

Coedmellyn Farm

6

Warren

Cross (restored)

WEST LANE

Merrion

MERRION CROSS

Treforce Farm

Valast Hill Farm

Coldwell Wood

Castle Dock Wood

97

B4319

LONGSTONE LANE

Loveston Farm

Lyserry Farm

Sampson Farm

5

Hayston Farm

Thorne

SA71

Devil's Quoit (Standing Stone)

Lodge Park

DANGER AREA

FARMGATE LANE

Trenorgan

Lyserry Covert

Quarry (dis)

Harold Stone

The Home Farm

Stackpole Centre

96

Flimston

ADDLEGUTTER LANE

LONGSTONE LANE

Carew Farm

Quarry (dis)

Creature Farm

Sampson Brake

Tumulus

4

Pits (dis)

Quarries (dis)

Cross (restored)

Fort

Settlement

95

Fort

Glebe Farm

Bosherston

Tumulus

Lily Ponds

3

Elegug Stacks

The Green Bridge of Wales

Flimston Bay

Fort

Buckspool Farm

Pits (dis)

The Wash

Bullslaughter Bay

94

Broad Haven

Mewsford Point

Pembrokeshire Coast Path

Trevallen

Star Rock

2

The Castle (Fort)

Mast

Quarry (dis)

Castle Tank

Castle Tank

DANGER AREA

Trevallen Downs

Huntsman's Leap

93

St Govan's Chapel

Long Matthew Point

Saddle Head

St Govan's Head

1

92

92   93   94   95   96   97

A   B   C   D   E   F

112   For full street detail of the highlighted area see page 133.

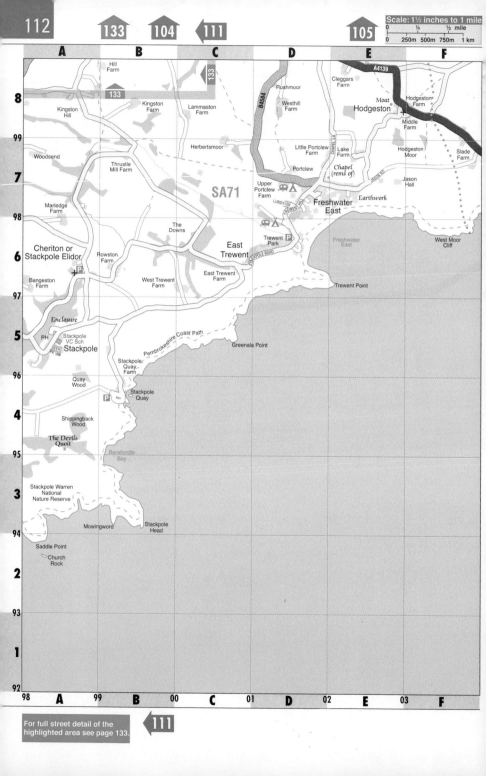

Scale: 1½ inches to 1 mile

0   ¼   ½ mile
0   250m   500m   750m   1 km

A   **B**   **C**   **D**   **E**   **F**

A4139

8

Hill Farm

133

133

Kingston Hill

Kingston Farm

Lammaston Farm

B4584

Rushmoor

Westhill Farm

Cleggars Farm

Moat

Hodgeston

Hodgeston Farm

Middle Farm

99

Woodsend

Herbertsmoor

Little Portclew Farm

Lake Farm

CHAPEL LA

Hodgeston Moor

Slade Farm

7

Thrustle Mill Farm

SA71

Portclew

Chapel (rems of)

Jason Hall

JASON RD

Marledge Farm

98

The Downs

Upper Portclew Farm

Freshwater East

Earthwork

Cheriton or Stackpole Elidor

Rowston Farm

East Trewent

LUNDY VW

TREWENT HILL

West Moor Cliff

6

Bangeston Farm

West Trewent Farm

East Trewent Farm

Trewent Park

P

STACKPOLE ROAD

Freshwater East

97

Enclosure

Trewent Point

5

PH

Stackpole VC Sch

DEER PK VW

Stackpole

Greenala Point

Pembrokeshire Coast Path

Stackpole Quay Farm

96

Quay Wood

P

Stackpole Quay

4

Shippingback Wood

The Devils Quoit

95

Barafundle Bay

3

Stackpole Warren National Nature Reserve

Mowingword

Stackpole Head

94

Saddle Point

Church Rock

2

93

1

92

98   **A**   99   **B**   00   **C**   01   **D**   02   **E**   03   **F**

For full street detail of the highlighted area see page 133.

111

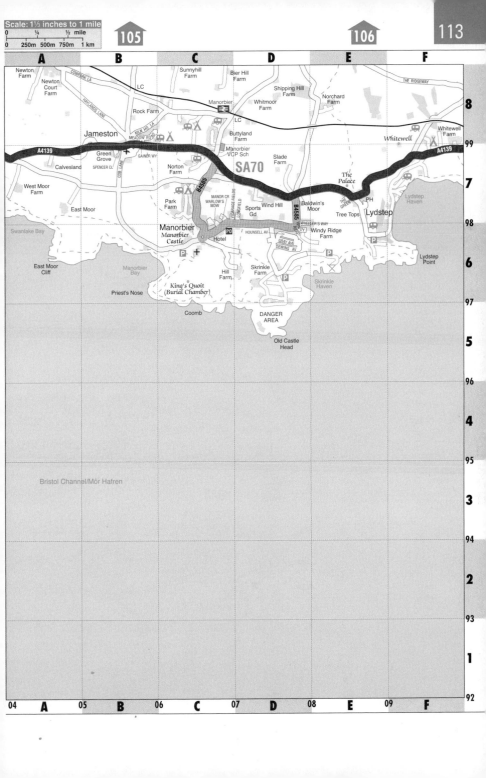

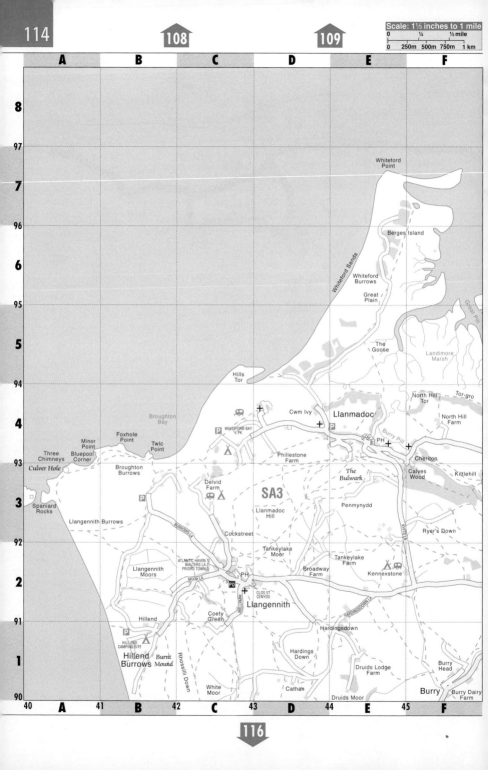

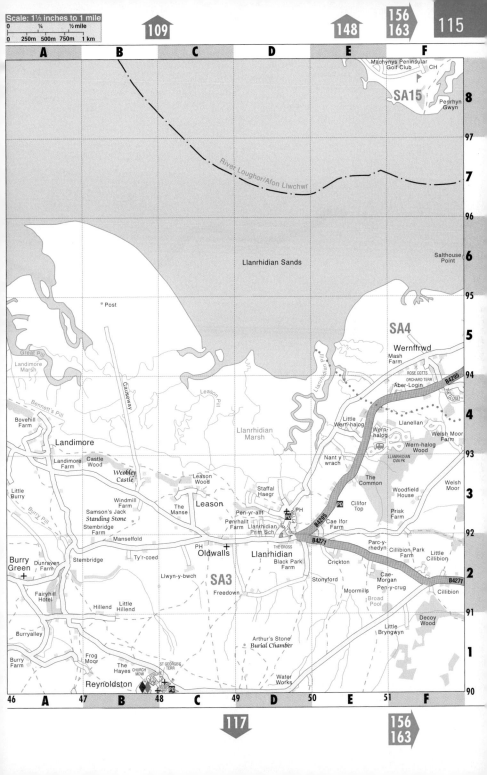

Sweyne's Howes
Burial Chambers

Sluxton

Rhossili
Down

Kingshall

Betlands

New Henllys

The Beacon

Old Henllys

Llanddewi
Castle

Rhossili
Bay

Rhossili

Talgarth's
Well

SA3

PH

Old Castle

Middleton

Kitchen
Corner

Rhossili
Visitor Ctr

B4247

Pitton
Cross

Monksland

CCW
Information
Point

Pitton

Kimleymoor

Pilton
Green

B4247

Fall Bay

West
Pilton

East Pilton
Farm

Crabart

Mewslade Bay

Margam
Farm

Tears
Point

Thurba

Paviland
Manor

Margam
Cottage

Red Chamber

Littlehills

The Knave

Foxhole
Slade

Paviland
Cave

Blackhole
Gut

Common
Cliff

Longhole
Cave

Overton
Cliff

Scale: 1⅓ inches to 1 mile

0 ¼ ½ mile
0 250m 500m 750m 1 km

A B C D E F

8
Reynoldston
King Arthur Hotel (PH)
THE DORKING
BRY VIEW CL.
Ty Bryn
Little Reynoldston
Great Walterston
Little Walterston
Lake Farm
Llanddewi
Stout Hall
Cefn Bryn
Home Farm

89
Knelston Prim Sch
Kittle Top
Perriswood
Nicholaston

7
Knelston
Penrice Castle
A4118

88
Penrice Forest Walks
Penrice
Nicholaston Woods
Scurlage
Berry
Sanctuary Farmhouse

6
SALISBURY FARM
B4247
PH
MONKS
GOWER HOLIDAY VILLAGE
SA3
Pitt
Oxwich Burrows

87
HANGMAN'S CROSS
Oxwich
Oxwich Nature Reserve

5
Moor Corner Farm
Norton
OXWICH LEISURE PK
Oxwich Bay

86
GREAT HOUSE CT.
Horton
ROCK LA
Slade
Oxwich Castle
Oxwich Green
Port Eynon
UNDERHILL LA
NEW PARK HOLIDAY PK
HIGHFIELDS HOLIDAY PK
SPRINGFIELD
PH

4
THE BOARLANDS
A4118
PO
The Cove
The Sands
Holy's Wash
Oxwich Point

85
Overton
Port-Eynon YH
The Salt House (rems of)
Port-Eynon Point
Culver Hole
Mon
Port-Eynon Bay
Overton Mere

84

3

2

83

1

82

46 A 47 B 48 C 49 D 50 E 51 F

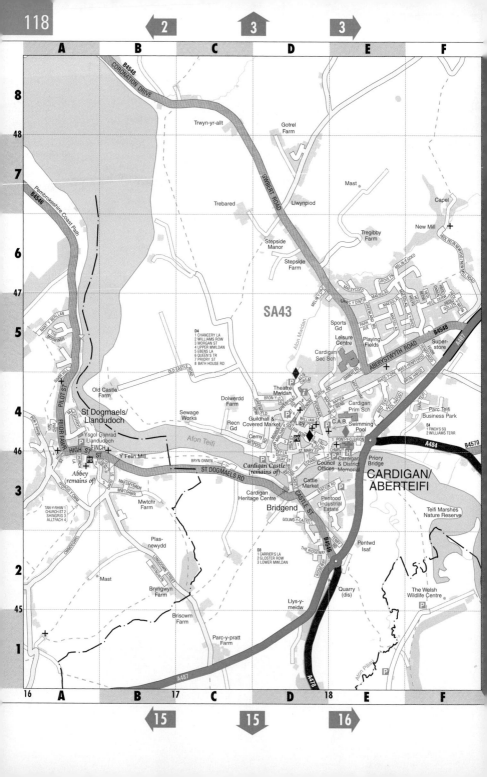

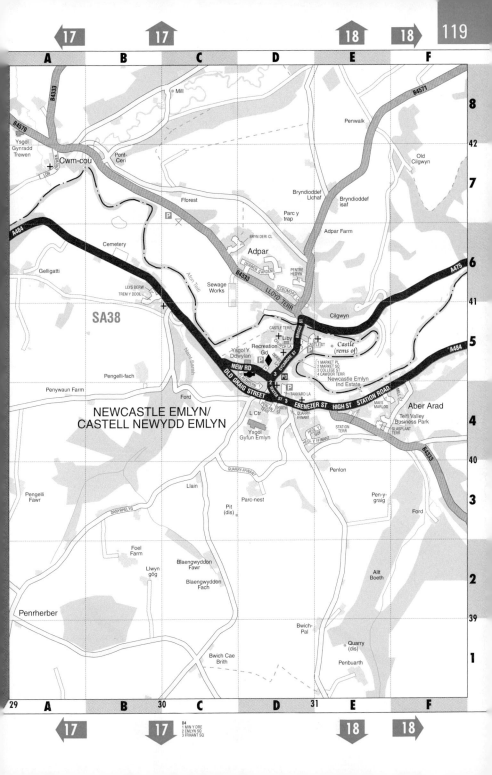

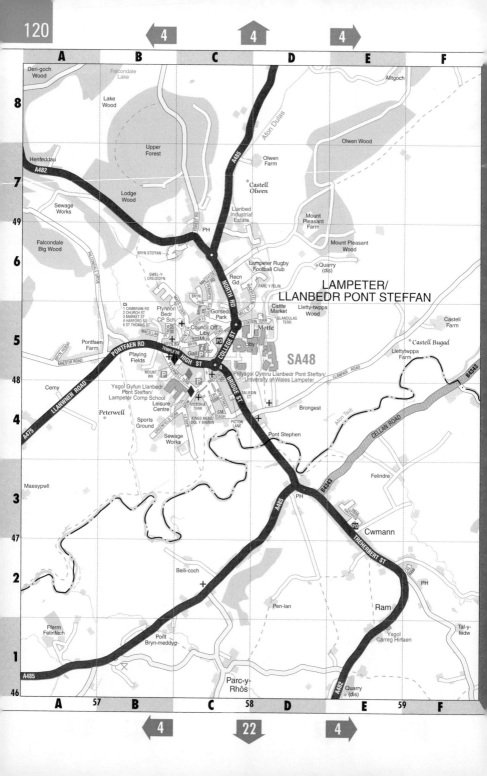

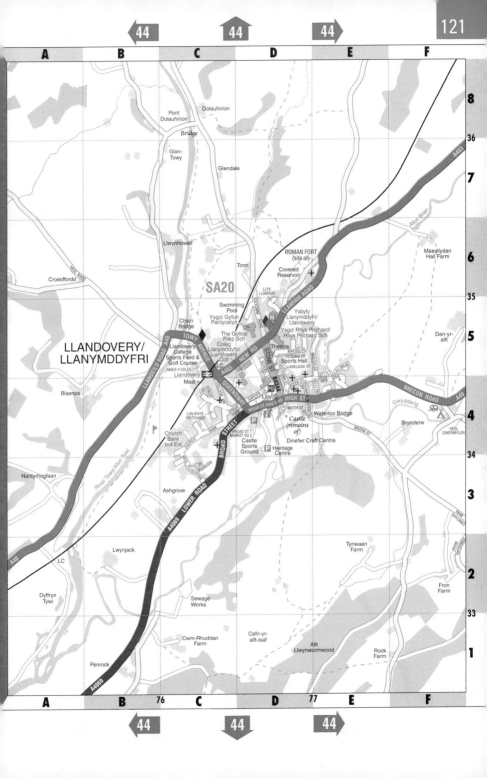

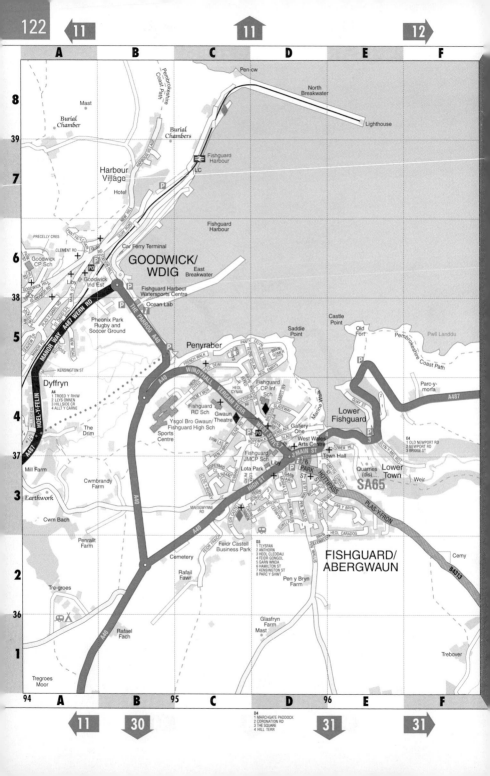

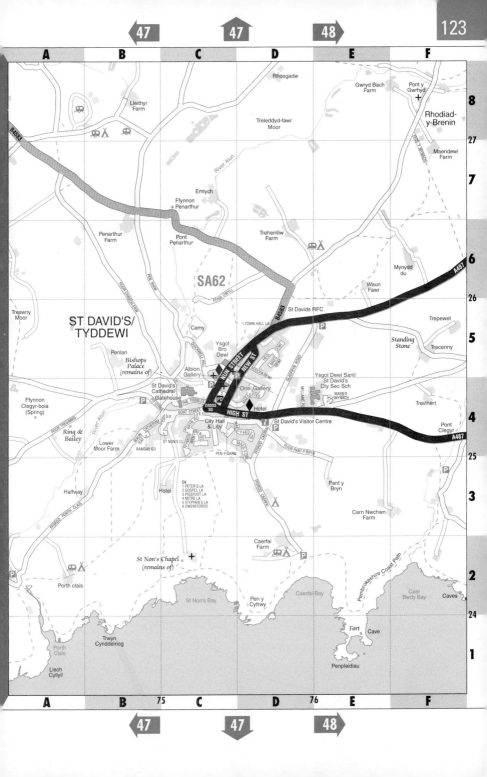

A B C D E F

8

17

7

6

16

5

HAVERFORDWEST/ HWLFFORDD

SA62

4

15

3

2

14

1

92 A 93 B C 93 D 94 E F

A487
Sunnyhill
Pelcomb Farm
Elliotts Hill Farm
Cuckoo Mill Farm
PH
Pelcomb Bridge
CORMORANT CL
SIGNAL VW
Easthook Wood
Slade Farm
SLADE LANE
ST DAVID'S ROAD
Slade
SLADE LANE
A487
A487 THOMAS PARRY WAY

F5
1 CUFFERN CL
2 RACKHILL CT
3 POYSTON CL
4 CLARESTON CL
5 MILWARD CL
6 QUEEN'S DITCH
7 PRESCELLY RD

Cuckoo Grove
CUCKOO LANE
Slade Hall

E5
1 PEREGRINE CL
2 CURLEW CL
3 SANDERLING CL
4 PEGGYS LA
5 OSPREY DR

FLEMING CRESCENT
GOSHAWK RD
BARING GOULD WAY
HIGHLANDS
UAWEL CL
CITY ROAD
City Rd Cemy
NORTH CT
SOUTH CT
SISSON
TRAFALGAR ROAD
GERALD RD
KESTREL
HAWTHORN RISE
RD
Cty and Magistrates Courts
Haverfordwest VC Sch

PH
Highmead Farm
B4341
HAVEN ROAD
Little Slade Farm
Douglas James CL
HAWTHORN RISE
GOLDCREST WAY
DOUGLAS JAMES WAY
HYWEL RD
Albert Town
Sports Gd
PO
B4341
B4327
Fenton CP Sch
BARN ST
MILFORD RD
PO

RUTHER PK
WREN PK
HAVEN PK CL
HAVEN PK DR
PARK CORNER ROAD
E4
1 WILLIAMSTON CL
2 CARADOC PL
3 SNOWDROP CL
DALE RD
TUDOR WAY
RUBIAN AVENUE
St Mary's Cemy
Tasker Milward Sch
Superstore
Fenton Trading Estate
Glan Cleddau Sch
Mary Immaculate RC Sch

DALE ROAD
PALMERSTON ROAD
SA61
Skerryford
Dreenhill Farm
Overdale Farm
PH
B4327
Dreenhill
Palmerston Farm
BEECHLANDS PK
BETHANY ROAD
Coleg Sir Benfro / Pembrokeshire Coll
CARADOG'S WELL ROAD
Chapel (rems of)
A487 MERLIN'S HILL
PO
Merlin's Bridge
MERLIN'S AV

St Caradoc's Well
Bethany Farm
UNDER THE HILLS
GLEN VIEW
OLD HAKIN ROAD
DREDGMAN HILL
Brooksgrove
Merlin's Brook
A4076
Haverfordwest Rugby Football Club

F4
1 BARN CT
2 FOUNTAIN ROW

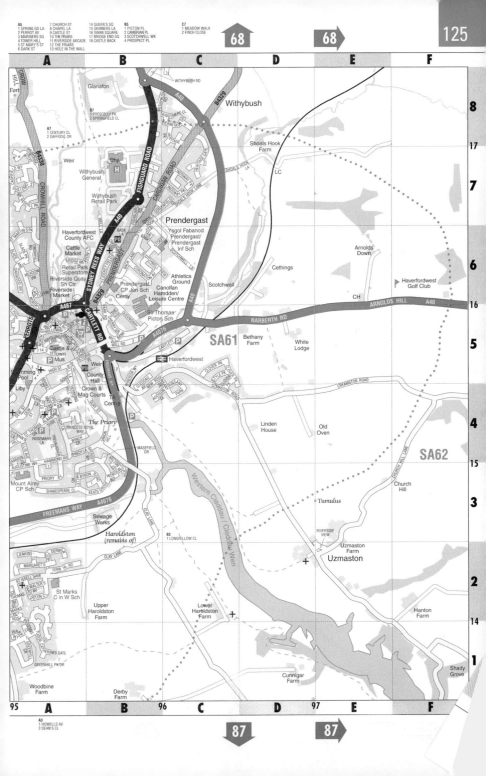

A5
1 SPRING GD LA
2 PERROT AV
3 MARINERS SQ
4 TOWER HILL
5 ST MARY'S ST
6 DARK ST

7 CHURCH ST
8 CHAPEL ST
9 CASTLE ST
10 THE FRIARS
11 RIVERSIDE ARCADE
12 THE FRIARS
13 HOLE IN THE WALL

14 QUEEN'S SQ
15 SKINNERS LA
16 SWAN SQUARE
17 BRIDGE END SQ
18 CASTLE BACK

B5
1 PICTON PL
2 CAMBRIAN PL
3 SCOTCHWELL WK
4 PROSPECT PL

C7
1 MEADOW WALK
2 FINCH CLOSE

68

68

125

A **B** **C** **D** **E** **F**

Crow Hill
Fort

Glanafon

WITHYBUSH RD

8

Withybush

B7
1 PIRESCELLY PK
2 SPRINGFIELD CL

Weir

Withybush
General

H

Withybush
Retail Park

A7
1 CENTURY CL
2 DAFFODIL DR

17

Shoals Hook
Farm

LC

7

Prendergast

Ysgol Fabanod
Prendergast/
Prendergast
Inf Sch

Arnolds
Down

Haverfordwest
County AFC

Cattle
Market

Retail Park
Superstore
Riverside Quay
Sh Ctr
Riverside
Market

Prendergast
CP Jun Sch
Cemy

Athletics
Ground

Canolfan
Hamdden/
Leisure Centre

Scotchweil

Cethings

CH

Haverfordwest
Golf Club

6

ARNOLDS HILL A40

16

Sir Thomas
Picton Sch

NARBERTH RD

SA61

Bethany
Farm

White
Lodge

Haverfordwest

Castle &
Town Mus

County
Hall

Crown &
Mag Courts

TA
Centre

5

CREAMSTON ROAD

Swimming
Pool

Liby

The Priory

Linden
House

Old
Oven

SA62

4

Rosemary
La

Church
Hill

Mount Airey
CP Sch

Tumulus

15

FREEMANS WAY

Sewage
Works

Haroldston
(remains of)

Western Cleddau / Cleddau Wen

RIVERSIDE
VIEW

Uzmaston
Farm

Uzmaston

3

Jenkins

B3
1 LONGFELLOW CL

St Marks
C in W Sch

Upper
Haroldston
Farm

Lower
Haroldston
Farm

Hanton
Farm

2

GREENHILL PK DR

14

Woodbine
Farm

Derby
Farm

Cunnigar
Farm

Shady
Grove

1

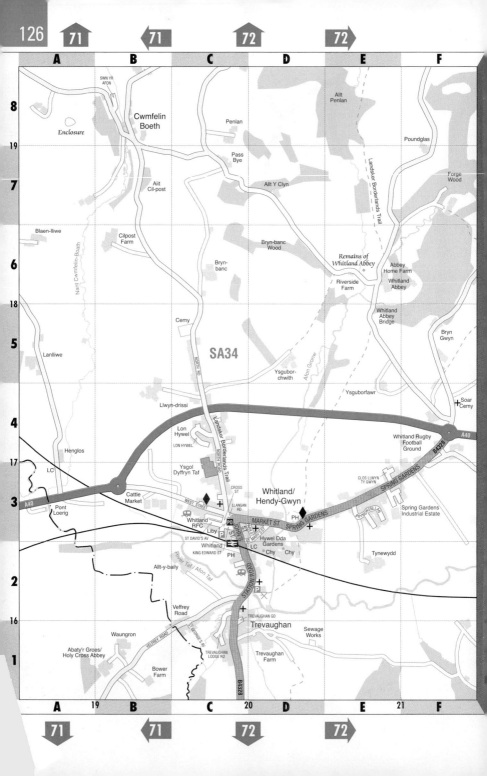

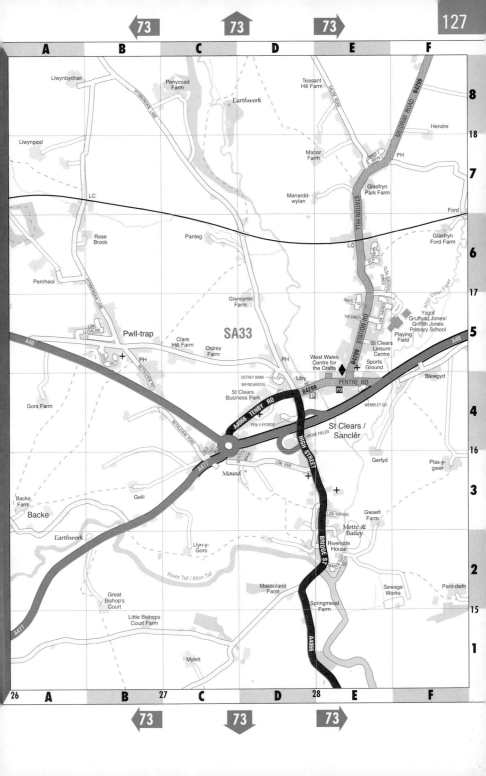

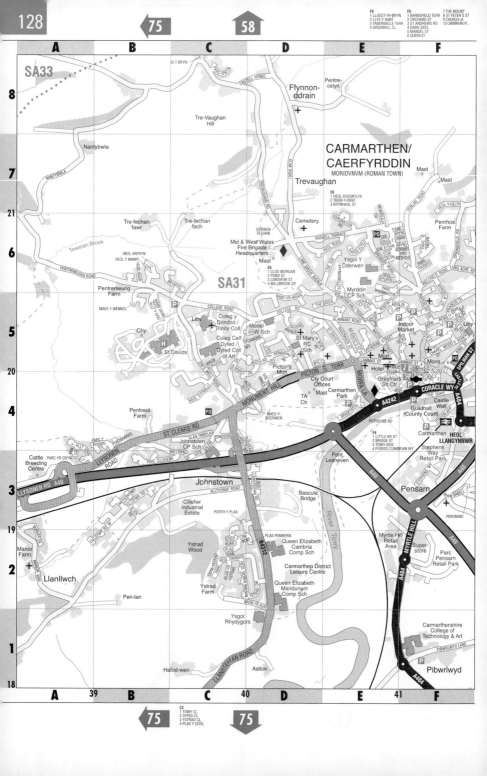

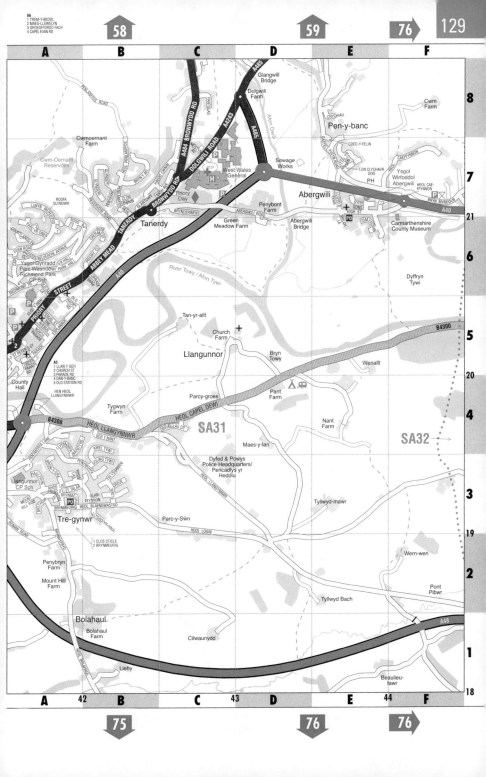

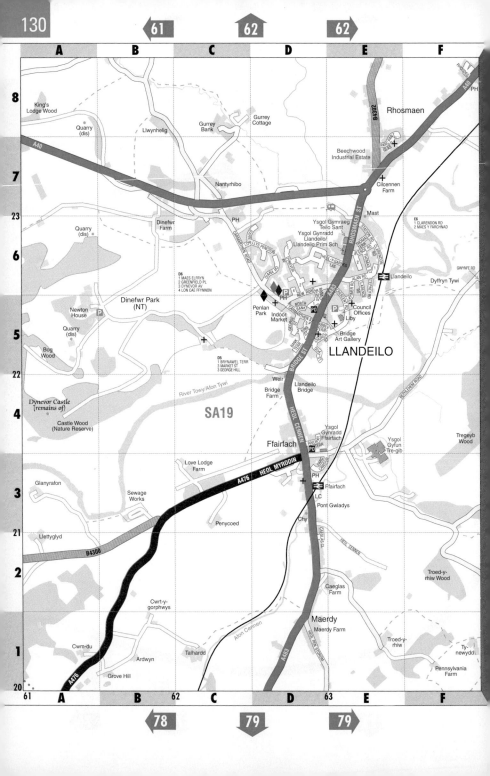

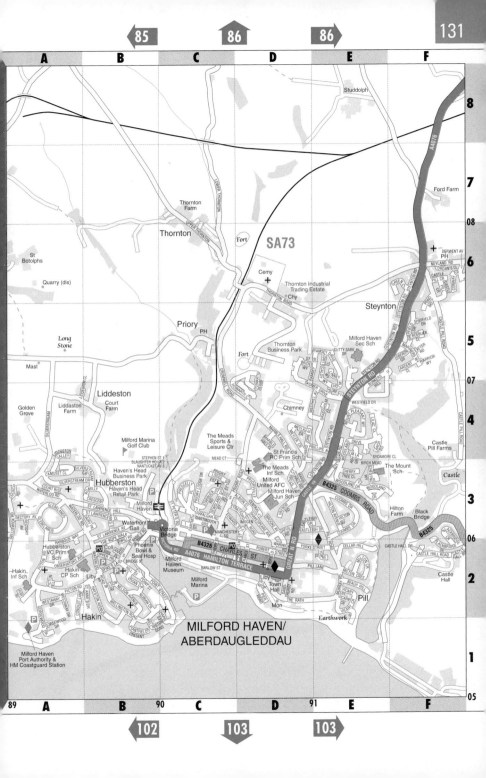

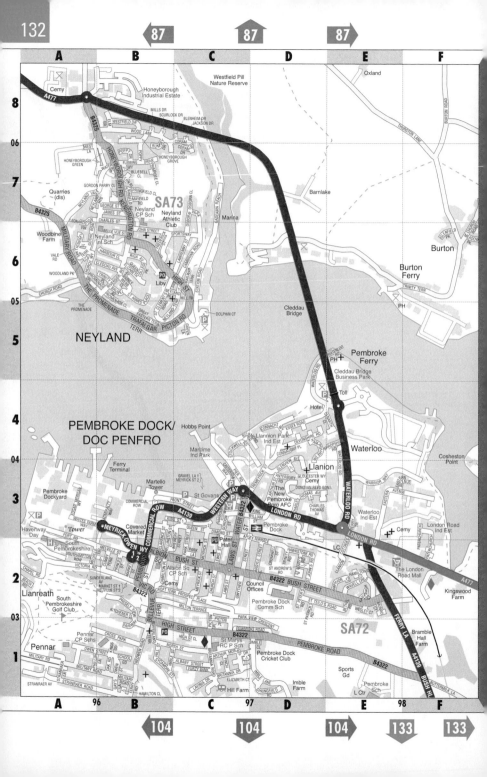

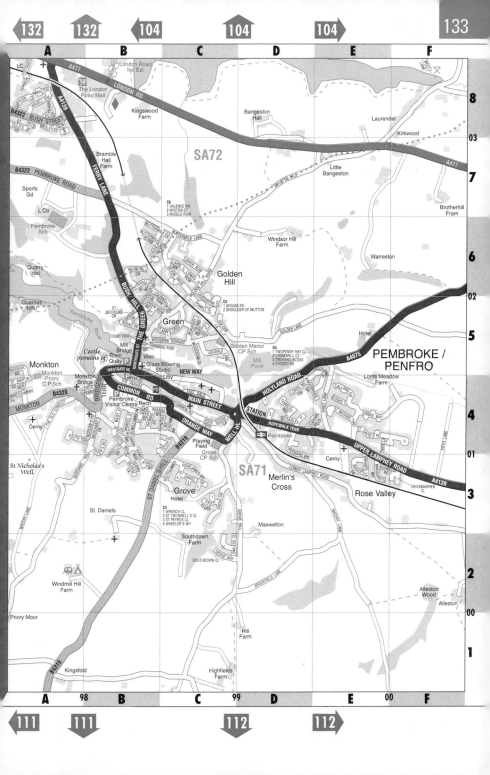

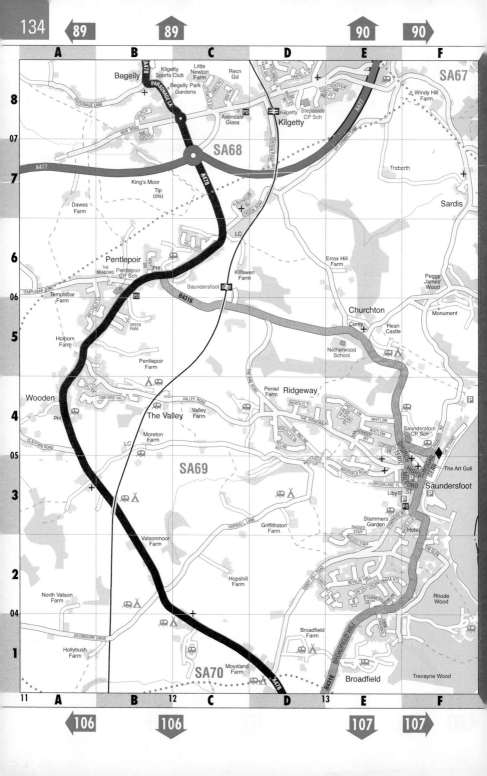

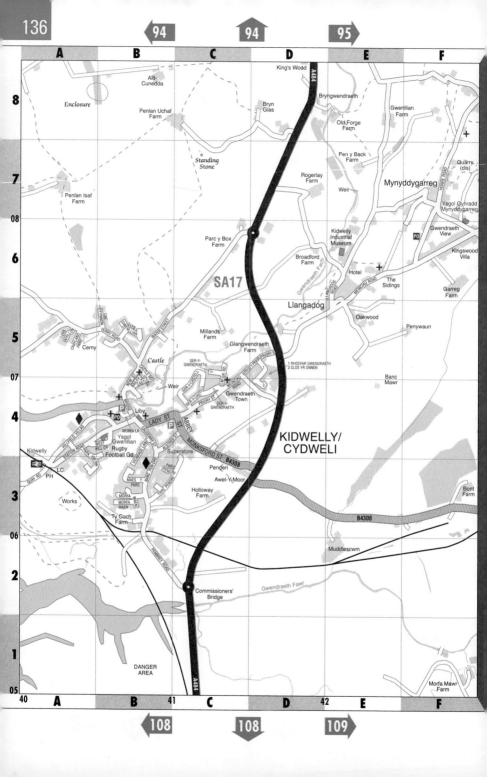

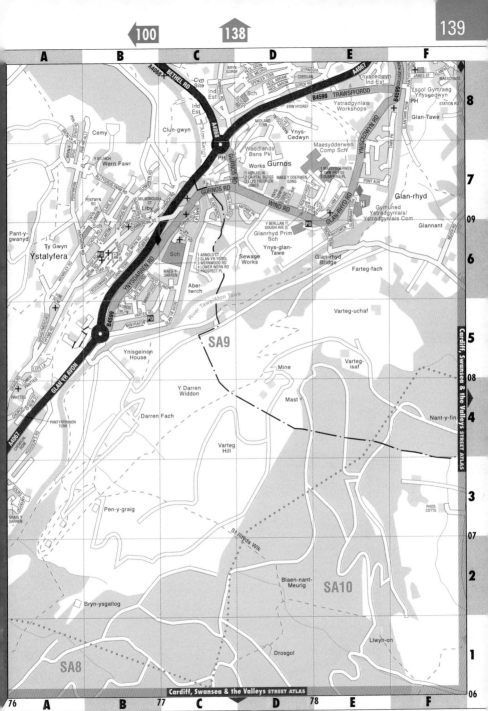

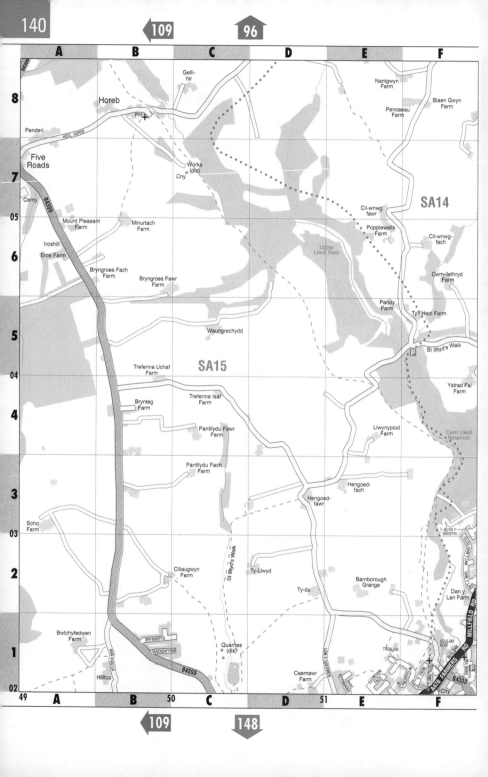

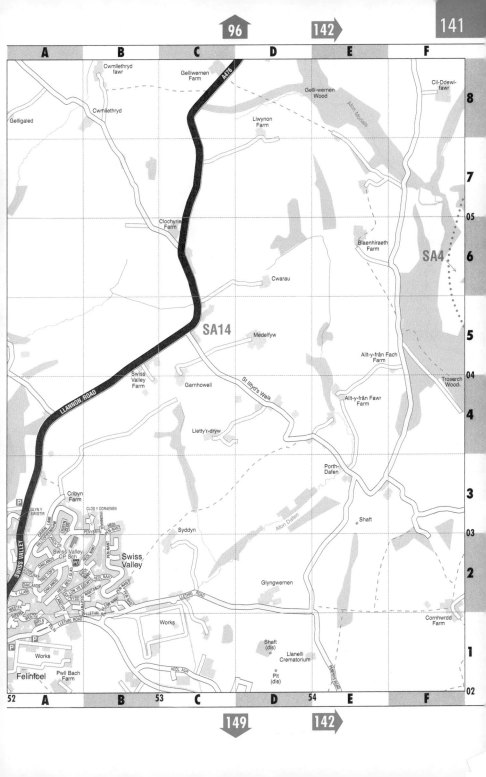

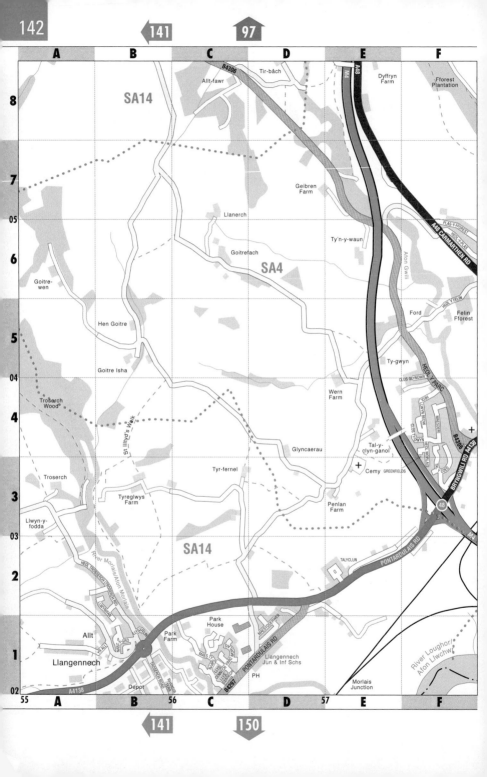

141
97

B4306

Tir-bâch

Allt-fawr

Dyffryn Farm

Fforest Plantation

SA14

8

Geibren Farm

7

Llanerch

05

Ty'n-y-waun

PLAS-Y-FFOREST

A48 CARMARTHEN RD

Goitrefach

6

SA4

Goitre-wen

Afon Gwili

HEOL Y FELIN

Ford

Felin Fforest

Hen Goitre

5

Ty-gwyn

CLOS GLYNDWR

HEOL Y PARC

Goitre Isha

04

Trosarch Wood

Wern Farm

YDRI

MAESDER

LLWYN BELEW

CLOS Y GWYN

HEOL MONA

HEOL BRYN

4

St Illtyd's Walk

Glyncaerau

Tal-y-clyn-ganol

+

BRYNGWILI RD A4138

B4306

Troserch

Tyr-fernel

+ Cemy GREENFIELDS

Tyreglwys Farm

3

Llwyn-y-fodda

Penlan Farm

48

03

SA14

TALYCLUN

PONTARDULAIS RD

M4

HEOL TROSSERCH/FFORDD TR

River Morlais/Afon Morlais

2

CAE ALLT

LLYS ELFI

Park House

MAES DERWEN

River Loughor/ Afon Llwchwr

Allt

Park Farm

SW HOLM

MAES Y

PONTARDULAIS RD

Llangennech Jun & Inf Schs

1

Llangennech

TROSSERCH

PANNAU

MAES

B4297

PH

Morlais Junction

Depot

A4138

02

55   **A**   56   **B**   **C**   **D**   57   **E**   **F**

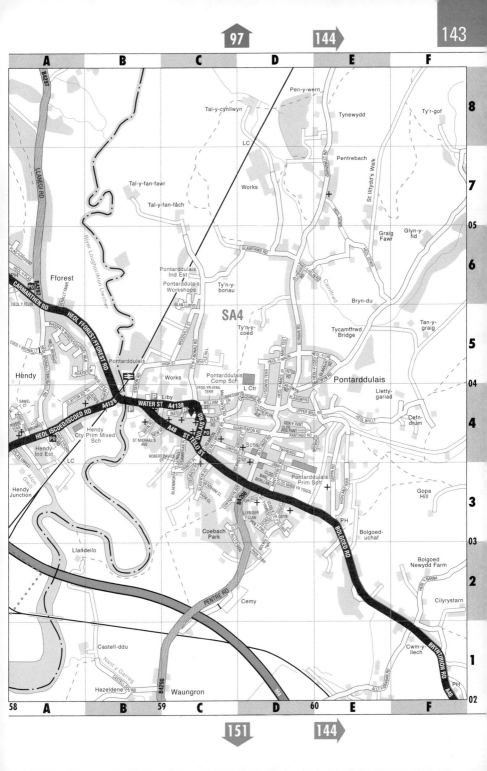

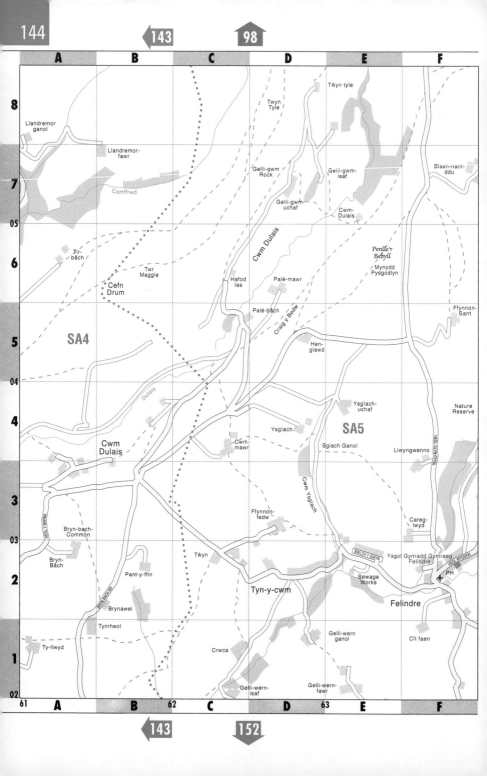

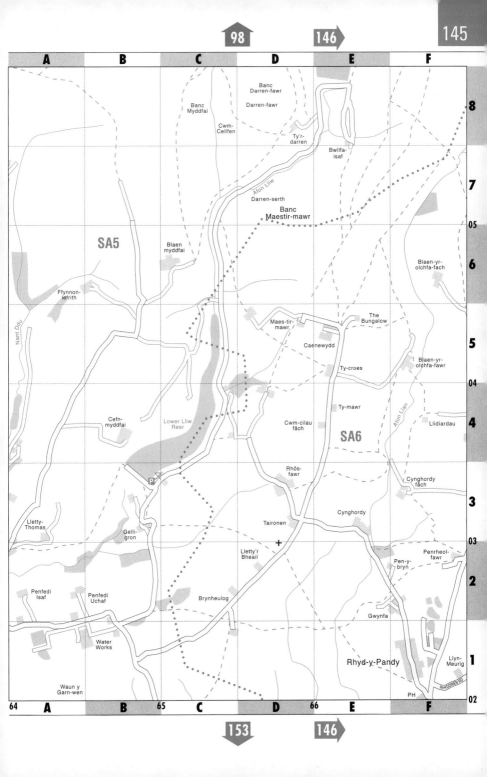

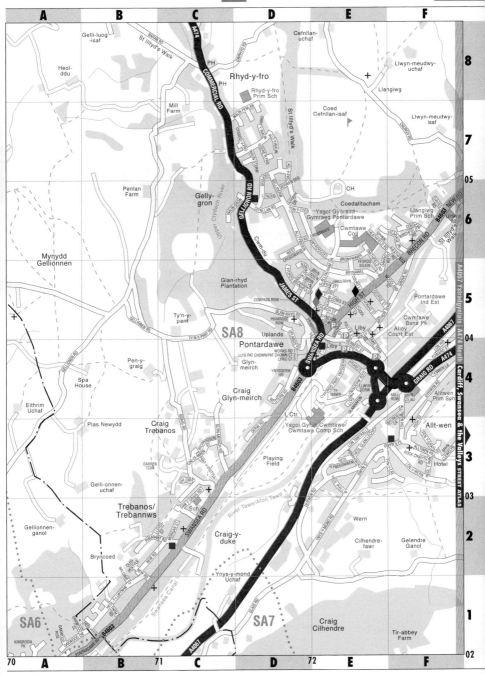

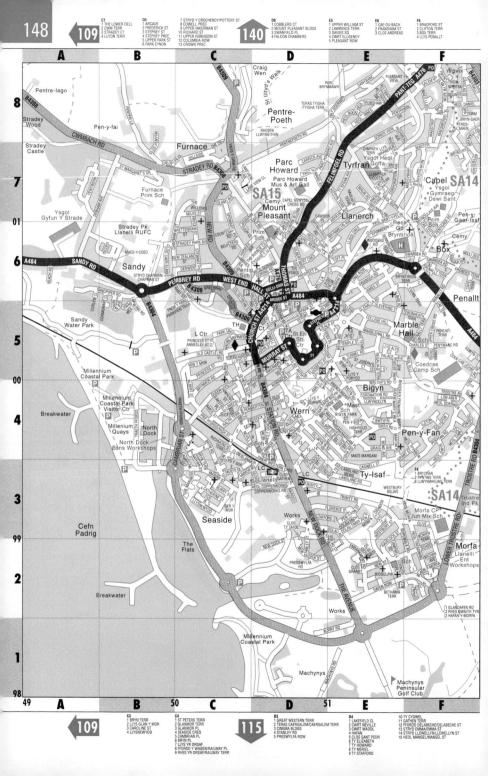

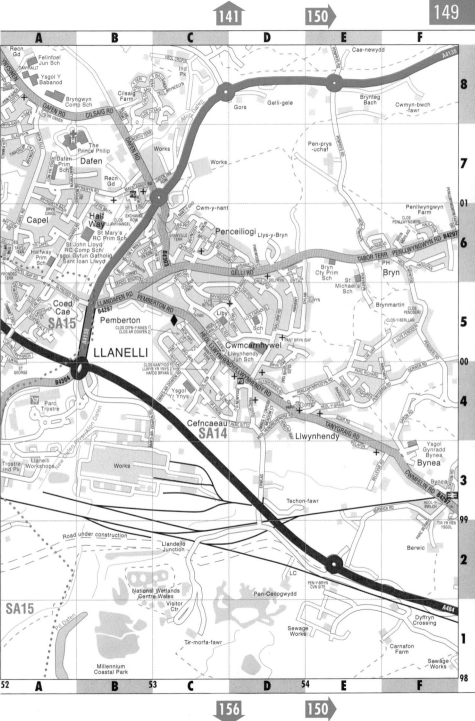

149 142

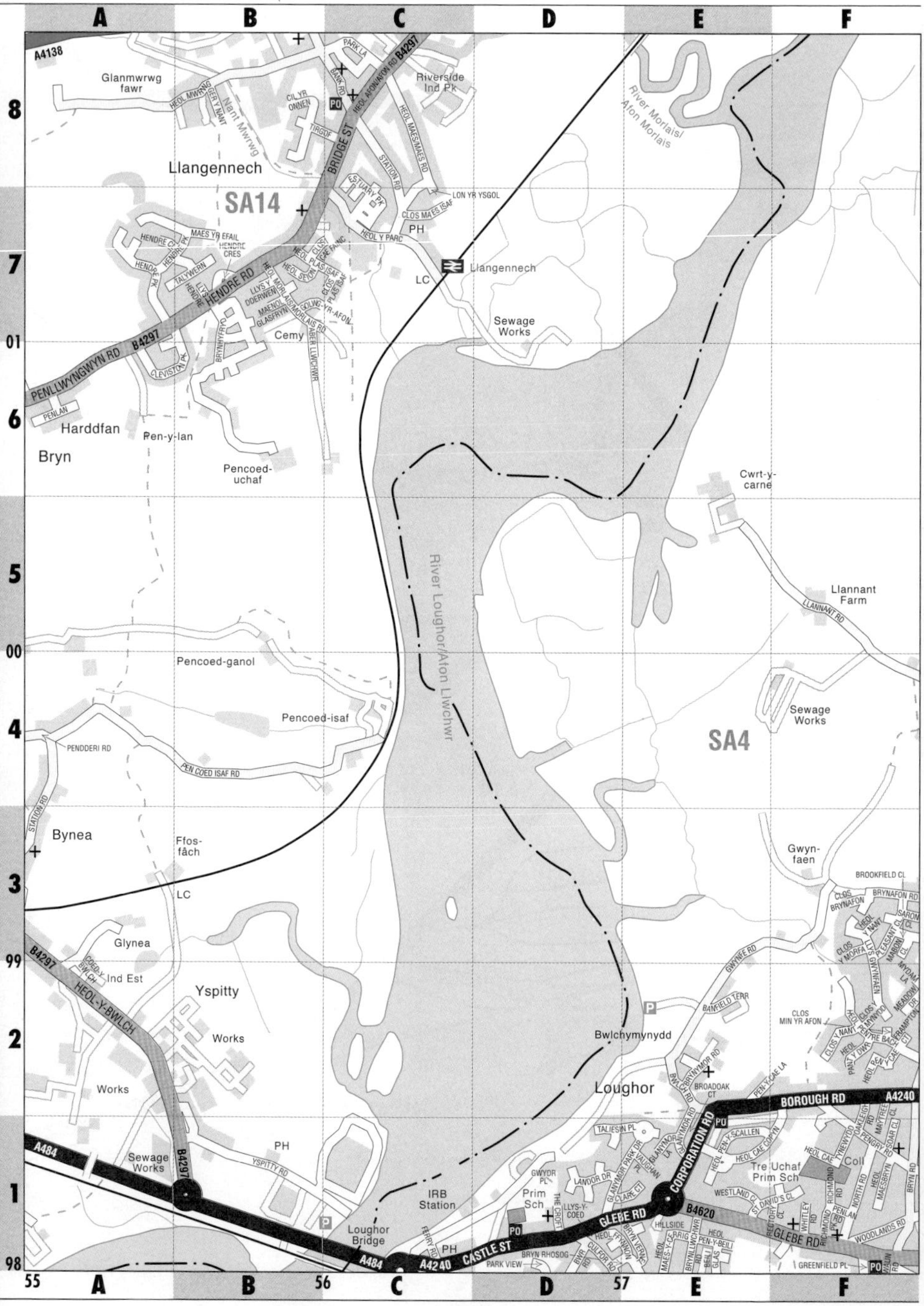

A B C D E F

A4138

8

Glanmwrwg fawr

Riverside Ind Pk

River Morlais/ Afon Morlais

Llangennech

SA14

7

Llangennech

LC

Sewage Works

01

Cwrt-y-carne

6

Harddfan

Pen-y-lan

Bryn

Pencoed-uchaf

Llannant Farm

5

LLANNANT RD

River Loughor/Afon Llwchwr

Pencoed-ganol

00

Sewage Works

Pencoed-isaf

SA4

4

PENDDERI RD

PEN COED ISAF RD

Gwyn-faen

BROOKFIELD CL

Bynea

Ffos-fâch

LC

3

Glynea

Ind Est

Yspitty

99

B4297

HEOL-Y-BWLCH

Works

Bwlchymynydd

2

Works

Loughor

BOROUGH RD A4240

CORPORATION RD

A484

PH

Sewage Works

B4297

YSPITTY RD

IRB Station

Prim Sch

Tre Uchaf Prim Sch

1

Loughor Bridge

PH

GLEBE RD

B4620

GLEBE RD

98

A484 A4240 CASTLE ST

PARK VIEW

BRYN RHOSOG

GREENFIELD PL

55 A B 56 C D 57 E F

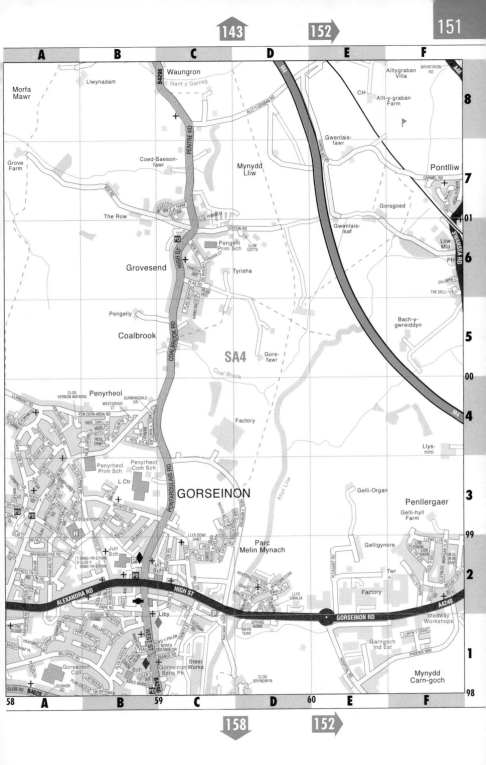

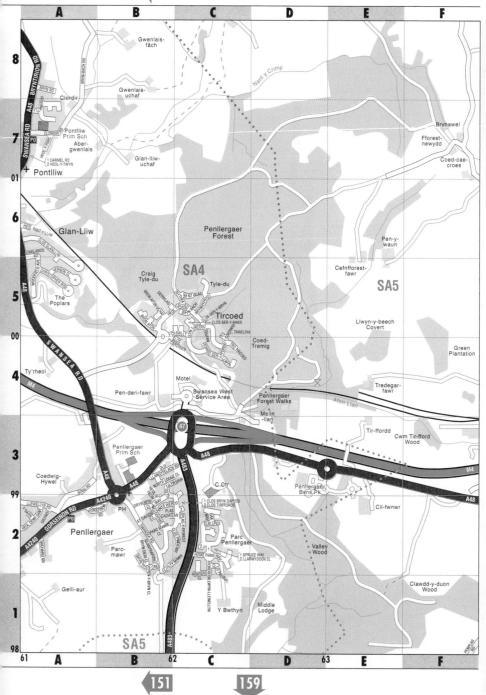

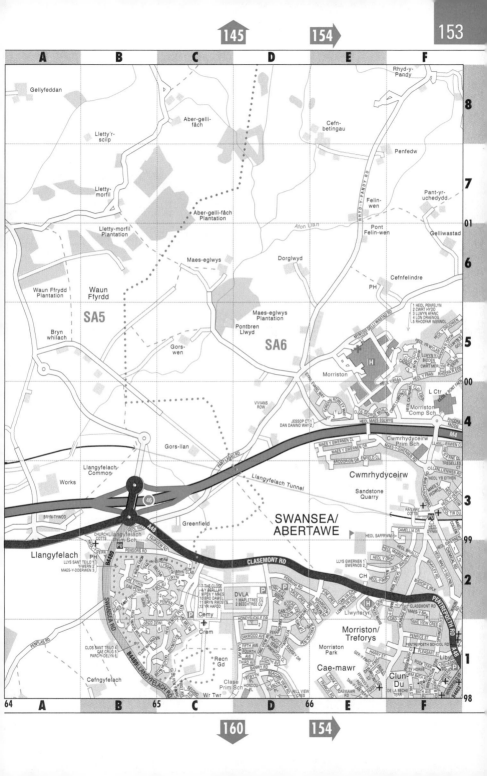

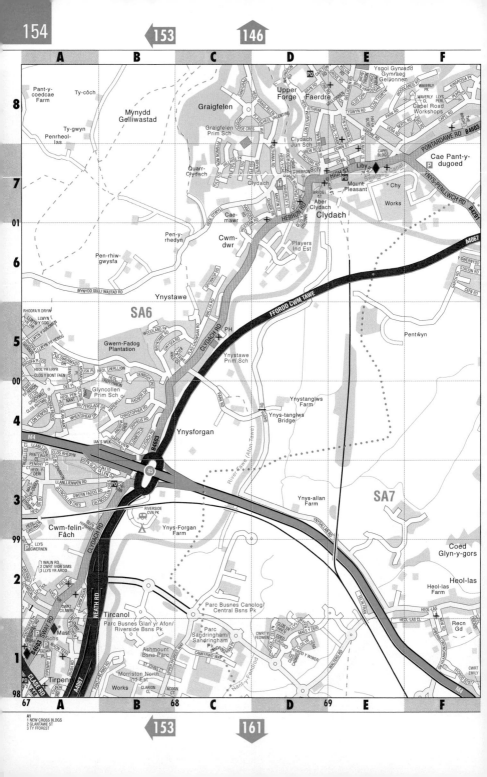

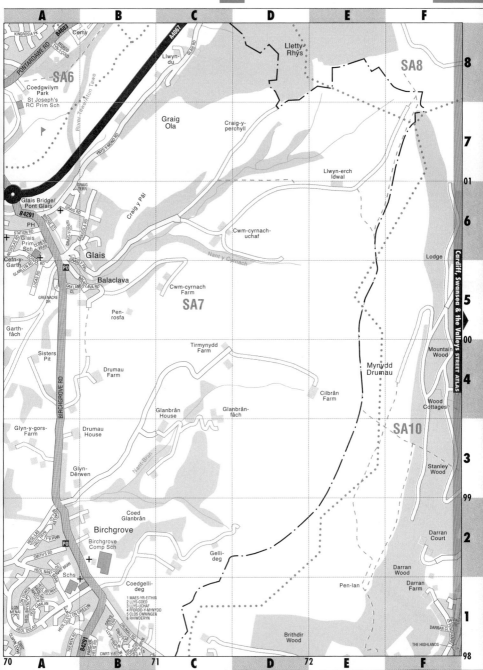

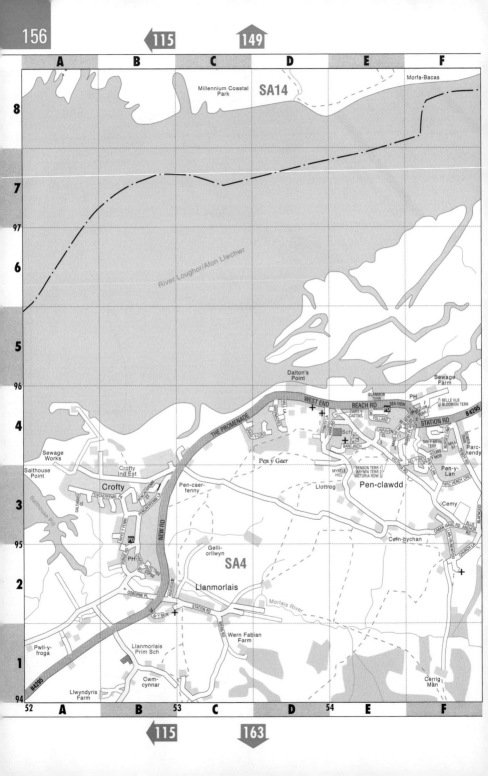

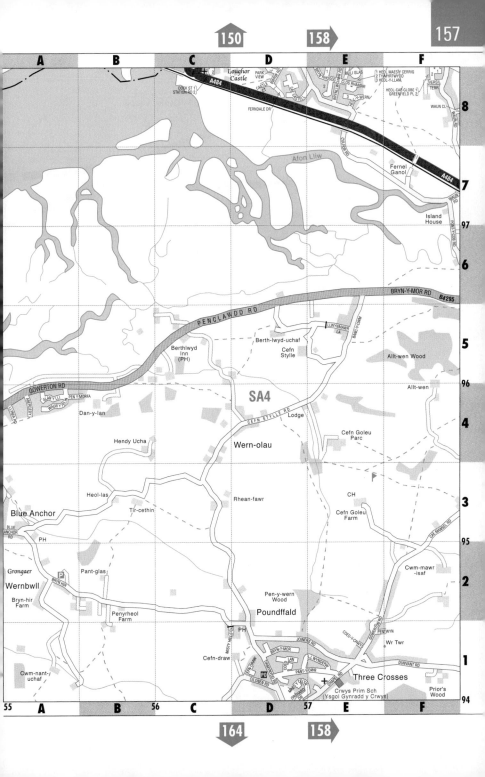

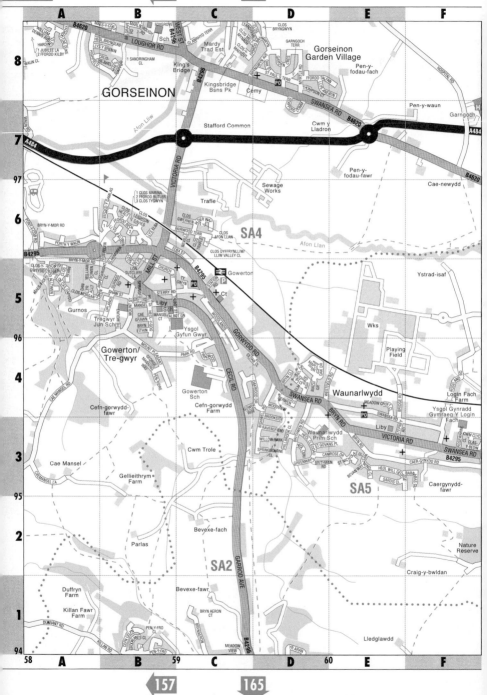

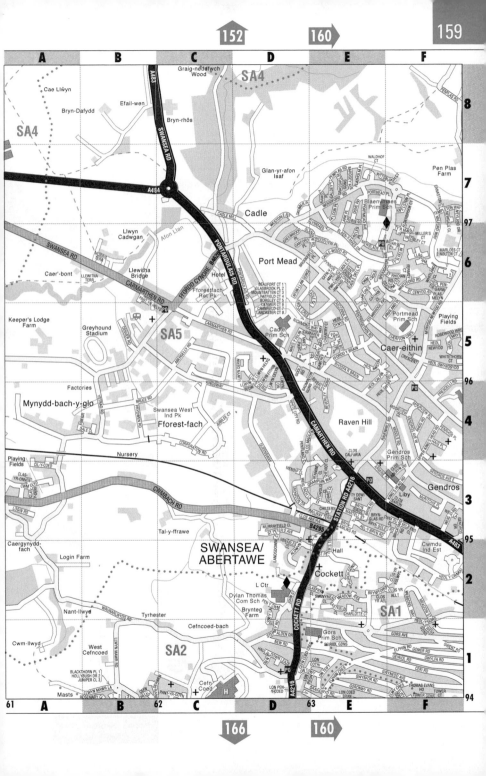

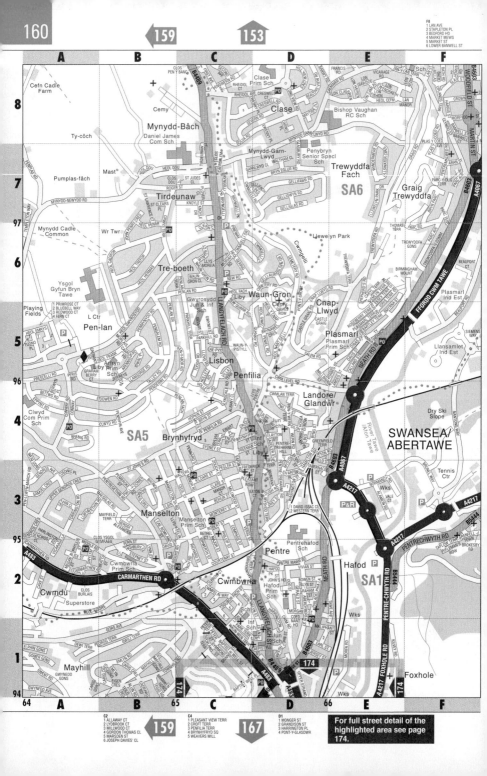

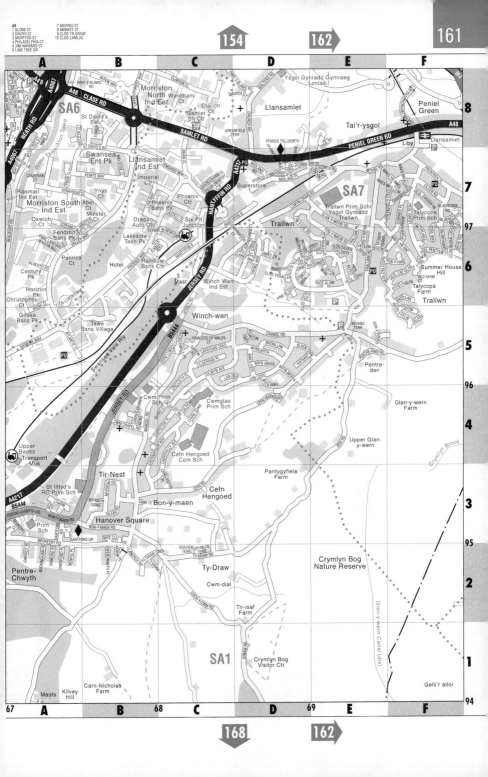

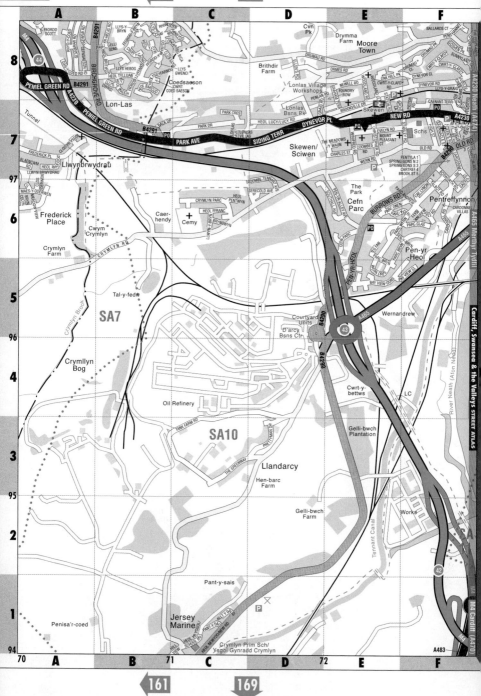

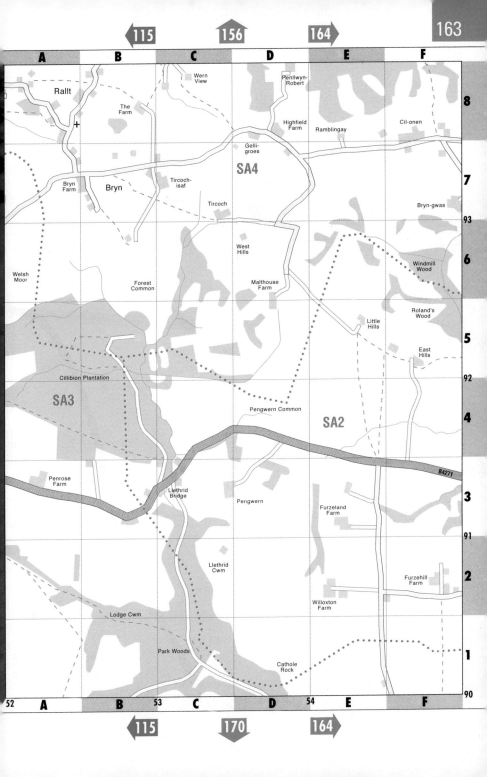

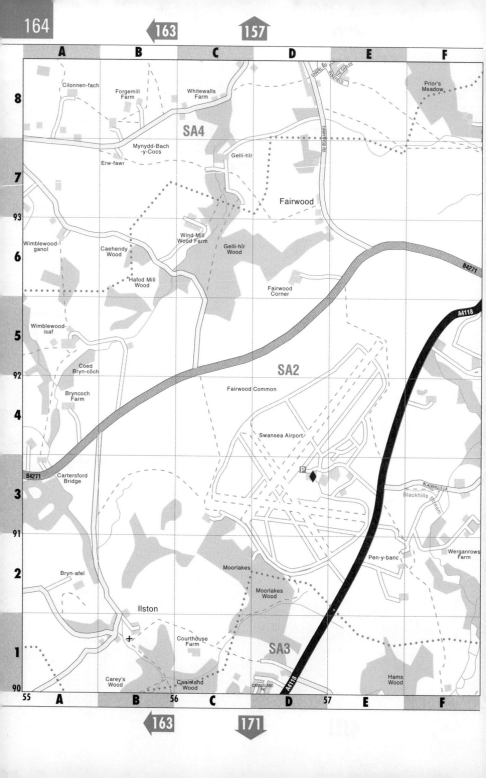

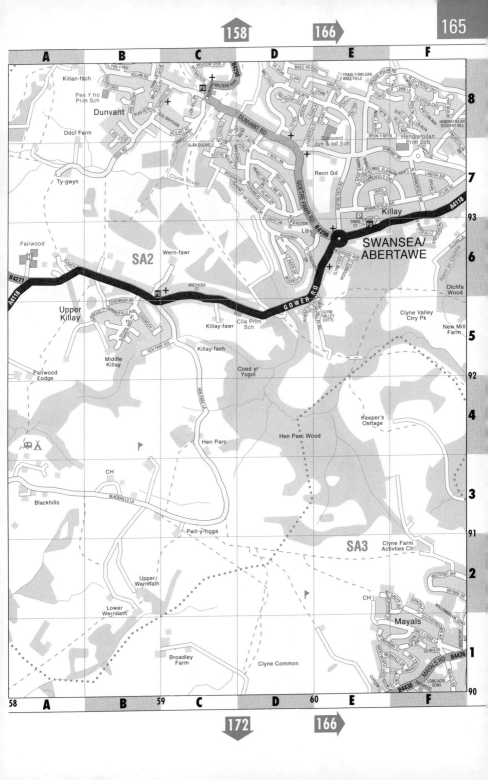

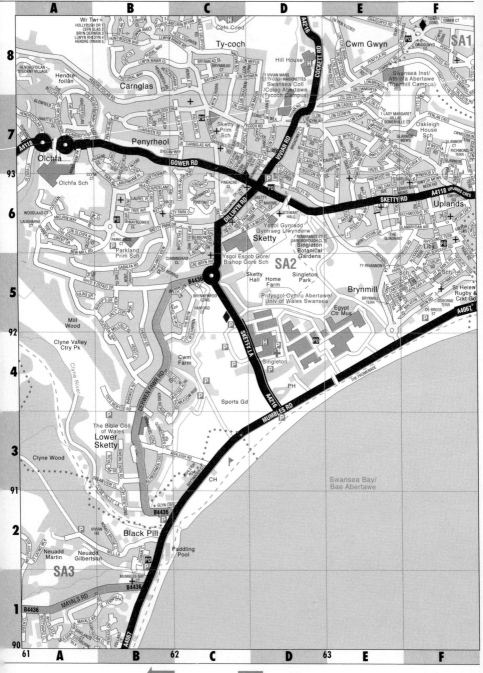

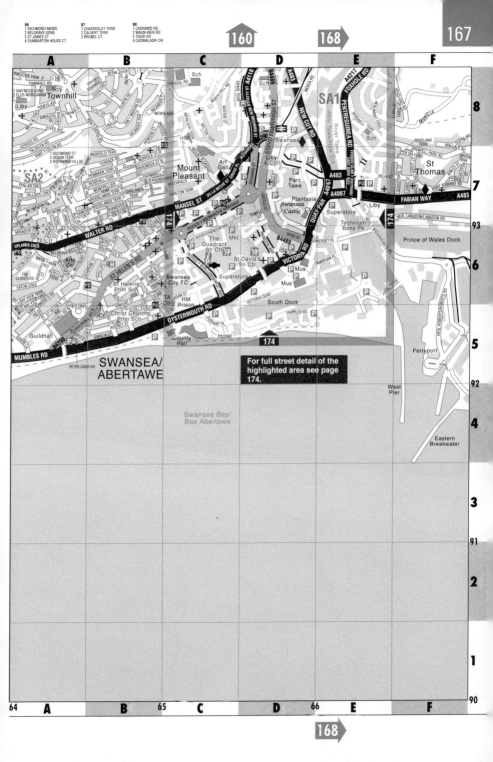

SWANSEA/
ABERTAWE

8

Windmill
(remains of)

Pen-y-graig

Port Tennant

Cemy

Dan-y-graig

ROBERT OWEN GDNS

DAVID WILLIAMS TERR

SIR JOHN NORTH RD

GWYNNE TERR

HARDON RD

TY
BEDDOE

DANYGRAIG RD

WEST TERR

Works

SA1

Tennant Canal (dis)

KINLEY
ST

LONGFORD
CRES

UPTON TERR · OSTERLEY
ST

RAGLAN

ELLISTON CRES

GRAIG ST

WALT LLANDWRN

WERN FAWR RD

7

A483

Port Tennant Rd

Danygraig
Prim Sch

P&R

VALE OF NEATH RD

FABIAN WAY

Works

Baldwin's Cres

Baldwin's Cres

Works

93

HEOL LANSDOWN/LANSDOWN RD

BEULAS ROW

Works

P

A483

PD

LC's

6

King's Dock

LC

P

Jetties

5

Queen's Dock

Jetties

Jetties

Jetties

Dry
Dock

Jetty

92

4

3

91

2

1

90

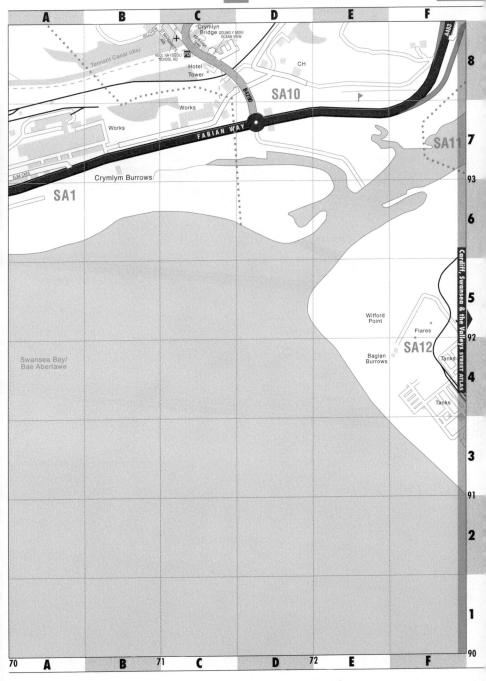

Crymlyn
Bridge
GOLWG Y MOR/
OCEAN VIEW
HEOL YR YSGOL/
SCHOOL RD
Tennant Canal (dis)
Hotel
Tower
CH
Works
Works
SA10
B4290
FABIAN WAY
ELBA CRES
Crymlym Burrows
SA1
SA11
Witford
Point
Flares
92
SA12
Baglan
Burrows
Tanks
Tanks
Swansea Bay/
Bae Abertawe

A4-83

8
7
93
6
5
92
4
3
91
2
1
90

70   71   72

A   B   C   D   E   F

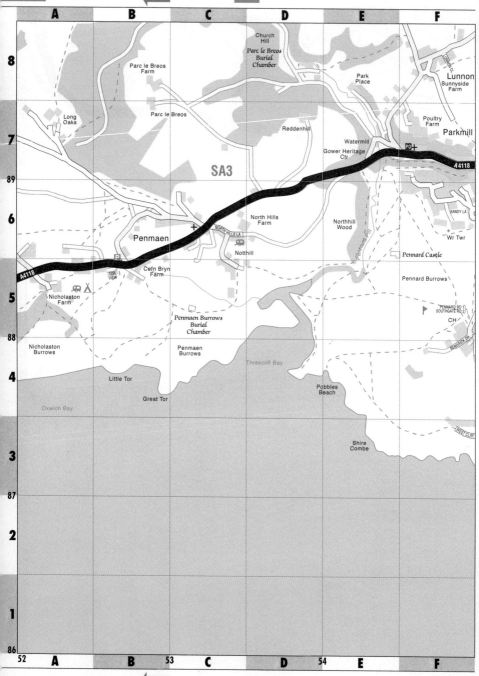

117
163

A **B** **C** **D** **E** **F**

8

Church
Hill

Parc le Breos
Burial
Chamber

Parc le Breos
Farm

Park
Place

Lunnon

Sunnyside
Farm

7

Parc le Breos

Long
Oaks

Reddenhill

Poultry
Farm

Parkmill

Watermill
Gower Heritage
Ctr

PO

A 4118

89

SA3

6

North Hills
Farm

Northhill
Wood

SANDY LA

Penmaen

NORTH HILLS LA

Notthill

Wr Twr

Pennard Castle

Pennard Burrows

Cefn Bryn
Farm

TOR
VIEW

A4118

5

Nicholaston
Farm

Penmaen Burrows
Burial
Chamber

PENNARD RD
SOUTHGATE RD 2

CH

88

Nicholaston
Burrows

Penmaen
Burrows

HENDRICK DR

Threecliff Bay

4

Little Tor

Pobbles
Beach

Great Tor

WEST CLIFF

Oxwich Bay

Shire
Combe

3

87

2

1

86

52 **A** **B** **53** **C** **D** **54** **E** **F**

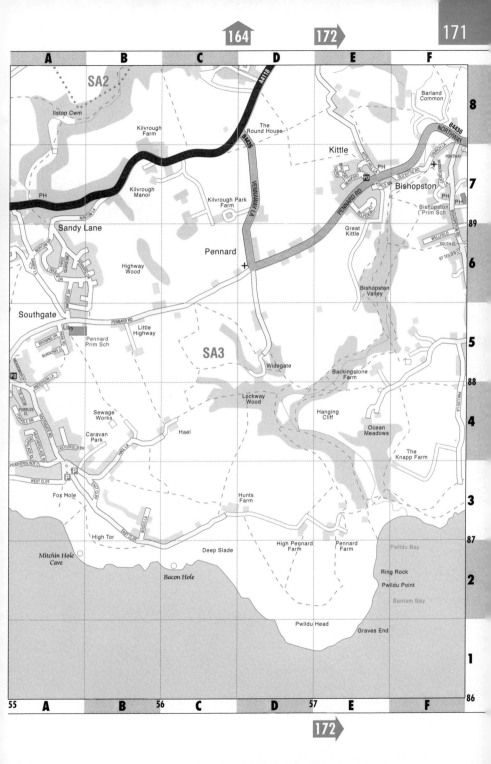

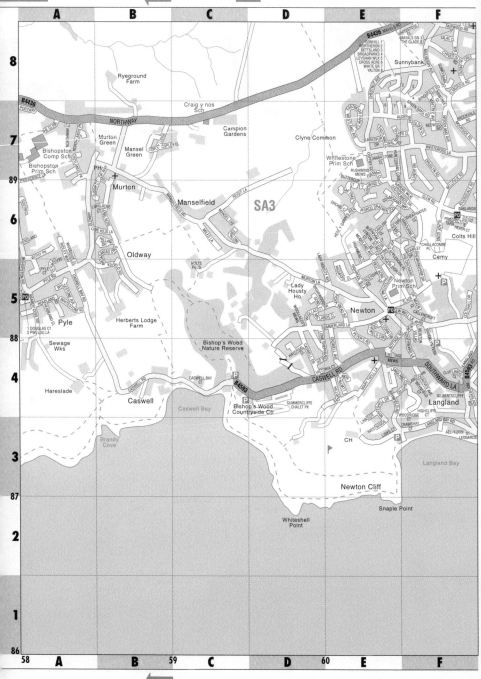

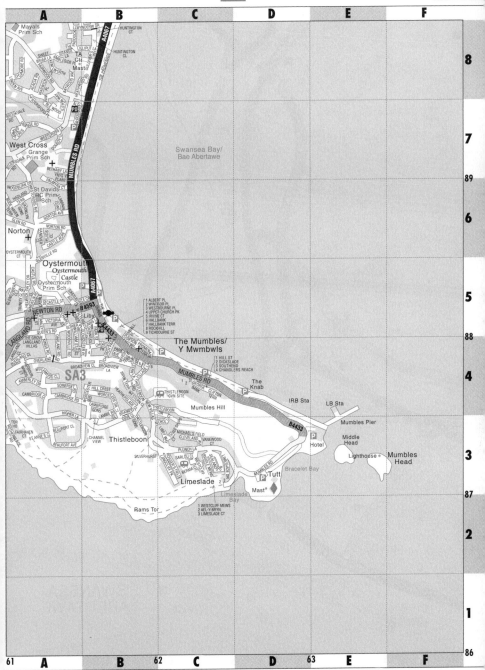

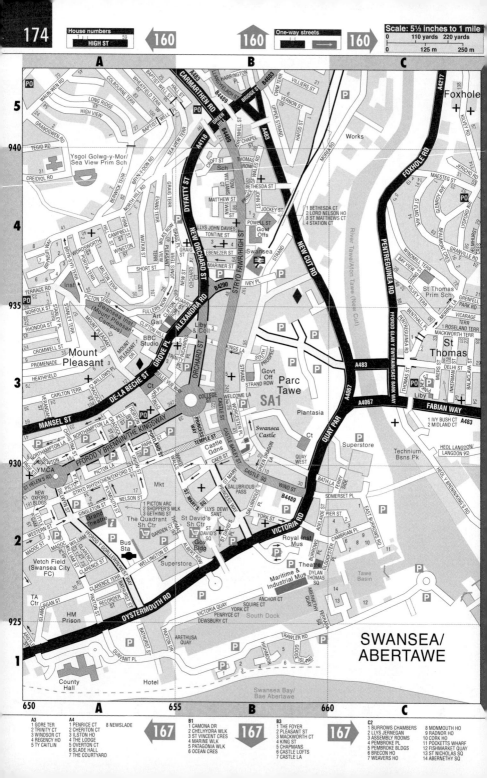

House numbers
HIGH ST
160

160   One-way streets   160

Scale: 5½ inches to 1 mile
0   110 yards   220 yards
0   125 m   250 m

SWANSEA/
ABERTAWE

A3
1 GORE TER
2 TRINITY CT
3 WINDSOR CT
4 REGENCY HO
5 TY CAITLIN

A4
1 PENRICE CT
2 CHERITON CT
3 ILSTON HO
4 THE LODGE
5 OVERTON CT
6 SLADE HALL
7 THE COURTYARD

8 NEWSLADE

B1
1 CAMONA DR
2 CHELHYDRA WLK
3 ST VINCENT CRES
4 MARINE WLK
5 PATAGONIA WLK
6 OCEAN CRES

B3
1 THE FOYER
2 PLEASANT ST
3 MACKWORTH CT
4 KING ST
5 CHAPMANS
6 CASTLE LOFTS
7 CASTLE LA

C2
1 BURROWS CHAMBERS
2 LLYS JERNEGAN
3 ASSEMBLY ROOMS
4 PEMBROKE PL
5 PEMBROKE BLDGS
6 BRECON HO
7 WEAVERS HO

8 MONMOUTH HO
9 RADNOR HO
10 CORK HO
11 POCKETTS WHARF
12 FISHMARKET QUAY
13 ST NICHOLAS SQ
14 ABERNETHY SQ

Church Rd 6 Beckenham BR2.......... **53** C6

Place name
May be abbreviated
on the map

Location number
Present when a number
indicates the place's
position in a crowded area
of mapping

Locality, town or village
Shown when more than one
place has the same name

Postcode district
District for the indexed place

Page and grid square
Page number and grid
reference for the standard
mapping

Public and commercial buildings are highlighted in magenta   **Places of interest** are highlighted in blue with a star★

Abbreviations used in the index

Acad	**Academy**	Comm	**Common**	Gd	**Ground**	L	**Leisure**
App	**Approach**	Cott	**Cottage**	Gdn	**Garden**	La	**Lane**
Arc	**Arcade**	Cres	**Crescent**	Gn	**Green**	Liby	**Library**
Ave	**Avenue**	Cswy	**Causeway**	Gr	**Grove**	Mdw	**Meadow**
Bglw	**Bungalow**	Ct	**Court**	H	**Hall**	Meml	**Memorial**
Bldg	**Building**	Ctr	**Centre**	Ho	**House**	Mkt	**Market**
Bsns,Bus	**Business**	Ctry	**Country**	Hospl	**Hospital**	Mus	**Museum**
Bvd	**Boulevard**	Cty	**County**	HQ	**Headquarters**	Orch	**Orchard**
Cath	**Cathedral**	Dr	**Drive**	Hts	**Heights**	Pal	**Palace**
Cir	**Circus**	Dro	**Drove**	Ind	**Industrial**	Par	**Parade**
Cl	**Close**	Ed	**Education**	Inst	**Institute**	Pas	**Passage**
Cnr	**Corner**	Emb	**Embankment**	Int	**International**	Pk	**Park**
Coll	**College**	Est	**Estate**	Intc	**Interchange**	Pl	**Place**
Com	**Community**	Ex	**Exhibition**	Junc	**Junction**	Prec	**Precinct**

Prom	**Promenade**
Rd	**Road**
Recn	**Recreation**
Ret	**Retail**
Sh	**Shopping**
Sq	**Square**
St	**Street**
Sta	**Station**
Terr	**Terrace**
TH	**Town Hall**
Univ	**University**
Wk, Wlk	**Walk**
Wr	**Water**
Yd	**Yard**

Translations Welsh – English

Aber	**Estuary, confluence**	Cwm	**Valley**	Lôn	**Lane**	Rhiw	**Hill, incline**
Afon	**River**	Cwrt	**Court**	Maes	**Open area, field, square**	Rhodfa	**Avenue**
Amgueddfa	**Museum**	Dinas	**City**			Sgwâr	**Square**
Bro	**District, area**	Dôl	**Meadow**	Môr	**Sea**	Stryd	**Street**
Bryn	**Hill**	Eglwys	**Church**	Mynydd	**Mountain**	Swyddfa post	**Post office**
Cae	**Field**	Felin	**Mill**	Oriel	**Gallery**		
Caer	**Fort**	Fferm	**Farm**	Parc	**Park**	Tref, Tre	**Town**
Canolfan	**Centre**	Ffordd	**Road, way**	Parc busnes	**Business park**	Tŷ	**House**
Capel	**Chapel**	Gelli	**Grove**	Pen	**Top, end**	Uchaf	**Upper**
Castell	**Castle**	Gerddi	**Gardens**	Pentref	**Village**	Ysbyty	**Hospital**
Cilgant	**Crescent**	Gorsaf	**Station**	Plas	**Mansion, place**	Ysgol	**School**
Clòs	**Close**	Heol	**Road**	Pont	**Bridge**	Ystad, stad	**Estate**
Coed	**Wood**	Isaf	**Lower**	Prifysgol	**University**	Ystad ddiwydiannol	**Industrial estate**
Coleg	**College**	Llan	**Church, parish**	Rhaeadr	**Waterfall**		
		Llyn	**Lake**	Rhes	**Terrace, row**	Ystrad	**Vale**

Translations English – Welsh

Avenue	**Rhodfa**	Estuary	**Aber**	Mansion	**Plas**	Station	**Gorsaf**
Bridge	**Pont**	Farm	**Fferm**	Meadow	**Dôl**	Street	**Stryd**
Business	**Parc busnes**	Field	**Cae**	Mill	**Felin**	Terrace	**Rhes**
Park		Fort	**Caer**	Mountain	**Mynydd**	Top, end	**Pen**
Castle	**Castell**	Gallery	**Oriel**	Museum	**Amgueddfa**	Town	**Tref, tre**
Centre	**Canolfan**	Gardens	**Gerddi**	Parish	**Plwyf eglwys, llan,**	University	**Prifysgol**
Chapel	**Capel**	Grove	**Gelli**			Upper	**Uchaf**
Church	**Eglwys**	Hill	**Bryn, rhiw**	Park	**Parc**	Vale	**Ystrad, glyn, dyffryn**
City	**Dinas**	Hospital	**Ysbyty**	Place	**Plas, maes**		
Close	**Clòs**	House	**Tŷ**	Post office	**Swyddfa post**	Valley	**Cwm**
College	**Coleg**	Industrial	**Ystad**	River	**Afon**	Village	**Pentref**
Court	**Cwrt**	estate	**ddiwydiannol**	Road	**Heol, ffordd**	Waterfall	**Rhaeadr**
Crescent	**Cilgant**	Lake	**Llyn**	School	**Ysgol**	Way	**Ffordd**
District	**Bro**	Lane	**Lôn**	Sea	**Môr**	Wood	**Coed**
Estate	**Ystad, stad**	Lower	**Isaf**	Square	**Sgwâr, maes**		

Index of localities, towns and villages

A

Aber Arad 119 F4
Aber-banc 18 F4
Abercastle 29 C6
Abercych 16 F3
Aberdaugleddau / Milford Haven 131 C1
Abereiddy 28 D4
Aber-Giâr 21 B4
Abergorlech 41 D4
Abergwaun / Fishguard 122 E2
Abergwesyn 9 A7
Abergwili 129 E7
Abernant 57 C2
Abertawe / Swansea 174 C1
Aberteifi / Cardigan 118 E3
Achddu 137 E3
Adpar 119 D6
Albert Town 124 E4
Allt 142 A1
Alltwalis 39 B2
Allt-wen 147 F3
Ambleston 51 F4
Ammanford / Rhydaman 98 A8
Amroth 90 D1
Angle 102 D6
Arberth / Narberth 70 D1
Ashfield 63 B7

B

Babel 45 D6
Backe 127 A3
Balaclava 155 B5
Bancffosfelen 95 F6
Bancycapel 76 A2
Bancyfelin 74 A4
Bancyffordd 38 E8
Bangor Teifi 19 A3
Begelly 134 B8
Bengal 31 A3
Berea 28 C2
Berry 117 B6
Bethesda 70 C4
Bethlehem 63 B4
Betws 98 C6
Betws Bledrws 4 E6
Bicton 85 B2
Bigyn 148 E4
Birchgrove 155 B2
Bishopston 171 F7
Black Pill 166 B2
Blaenffos 35 A8
Blaenwaun 55 E6
Blaen-y-coed 57 E6
Bletherston 69 F8
Blue Anchor 157 A3
Bolahaul 129 B1
Boncath 16 B1
Bon-y-maen 161 C3
Bosherston 111 E3
Boulston 87 C7
Box 148 F6
Brechfa 40 D1
Bridell 15 E5
Bridgend 118 D3
Brimaston 50 E4
Broadfield 134 E1
Broad Haven 85 C8
Broadlay 94 A4
Broadmoor 106 C8
Broad Oak 61 D1
Broadway Laugharne Township 92 E4
Broadway St Ishmael 94 B3
Broadway The Havens 85 E8
Brongest 18 A8
Brongwyn 17 D6
Bronwydd Arms 58 E2
Brook 92 B4
Broom 89 D3
Bryn Crofty 163 B7
Bryn Llanelli 149 F6
Brynamman 99 E8
Brynamman Quarter Bach 80 D1
Brynberian 33 C6
Bryngwyn Beulah 17 E8
Bryngwyn Brawdy 49 B3
Bryn-henllan 12 F4
Brynhyfryd 160 C4
Bryn Iwan 37 A2
Brynmill 166 E5
Brynteg 20 F6
Burry Green 115 A2
Burry Port / Porth Tywyn 137 D4
Burton 132 F6
Burton Ferry 132 F6
Bwlch-newydd 57 F3
Bwlchygroes 35 F6
Bynea 149 F3

C

Cadle 159 D7
Cae-mawr 153 E1
Caer-eithin 159 F5
Caerfarchell 48 C6
Caerfyrddin / Carmarthen 128 E7
Caio 24 A2
Camrose 67 E7
Capel 148 F7
Capel Dewi Llanarthney 76 E7
Capel Dewi Llandysul 20 C5
Capel Gwynfe 63 F1
Capel Hendre 97 E6
Capel Isaac 61 D6
Capel Iwan 36 D7
Capel Newydd / Newchapel 16 D2
Capel Seion 96 C8
Capel Tygwydd 17 C6
Cardigan / Aberteifi 118 E3
Carew 105 D6
Carew Cheriton 105 D5
Carew Newton 105 D7
Carmarthen / Caerfyrddin 128 E7
Carmel 78 D3
Carnglas 166 B8
Carnhedryn 48 C6
Carway 95 D1
Cas-Mael / Puncheston 51 F8
Castell Newydd Emlyn / Newcastle Emlyn 119 B4
Castlebythe 52 A7
Castlemartin 110 F7
Castlemorris 30 B2
Caswell 172 B4
Cefn-bryn-brain 100 B8
Cefncaeau 149 C4
Cefneithin 97 A8
Cefn-gorwydd 27 F8
Cefn Hengoed 161 C3
Cefn Parc 162 E6
Cefn-y-Garth 155 A6
Cefn-y-pant 55 A4
Cellan 4 F4
Cenarth 17 B4
Chapelhill 104 A1
Cheriton or Stackpole Elidor 112 A6
Churchton 134 E5
Cilau 11 B4
Cilgerran 16 A5
Cilgwyn Myddfai 64 B8
Cilgwyn Nevern 33 A7
Cilrhedyn 36 C5
Cilsan 61 E1
Cilycwm 25 C3
Cippyn 2 D3
Clarbeston 69 D8
Clarbeston Road 69 B7
Clase 160 D8
Cloigyn 76 A1
Clunderwen 70 F6
Clun-Du 153 F1
Clydach 154 D7
Clydau 36 A6
Cnap-Llwyd 160 D5
Coalbrook 151 B5
Cockett 159 E2
Coed Cae 149 A5
Coed-y-bryn 18 E8
Cold Blow 89 F7
Cold Inn 106 D8
Colston 51 D6
Cosheston 104 F6
Court Henry 61 A1
Craig-cefn-parc 146 A2
Craig Glyn-meirch 147 D4
Craig Trebanos 147 C3
Craig-y-duke 147 C2
Cresselly 88 F1
Cresswell Quay 88 E1
Crinow 70 F1
Croes-goch 29 A3
Croes-lan 19 B7
Croesyceilog 75 D3
Croes-y-Llan 3 D1
Crofty 156 B3
Crosshands 55 A1
Cross Hands 97 A7
Cross Hands Jeffreyston 89 A6
Crosswell / Ffynnoncroes 33 F7
Crugybar 42 F8
Crundale 68 C5
Crwbin 95 D8
Crymych 34 E4
Cuffern 67 A8
Cuttybridge 67 F6
Cwmann 120 E3
Cwmbach 56 A5
Cwmbwrla 160 C2
Cwm Capel 137 F5
Cwmcarnhywel 149 D5
Cwmcerdinen 98 C2
Cwm-cou 119 A7
Cwmcych 36 C7
Cwmdu 160 A2
Cwmdu Talley / Talyllychau 42 C1
Cwmduad 38 A2
Cwm Dulais 144 B4
Cwmdwr 43 E3
Cwmdwyfran 58 D3
Cwmfelin Boeth 126 B8
Cwm-felin-Fâch 154 A3
Cwmfelin Mynach 55 D3
Cwmffrwd 75 F4
Cwmgiedd 138 F3
Cwmgors 99 D5
Cwmgwili 97 C6
Cwm Gwyn 166 E8
Cwmhiraeth 37 D8
Cwmifor 62 E4
Cwm Irfon 9 A4
Cwmisfael 77 A2
Cwmllynfell 100 B7
Cwm-mawr 96 E7
Cwm-miles 54 C1
Cwmorgan 36 E5
Cwmpengraig 37 D7
Cwmrhydyceirw 153 E3
Cwm-twrch Isaf 138 B1
Cwm-twrch Uchaf 100 C6
Cwmwdig Water 28 D3
Cwm-y-glo 97 A8
Cwrt-y-cadno 24 B7
Cydweli / Kidwelly 136 D4
Cynghordy 26 C2
Cynheidre 95 F2
Cynwyl Elfed 58 A6

D

Dafen 149 B7
Dale 101 E4
Dan-y-graig 168 A7
Deerland 87 D5
Derwydd 79 B4
Dinas 36 C1
Dinas Cross 12 F3
Dinbych-y-pysgod / Tenby 135 C4
Doc Penfro / Pembroke Dock 132 B4
Dolgran 39 A5
Dreenhill 124 A2
Drefach Gorslas 96 D8
Drefach Llangeler 18 E1
Drefach Meidrim 73 E8
Dre-fach Dyffryn Cennen 79 E3
Dre-fach Llanwenog 21 B8
Drefelin 37 F8
Druidston 66 D3
Dryslwyn 78 A7
Dunvant 165 B8
Dyffryn 122 A4
Dyffryn Ceidrych 63 D4

E

East Trewent 112 C6
East Williamston 106 D8
Edwinsford 42 B5
Efailwen 54 A4
Eglwyswen 34 C7
Eglwyswrw 15 A1
Esgair 58 A7

F

Faedre 154 D8
Fagwr-isaf 146 B2
Fairwood 164 D7
Felindre Llangadog 63 D6
Felindre Llangathen 78 A8
Felindre Llangeler 18 E1
Felindre Llansadwrn 43 B1
Felindre Pontarddulais 144 F2
Felindre Farchog 14 D1
Felinfoel 141 A1
Felingwmisaf 60 B2
Felingwmuchaf 60 B3
Felin Newydd 23 F1
Ferryside 93 F5
Ffairfach 130 D4
Ffaldybrenin 23 C7
Ffarmers 23 E7
Fforest 143 A6
Fforest-fach 159 C4
Ffynnoncroes / Crosswell 33 F7
Ffynnon-ddrain 128 D8
Fishguard / Abergwaun 122 E2
Five Roads 140 A7
Foelgastell 77 F1
Folly 67 D7
Ford 51 A5
Four Roads 95 C4
Foxhole 174 C5
Freshwater East 105 B1
Freystrop 87 B6
Furnace 148 C7
Furnace Pembrey & Bury Port Town 137 C3

G

Garnant 99 B7
Garnswllt 98 B4
Gelli 70 B6
Gellygron 147 C6
Gellywen 56 D2
Gendros 159 F3
Gignog 49 F3
Glais 155 B6
Glanaman 99 A8
Glanaman Cwmamman 80 A1
Glan-Duar 21 E6
Glandŵr / Landore 160 D4
Glandwr 54 F7
Glandy Cross 54 B5
Glanrhyd 15 B5
Glan-rhyd 139 F7
Glan-y-mÛr 92 F6
Glenowen 104 A8
Glogue 35 C3
Glyntawe 82 F3
Godreír-graig 100 B1
Golden Grove 78 D6
Golden Hill Pembroke / Penfro 133 C6
Golden Hill Spittal 51 C3
Goodwick / Wdig 122 B6
Gorof 138 E1
Gorseinon 151 C3
Gorseinon Garden Village 158 D8
Gorslas 97 C8
Gowerton / Tre-gwyr 158 B4
Graig 137 E4
Graig Fawr 143 E6
Graigfelen 154 C8
Graig Trewyddfa 160 F7
Granston 30 A5
Green 133 C5
Grove 133 C3
Grovesend 151 C6
Guilford 87 D4
Gumfreston 106 D4
Gurnos 139 D7
Gwastad 52 D3
Gwaun-Cae-Gurwen 99 E6
Gwaun-Leision 99 D7
Gwbert 3 A6
Gwernogle 40 E5
Gwyddgrug 39 D6

H

Hafod 160 E2
Hakin 131 B2
Halfpenny Furze 92 B8
Halfway 42 D1
Half Way 149 B6
Halfway Farm 45 D3
Hanover Square 161 B3
Harbour Village 122 B7
Harddfan 150 A6
Haroldston West 66 D2
Hasguard 85 C4
Haverfordwest / Hwlffordd 124 D5
Haycastle Cross 50 B4
Hayscastle 50 A4
Haysford 67 D8
Hebron Cilymaenllwyd 54 F6
Hebron Llanfihangel-ar-Arth 38 E6
Hendy 143 A5
Hendy-Gwyn / Whitland 126 D3
Henllan 18 E3
Henllan Amgoed 71 F6
Henry's Moat 52 D6
Heol-ddu 109 C6
Heol-las 154 F2
Herbrandston 85 D2
Hermon Crymych 35 B2
Hermon Cynwyl Elfed 37 F1
High Street 71 F2
Hillend Burrows 114 B1
Hill Mountain 87 D3
Hiraeth 71 D8
Hodgeston 105 B2
Hook 87 D6
Hopkinstown 98 C7
Horeb Llandysul 19 C5
Horeb Llanegwad 60 C7
Horeb Llanelli Rural 140 B8
Horton 117 B4
Houghton 87 D2
Hubberston 131 B3
Hundleton 104 B3
Hwlffordd / Haverfordwest 124 D5

I

Idole 75 F2
Iet-y-bwlch 54 C7
Ilston 164 B2

J

Jameston 105 E2
Jeffreyston 89 C1
Jersey Marine 162 C1
Johnston 86 E5
Johnstown 128 C3
Jordanston 30 D3

K

Keeston 67 B6
Kete 101 D3
Kidwelly / Cydweli 136 D4
Kilgetty 134 D8
Killay 165 E7
Kittle 171 E7
Knelston 117 A7

L

Lambston 67 B4
Lampeter / Llanbedr Pont Steffan 120 E6
Lampeter Velfrey 71 C1
Lamphey 105 A3
Landimore 115 A4
Landore / Glandŵr 160 D4
Landshipping 88 A6
Langland 172 F4
Laugharne 92 E6
Lawrenny 88 A2
Lawrenny Quay 88 A1
Leason 115 C3
Leonardston 103 F8
Letterston 50 F8
Leweston 50 F1
Liddeston 131 B4
Limeslade 173 C3
Lisbon 160 C5
Little Haven 85 C8
Little Honeyborough 86 F1
Little Milford 87 B6
Little Newcastle 51 D7
Little Reynoldston 117 D8
Llanarthne 77 E7
Llanbedr Pont Steffan / Lampeter 120 E6
Llanboidy 55 D2
Llandarcy 162 D3
Llandawke 92 D6
Llanddarog 77 B3
Llanddeusant 64 E3
Llanddewi 117 A8
Llanddewi Velfrey 71 B3
Llanddowror 73 A1
Llandeilo 130 E5
Llandeilo'r-Fan 46 E5
Llandeloy 49 D5
Llandilo 53 D6
Llandissilio 70 F8
Llandovery / Llanymddyfri 121 B5
Llandre 24 A4
Llandruidion 48 B3
Llandudoch / St Dogmaels 118 A4
Llandybie 79 B2
Llandyfaelog 94 F6
Llandyfan 79 D4
Llandyfriog 18 C4
Llandygwydd 16 F6
Llandyry 109 A8
Llandysul 19 D3
Llanedi 97 D2
Llanegwad 77 D8
Llanelli 149 B5
Llanerch 148 E7
Llanfair Clydogau 5 B6
Llanfair-Nant-Gwyn 34 D8
Llanfallteg 71 C6
Llanfallteg West 71 B6
Llanfihangel-ar-arth 20 C2
Llanfihangel-uwch-Gwili 59 F1
Llanfynydd 61 B6
Llanfyrnach 35 D2
Llangadog Kidwelly / Cydweli 136 D5
Llangadog 63 E7
Llangain 75 B2

Llangathen 61 D1
Llangeler 19 A2
Llangennech 54 E7
Llangenwith 114 C2
Llangloffan 30 B3
Llanglydwen 54 F5
Llangoedmor 3 D1
Llangolman 53 F6
Llangunnor 129 C5
Llangwm 87 D4
Llangybi 4 F8
Llangyfelach 153 A2
Llangyndeyrn 76 D1
Llangynin 73 A6
Llangynog 74 D3
Llanhowel 48 E6
Llanion 132 D3
Llanllawddog 59 C8
Llanllwch 128 A2
Llanllwni 21 A2
Llanmadoc 114 E4
Llan-mill 71 B1
Llanmiloe 92 A4
Llanmorlais 156 C2
Llannon 96 E3
Llanon 29 A4
Llanpumsaint 58 F8
Llanreath 132 A2
Llanrhian 28 E4
Llanrhidian 115 D2
Llansadurnen 92 C5
Llansadwrn 43 C2
Llansaint 94 B3
Llansamlet 161 D8
Llansawel 42 A7
Llansteffan 93 D5
Llanteg 90 E5
Llanteglos 90 E4
Llanwenog 21 A8
Llanwinio 56 B5
Llanwnda 11 A4
Llanwrda 43 E2
Llanwrtyd 9 B2
Llanwrtyd Wells 9 C2
Llanybri 93 C7
Llanybydder 21 D7
Llanycefn 53 C2
Llanychaer 31 D6
Llanymddyfri /
  Llandovery 121 B5
Llawhaden 69 F4
Llechryd 16 C7
Llidiad-Nenog 40 F8
Llwynbrwydrau 162 A7
Llwyndrain 36 B5
Llwynhendy 149 D4
Llwyn-rhyd-Owen 20 C7
Llwyn-y-brain 72 A1
Llys-y-frân 52 D3
Llywel 46 C1
Login 54 D2
Longstone 90 B4
Lon-Las 162 B7
Loughor 150 E2
Loveston 89 B3
Lower Brynamman 99 D8
Lower Fishguard 122 E4
Lower Freystrop 87 B7
Lower Sketty 166 B3
Lower Solva 48 E3
Lower Town 122 E3
Ludchurch 90 B5
Lunnon 170 F8
Lydstep 106 B1

M

Maenclochog 53 B6
Maerdy 130 D1
Maes llyn 18 F7
Maesybont 75 B3
Maesycrugiau 20 E4
Maesymeillion 19 E8
Maiden Wells 104 B2
Manorbier 113 C6
Manorbier Newton 105 D3
Manordeilo 63 A5
Manorowen 11 B1
Mansel field 172 C6
Manston 160 B3
Marble Hall 148 E5
Marloes 84 C3
Marros 91 B4
Martletwy 88 C5
Mascle Bridge 104 A8
Mathry 29 E4
Mayals 165 F1
Mayeston 105 A6
Mayhill 160 A1
Meidrim 73 D8
Meinciau 95 C5
Merlin's Bridge 124 E2
Merlin's Cross 133 D3
Merrion 111 C6
Merthyr 74 E7
Mesur-y-dorth 29 A3
Middle Mill 48 E4
Middleton 116 C6
Milford Haven /
  Aberdaugleddau 131 C1
Milin Cross 87 E8
Milo 78 E4
Milton 105 C6
Minwear 88 D8
Monington 15 A6
Monkton 133 A5

Moore Town 162 E8
Morfa
  Ammanford / Rhydaman . . .97 C7
Morfa Llanelli 148 F2
Morfa Bach 93 F8
Morriston / Treforys 153 E1
Mount Pleasant
  Cosheston 105 A8
Mount Pleasant Llanelli . .148 D7
Mount Pleasant
  Swansea / Abertawe . . .174 A3
Moylgrove / Trewyddel . .14 E7
Murton 172 B6
Musselwick 84 F1
Myddfai 44 E1
Mynachlog-ddu 34 B1
Mynydd-Bâch 160 B8
Mynydd-bach-y-glo 159 A4
Mynydd-Garn-Lwyd 160 D7
Mynyddygarreg 136 F7

N

Nanhyfer / Nevern 14 B3
Nantgaredig 77 A8
Nant-y-Bai 25 E7
Nantycaws 76 D5
Nant-y-ffin 41 A3
Narberth / Arberth 70 D1
Narberth Bridge 70 D1
Neuadd 80 C8
Nevern / Nanhyfer 14 B3
Newcastle Emlyn / Castell
  Newydd Emlyn 119 B4
Newchapel /
  Capel Newydd 16 D2
Newchurch 58 B3
Newgale 49 C1
New Hedges 107 A5
New Inn Llanfihangel-ar-Arth 39 E7
New Inn Puncheston /
  Cas-Mael 32 E1
New Moat 52 E4
New Park 88 B6
Newport / Trefdraeth 13 F4
Newton 172 E5
Newton Cross 50 A6
Neyland 132 B5
Nicholaston 117 F7
Nine Wells 48 E3
Nolton 66 D5
Nolton Haven 66 D5

O

Oaklands 75 F3
Olchfa 166 A7
Oldwalls 115 C2
Oldway 172 B6
Overton 117 A4
Oxwich 117 D5
Oxwich Green 117 D5
Oystermouth 173 A5

P

Panteg 30 D5
Pantgwyn 61 E4
Pant-y-Caws 54 C5
Pantyffynnon 98 B5
Parc Melin Mynach 151 D2
Parc Tawe 174 B3
Parc-y-Rhôs 120 C1
Parkmill 170 F7
Parrog 13 D4
Pelcomb 67 D5
Pelcomb Bridge 124 C8
Pelcomb Cross 67 D5
Pemberton 149 B5
Pembrey / Pen-bre 137 A3
Pembroke Dock /
  Doc Penfro 132 B4
Pembroke Ferry 132 E5
Pembroke / Penfro 133 F5
Penallt 148 F6
Penally / Penalun 135 C2
Penalun / Penally 135 C2
Penboyr 37 E7
Pen-bre / Pembrey 137 A3
Pencader 39 B6
Penceiliogi 149 C6
Pen-clawdd 156 E3
Pendine / Pentywyn 91 D3
Penffordd 53 B1
Penfilia 160 C5
Penfro / Pembroke 133 F5
Peniel 59 A3
Peniel Green 161 F8
Pen-lan 160 A5
Pen-lan-mabws 29 E2
Penllergaer 152 A2
Penmaen 170 B6
Pennar 132 A1
Pennard 171 C6
Pennar Park 103 F5
Penparc 3 F3
Penplas 74 E4
Penrherber 119 A2
Pen-Rhiw-fawr 100 B5
Penrhiwgoch 78 B4
Penrhiw-llan 19 A4
Penrhiw-pâl 18 D8
Penrice 117 D6
Pensarn 128 F3

Pentlepoir 134 B6
Pentre 160 D2
Pentre-bâch 4 A2
Pentrebach Myddfai 45 C4
Pentrebach Pontarddulais .143 E7
Pentrecagal 18 C3
Pentre-Chwyth 161 A2
Pentre-cwrt 19 B1
Pentrefelin Llanfair Clydogau .5 A3
Pentrefelin Llangathen 61 C2
Pentreffynnon 162 F6
Pentre Galar 34 F1
Pentre-Gwenlais 79 A3
Pentrellwyn 19 E5
Pentre-Poeth 148 D8
Pentre-ty-gwyn 45 C6
Pentywyn / Pendine 91 D3
Penybanc 98 A6
Penybanc Abergwili 129 E8
Pen-y-banc
  Manordeilo & Salem 62 A3
Penybedd 108 E5
Pen-y-bont 56 F6
Pen-y-Bryn 15 F5
Penycwm 49 B2
Penydre 146 F1
Pen-y-Fan 148 F3
Penyfeidr 49 E5
Pen-y-garn 41 C2
Penygroes 34 C6
Pen-y-groes 97 D8
Penyraber 122 C5
Penyrheol Gorseinon 151 B4
Penyrheol
  Swansea / Abertawe . .166 B3
Pen-yr-Heol 162 F6
Pibwrlwyd 128 F1
Pill 131 E2
Pilton Green 116 E6
Pinged 108 F6
Pitton 116 C6
Plashett 92 C4
Plasmarl 160 E5
Pontantan / Pontamman .98 C7
Pontamman / Pontaman .98 C7
Pontantwn 95 B8
Pontardawe 147 D4
Pontarddulais 143 E5
Pont-ar-gothi 77 B8
Pont-ar-llechau 63 F3
Pontarsais 59 B7
Pont Creuddyn 4 A7
Pontfaen 32 B4
Pont-Henri 95 F4
Ponthirwaun 17 B8
Pontiago 11 A3
Pont-iets / Pontyates 95 D3
Pontlliw 152 A7
Pont-newydd 95 B2
Pontyates / Pont-iets 95 D3
Pontyberem 96 A6
Pont-y-Fenni 72 E4
Pontyglasier 34 B7
Pont-yr-hafod 50 B5
Pope Hill 86 F7
Port-Eynon 117 A4
Portfield Gate 67 C2
Portheiddy 28 D4
Porthgain 28 E5
Porth Tywyn /
  Burry Port 137 D4
Porthyrhyd Llanddarog . . .77 C2
Porthyrhyd Llanwrda 43 D8
Port Lion 87 D3
Port Mead 159 D6
Port Tennant 168 C8
Poundffald 157 D2
Poyston 68 B6
Poyston Cross 68 C6
Prendergast 125 C7
Pren-gwyn 19 F7
Priory 31 C5
Pumsaint 24 D7
Puncheston / Cas-Mael . .51 F8
Pwll 109 F4
Pwllcrochan 103 D5
Pwll-trap 127 B5
Pyle 172 A5

R

Rallt 163 A8
Ram 120 E2
Redberth 106 A7
Red Roses 91 B6
Reynalton 89 B3
Reynoldston 115 B1
Rhandirmwyn 25 E6
Rhodiad-y-Brenin 123 F8
Rhos 38 B6
Rhosaman 81 A1
Rhoscrowther 103 A5
Rhosfach 53 E7
Rhos-Hill 15 F3
Rhosmaen 130 F8
Rhossili 116 B7
Rhosson 47 B4
Rhosycaerau 10 C7
Rhydaman / Ammanford .98 A8
Rhydargaeau 59 B5
Rhydcymerau 22 C1
Rhydowen Crymych 55 A7
Rhydowen Llandysul 20 A8
Rhydlefin 36 D8
Rhyd-y-fro 147 D8
Rhydygele 49 C3

Rhyd-y-gwin 146 A4
Rhyd-y-Pandy 145 F1
Rhydwrach 71 D6
Ridgeway 134 D4
Rinaston 51 D4
Robeston Back 70 A2
Robeston Wathen 70 B2
Robeston West 85 F4
Roch 66 E8
Rosebush 53 A3
Rosemarket 87 A3
Rosepool 85 D6
Rose Valley Farm 133 E3
Rudbaxton 68 A7

S

Sageston 105 E6
St Brides 84 C5
St Clears / Sanclêr 127 E4
St David's / Tyddewi 123 B5
St Dogmaels /
  Llandudoch 118 A4
St Florence 106 B4
St Ishmael 93 F3
St Ishmael's 85 A1
St Justinian 47 A4
St Nicholas 30 A6
St Petrox 111 E6
St Thomas 174 C3
St Twynnells 111 C6
Salem 62 B5
Sanclêr / St Clears 127 E4
Sandy 148 B6
Sandy Haven 85 B2
Sandy Lane 171 A6
Sardis 134 F7
Sarnau 74 D6
Saron 97 E7
Saron Llangeler 19 A1
Saundersfoot 134 F3
Sciwen / Skewen 162 D7
Scleddau 30 F4
Scurlage 117 A6
Seaside 148 C3
Shipping 89 E3
Silian 4 C6
Siloh 44 B8
Simpson Cross 67 A6
Skerryford 124 B3
Sketty 166 D6
Skewen / Sciwen 162 D7
Slade 117 C4
Slade
  Haverfordwest / Hwlffordd .124 E7
Slebech 69 B2
Smalls 62 A7
Solva 48 D3
Southgate 171 A5
Spittal 51 D2
Square and Compass 29 C4
Stackpole 112 A5
Star 35 F6
Stepaside 90 A3
Steynton 131 E5
Summerhill 90 C2
Sutton 67 C2
Swansea / Abertawe 174 C1
Swiss Valley 141 B2
Sylen 96 B1

T

Tafarnspite / Tavernspite .90 F7
Tafarn-y-bwlch 33 A4
Tairgwaith 99 F7
Tai'r-ysgol 161 E8
Talbenny 85 B6
Talley / Talyllychau 42 D3
Talog 57 B4
Talsarn 64 E5
Talyllychau / Talley 42 D3
Tanerdy 129 B6
Tangiers 68 A5
Tanglwst 37 A4
Tavernspite / Tafarnspite .90 F7
Tegryn 35 E4
Temple Bar 78 E4
Templeton 89 E6
Tenby /
  Dinbych-y-pysgod 135 C4
The Mumbles /
  Y Mwmbwls 173 C4
The Rhos 68 F1
The Valley 134 B4
Thistleboon 173 B3
Thomas Chapel 89 D3
Thornton 131 C6
Three Crosses 157 E1
Tiers Cross 86 B5
Tirabad 27 C4
Tircanol 160 E6
Tircoed 152 C5
Tirdeunaw 160 B7
Tir-Nest 161 B3
Tirpenry 154 A1
Townhill 167 A8
Trallwn 161 F6

Trefasser 10 D2
Trefdraeth / Newport 13 F4
Treffgarne 51 A2
Treffynnon 29 B1
Trefgarn Owen 49 D4
Trefin 29 B5
Treforys / Morriston 153 E1
Treginnis 47 C3
Treglemais 28 F1
Tre-gôig 41 F6
Tregroes 19 F7
Tre-gwyr / Gowerton . . .158 B4
Tregyddulan 10 D1
Tre-gynwr 129 A3
Trelech 36 D1
Trelech-a'r-Bettws 56 F5
Treleddyd-fawr 47 E6
Trelerw 48 A3
Tresinwen 10 E5
Tretio 28 B1
Trevaughan
  Carmarthen / Caerfyrddin .128 D7
Trevaughan
  Whitland / Hendy-Gwyn .126 D1
Trewyddel / Moylgrove . .14 E7
Trewyddfa Fach 160 E7
Triffleton 51 C3
Trimsaran 109 C8
Troedyraur 18 B8
Trooper's Inn 87 B5
Tufton 52 C7
Tumble / Tymbl 96 F7
Tutt 173 D3
Twynllanan 64 C3
Twynmynydd 79 F1
Ty-coch 166 C8
Tycroes 97 F5
Tyddewi / St David's 123 B5
Ty-Draw 161 C2
Ty-hên 56 E3
Ty-Isaf 148 E3
Ty Mawr 21 E5
Tymbl / Tumble 96 F7
Tyn-y-cwm 144 D2
Tyrfran 148 E7

U

Uplands 166 F6
Upper Brynamman 80 F1
Upper Forge 154 D8
Upper Killay 165 A5
Upper Nash 105 B5
Upper Solva 48 C3
Uzmaston 125 E2

V

Vachelich 48 A4

W

Wallis 52 A4
Walton East 52 B2
Walton West 85 D7
Walwyn's Castle 85 E6
Warren 111 A6
Waterloo 132 E4
Waterston 103 F8
Waunarlwydd 158 E4
Waun Beddau 28 A2
Waungilwen 18 D2
Waungron 143 C1
Waun-Gron 160 D6
Waun y Clyn 109 B7
Wdig / Goodwick 122 B6
Welsh Hook 50 E6
Wern 148 D4
Wernbwll 157 A2
Wernffrwd 115 F5
Wern-olau 157 D4
West Cross 173 A7
Weston 88 C5
West Williamston 105 C8
Whitchurch 48 D4
Whitehill 105 E7
White Mill 60 C4
Whitland / Hendy-Gwyn .126 D3
Winch-wen 161 C5
Wiseman's Bridge 90 B1
Wiston 69 A5
Withybush 125 D8
Wolf's Castle 51 A5
Wolfsdale 67 E8
Wood 66 C8
Wooden 134 A4
Woodstock 52 B4

Y

Yerbeston 88 F3
Y Ferwig 3 C5
Y Mwmbwls /
  The Mumbles 173 C4
Ynysforgan 154 C4
Ynystawe 154 C6
Yspitty 150 B2
Ystalyfera 139 A6
Ystradffin 7 F1
Ystradowen 100 C7

3rd St SA73 .... 103 E8
4th St SA73 .... 103 E8
5th St SA73 .... 103 E8
6th St SA73 .... 103 E7
7th St SA73 .... 103 E8
8th St SA73 .... 103 E8
9th St SA73 .... 103 E7
10th St SA73 .... 103 E7
11th St SA73 .... 103 E7
12th St SA73 .... 103 D8
13th St SA73 .... 103 D8

A

Abbey Mead SA31 .... 129 B6
Abbey St SA17 .... 136 C4
Abbey Terr SA19 .... 130 D5
Abbots Cl SA61 .... 125 A4
Aberbanc Cty Prim Sch SA44 .... 18 E4
Abercedy SA4 .... 157 A4
Aberclydach Pl SA6 .... 154 D7
Aber Ct SA6 .... 161 B7
Aberdyberthi St SA1 .... 160 D2
Aberelddy Rd SA62 .... 28 F3
Abergelly Rd SA4 .... 159 C5
Aberglasney Gdns* SA32 .... 61 D1
Abergwili Rd SA31 .... 129 D7
Aberlash Rd SA18 .... 98 B8
Aber Llwchwr SA14 .... 150 B7
Abernant CP Sch SA33 .... 57 D2
Abernant Rd SA18 .... 99 D5
Abernethy Quay SA1 .... 174 B2
Abernethy Sq 14 SA1 .... 174 C2
Aberystwyth Rd SA43 .... 118 C5
Acacia Rd SA3 .... 173 A8
Acorn Ct SA6 .... 154 E5
Adams Dr 8 SA67 .... 70 D1
Adams Rd SA71 .... 104 C4
Adam St SA43 16
Addison Cl SA61 .... 125 B4
Addlegutter La SA71 .... 111 B4
Adelaide St
Llandovery / Llanymddyfri SA20 .... 121 D5
Swansea / Abertawe SA1 .... 174 B2
Admirals Wlk SA4 .... 166 C6
Admiralty Way SA72 .... 132 B3
Adulam Row SA14 .... 140 F1
Aelybryn SA15 .... 109 E4
Ael-y-Bryn
Pen-clawdd SA4 .... 156 F4
The Mumbles / Y Mwmbwls SA3 .... 173 C3
Aelybryn Cl SA15 .... 148 E8
Aelybryn Dr SA15 .... 148 E8
Ael-y-Bryn Rd SA5 .... 159 E3
Ael-y-don SA3 .... 172 F3
Ael-y-Felin SA62 .... 29 B4
Ael-y-Fro SA8 .... 147 D7
Aeron Pl SA1 .... 161 B2
Afon-Llan Gdns SA5 .... 159 D6
Afon Rd / Heol Afon SA14 .... 150 C8
Alamein Rd SA1 .... 160 E3
Alan Rd SA19 .... 130 E6
Alban Cres SA73 .... 103 E8
Alban Rd SA15 .... 148 E8
Albany Ave SA1 .... 161 C8
Albany Cl SA5 .... 160 C4
Albany St SA72 .... 132 C1
Albany Terr SA61 .... 125 A4
Alberto Rd SA6 .... 161 A6
Albert Pl SA3 .... 173 A5
Albert Row SA1 .... 174 B2
Albert St SA15 .... 148 C4
Albion Sq SA72 .... 132 C2
Albion Sq CP Sch SA72 .... 132 C2
Albion St SA71 .... 131 C3
Alden Dr SA2 .... 159 D1
Alder Ave SA9 .... 139 D7
Alderbrook Ct SA15 .... 159 F6
Alder Way
Gowerton / Tre-gwyr SA4 .... 158 C6
The Mumbles / Y Mwmbwls SA3 .... 172 F7
Alderwood Rd SA3 .... 173 A7
Aldwyn Rd SA5 .... 159 D2
Alexandra Rd
Gorseinon SA4 .... 151 A2
Swansea / Abertawe SA1 .... 174 B3
Alexandra Terr SA2 .... 166 F6
Alfred Rd SA6 .... 154 D3
Alice St SA5 .... 160 A2
Allaway Ct 1 SA1 .... 160 C2
Allendale Rd SA62 .... 85 A2
Alloy Court Est SA8 .... 147 F5
Alltacham Dr SA8 .... 147 E5
Alltfach SA43 .... 118 A3
Allt-Iago Rd SA4 .... 143 D4
Allt Ioan SA31 .... 128 C4
Allt Rhyd Y Groes National
Nature Reserve* SA20 .... 7 D3
Alltwalis Prim Sch / Ysgol
Gynradd Alltwalis SA32 .... 39 B2
Alltwen Hill SA8 .... 147 F3
Alltwen Prim Sch SA8 .... 147 F4
Allt Y Carne
Fishguard & Goodwick SA64 .... 11 B2
4 Goodwick / Wdig SA64 .... 122 A4
Alltycnap Rd
Carmarthen / Caerfyrddin SA31 .... 128 C3

Alltycnap Rd continued
Llangain SA33 .... 75 A5
Allt Y Gog SA31 .... 128 B5
Allt-y-Graban Rd SA4 .... 151 D8
Allt Y Grug SA10 .... 162 C1
Alltygrug Farm Rd SA9 .... 139 B7
Alltygrug Rd SA9 .... 139 B7
Allt-y-Waun SA9 .... 147 D7
Alltywerin SA8 .... 147 D6
Als St SA15 .... 148 E5
Alstred St SA17 .... 136 B4
Alun Rd SA1 .... 160 B1
Amanwy SA14 .... 149 D5
Amberley Dr SA3 .... 173 A4
Ambleside Pl SA3 .... 173 A8
Ammanford Jun Sch 98 C7
Ammanford Rd / Heol
Rhydaman SA18 .... 97 F6
Ammanford Sta SA18 .... 98 B7
Amman Rd / Heol Amman
Brynamman SA18 .... 99 E8
Glanaman SA18 .... 98 F8
Amman Valley Comp Sch SA18 .... 98 C7
Amman Valley Hospl SA18 .... 99 A8
Amos St SA15 .... 148 C4
Amphion Ct SA72 .... 133 A8
Amroth Rd SA67 .... 90 D4
Anchor Ct SA1 .... 174 B2
Anchor Down 8 SA62 .... 48 D3
Anderson La SA3 .... 171 A5
Andrew Cres SA4 .... 154 B4
Andrew St SA15 .... 148 E6
Aneurin Cl SA2 .... 166 A6
Aneurin Way SA2 .... 166 A6
Angle Rd SA4 .... 104 C4
Angle VC Sch SA71 .... 102 D6
Annesley St SA15 .... 148 E5
Ann St SA15 .... 148 D4
Anson Way SA70 .... 105 D6
Anthony Way SA31 .... 128 B3
Anthorn 2 SA65 .... 122 D3
Apley Terr SA72 .... 132 C3
Appledore Pl SA3 .... 172 E6
Applegrove SA4 .... 115 B1
Approach Rd SA5 .... 160 C2
Aran St SA6 .... 160 F7
Arcade 1 SA15 .... 148 D5
Arcade Terr / Teras Yr Arced
11 SA18 .... 99 B8
Arcade The 20 SA18 .... 98 B7
Ardent Cl SA73 .... 131 F5
Ardwyn Rd 7 SA18 .... 80 E1
Aremrig Rd SA1 .... 160 B8
Arethusa Dr SA1 .... 174 B1
Arethusa Ct SA2 .... 165 C6
Arethusa Quay SA1 .... 174 B1
Arfryn SA18 .... 80 E1
Arfryn Ave SA15 .... 148 E7
Arfryn Prim Sch SA5 .... 160 B5
Arfryn Rd SA2 .... 166 E8
Argoed Cres SA17 .... 109 B8
Argoed Rd / Heol Argoed SA18 .... 98 C5
Argyle St
Pembroke Dock / Doc Penfro SA72 .... 132 C3
Swansea / Abertawe SA1 .... 167 B6
Argyll Ave SA1 .... 151 B2
Arian Gwilli SA4 .... 143 A4
Ar-Lan-Morlais SA17 .... 109 B8
Armine Rd SA5 .... 159 E3
Arnold Ct SA4 .... 139 B6
Arnolds Hill SA61 .... 125 E5
Arthur Morris Dr SA72 .... 132 C1
Arthur St Llanelli SA15 .... 148 E6
Pembroke Dock / Doc Penfro SA72 .... 132 D3
Arthur St / Stryd Arthur SA18 .... 98 B8
Arthur Terr SA8 .... 147 E5
Arwelfa SA6 .... 153 D1
Ar-y-Bryn SA16 .... 137 A4
Ashburnham Dr SA15 .... 165 E2
Ashburnham Rd SA16 .... 137 D2
Ashdale La Burton SA73 .... 87 C3
Pembroke / Penfro SA71 .... 133 C5
Ashes The SA17 .... 109 D5
Ash Gr
Ammanford / Rhydaman SA18 .... 98 D7
Carmarthen / Caerfyrddin SA31 .... 128 C5
Gorseinon SA4 .... 151 A3
Killay SA2 .... 165 D7
Milford Haven / Aberdaugleddau SA73 .... 131 E3
Waunarlwydd SA5 .... 158 D4
Ashgrove 7 SA6 .... 96 B6
Ash La SA4 .... 90 E7
Ashleigh Cl SA2 .... 166 C3
Ashleigh Rd SA2 .... 166 C3
Ashleigh Terr SA10 .... 169 C8
Ashmount Bsns Parc SA6 .... 154 B1
Ash Pk SA6 .... 134 C8
Ash St SA6 .... 161 A7
Ashtree Cl SA73 .... 87 C3
Asquith Ct SA1 .... 167 A6
Assembly Rooms 5 SA1 .... 174 C2
Athrofa Abertawe / Swansea
Inst (Townhill Campus) SA1 .... 166 F8

Atlantic Cl SA7 .... 161 A5
Atlantic Dr 6 SA62 .... 85 D8
Atlantic Haven SA1 .... 114 C2
Augustine Way SA61 .... 125 A3
Augustus Pl 7 SA70 .... 135 E5
Avenue Cilfig The SA15 .... 148 D6
Avenue F SA1 .... 103 E8
Avenue H SA73 .... 103 E8
Avenue K-K SA1 .... 103 E8
Avenue M SA73 .... 103 E7
Avenue N SA1 .... 103 E8
Avenue P SA73 .... 103 E7
Avenue Q SA73 .... 103 E8
Avenue The
Carmarthen / Caerfyrddin SA31 .... 129 A5
Llanelli, Cwmcarnhywel SA14 .... 149 C5
Llanelli SA15 .... 148 E2
Siebech SA62 .... 87 F8
Averil Vivian Gr SA2 .... 166 E6
Avis Terr SA15 .... 148 E5
Avondale Gdns* SA68 .... 134 C8
Awel Tywi SA31 .... 129 B4
Axton Hill SA71 .... 103 E1
Aylesbury Rd SA2 .... 166 F5

B

Back Dr SA10 .... 162 B7
Back La
Goodwick / Wdig SA64 .... 122 A6
Haverfordwest / Hwlffordd SA61 .... 125 B6
Laugharne Township SA33 .... 92 F5
Llawhaden SA67 .... 70 C1
Back Terr SA71 .... 133 A4
Badminton Gdns SA5 .... 159 E5
Baglan St SA1 .... 168 A7
Bailey St SA17 .... 136 B4
Balaclava Rd SA7 .... 155 B5
Balaclava St SA1 .... 174 C3
Baldwin's Cres SA1 .... 168 E7
Ballards Ct SA10 .... 162 F8
Banc Bach SA4 .... 74 B5
Banc Pen-dre SA14 .... 136 B3
Banc-y-cwm SA4 .... 157 E5
Banc Y Ddraenen SA18 .... 97 D6
Bancyfelin CP Sch SA33 .... 74 B5
Bancyffynnon SA14 .... 97 B7
Banc Y Gors SA15 .... 96 F6
Banfield Terr SA1 .... 150 E3
Bank Bldgs SA19 .... 130 D6
Bank La 8 SA70 .... 135 E4
Bank Rd SA14 .... 150 C8
Bank Terr SA19 .... 130 D5
Banwell Ct SA6 .... 160 F8
Banwell St SA6 .... 160 F8
Banwen La SA4 .... 147 F4
Banwen Pl / Y Bannen SA18 .... 99 D8
Banwy Rd SA6 .... 153 D1
Baptist La / Lon Y Bedydd 18 SA18 .... 98 B7
Baptist Well Pl SA1 .... 174 A5
Baptist Well St SA1 .... 160 C1
Baran Rd Pontardawe SA8 .... 99 D1
Rhyd-y-fro SA8 .... 147 B8
Bardsey Ave SA5 .... 159 E7
Barham Rd SA62 .... 31 C3
Baring Gould Way SA61 .... 124 F5
Barley Mow SA48 .... 120 C4
Barlow St SA71 .... 131 C2
Barnabas Cl SA1 .... 158 F3
Barn Ct 1 SA61 .... 124 F4
Barn Rd SA31 .... 128 F5
Barnsfield Terr 1 SA31 .... 128 F5
Barn St SA61 .... 124 F4
Barry Rd / Heol Barri SA18 .... 99 D7
Bartletts Well Rd SA70 .... 105 E6
Bartley Terr SA1 .... 160 E5
Bassett Terr SA15 .... 109 F3
Bath Ave SA15 .... 148 F3
Bath House Rd 8 SA43 .... 118 D4
Bath La SA1 .... 174 B2
Bath Rd SA6 .... 160 F8
Bathurst St
Swansea / Abertawe SA1 .... 174 A1
Swansea / Abertawe SA1 .... 174 A1
Bath Villas SA6 .... 160 F8
Battery Rd SA70 .... 135 E4
Bay St SA1 .... 168 A4
Bayswater Ct SA3 .... 166 C3
Bayswater Rd SA2 .... 166 C3
Bay View SA1 .... 174 C4
Bay View Cl SA10 .... 162 F5
Bay View Cres SA1 .... 167 A6
Bay View Dr SA73 .... 167 A6
Bay View Gdns SA10 .... 162 E5
Bay View Rd SA14 .... 149 A6
Bay View Terr SA1 .... 167 A6
Baywood Ave SA3 .... 173 A8
Beachfields 8 SA62 .... 85 D8
Beach Hill SA73 .... 131 E2
Beach Rd Llanelli SA15 .... 148 A6
Pembroke Dock / Doc Penfro SA72 .... 132 C3
Pen-clawdd SA4 .... 156 E4
Beach St SA1 .... 167 B5
Beaconing Rd SA73 .... 131 E3
Beaconsfield Ct SA2 .... 166 B7
Beaconsfield Way SA2 .... 166 B7
Beacons View Rd SA6 .... 153 D1
Beattie St SA5 .... 160 B2

Beaufort Ave SA3 .... 173 A3
Beaufort Cl SA3 .... 173 A3
Beaufort Ct
Swansea / Abertawe, Caer-eithin SA5 .... 159 E5
Swansea / Abertawe SA6 .... 160 F6
Beaufort Dr SA3 .... 171 E7
Beaufort Gdns SA3 .... 171 E7
Beaufort Rd
Pembroke / Penfro SA71 .... 133 C5
Swansea / Abertawe SA6 .... 160 F6
Beaumont Cres SA1 .... 174 C4
Beck Ho SA2 .... 166 F6
Bedford Ho 3 SA6 .... 160 F8
Bedford St SA1 .... 161 A8
Beech Cres SA4 .... 151 A4
Beeches Cl The SA4 .... 166 A8
Beeches The SA44 .... 19 E4
Beech Gr SA15 .... 109 E4
Beechlands Pk SA61 .... 124 E3
Beech Rd SA31 .... 128 D5
Beechtree Cl SA6 .... 153 D1
Beech Tree La SA2 .... 165 E4
Beechwood Ind Est SA19 .... 130 E7
Beechwood Pl SA67 .... 70 D2
Begelly Pk Gdns* SA68 .... 134 C8
Beidr Non SA14 .... 96 E3
Beili Glas SA4 .... 150 E1
Belgrave Cl SA4 .... 151 A1
Belgrave Ct SA1 .... 167 A6
Belgrave Gdns 2 SA1 .... 167 A6
Belgrave La SA1 .... 167 A6
Belgrave Rd SA1 .... 167 A6
Belle Vue SA4 .... 156 F4
Bellevue Rd Llanelli SA14 .... 149 E3
The Mumbles / Y Mwmbwls SA3 .... 172 F6
Belle Vue St SA73 .... 132 B6
Bellevue Terr SA72 .... 132 B1
Belle Vue Way SA1 .... 174 A3
Belmore Gdns 2 SA67 .... 70 D1
Belvedere Ave SA3 .... 129 A6
Belvedere Cl SA3 .... 171 C7
Belvedere Rd SA5 .... 148 C6
Benallt Fawr SA4 .... 143 A6
Benbow Cl SA2 .... 166 C6
Bendrick Dr SA3 .... 170 F4
Bennett St SA1 .... 160 D3
Benson Cl SA4 .... 156 F4
Benson St SA4 .... 156 F4
Benson Terr SA4 .... 156 F4
Benson Way / Parc Landwr SA6 .... 161 A6
Benthall Pl SA1 .... 174 C3
Bentlass Hill SA71 .... 104 A4
Bentlass Rd SA71 .... 104 B3
Bentlass Terr SA72 .... 104 B5
Bentley Villas 8 SA67 .... 70 E1
Berkeley Cl SA1 .... 155 A2
Berlan SA14 .... 140 F1
Berlan Deg SA15 .... 149 A6
Berma Cl SA2 .... 173 C3
Bernard St SA2 .... 166 F6
Berrington Villas / Filas
Berrington SA1 .... 100 C7
Berthllwyd 3 LD5 .... 9 D1
Berwick Rd SA4 .... 149 F3
Berwick Terr SA1 .... 160 A4
Berw Rd SA1 .... 167 B8
Berwyn Pl SA5 .... 160 A4
Beryl Rd SA4 .... 154 F8
Bethania Rd Clydach SA6 .... 154 D7
Cross Hands SA14 .... 97 A7
Llannon SA14 .... 96 F6
Bethania Terr SA15 .... 148 E2
Bethany La SA3 .... 173 A7
Bethany Rd SA61 .... 124 D3
Bethel Cl SA2 .... 160 C3
Bethel Rd
Pembroke Dock / Doc Penfro SA72 .... 133 A8
Swansea / Abertawe SA1 .... 161 C7
Ystradgynlais SA9 .... 139 C8
Bethesda Cl SA1 .... 174 A4
Bethesda Rd SA14 .... 96 E6
Bethesda St SA1 .... 174 A4
Bethlehem Rd
Dyffryn Cennen SA19 .... 117 D6
Neath / Castell-Nedd SA10 .... 162 F7
St Clears / Sanclêr SA33 .... 127 B5
Bettisland SA3 .... 172 F8
Bettws Rd SA4 .... 160 A4
Betws Cty Prim Sch SA18 .... 98 C6
Betws Ind Pk / Parc
Ddiwydiannol Betws SA18 .... 98 C6
Betws Rd / Ffordd-y-Betws SA18 .... 98 C6
Beulah Hill SA62 .... 51 D7
Beulah Rd Beulah SA38 .... 17 F8
Llanwrtyd Wells LD5 .... 9 D1
Bevans Row SA1 .... 168 B7
Bevans Terr SA1 .... 161 C5
Bevan Way SA5 .... 158 E3
Bevelin Hall SA69 .... 134 E2
Bevelyn La SA69 .... 134 F2
Beverley La SA14 .... 159 E4
Beverley Cl SA4 .... 159 E4
Bible Coll of Wales The SA2 .... 166 B3
Bicton Rd SA62 .... 85 B3
Biddulph SA15 .... 148 E2

Bigny Cross SA66 .... 53 C2
Bigyn La SA15 .... 148 D4
Bigyn Park Ct SA15 .... 148 E4
Bigyn Park Terr / Teras Parc
Bigyn SA15 .... 148 E4
Bigyn Prim Sch SA15 .... 148 E4
Bigyn Rd SA15 .... 148 E4
Birches The SA6 .... 154 F8
Birchfield Rd
Pontardawe SA8 .... 147 F6
The Mumbles / Y Mwmbwls SA3 .... 172 F8
Birch Gr SA5 .... 158 D4
Birchgrove Comp Sch SA7 .... 155 B2
Birchgrove Jun & Inf Schs SA7 .... 155 A1
Birchgrove Rd Glais SA7 .... 155 A6
Swansea / Abertawe SA7 .... 162 A8
Birch Mead SA73 .... 131 E3
Birch Tree Cl SA2 .... 166 C6
Bird's La SA70 .... 105 E6
Birkdale Cl SA3 .... 165 F2
Birmingham Mount SA6 .... 160 F6
Bishop Gore Sch / Ysgol
Esgob Gore SA2 .... 166 C6
Bishop La SA71 .... 133 C3
Bishops Pk SA71 .... 133 C3
Bishop's Rd SA67 .... 71 B1
Bishopston Comp Sch SA3 .... 172 A7
Bishopston Prim Sch SA3 .... 171 F7
Bishopston Rd SA3 .... 171 F6
Bishop's Wood Countryside
Ctr* SA3 .... 172 D4
Bishop's Wood Nature
Reserve* SA3 .... 172 C4
Bishop Vaughan RC Sch SA6 .... 160 E8
Bishwell Rd SA4 .... 158 D4
Blackberry La SA71 .... 105 B5
Blackbridge Cres SA73 .... 131 F3
Blackbridge Dr SA73 .... 131 F2
Blackhill Rd SA4 .... 151 A3
Blackhills La
Fairwood SA2 .... 164 F3
Upper Killay SA2 .... 165 A3
Black Lion Rd / Heol y Llew
Du SA14 .... 97 C7
Blackthorn Pl SA2 .... 159 B1
Blaenau Rd
Ammanford / Rhydaman SA18 .... 98 A8
Llandybie SA18 .... 79 A1
Blaencedi SA4 .... 156 F3
Blaen Cefn SA1 .... 161 D5
Blaencoed Rd SA7 .... 161 F7
Blaencwm Rd SA7 .... 162 A7
Blaen Emlyn SA14 .... 97 C3
Blaenmorfa SA4 .... 143 C3
Blaen Treweryll SA37 .... 34 F2
Blaenwern SA38 .... 119 D5
Blaen-y-Maes Dr SA5 .... 159 E6
Blaenymaes Prim Sch SA5 .... 159 E7
Blaen-y-Morfa SA15 .... 148 E2
Blean Nant SA14 .... 141 B2
Blende Rd SA19 .... 130 E6
Bienheim Dr SA73 .... 132 C8
Bienhein Dr SA73 .... 132 C8
Blockett La SA62 .... 49 E5
Blodwen Terr SA4 .... 156 F4
Bloomfield Gdns SA67 .... 70 D2
Blue Anchor Rd SA4 .... 156 F3
Blue Anchor Way SA62 .... 101 D4
Bluebell Cl SA3 .... 132 B7
Bluebell Way SA5 .... 160 A5
Blue St SA31 .... 128 C4
BMI Werndale Hospl SA33 .... 74 B4
Boarlands The SA3 .... 117 A4
Bog Rd SA7, SA10 .... 161 E4
Bohun St SA5 .... 160 C3
Bolgoed Rd SA4 .... 143 E2
Bond Ave SA15 .... 148 E4
Bond St SA1 .... 167 B5
Bonllwyn SA18 .... 98 B8
Bonvilles Cl SA69 .... 134 D4
Bonville Terr SA1 .... 167 A6
Bon-y-Maen Rd SA1 .... 161 A3
Borough Rd SA4 .... 150 F2
Bosco La SA2 .... 171 B3
Bosworth Rd SA10 .... 162 F7
Bowen St SA1 .... 160 D2
Bowen Terr SA15 .... 148 F3
Bowett La SA71 .... 104 B2
Box Rd SA4 .... 151 B7
Box Terr 3 SA1 .... 167 B5
Bradford St 1 SA15 .... 148 F6
Bramble Hill SA62 .... 49 E1
Bramley Dr SA3 .... 172 F6
Bran Cl SA7 .... 161 E4
Brandon Cres SA1 .... 161 D5
Brandy Cove Cl SA3 .... 173 B4
Brandy Cove Rd SA3 .... 172 A5
Brandyway SA15 .... 96 A6
Brangwyn Cl SA6 .... 153 E2
Branwen Gdns SA1 .... 160 B1
Brawdy Bsns Pk SA62 .... 49 B3
Brawdy Cres SA1 .... 49 B2
Brayley Rd SA6 .... 153 F2
Brecon B SA1 .... 174 C2

Brecon Rd
Llandovery / Llanymddyfri
SA20 ....121 F4
Pontardawe SA8 ....147 F6
Ystradgynlais SA9 ......138 F1
Brenig Rd SA5 ....160 A4
Bres Rd SA15 ....148 D5
Brettenham St SA15 ....148 C4
Brewery Rd 3 SA31 ....128 E6
Brewery St SA72 ....132 C2
Briar Dene SA2 ....166 B6
Briar's Ct SA5 ....159 F6
Briarwood Gdns SA3 ...172 D5
Brickhurst Cl SA62 .....86 D6
Brickhurst Pk SA62 .....86 E6
Brickyard La SA31 ......128 E4
Brickyard Rd SA14 .....159 F3
Bridge End Sq 17 SA61 .125 A5
Bridge La SA62 ....67 B6
Bridgend Terr SA11 ....133 B4
Bridge Rd SA5 ....158 E4
Bridge St
Burry Port SA16 ......137 E2
Cardigan / Aberteifi SA43 .118 D3
2 Carmarthen / Caerfyrddin
SA31 ....128 F4
Clydach SA6 ....154 D7
Cwm Gwaun SA65 ......31 D6
Cwm-twrch Isaf SA9 ...138 B1
3 Fishguard & Goodwick
SA65 ....122 E4
Glais SA7 ....155 A6
Haverfordwest / Hwlffordd
SA61 ....125 A2
Kidwelly / Cydweli SA17 .136 B4
Lampeter / Llanbedr Pont Steffan
SA48 ....120 C5
Llandeilo SA19 ....130 D5
Llandovery / Llanymddyfri
SA20 ....121 A4
Llanelli SA15 ....148 D6
Llangennech SA14 .....150 C8
Llanybyther SA40 ......21 D7
Milford Haven / Aberdaugleddau
SA73 ....131 B2
Newcastle Emlyn / Castell
Newydd Emlyn SA38 ...119 D5
10 Newport / Trefdraeth
SA42 ....13 E4
Penygroes SA14 ....97 D8
St Clears / Sanclêr
SA33 ....127 E2
Swansea / Abertawe SA1 .174 B5
Tenby / Dinbych-y-pysgod
SA70 ....135 F4
Bridle Mews SA3 ......173 C3
Brighton Rd SA4 ......151 C2
Britannia Dr SA72 .....132 C1
Britannia Rd
Pembroke Dock / Doc Penfro
SA72 ....132 C1
Swansea / Abertawe SA6 ..160 E5
Brithdir SA31 ....129 A3
Brithwen Rd SA5 ......158 D3
Broadacre SA2 ....165 C7
Broadfield Hill SA14 ...148 C1
Broad Haven CP Sch
SA62 ....85 D8
Broad La SA8 ....88 B2
Broadmead SA2 ....165 D7
Broadmead Cres SA3 ..172 B6
Broadoak St SA14 .....150 E1
Broadparks SA3 ......172 F8
Broad St SA20 ....121 C3
Broadview Cl SA3 .....173 B4
Broadview La SA3 .....173 B4
Broadway SA2 ....166 D7
Broadway Ct SA2 .....166 D7
Broadwell Hayes SA70 .135 D4
Bro Annedd 2 SA39 ...39 B6
Brockfield La SA71 .....133 D2
Bro Dauddwr 3 SA32 ...59 A2
Brodawel
Ammanford / Rhydaman
SA18 ....98 C6
8 Burry Port SA16 ....137 D2
Llannon SA14 ....96 E3
Bro Dawel Dunvant SA2 .165 D7
Solva SA62 ....48 E2
Swansea / Abertawe SA6 .153 C2
Bro Deg SA15 ....165 D8
Bro Deri SA16 ....137 D3
Bro Dirion SA2 ....165 D8
Brodog La SA65 ....122 D4
Brodog Terr SA65 .....122 C4
Brodorion Dr SA6 .....153 E3
Bro Dulais 2 SA19 .....43 E2
Bro Einon SA40 ....21 D6
Bro Gwen 1 SA39 .....39 B6
Bro Gwynfaen SA44 ...19 E7
Bro Hedydd SA11 .....128 F6
Bro Helyg 1 SA32 .....59 B6
Bro Hyfryd 2 SA32 ....59 A2
Brokesby Cl SA1 ......161 A3
Brokesby Rd SA1 .....161 A3
Bromeddyg 6 SA42 ...13 E4
Bro Meigan Gdns* SA41 .15 E1
Bromeilion SA48 ......4 F3
Bromeinis SA36 ....35 B2
Bron Afon SA4 ....152 B5
Bron Afon Uchaf SA4 ..152 B5
Bronallt Rd / Heol Bronallt
SA4 ....143 A5
Bro Nant Fer SA18 ....99 D7
Bro Nantlais SA39 .....39 D6
Brondeg SA5 ....160 B3
Brondeg Cres SA5 ....160 B3

Brondeg La SA8 ....147 F3
Brongwyn Ct SA43 ....3 F4
Bronhaul SA20 ....26 B3
Bronllan SA1 ....161 D5
Bronwydd SA4 ....154 C8
Bronwydd Arms Sta
SA33 ....58 E3
Bronwydd Rd SA1 ....129 B7
Bron-y-Bryn SA2 .....165 E8
Bron-y-Dre
Cardigan / Aberteifi SA43 .118 D4
2 Carmarthen / Caerfyrddin
SA31 ....129 A3
Bron-y-Glyn SA33 .....58 E2
Bron Yr Allt SA9 ......139 A8
Bron Yr Aur SA31 .....128 C2
Bron-yr-Ynn 1 SA14 ...96 E8
Bronywawr SA8 ......147 E5
Brooke Ave SA3 ......131 D3
Brookfield Cl SA4 .....150 F3
Brookfield Pl SA5 .....159 E6
Brookland Pl SA69 ....134 E3
Brooklands Cl SA2 ....158 B1
Brooklands Pk SA61 ...124 E3
Brooklands Terr SA11 .167 B7
Brooklyn Gdns SA3 ...173 A6
Brooklyns Cl SA63 ....69 A7
Brooklyn Terr SA3 ....172 F5
Brookside
Gowerton / Tre-gwyr SA4 .158 D3
St Ishmael's SA62 .....85 A2
Brookside Ave SA62 ...86 E6
Brookside Cl SA62 ....86 E6
Brookside Villas SA67 ..90 D2
Brook St SA10 ....162 F7
Brook Terr SA18 ......99 E7
Brookvale Rd SA43 ....172 F7
Brookville Dr SA10 ....162 E7
Broom La SA68 ....89 D3
Bro-pedr SA17 ....94 E6
Bro'r Dderwen SA66 ...70 F5
Bro'r-hengil 4 SA32 ...59 A3
Bro'r Orsaf SA39 .....20 C2
Bro Ryan SA18 ....99 A8
Bro Stinian 2 SA65 ...30 F5
Bro Tawel SA48 ......4 B6
Bro Teifi SA43 ....118 E4
Broughton Ave SA5 ...159 E4
Bro-Wen SA14 ....149 C5
Brown Ave SA15 ......148 F2
Brownhills SA4 ....151 A3
Browns Dr SA3 ....171 A5
Bruce Rd SA5 ....159 E5
Brunant Rd SA4 ......151 B3
Brunel Ave SA73 .....132 B6
Brunel Ct 3 SA1 ......167 B7
Brunel Way SA1 ......160 F3
Brunner Dr SA6 ......146 E1
Brunswick St SA1 ....167 B6
Brychan 1 SA1 ....167 A7
Bryanston Rd SA2 ....158 C1
Bryn Aeron Cl SA2 ...158 C1
Brynafon Rd SA4 .....151 A3
Brynallt Terr SA15 ....148 F5
Brynamlwg Clydach SA6 .146 F1
Llanelli SA15 ....148 F6
Brynamlwg Rd SA4 ...151 A2
Bryn-Amlwg Rd SA5 ..159 E3
Brynamman Cty Prim Sch
SA18 ....80 C1
Brynamman Rd / Heol
Brynamman SA18 .....99 D7
Brynau Dr SA3 ....165 F2
Bryn Ave 2 Brecon SA18 .80 E1
Burry Port SA16 ......137 F2
Brynawel SA8 ....147 E5
Brynawel Cres SA5 ...160 D5
Brynawelon
Ammanford SA18 .....97 F7
Cefn-bryn-brain SA9 ..100 B8
Llanelli SA14 ....149 C6
Llanwenog SA40 ......21 A8
2 Llanwrtyd Wells LD5 ...9 FI
Brynawel Rd
Gorseinon SA4 ....151 A2
Ystradgynlais SA9 ....138 F1
Brynawel Terr
1 Llandeilo SA19 .....130 D5
Ystradowen SA9 ......100 C7
Bryn Bach SA4 ....152 C5
Bryn Bach Rd
Brynamman SA18 .....99 D8
Pontllïw SA4 ....144 B2
Bryn-Bach Rd SA4 ....152 A8
Bryn Bach Rd SA18 ...80 D1
Brynbedw SA43 ......16 C7
Brynbrain SA9 ....100 B8
Bryncaerau SA17 .....109 B8
Bryn Canol SA14 .....149 A6
Bryncastella SA33 ....127 C4
Bryncelyn SA3 ....153 C1
Bryn Celyn
Pontardawe SA7 .....147 D5
Swansea / Abertawe SA7 .162 A6
Bryncelyn Rd SA4 ....151 A2
Bryncerdin Rd SA3 ...172 E5
Bryncethin Rd SA18 ..99 C7
Bryncenuant 2 SA18 ..80 E1
Bryn Cl Gorseinon SA4 .151 B3
Gowerton / Tre-gwyr SA4 .158 D4
Bryncoch SA14 ....149 C6
Brynconin CP Sch SA66 .70 F8
Bryncwar Rd SA14 ...97 D8
Bryndedwyddfa SA18 ...97 D8
Brynderi Ammanford SA18 .97 F7
Pontyates / Pont-iets SA15 .95 D4
Bryn Deri Cl
Llandyfriog SA38 .....119 D6

Bryn Deri Cl continued
Penllergaer SA4 ......152 B2
Brynderwen SA31 .....129 C7
Bryn Derwen
Pontardawe SA4 .....147 D5
Swansea / Abertawe SA2 .159 B1
Brynderwen Rd 2 SA18 .98 B7
Bryn Derw Gdns SA6 .153 E2
Bryndolau SA2 ....165 B8
Bryn-edda SA17 ......94 B3
Bryn Eglur Rd SA6 ...160 D7
Brynenion Rd SA4 ...151 A3
Bryneithin SA16 ......137 C2
Bryn Eithin SA4 ......158 B5
Bryneithin Rd SA4 ...151 A2
Bryneithin Terr SA6 ..153 F1
Bryneithyn SA9 ......138 C1
Bryn Elfed SA65 .....122 C5
Bryn Eli SA14 ....149 A7
Bryn Euraidd SA18 ...98 A6
Brynfa Terr SA14 .....156 E4
Brynffordd SA1 ......159 E2
Brynffynnon Rd SA14 .151 A3
Brynfield Ct SA3 .....172 F4
Brynfield Rd SA3 .....172 E4
Bryn-Gaer SA14 .....149 A7
Bryngelli Dr SA5 .....160 C7
Bryngelli Pk SA5 .....160 C7
Bryngelli Rd SA5 ....160 C7
Bryn Gerran 3 SA43 ..16 A5
Brynglas
Cross Hand SA14 .....96 D8
Penygroes SA14 ....97 D7
Bryn Glas SA6 ....153 C2
Brynglas Cres SA31 ..129 C4
Bryn-Glas Rd SA5 ....159 E3
Bryngolau Gorseinon SA4 .151 A2
Llanelli SA14 ....149 A7
Bryn Golau
Brawdy SA62 ....49 D4
Pontardawe SA8 .....147 F4
Bryn Goleu Rd SA5 ..159 F3
Bryngoleu Terr SA14 .166 D7
Bryn Gomer SA65 ...122 D5
Bryn Gorof SA9 ......139 D8
Bryn Gorwel SA31 ...128 E6
Bryngwastad Rd SA4 .151 A2
Bryn Gwdig SA14 ....109 C4
Bryngwenllan SA34 ..126 E3
Bryngwili Rd SA4 ....142 F3
Bryngwyn
Cardigan / Aberteifi SA43 .118 B2
Neath / Castell-Nedd
SA10 ....162 C6
Bryngwyn Ave SA4 ..158 D8
Bryngwyn Bach SA14 .149 A7
Bryngwyn Comp Sch
SA14 ....149 A8
Brynhafod SA18 .....97 F5
Bryn Hafod SA43 ....118 E4
Bryn Hawddgar SA6 .154 E8
Bryn Hebog SA48 ....120 A5
Brynhedydd SA62 ....29 F4
Bryn Hedydd SA6 ...153 C5
Bryn Helyg SA1 ......161 D5
Brynheulog SA14 ....148 F8
Bryn Hir SA4 ....157 A2
Brynhyfryd
Burry Port SA16 .....137 E3
Llangennech SA14 ...150 B6
Llangunnor SA31 ....129 A3
Tircoed SA4 ....152 C5
Brynhyfryd Rd
Gorseinon SA4 ......151 A3
Llanelli SA15 ....148 D6
Brynhyfryd Sq 4 SA5 .160 D7
Brynhyfryd St SA5 ...160 C4
Brynjago SA4 ....143 E4
Bryn-Melyn St SA1 ..160 D2
Brynmead SA31 .....129 A3
Brynmead Cl SA2 ...166 C8
Brynmead Ct SA2 ...166 C8
Brynmefys SA15 ....140 B1
Brynmill Ave SA15 ..148 E6
Brynmill Cres SA4 ...166 E5
Brynmill La SA2 .....166 E5
Brynmill Prim Sch SA2 .166 F5
Brynmill Terr SA2 ...166 E5
Bryn Morfa SA14 ....161 D5
Bryn Morlais SA14 ...149 F6
Brynmor Rd SA15 ...148 C4
Bryn Myrddin SA31 ..129 F7
Brynnewydd Gdns SA2 .166 E5
Bryn Onnen
Cardigan / Aberteifi SA43 .118 C3
Pontardawe SA8 .....147 E5

Bryn Parc SA6 ....160 F7
Bryn Pen SA48 ....120 C6
Bryn Pl 8 SA15 ......148 C4
Bryn Prim Sch SA14 ..149 E6
Bryn Rd Clydach SA6 .154 D8
Cwmllynfell SA9 .....100 B7
Fishguard / Abergwaun
SA65 ....122 D4
Lampeter / Llanbedr Pont Steffan
SA48 ....120 B5
Llanelli SA15 ....148 C4
Loughor SA4 ....150 F1
Penygroes SA14 ......97 D8
Pontarddulais SA4 ...143 B4
Pontlliw SA4 ....152 A8
Quarter Bach SA18 ..80 E1
St David's / Tyddewi SA62 .123 C4
Swansea / Abertawe, Brynmill
SA2 ....166 F5
Swansea / Abertawe SA5 .159 E3
Waunarlwydd SA5 ...158 E3
Bryn Rhos Llanelli SA14 .149 C6
Llannon SA14 ....96 E4
Bryn Rhos Cres SA4 ..152 A8
Bryn Rhosog SA4 ....157 E8
Bryn Rhosyn SA6 ....154 C5
Brynsaron Prim Sch / Ysgol
Gynradd Brynsaron
SA44 ....38 B7
Brynseilo SA17 ....95 D1
Bryn Seion SA62 ....48 D3
Brynsierfel SA14 .....149 C5
Brynsifi Way SA1 ....174 A4
Bryn-sion Hill SA67 ..71 B1
Brynsirfol
Fishguard / Abergwaun
SA65 ....122 D3
Gwaun-Cae-Gurwen SA18 .99 D7
Llanelli SA14 ....148 F7
Bryn Siriol SA5 ......159 E3
Bryn St SA5 ....160 C4
Bryn Steffan SA48 ...120 A5
Bryn-Syfi Terr SA1 ...174 A4
Brynteg Hall Cl SA4 ..154 C5
Brynteg Rd SA6 .....154 B5
Brynteg Capel Hendre SA18 .97 E6
Carmarthen / Caerfyrddin
SA31 ....128 B6
Clydach SA6 ....154 D7
St David's / Tyddewi SA62 .123 C4
Bryn Teg SA7 ....162 A7
Bryn-Teg Terr / Teras
Brynteg 13 SA18 .....98 B7
1 Llanelli, Seaside SA15 .148 C3
Llanelli SA14 ....149 C6
Swansea / Abertawe SA1 .160 D3
The Mumbles / Y Mwmbwls
SA3 ....173 B4
Bryn The SA2 ....166 C5
Bryn Tirion Clydach SA6 .154 E8
1 Pontrhydfendigaid SA25 .96 B6
Bryntirion Hospl SA15 .148 E6
Bryntirion
Pontardawe SA4 .....143 F1
Pontlliw SA4 ....152 A8
Bryntirion Terr SA15 .148 F6
Brynteg SA31 ....129 A3
Bryn-tywod SA4 .....153 A3
Bryn Vernel SA4 .....150 E1
Bryn View Cl SA3 ....117 C8
Bryn Y Ael SA31 .....129 B7
Bryn-y-Don Rd SA4 ..174 A4
Bryn Y Felin SA14 ...141 A1
Bryn Y Gors SA6 ....153 B2
Brynygroes Cotts SA9 .138 F2
Bryn-y-Grug SA9 ....139 A7
Brynymor SA16 ......137 C2
Bryn Y Mor SA14 ....109 F7
Bryn-y-Mor SA2 .....167 A6
Brynymor Rd
Loughor SA4 ....150 E2
Swansea / Abertawe SA2 .166 F5
Bryn-y-Mor Rd
Gowerton / Tre-gwyr SA4 .157 F6
Gowerton / Tre-gwyr SA4 .158 A5
Swansea / Abertawe SA2 .166 F5
Bryn Yr Eglwys SA48 .120 C5
Bryn-y-Wawr SA33 ..58 E8
Bude Haven Terr SA3 .173 A6
Bufferland Terr SA72 .132 B1
Bulford Cl SA62 ......86 D5
Bulford Rd SA62 .....86 D6
Bullin's La SA14 .....167 A7
Bunkers Hill SA73 ...131 E4
Bunker's Hill SA62 ...85 A2
Burgage Gn Cl SA62 .85 A2
Burgley Ct SA5 ......159 E5
Burman St SA1 ......167 B7
Burnham Dr SA3 ....172 E6
Burrows Chambers 1
SA1 ....174 C2
Burrows Cl SA3 .....171 A3
Burrows La SA3 .....174 C2
Burrows Pl SA1 .....174 C2
Burrows Rd
Neath / Castell-Nedd,
Pentrefrynnon SA10 ..162 C6
Swansea / Abertawe SA1 .167 B5
Burrows Terr SA16 ..137 F2
Burry Cl SA4 ....148 F3
Burry Port Inf Sch SA16 .137 D3
Burry Rd
Burry Port SA16 .....137 C3
Llanelli SA15 ....148 E1
Burry St SA15 ....148 C3

Burton Rd SA73 ......132 F8
Bushes La SA67 ......70 E1
Bush Hill SA71 ....133 B6
Bush Rd SA6 ....154 A1
Bush St SA72 ....132 C2
Buttercup Cl SA73 ...172 E6
Butterhill SA73 ......87 D3
Butterhill La SA72 ...133 B6
Buttermilk La SA62 ..133 B7
Butterslade Gr SA6 ..154 A4
Butts La SA70 ......105 D6
Butts The 2 SA33 ...92 E5
Bwlch La SA31 ......129 E6
Bwlch Rd SA4 ......154 C5
Bwlch Y Gwynt SA5 .144 E2
Bwlifa Rd SA6 ......154 C5
Bwrw Rd SA4 ......157 D8
Bynea Prim Sch / Ysgol
Gynradd Bynea SA14 .149 F3
Bynea Sta SA14 .....149 F3
Byng Morris Cl SA2 ..166 B5
Byng St SA1 ....160 D4
Byron Rd SA61 .....125 A3
Byron Way SA2 .....165 F8

C

Caban Isaac Rd SA4 .156 F3
Cadfan Rd SA1 .....167 A8
Cadle Cl SA5 ....159 D5
Cadle Cres SA5 ....159 D5
Cadle Dell Pl SA5 ..159 E6
Cadle Mill SA5 .....159 C7
Cadle Pl SA5 ....159 D5
Cadle Prim Sch SA5 .159 D5
Cadle-Wood Rd SA5 .159 D5
Cadnant Rd SA5 ....160 A5
Cadogan Cl SA62 ...86 E6
Cadrawd Rd SA14 ..160 B1
Cadwaladr Cir 4 SA31 .167 B8
Cadwgan Rd SA6 ...146 B2
Cae Banc SA2 ......166 D7
Cae-Bricks Rd SA5 ..160 B3
Cae Bryn Drain SA31 .128 E6
Cae Castell SA4 ....157 D8
Cae Celyn SA31 ....128 E6
Caecerrig Rd SA14 ..143 D4
Caecoed SA18 ......79 A1
Caeconna Rd SA5 ..159 C5
Cae Cotton SA14 ...148 F6
Cae Crug
Carmarthen / Caerfyrddin
SA31 ....128 E6
Swansea / Abertawe SA6 .165 B1
Cae Crwn SA2 ......165 E8
Cae Dash SA48 .....120 C4
Caedegar Rd SA9 ...138 F2
Cae Delyn Cl SA15 ..148 E3
Caedolau SA16 .....137 E3
Cae-Du-Bach 1 SA15 .148 F6
Caedu Rd SA14 .....100 B7
Cae Ethin
Carmarthen / Caerfyrddin
SA31 ....128 E6
Swansea / Abertawe SA6 .153 B2
Cae Ffynnon SA17 ..136 B5
Caeffynnon Rd SA18 .79 B2
Cae Folland SA4 ....156 E4
Cae Gar SA14 ......151 C2
Caeglas Cross Hands SA14 .97 B7
Llanelli SA14 ....148 F8
Cae Glas SA4 ......151 C2
Caeglas Cl SA19 ...130 D3
Cae Grawn SA4 ....158 B5
Cae-Gwyn Rd SA4 .143 D4
Cae-is-Maen SA8 ..147 C3
Cae Lynch SA10 ...162 F6
Caemansel La SA4 ..150 C3
Cae Mansel Rd
Gowerton / Tre-gwyr SA4 .158 A4
Three Crosses SA4 ..158 C5
Caemawr SA18 .....98 C6
Caemawr Rd SA6 ...160 E8
Cae Melyn SA14 ....153 C1
Caenarvon Way SA1 .161 B8
Cae Rowland St SA5 .160 B3
Caerphilly Ave SA1 ..161 C4
Caersalem Terr / Teras
Caersalem 2 SA15 ..148 D3
Caer St SA1 ....174 B3
Caerwenog SA33 ....36 D1
Caio CP Sch SA19 ...24 A2
Caldey Island Mus* ‡
SA70 ....107 J2
Caldey Pl SA5 ......159 E7
Caldicot Cl SA1 ....161 C4

Caldicot Rd SA1 . . . . .161 C4
Caldy Way SA73 . . . . .131 E5
Caledfwlch SA19 . . . . .62 E4
Calland St SA6 . . . . .160 E5
Callans Dr SA71 . . . . .133 E4
Calvert Terr **2** SA1 . . . . . .167 B7
Camarthen Rd SA5 . . . . . . .159 E4
Cambrian Cl SA6 . . . . .161 A7
Cambrian Mill Heritage Ctr*
LD5 . . . . .9 D2
Cambrian Pl
10 Carmarthen / Caerfyrddin
SA31 . . . . .128 F5
Cwm-twrch Uchaf SA9 . . .100 C6
2 Haverfordwest / Hwlffordd
SA61 . . . . .125 B5
3 Llanelli SA15 . . . . .148 C3
Pontarddulais SA4 . . . . . . .143 C4
Swansea / Abertawe SA1 .174 C2
Cambrian Rd
1 Lampeter / Llanbedr
Pont Steffan SA48 . . . . . . .120 C5
Neyland SA73 . . . . .132 C6
Cambrian St SA15 . . . . . . .148 C4
Cambridge Cl SA3 . . . . . . .173 A3
Cambridge Gdns SA3 . . . .173 B4
Cambridge Rd SA3 . . . . . .173 A4
Cambridge St SA2 . . . . . . .166 F7
Camellia Dr SA6 . . . . .153 F3
Cameron Pl SA4 . . . . .151 A2
Camffrwd Way SA6 . . . . . .154 C1
Camona Dr **2** SA1 . . . . . .174 B1
Campbell Rd **3** SA18 . . . . .79 A2
Campbell St
Llanelli SA15 . . . . .148 E2
Swansea / Abertawe SA1 .174 A4
Camrose Dr SA5 . . . . .158 E3
Camuset Cl SA73 . . . . .131 A3
Canal Terr SA9 . . . . .139 B6
Canaston Ct SA5 . . . . .159 F7
Candleston Pl SA1 . . . . . . .160 E2
Cannisland Pk SA3 . . . . . .164 D1
Cannon St / Stryd Cannon
SA18 .99 D8
Canterbury Rd
Pembroke Dock / Doc Penfro
SA72 . . . . .132 D3
Swansea / Abertawe SA2 .166 E5
Cantref Ct SA5 . . . . .159 E5
Can-Yr-Aderyn SA6 . . . . . .153 D2
Can-Yr-Eos SA6 . . . . .153 E2
Capel Bldgs SA6 . . . . .154 F7
Capel Colman Rd SA37 . . . .16 C1
Capel Evan Rd **4** SA31 . . .129 A6
Capel Hendre Ind Est
SA18 .97 F5
Capel Isaf Rd SA15 . . . . . .149 A6
Capel Newydd / Cross Rd
SA15 . . . . .148 D6
Capel-Newydd La SA15 . .148 D6
Capel Rd Clydach SA6 . . . .154 F8
Llanelli SA14 . . . . .149 A6
Capel Road Workshops
SA6 . . . . .154 F8
Capel Seion Rd SA15 . . . . .96 C7
Capel Sion Rd SA14 . . . . . .96 D8
Capel Teilo Rd SA17 . . . . . .95 A2
Capel Terr SA15 . . . . .148 F6
Capital Bldgs SA9 . . . . . . .139 C7
Caradoc Pl **2** SA61 . . . . . .124 E4
Caradog Pl SA1 . . . . .167 A8
Caradog's Well Rd SA61 . .124 E2
Cardifor St **3** SA31 . . . . . .128 E5
Cardigan Castle (remains
of)* SA43 . . . . .118 D3
Cardigan Cres SA1 . . . . . .161 C5
Cardigan & District Meml
Hospl SA43 . . . . .118 E3
Cardigan Her Ctr*
SA43 . . . . .118 D3
Cardigan Island Nature
Reserve* SA43 . . . . .3 A7
Cardigan Prim Sch
SA43 . . . . .118 E4
Cardigan Rd SA31 . . . . . . .128 B7
Cardigan Sec Sch SA43 . .118 D5
Cardigan Swimming Pool &
Leisure Ctr SA43 . . . . . . .118 E4
Cardonnel Rd SA10 . . . . . .162 F6
Cardonnel Villas SA10 . . . .162 F6
Carew Castle & Tidal Mill*
SA70 . . . . .105 D6
Carew La SA70 . . . . .105 E7
Carew Pl SA1 . . . . .161 C5
Carig Cres SA3 . . . . .160 B1
Carig Gdns SA1 . . . . .160 A1
Carlton Rd SA6 . . . . .146 E1
Carlton Terr SA1 . . . . .174 A3
Carmarthen District Leisure
Ctr SA31 . . . . .128 D2
Carmarthen Rd
Cross Hands SA14 . . . . . . .97 A8
Ferryside SA17 . . . . .93 F5
Fforest SA4 . . . . .142 F6
Llandeilo SA19 . . . . .130 C6
Swansea / Abertawe SA1 .174 B5
Carmarthenshire Coll of Tech
& Art
Ammanford / Rhydaman
SA18 . . . . .98 B7
Llangunnor SA31 . . . . .128 F1
Carmarthenshire Cty Mus
SA31 . . . . .129 F6
Carmarthen St SA19 . . . . .130 D5
Carmarthen Sta SA31 . . . .128 F4

Carmel Rd Pontlliw SA4 . . .151 F7
Swansea / Abertawe SA1 .161 D5
Carnglas Ave SA2 . . . . . . .166 C7
Carnglas Rd SA2 . . . . .166 C7
Carnhywel SA14 . . . . .149 C6
Carno Pl SA14 . . . . .160 D8
Caroline St **3** SA15 . . . . . .148 C3
Carregamman **19** SA18 . . . .98 B7
Carregamman Isaf SA18 . .98 B6
Carreg Cennen Castle
(remains of)* SA19 . . . . . .79 F6
Carreg Cennen Gdns
SA1 . . . . .161 B4
Carreg Coetan **9** SA42 . . . .13 E4
Carreg Onnen SA65 . . . . . .122 C3
Carreg Yr Afon SA9 . . . . . .100 C2
Carrick Ave SA15 . . . . .148 D7
Carrier's La **1** SA13 . . . . . .118 D3
Carrog Rd SA5 . . . . .160 B5
Carr Terr SA72 . . . . .104 E6
Cartersford Pl SA3 . . . . . .173 A8
Cartlett SA61 . . . . .125 B5
Cartlett Rd **4** SA61 . . . . . .125 B5
Cartref SA10 . . . . .162 F7
Carway Cty Prim Sch
SA17 .95 C1
Carway St SA16 . . . . .137 D2
Caryl Terr SA6 . . . . .160 E6
Cashfield Way SA61 . . . . . .125 A7
Casllwchwr Prim Sch
SA4 . . . . .150 D1
Castell Cl SA7 . . . . .161 C7
Castell Corwg SA43 . . . . . .16 A5
Castell Ddu Rd SA4 . . . . . .143 B1
Castell Henllys Iron Age
Fort* SA41 . . . . .14 E2
Castell Hywel SA31 . . . . . .128 C8
Castell Pigyn Rd SA31 . . . .129 E8
Castle Acre SA3 . . . . .173 A6
Castle Ave SA3 . . . . .173 A5
Castle Back **18** SA61 . . . . . .125 A5
Castle Bailey St SA1 . . . . .174 B3
Castle Cl
Llangadog SA19 . . . . .63 D7
Nolton & Roch SA62 . . . . . .66 E8
Castle Cres SA3 . . . . .173 A5
Castle Ct Loughor SA4 . . . .157 D8
Swansea / Abertawe SA7 .161 B6
Castle Graig SA6 . . . . .160 D5
Castle Graig Rd SA6 . . . . .160 D5
Castle Hall Dr SA73 . . . . . .131 F2
Castle High Rd SA73 . . . . .131 F2
Castle High SA61 . . . . .124 F5
Castle La Carew SA70 . . . .105 D6
7 Swansea / Abertawe
SA1 . . . . .174 B3
Castle Lofts **6** SA1 . . . . . .174 B3
Castle Pill Cres SA73 . . . . .131 F6
Castle Pill Rd SA73 . . . . . .131 F4
Castle Rd
Kidwelly / Cydweli SA17 . .136 B5
Llanfihangel-ar-Arth SA39 . .39 B7
St Ishmael's SA62 . . . . .85 A2
The Mumbles / Y Mwmbwls
SA3 . . . . .173 A5
Castle Rise SA62 . . . . .51 C2
Castle Sports Gd SA20 . .121 D4
Castle Sq
Swansea / Abertawe SA1 .174 B2
Tenby / Dinbych-y-pysgod
SA70 . . . . .135 F5
The Mumbles / Y Mwmbwls
SA3 . . . . .173 A5
Castle St
Cardigan / Aberteifi SA43 .118 D3
9 Haverfordwest / Hwlffordd
SA61 . . . . .125 A5
Kidwelly / Cydweli SA17 . .136 B4
Llandovery / Llanymddyfri
SA20 . . . . .121 D4
Loughor SA4 . . . . .150 D1
Narberth / Arberth SA67 . . .70 D1
Narth / Castell-Nedd SA10 .162 F7
Newcastle Emlyn / Castell
Newydd Emlyn SA38 . . . . .119 D5
2 Newport / Trefdraeth
SA42 . . . . .13 E3
Pembroke Dock / Doc Penfro
SA72 . . . . .104 B5
Swansea / Abertawe SA1 .174 B3
The Mumbles / Y Mwmbwls
SA3 . . . . .173 A5
Castle Terr
Milford Haven / Aberdaugleddau
SA73 . . . . .131 D3
8 Narberth / Arberth SA67 .70 E1
Newcastle Emlyn / Castell
Newydd Emlyn SA38 . . . . .119 D5
Castle View
Camrose SA62 . . . . .67 A6
Haverfordwest / Hwlffordd
SA61 . . . . .125 A6
Pembroke / Penfro SA71 . .133 B5
Saundersfoot SA69 . . . . . .134 E4
Castle Way SA62 . . . . .101 D4
Caswell Ave SA3 . . . . .172 E4
Caswell Bay Ct SA3 . . . . . .172 C4
Caswell Bay Rd SA3 . . . . .172 A5
Caswell Dr SA3 . . . . .172 D4
Caswell Rd
Bishopston SA3 . . . . .172 B4
The Mumbles / Y Mwmbwls
SA3 . . . . .172 E4
Caswell St Llanelli SA15 . .148 E3
Swansea / Abertawe SA1 .167 B6
Cathan Cl SA5 . . . . .159 E6
Cathan Cres SA5 . . . . .159 E6
Catherines Gate SA61 . . . .125 A1

Catherine St
Llanelli SA15 . . . . .148 C3
St David's / Tyddewi SA62 .123 B4
Swansea / Abertawe SA1 .167 B6
Causeway St SA17 . . . . . . .136 B4
Causeway The SA2 . . . . . . .166 E7
Causway The SA62 . . . . . . .50 B1
Cave St SA5 . . . . .160 A2
Cawdor Cl SA15 . . . . .124 E3
Cawdor Pl SA15 . . . . .148 D6
Cawdor Terr SA38 . . . . . . .119 D5
Cecil Rd Gorseinon SA4 . . .151 C2
Gowerton / Tre-gwyr SA4 .158 C4
Cecil St SA5 . . . . .160 C2
Cedar Ave SA4 . . . . .151 A4
Cedar Cl SA4 . . . . .158 D4
Cedar Cres SA4 . . . . .172 F8
Cedric Cl SA2 . . . . .166 B5
Cedric St SA15 . . . . .148 E5
Cefn Brith SA14 . . . . .149 B6
Cefn Celyn SA2 . . . . .158 B1
Cefn Coed SA65 . . . . .30 F5
Cefn Coed Cres SA2 . . . . .159 D1
Cefn Coed Hospl SA2 . . . .159 C1
Cefncrug SA18 . . . . .97 E7
Cefn-Draw SA4 . . . . .157 D1
Cefneithin Prim Sch
SA14 . . . . .97 A8
Cefneithin Rd SA14 . . . . . . .97 B8
Cefn Gallod **2** SA62 . . . . . .29 B5
Cefn Glas
Swansea / Abertawe SA2 .166 B8
Ynysforgan SA6 . . . . .154 A3
Cefn Helyg SA2 . . . . .159 B1
Cefn Hengoed Com Sch
SA1 . . . . .161 C4
Cefn Hengoed Rd SA1 . . . .161 C4
Cefnfilan Rd SA8 . . . . .147 D6
Cefn Llwyn SA1 . . . . .161 C5
Cefn-Parc SA10 . . . . .162 E6
Cefn Rd Glais SA7 . . . . . . .154 F6
Gwaun-Cae-Gurwen SA18 . .99 D6
Swansea / Abertawe SA1 .161 C3
Cefnsaeson Rd SA7 . . . . . .162 A8
Cefn Stylle Rd SA4 . . . . . . .142 B6
Cefn-y-Maes SA5 . . . . .159 E6
Ceidrim Rd SA18 . . . . .99 B8
Ceiriog Rd SA1 . . . . .167 A8
Cellan Rd SA48 . . . . .120 E4
Cellar Hill SA3 . . . . .131 E2
Cemaes St SA43 . . . . .16 A5
Cemetery Rd
Gwaun-Cae-Gurwen SA18 . .99 D6
Swansea / Abertawe SA5 .160 D6
Cenarth SA72 . . . . .132 D3
Central Bsns Pk / Parc
Busnes Canolog SA2 . . .154 C2
Central Ct SA73 . . . . .131 D3
Century Cl **1** SA61 . . . . . .125 A7
Century Pk SA6 . . . . .145 A4
Ceri Rd SA1 . . . . .159 F1
Chaddesley Terr **1** SA1 . .167 B7
Challacombe Pl SA3 . . . . .172 E6
Chancery La **1** SA43 . . . . .118 D4
Chandlers Reach SA3 . . . .173 C4
Channel View
Swansea / Abertawe SA2 .166 B5
The Mumbles / Y Mwmbwls
SA3 . . . . .173 B3
Chantry St SA1 . . . . .159 E5
Chapelfield Gdns 7
SA67 . . . . .70 D1
Chapel Hill La SA67 . . . . . .89 F7
Chapel La
8 Haverfordwest / Hwlffordd
SA61 . . . . .125 A5
Lamphey SA71 . . . . .105 B1
Chapel Rd Crofty SA4 . . . .156 B2
Crundale SA62 . . . . .68 C5
Pembroke Dock / Doc Penfro
SA72 . . . . .132 A2
Scleddau SA65 . . . . .30 F5
10 Solva SA62 . . . . .50 E5
Three Crosses SA4 . . . . . .157 E1
Chapel Row **8** SA62 . . . . . .87 E4
Chapel St **6** Brecon SA18 .80 E1
Carmarthen / Caerfyrddin
SA31 . . . . .128 F5
Gorseinon SA4 . . . . .151 D2
Milford Haven / Aberdaugleddau
SA73 . . . . .131 B2
Swansea / Abertawe SA1 .174 B5
Templeton SA67 . . . . .89 E6
The Mumbles / Y Mwmbwls
SA3 . . . . .173 A5
Chapmans **5** SA1 . . . . . . .174 B3
Chapman St / Stryd
Chapman SA15 . . . . .148 C6
Charles Ct SA4 . . . . .151 A1
Charles Rd SA71 . . . . .133 D4
Charles St
10 Llandyssul SA44 . . . . .19 E3
Llanelli SA15 . . . . .148 F5
Milford Haven / Aberdaugleddau
SA73 . . . . .131 C2
Skewen / Sciwen SA10 . . .162 E7
Neyland SA73 . . . . .132 B7
Charles Terr SA15 . . . . . . .148 C4
Charles Thomas Ave
SA72 . . . . .132 D3
Charlotte Ct SA1 . . . . .159 E2
Charlton Pl SA72 . . . . .132 D2
Charnwood Ct SA1 . . . . . .161 D6
Chedhydra Wlk **2** SA1 . . .174 B1
Chemical Rd
Morriston / Treforris SA6 . .154 A2
Swansea / Abertawe SA6 .153 F2

Chemical Row SA9 . . . . . . .139 A4
Chepstow Pl SA1 . . . . .161 C4
Cheriton Cres SA5 . . . . . . .159 F5
Cheriton Ct **2** SA1 . . . . . .174 A4
Cheriton Rd SA72 . . . . . . .104 B5
Cherry Gr
Haverfordwest / Hwlffordd
SA61 . . . . .125 B5
Swansea / Abertawe SA7 .166 B4
Cherry Tree Cl SA73 . . . . .131 E3
Chesshyre St SA2 . . . . . . .166 E5
Chestnut Ave
Gorseinon SA4 . . . . .151 A4
The Mumbles / Y Mwmbwls
SA3 . . . . .172 E8
Chestnut Tree Dr SA62 . . .86 E6
Chestnut Way SA73 . . . . . .131 E3
Cheviot Cl SA5 . . . . .159 E3
Childrens Orthopaedic Hospl
SA1 . . . . .167 B6
Chiltern Cl SA5 . . . . .159 E3
Chirk Gdns SA1 . . . . .161 C4
Christ Church Prim Sch
SA1 . . . . .167 B5
Christina St SA1 . . . . .174 A3
Christopher Cl SA6 . . . . . .161 A6
Christopher Rd
Neath / Castell-Nedd
SA10 . . . . .162 E7
Ynysforgan SA6 . . . . .154 B4
Christopher Rise SA4 . . . .152 A5
Christopher St SA15 . . . . .148 E4
Church Bank SA20 . . . . . . .121 C4
Church Bank Ind Est
SA20 . . . . .121 C4
Church Cl
Kilgetty / Begelly SA68 . . .134 B8
1 Marloes & St Brides
SA62 . . . . .84 C3
Swansea / Abertawe SA7 .161 D8
Church Cotts SA1 . . . . . . .153 B2
Church Gdns SA2 . . . . .159 E2
Church Hill La SA62 . . . . . .125 F3
Churchill Cl SA70 . . . . . . .135 C5
Churchill St SA68 . . . . .89 B1
Church La
Bishopston SA3 . . . . .171 F7
9 Carmarthen / Caerfyrddin
SA31 . . . . .128 F5
Gwaun-Cae-Gurwen SA18 . .99 D6
Haverfordwest / Hwlffordd
SA61 . . . . .125 A4
Newcastle Emlyn / Castell
Newydd Emlyn SA38 . . . . .119 D5
Pen-clawdd SA4 . . . . .156 F2
Pontarddulais SA4 . . . . . . .143 D3
St Dogmaels / Llandudoch
SA43 . . . . .118 A3
Church Lake Terr SA73 . . .132 A6
Church Mdw SA3 . . . . .115 B1
Church Park La SA3 . . . . . .173 B4
Church Pk
Tenby / Dinbych-y-pysgod
SA70 . . . . .135 E4
The Mumbles / Y Mwmbwls
SA3 . . . . .173 B4
Church Rd / Heol Yr Eglwys
SA4 .97 A1
Church Rd Ind Est SA14 . .78 B1
Church Row **8** SA18 . . . . . .99 B8
Church St
Cardigan / Aberteifi SA43 .118 C4
2 Carmarthen / Caerfyrddin
SA31 . . . . .129 A5
Cilgerran SA43 . . . . .15 F5
Cwmyr Gaes SA7 . . . . .24 A2
Gowerton / Tre-gwyr SA4 .158 B5
7 Haverfordwest / Hwlffordd
SA61 . . . . .125 A5
3 Lampeter / Llanbedr
Pont Steffan SA48 . . . . . . .120 C5
Laugharne Township SA33 .92 E6
Llandeilo SA19 . . . . .130 D5
4 Llandybie SA18 . . . . . . .79 A2
5 Llandyssul SA44 . . . . . .19 E3
Llanelli SA15 . . . . .148 D5
Llangadog SA19 . . . . .63 D7
10 Narberth / Arberth
SA67 . . . . .70 D1
Pembroke Dock / Doc Penfro
SA72 . . . . .132 C2
St Dogmaels / Llandudoch
SA43 . . . . .118 A3
5 Tenby / Dinbych-y-pysgod
SA70 . . . . .135 E4
Church St / Stryd-yr-Eglwys
8 SA18 . . . . .98 B7
Church Terr
Pembroke / Penfro SA71 . .133 A4
Saundersfoot SA69 . . . . . .134 E4
Church View SA67 . . . . . . .90 B2

Church Way SA73 . . . . . . .132 A6
Cila Prim Sch SA2 . . . . . .165 C5
Cilfrow Ct SA1 . . . . .160 C2
Cilgerran Castle (NT)*
SA43 . . . . .16 A6
Cilgerran C in W VC Sch
SA43 . . . . .16 A6
Cilgerran Pl SA1 . . . . .161 C5
Cilyrychen Ind Est SA31 . .128 C3
Cillefwr Rd E SA31 . . . . . .128 B3
Cillefwr Rd W SA31 . . . . . .128 A2
Cilmaengwyn SA8 . . . . . . .100 B1
Cilsaig Rd SA14 . . . . .149 B8
Cil-y-Coed SA5 . . . . .159 A3
Cilycwm Rd SA20 . . . . .121 D5
Cilycwm VC Prim Sch
SA20 . . . . .25 C2
Cil Yr Onnen SA14 . . . . . . .150 B8
Cinema Bldgs **3** SA15 . . .148 D3
City Rd SA51 . . . . .124 F5
Clarbeston Rd Sta SA63 . .69 A8
Clare Cl SA4 . . . . .150 E1
Clarence Ct SA1 . . . . .174 A2
Clarence Rd SA19 . . . . . . .130 E6
Clarence St
Pembroke Dock / Doc Penfro
SA72 . . . . .132 B2
Swansea / Abertawe SA1 .174 A2
Clarence Terr SA1 . . . . . . .174 A2
Clarendon Rd
1 Llandeilo SA19 . . . . . . .130 E6
Swansea / Abertawe SA2 .166 C7
Clare Rd SA9 . . . . .139 B7
Clare St SA5 . . . . .160 C3
Clareston Cl **4** SA61 . . . . .124 F5
Clareston Rd **6** SA70 . . . . .135 E5
Clare Wlk SA71 . . . . .133 C6
Clarion Cl
Llansamlet SA6 . . . . .154 B1
Swansea / Abertawe SA6 .161 C8
Clarion Ct SA6 . . . . .161 C8
Clarke Way SA1 . . . . .161 D6
Clasemont Rd
Swansea / Abertawe,
Morriston / Treforys SA6 . .153 F2
Swansea / Abertawe SA6 .153 D2
Clase Prim Sch SA6 . . . . .160 D8
Clase Rd
Morriston / Treforris SA6 . .154 A1
Swansea / Abertawe SA6 .161 B8
Clas-y-Bedw SA5 . . . . .158 F3
Clas-y-Deri SA5 . . . . .159 A3
Clas-yr-Onnen SA5 . . . . . .159 A3
Claybogs La SA62 . . . . .50 E1
Clayford Rd SA69 . . . . . . .134 A4
Clay La Houndleton SA71 . .104 A2
Merlin's Bridge SA61 . . . . .125 B2
Milford Haven / Aberdaugleddau
SA73 .9 F5
Clayton Rd SA4 . . . . .143 A4
Clayton St SA1 . . . . .160 D4
Cleddau Ave
Haverfordwest / Hwlffordd
SA61 . . . . .125 B4
Neyland SA73 . . . . .132 C5
Cleddau Bridge Bsns Pk
SA73 . . . . .132 E5
Cleddau Cl SA73 . . . . .87 C3
Clees La SA9 . . . . .139 A5
Cleggars Pk SA71 . . . . . . .105 A3
Clement Rd SA64 . . . . .122 A6
Clement Terr SA70 . . . . . . .135 C6
Clerkenhill Adventure Farm*
SA61 . . . . .69 D2
Clevedon Ct SA2 . . . . .166 F7
Cleveland Ave SA3 . . . . . .173 C3
Cleviston Pk SA14 . . . . . . .150 A6
Clickett La SA70 . . . . .135 C7
Clicketts Ct SA70 . . . . .135 B5
Clicketts The SA70 . . . . . . .135 B5
Clifflands Cl SA3 . . . . .172 F4
Cliff Rd Amroth SA67 . . . . .90 C2
Laugharne Township SA33 . .92 F5
Pembroke Dock / Doc Penfro
SA72 . . . . .103 F5
Cliff Terr SA16 . . . . .137 C2
Clifton Cl SA5 . . . . .160 C6
Clifton Hill SA1 . . . . .174 A3
Clifton Row SA1 . . . . .174 A3
Clifton St SA33 . . . . .92 F6
Clifton Terr
2 Llanelli SA15 . . . . .148 F6
The Mumbles / Y Mwmbwls
SA3 . . . . .173 C4
Clive Rd SA5 . . . . .122 C4
Cloisters The SA1 . . . . . . .167 A6
Clordir Rd SA4 . . . . .152 A7
Clos Aderyn Du SA4 . . . . . .99 D6
Clos Affallon SA18 . . . . . . .99 D6
Clos Afon Llan SA4 . . . . . .158 C6
Clos Alaw SA7 . . . . .161 E6
Clos Allt-y-Gog SA4 . . . . . .143 C3
Clos Andreas **3** SA15 . . . .148 E6
Clos Aneira SA5 . . . . .159 D3
Clos Ar Ddafen SA14 . . . . .149 C5
Clos Bancy Berllan
SA4 . . . . .143 D3
Clos Bevan SA4 . . . . .158 A5
Clos Blean Crymlyn SA7 . .161 F6
Clos Brynaford SA4 . . . . . .150 F3
Clos Brynbarcud SA4 . . . . .152 C2
Clos Bryngwyn SA4 . . . . . .158 D8
Clos Bryn Isaf SA14 . . . . . .149 D4
Clos Burlais SA5 . . . . .160 A2

Clos Cadno
Llansamlet SA7 ....154 D1
Swansea / Abertawe SA6 .153 F5
Clos Cae Dafydd SA4 ....158 A5
Clos Cae Fainc SA14 ....150 B7
Clos Cae Elms SA15 ....148 B6
Clos Caersalem SA4 ....160 C7
Clos Calfaria SA5 ......159 E3
Clos Camlas **2** SA6 ....161 A8
Clos Cefn-y-Maes SA14 .149 C5
Clos Celyn SA7 ....161 D6
Clos Cenawon SA4 ......154 A5
Clos Cerdinen SA4 .....152 C4
Clos Ceri SA6 ....154 E8
Clos Cilfwnwr SA4 .....152 B3
Clos Cilsaig SA14 ......149 C8
Clos Crucywel SA6 .....154 A4
Clos Cwmin SA31 ....129 B7
Clos Cwningen SA7 .....155 B1
Clos Cwrt Y Carne SA4 .151 A4
Clos Cynan SA2 ....165 F8
Clos Dan Y Lan SA14 ...140 F2
Clos Ddu SA5 ....160 B7
Clos Delyth SA4 ....151 C2
Clos Derwen SA7 ......162 A6
Clos Dewi Medi SA15 ...148 E2
Clos Dyffrynlliw / Lliw Valley
  CI SA4 ....158 C6
Clos Ebol SA6 ....153 F4
Clos Eileen Chilcott
  SA7 ....161 E6
Clos Emily SA14 ....97 C7
Close The Gorseinon SA4 .151 A1
  Hook SA62 ....87 D6
  Johnston SA62 ....86 E5
  Llanrhidian SA4 ......115 F4
  Spittal SA62 ....51 C1
  Swansea / Abertawe SA5 .153 C2
Clos Felen **3** SA18 ....99 B8
Clos Gathen SA15 .....148 D4
Clos George Morgan
  SA4 ....153 E4
Clos Ger-y-Bryn SA4 ..152 C5
Clos Ger-y-Maes SA4 ..152 C5
Clos Gianlliw SA4 .....152 A6
Clos Glanmor SA15 ....148 C4
Clos Glan-y-Wern SA7 .161 A6
Clos Glyndwr SA4 .....142 F5
Clos Gors Fawr SA4 ...151 C6
Clos Granby SA15 .....148 E2
Clos Gwernen SA4 .....158 C6
Clos Healy SA4 ....158 B6
Clos Helyg SA4 ....158 B5
Clos Hendra SA16 .....146 B2
Clos Hermon SA16 .....137 B3
Clos Islwyn SA2 ....162 A6
Clos Leighton Davies
  SA4 ....158 E6
Clos Llandyfan SA4 ...158 D8
Clos Llanfihangel SA14 .149 B6
Clos Llwyn Cwm SA6 ..161 A6
Clos Llwyn Ty Gwyn
  SA34 ....126 E3
Clos Llyg SA7 ....162 B8
Clos Madlen SA4 ......159 D4
Clos Maes Isaf SA14 ..150 C7
Clos Maes Yr Ysgol
  SA4 ....143 D3
Clos Marina SA4 ......158 B6
Clos Melin Mynach SA4 .158 C8
Clos Min Yr Afon SA4 .150 F2
Clos Morgan **1** SA31 ..128 E5
Clos Morgannwg SA4 ..167 A8
Clos Morgan Owen SA4 .153 E4
Clos Nant Bran SA7 ...155 A2
Clos Nant-y-Ci SA18 ...97 F7
Clos Nantydd SA14 ....149 C4
Clos Penbwl SA4 ......152 C2
Clos Pendderi SA14 ...149 F5
Clos Penderri SA4 ....152 C2
Clos Pengelli SA4 .....151 C7
Clos Penllwyngwyn
  SA14 ....149 F6
Clos Pen Pant SA4 ....143 D4
Clos Pentyle SA4 .....147 B2
Clos Pen y Banc SA6 ..160 C8
Clos Penyfai SA15 ....148 B7
Clos Pen Y Waun SA14 ..97 C7
Clos Plas Isaf SA14 ...150 C7
Clos Pluguen SA20 ....121 C3
Clos Rebecca SA14 ....96 F2
Clos Rhandir SA4 .....157 E8
Clos Rhedyn SA4 ......154 A4
Clos Rhymni SA4 ......154 A4
Clos Sant Paul SA15 ..148 D4
Clos Sant Pedr **1** SA15 .148 D4
Clos Sant Teilo SA15 ..153 A1
Clos Saron SA5 ....159 F3
Clos St Cenydd SA13 ..114 C2
Clos Sticle SA31 ......129 A3
Clos Tawel SA48 ......4 B6
Clos Tirffordd SA4 ....152 C2
Clos Trafle SA4 ....158 C6
Clos Tygwyn Clydach SA6 .154 E8
  Gowerton / Tre-gwyr SA4 .158 B6
Clos Ty-Gwyn SA14 ....142 F4
Clos Ty Mawr SA4 .....152 B2
Clos Ty Tafol SA15 ....148 B3
Clos Vernon Watkins
  SA4 ....151 A4
Clos Waun Wen SA4 ..153 E5
Clos Y Banc-yr-Eithin
  SA4 ....151 A3
Clos-y-Berllan SA14 ..149 F5
Clos-y-bigney SA65 ...122 C3
Clos Y Binwydd / Pine Tree
  CI SA16 ....137 F3

Clos Y Bont Faen
Cwmrhydyceirw SA4 ..154 A5
Swansea / Abertawe SA6 .153 F4
Clos Y Coedwr SA4 ....154 D7
Clos-y-Cwm SA14 .....97 D7
Clos Y Dderwen SA16 .137 B3
Clos Y Dderwen / Oak Tree
  CI SA18 ....99 B8
Clos Y Ddraenen SA14 .141 B3
Clos Y Deri SA31 ......129 A5
Clos-y-Deri SA4 ......97 D2
Clos Y Deri
  Llanegwad SA32 ......77 A8
  Llanelli SA14 ....149 B8
Clos-y-Derwen / Oaklands CI
  SA67 ....90 C3
Clos-y-Felin SA18 .....98 D7
Clos Y Fran SA7 ......155 A6
Clos Y Fynwent SA4 ...143 D3
Clos Y Gafel **2** SA41 ..34 E4
Clos-y-gerddi SA37 ....34 F8
Clos-y-Gwydd SA4 ....158 A5
Clos-y-Maerdy SA4 ....158 A6
Clos Y Meini SA41 .....34 E4
Clos Y Morfa SA4 .....150 F3
Clos Y Mynydd SA4 ...150 F2
Clos Y Nant SA4 ......150 F3
Clos Yr Ael SA1 ......159 E2
Clos Yr Allt SA1 ......159 E2
Clos Yr Eglwys SA1 ...159 F2
Clos-yr-Hendre SA18 ..97 E6
Clos-yr Hesg SA2 .....154 D1
Clos Yr Onnen
  Abergwili SA31 ....129 E7
  Kidwelly / Cydweli SA17 .136 D4
  Llansamlet SA7 ......154 D1
Clos Yr Orsaf **9** SA4 ..161 A8
Clos Y Ysgol SA7 .....162 A7
Clos Ysgallen SA7 ....161 D6
Clos Ysgol Gymraeg
  SA5 ....160 B2
Clos Y Waun SA14 ....97 B7
Clovelly Pl SA3 ....172 E6
Clover Pk SA61 ....125 C5
ClUs Griffith Jones
  SA33 ....127 E6
Club La SA9 ....138 F1
Clunderwen Sta SA66 .70 E6
Clwyd Com Prim Sch
  SA4 ....160 A4
Clwyd Rd
  Gwaun-Cae-Gurwen SA18 .99 D6
  Swansea / Abertawe SA6 .160 B4
Clwyd -Wen SA4 ......158 A5
Clydach Hospl SA6 ....154 D7
Clydach Inf Sch SA6 ..154 D8
Clydach Jun Sch SA6 ..154 D8
Clydach Rd
  Craig-cefn-parc SA6 ..146 B2
  Ynysforgan SA6 ......154 A2
  Ynystawe SA6 ....154 C5
Clyndu St SA6 ....160 F8
Clyne CI SA3 ....165 F1
Clyne Cres SA3 ....165 F1
Clyne Ct SA2 ....166 B7
Clyne Dr SA3 ....165 F1
Clyne Farm Activities Ctr*
  SA3 ....166 A4
Clyne Valley Cotts SA2 .165 E5
Clyne Valley Ctry Pk*
  SA2 ....166 A4
Clyne Valley La SA2 ..166 B2
Clyne Valley Rd SA2 ..165 E5
Clyne View SA2 ......165 E6
Clyngwyn Rd SA9 ....139 B7
Clynmaes Pl SA5 .....159 E6
Clyro Ct SA1 ....161 C4
Cnap Llwyd Rd SA6 ..160 D6
Coalbrook Rd
  Grovesend SA4 ....151 C5
  Pontyberem SA15 ....96 B6
Coal La SA70 ....105 E3
Cobblers St **1** SA15 ..148 D6
Cobham Ct SA4 ......151 A3
Cob La Manorbier SA70 .105 E1
  Tenby / Dinbych-y-pysgod
  SA70 ....135 F4
Coch-y-Cwm Rd SA1 ..161 C2
Cockett Rd SA2 ......159 D2
Coedbach Rd SA4 ....143 C3
Coedcae SA8 ....147 F6
Coedcae Comp Sch
  SA15 ....148 F5
Coed Cae Rd
  Llanelli SA15 ....148 F5
  Llanelli SA14 ....149 A5
Coed Cae Uchaf SA15 .148 F5
Coed Ceirios SA4 .....154 D1
Coed Celyn Rd SA2 ...166 A6
Coedfan SA2 ....166 A6
Coedffaldau SA9 .....100 B6
Coedffranc Inf Sch
  SA10 ....162 F7
Coedffranc Jun Sch
  SA10 ....162 F7
Coedlan SA9 ....139 D8
Coed Lan SA4 ....157 D1
Coedmawr SA15 ......95 F4
Coed Mor SA2 ....166 B5
Coedmore La SA43 ...75 E8
Coedmore La SA38 ...119 F6
Coedmor National Nature
  Reserve* SA43 ......16 A6
Coed Nant Ho SA1 ...160 D2
Coedrath Pk SA69 ....134 E4
Coed-Saeson Cres SA2 .166 D2
Coedwig Pl SA15 .....160 B3

Coed Y Bronallt SA4 ..143 A5
Coedybryn Cty Prim Sch
  SA44 ....18 E2
Coed-y-Bwlch SA4 ....150 A2
Coed y Cadno SA14 ...97 C5
Coed Y Clun SA17 ....109 B7
Coed-y-crwys SA41 ...157 E1
Coed-y-Felin SA31 ...129 E7
Coed Y Pin / Pinewood
  SA18 ....98 D7
Coed Y Plas SA31 .....128 C2
Colbourne Terr SA1 ..174 A5
Colbren Sq SA18 ......99 D6
Colby Rd SA16 ....137 E3
Colby Woodland Gdn (NT)
  SA67 ....90 C3
Coldstream St SA15 ..148 C6
Coldwell Terr SA71 ...133 C5

Coleg = college

Coleg Abertawe / Swansea
  Coll (Tycoch Campus)
  SA2 ....166 D7
Coleg Celf Dyfed / Dyfed Coll
  of Art SA31 ....128 C5
Coleg Llanymddyfri /
  Llandovery Coll SA20 .121 C5
Coleg Sir Benfro /
  Pembrokeshire Coll
  SA61 ....124 E3
Coleg y Drindod / Trinity
  Coll SA31 ....128 C5
Coleridge Cres SA2 ...165 F8
Coleshill Terr SA15 ...148 C5
College Hill SA15 .....148 E5
College Rd SA31 .....132 B6
College Sq SA71 .....174 A3
College Row
  Cardigan / Aberteifi SA43 .118 D4
  Ystradgynlais SA9 ...139 F8
College Sq SA15 .....148 E5
College St
  Lampeter / Llanbedr Pont Steffan
  SA48 ....127 C8
  Newcastle Emlyn / Castell
  Newydd Emlyn SA38 ..119 D5
  Swansea / Abertawe SA1 .174 B3
College St / Stryd-y-Coleg
  SA18 ....98 B7
College View SA20 ...121 C4
Colley Ct SA71 ....104 C4
Colonel Rd /
  Ffordd-y-Cyrnol SA18 .98 C6
Colonel Road SA18 ..98 C6
Coltshill Dr SA3 .....172 F5
Columbia Row **12** SA15 .148 D5
Colwyn Ave SA1 .....161 C5
Commercial Rd SA8 ..147 C8
Commercial Row SA2 .132 B2
Commercial St
  Ystalyfera SA9 ....139 B6
  Ystradgynlais SA9 ...138 F1
Common Rd SA71 ....133 B4
Compass Row SA18 ..147 D5
Compass St SA5 .....160 C3
Compton Ave SA10 ..162 F7
Conduit La SA71 .....131 A2
Coniston Wlk SA2 ....166 D7
Conkland Hill SA62 ..40 E2
Connaught Ave SA2 ..132 D4
Connaught PI SA72 ..132 C4
Constitution Hill SA1 .167 B7
Convent St SA1 ......160 D1
Conway Ct SA5 ......160 A4
Conway Dr SA3 ......131 F6
Conway Rd SA5 .....160 A4
Cooks CI SA71 ....133 B4
Cooksport View SA68 .134 E8
Coombes Rd SA10 ....162 E7
Coombe-Tennant Ave
  SA10 ....162 D7
Coombs Dr SA73 .....131 E3
Coombs Rd SA73 .....131 E3
Coopers Est SA18 ....97 E5
Coopers Rd / Heol Cwper
  SA70 ....135 E6
Copley CI SA3 ....172 B7
Copley Lodge SA3 ...172 B7
Copperworks Inf Sch
  SA15 ....148 D5
Coracle Way SA31 ...128 F4
Coram Dr SA73 ......132 C7
Cork Ho **13** SA1 ......174 C2
Cormorant CI SA15 ..148 B6
Cormorant Way SA3 ..172 E6
Cormoront CI SA62 ..124 F7
Cornish PI SA15 .....148 E2
Cornwall PI SA15 ....173 B5
Coronation Ave
  Haverfordwest / Hwlffordd
  SA61 ....125 B6
  6 Llangwm SA62 .....87 E4
Coronation Dr SA43 ..118 B8
Coronation Rd
  1 Brecon SA18 ......80 E1
  Carmarthen / Caerfyrddin
  SA31 ....128 E6
  2 Fishguard / Abergwaun
  SA65 ....122 D4
  Llanelli SA15 ....148 E4
Coronation Rd / Heol Y
  Coroni **16** SA1 ....99 B8
Coronation Terr SA18 .98 D6
Coronet Way SA6 ....161 A7
Corporation Ave SA15 .148 E7

Corporation CI SA15 ..148 E6
Corporation Rd
  Loughor SA4 ....150 E1
  Swansea / Abertawe SA4 .159 C4
Corrymore Mans SA2 .166 F6
Cors Goch; Llanllwch
  National Nature Reserve*
  SA33 ....74 F5
Cory St SA2 ....166 D6
Cots La SA62 ....69 A5
Cotswold CI SA5 .....159 E3
Cotswold Gdns SA68 .134 C8
Cott La SA67 ....88 E7
Cotts Rd SA62 ....85 C5
Courtenay Rd SA15 ..148 C6
Courtenay St SA1 ....160 C2
Courtfield Dr SA62 ..67 A6
Court La SA8 ....147 E5
Courtlands Pk SA31 ..129 A6
Courtlands Way SA5 ..159 F5
Court Rd SA61 ....124 D5
Court Rise SA73 .....131 E6
Court Terr SA71 .....133 B5
Courtyard The **7** SA1 .174 A4
Courtyard Units SA10 .162 D5
Cowell Prec **2** SA15 ..148 D5
Cowell Rd / Heol Cowell
  SA18 ....99 C7
Cowell St SA15 ......148 D5
Cowpark La SA70 ....105 D2
Cowper CI SA2 ......165 F7
Cox Hill SA67 ....70 C2
Crackwell CI SA70 ...135 A1
Crackwell St SA70 ...135 E4
Cradock St Llanelli SA15 .148 D4
  Swansea / Abertawe SA1 .174 A3
Craig-cefn-parc Prim Sch
  SA6 ....146 B4
Craig-las SA62 ......50 F8
Craigwen SA14 ......149 E4
Craig-y-Bwldan SA2 ..165 E8
Craig y nos Sch SA3 ..172 C7
Cranfield CI SA1 .....159 E5
Cranham Pk **3** SA62 ..86 C5
Cranmer CI SA5 .....159 D5
Cranog CI SA42 .....29 B5
Crawshay Ct SA3 ....172 F3
Crayland Parc SA17 ..136 A5
Creamston Rd SA61 ..125 E4
Creidiol Rd SA1 .....174 A4
Crescent Rd
  Gwaun-Cae-Gurwen SA18 .99 D6
  Llandeilo SA19 ......130 E6
Crescent The
  Burry Port SA16 ......137 E3
  1 Narberth / Arberth SA67 .70 E1
  Swansea / Abertawe SA5 .159 F5
Cresswell Castle* SA68 .88 D2
Cresswell St SA70 ....135 E4
Crest Acre CI SA3 ...172 E5
Creswell Rd SA6 .....160 E7
Cribin La SA14 ......141 A2
Cribyn Clos SA14 ....141 A3
Criccieth PI SA1 .....161 C5
Cricket Gr SA71 .....104 A3
Crickhowell PI SA1 ..161 C5
Crickmarren CI SA71 .133 F3
Criney Hill SA5 ......128 D5
Crispin Ave SA31 ....128 D5
Criterion Way SA72 ..132 C3
Croesffyrdd SA9 .....139 D7
Croesgoch CP Sch SA62 .28 F3
Croeso Rd **4** SA71 ...133 D4
Croes Y-ceiliog SA14 .96 C4
Croft Ave SA1 ....85 F1
Croftfield Cres SA3 ..132 E3
Croft La SA70 ....105 D7
Croft Rd **3** SA62 ....85 D8
Croft St SA1 ....174 B4
Croft Terr
  Pembroke Dock / Doc Penfro
  SA72 ....132 B2
  2 Swansea / Abertawe
  SA5 ....160 C4
Croft The Loughor SA4 .150 D1
  Tenby / Dinbych-y-pysgod
  SA70 ....135 E6
Croft Villas SA67 ....70 E1
Crofty CI SA62 ......28 F3
Crofty Ind Est SA4 ..156 B3
Crole St SA1 ....167 B7
Cromie Ave SA61 ....124 E6
Cromwell Ct **4** SA71 ..133 D4
Cromwell Drive SA70 .106 B7
Cromwell Rd SA73 ...131 C5
Cromwell St
  Pembroke Dock / Doc Penfro
  SA72 ....132 D2
  St Mary out Liberty SA71 .133 B3
Cross Acre SA3 .....172 E7
Cross Hands Bsns Pk
  SA14 ....97 B7
Cross Hands Prim Sch
  SA14 ....97 B8
Cross Hands Rd / Heol Cross
  Hands SA14 ....97 B8
Cross Inn Bldgs **16** SA18 .98 B7
Cross La SA62 ....68 C5
Crosslands Rd SA67 ..90 C6
Cross Pk
  Pembroke Dock / Doc Penfro
  SA72 ....132 B2
  St Mary out Liberty SA71 .133 B4
Cross Rd / Capel Newydd
  SA14 ....148 D6
Cross Sq SA62 ....123 C4

Cross St
  Goodwick / Wdig SA64 ..122 A5
  Gorseinon SA4 ....151 C2
  Pontardulais SA4 ....160 D4
  Swansea / Abertawe SA5 .160 C4
  Whitland / Hendy-Gwyn
  SA34 ....126 C3
Cross The
  Cosheston SA72 .....104 F6
  Llanrhidian SA3 .....115 D2
  Crossways SA73 ......87 A1
Crow Hill SA62 ......125 A8
Crowhill Rd SA61 ....125 A6
Crown Cotts SA9 ....138 F2
Crown Prec **15** SA15 ..148 D5
Crown St
  Swansea / Abertawe SA6 .161 A8
  Swansea / Abertawe SA4 .158 B8
  Crug Yr Eryd SA1 ....34 F4
Crwys Prim Sch / Ysgol
  Gynradd y Crwys SA4 .157 E1
Crwys Terr SA1 ......160 B6
Crychiau SA31 ....129 E8
Crymlyn Bog Nature
  Reserve* SA1, SA7 ..161 E2
Crymlyn Bog Visitor Ctr*
  SA1 ....161 D1
Crymlyn Parc SA10 ..162 C6
Crymlyn Prim Sch / Ysgol
  Gynradd Crymlyn
  SA10 ....162 C1
Crymlyn Rd SA7, SA10 .162 B6
Crymlyn St SA1 ......168 B7
Crymlyn Terr SA1 ...160 C1
Cuckoo La SA62 ....124 B6
Cuffern CI **1** SA61 ...124 F5
Cuffern Rd SA62 ....67 A6
Cuffern View SA62 ..67 A6
Culfor Rd SA4 ......157 E8
Culla Rd SA17 ......109 C8
Culver Pk SA70 .....135 E4
Cumby Terr SA72 ...132 B2
Cunningham Ct SA2 ..166 C6
Curlew CI
  2 Haverfordwest / Hwlffordd
  SA61 ....124 C5
  Llanelli SA15 ....148 A6
The Mumbles / Y Mwmbwls
  SA3 ....165 E1
Curry CI SA2 ....165 E8
Cutty Sark Dr SA73 ..131 E5
Cwmamman Rd SA18 .98 F8
Cwm Arian SA4 .....154 A2
Cwmbach Rd
  Llanelli Rural SA15 ..109 F4
  Llanelli SA15 ....148 A8
Cwm Bath Rd SA6 ...153 F1
Cwmbwrla Prim Sch
  SA5 ....160 B2
Cwm Cadle SA5 .....159 B6
Cwm Catti SA32 .....77 F6
Cwm Chapel Rd SA14 .161 B4
Cwm Clyd SA15 .....159 A3
Cwm Clydach Nature
  Reserve* SA6 ......146 B3
Cwmdegwel SA43 ...118 A2
Cwm Deri Vineyard*
  SA67 ....88 C5
Cwmdonkin Dr SA2 ..167 A7
Cwmdonkin Terr SA2 .166 F7
Cwm Du CI SA1 .....159 F3
Cwm Gelli SA15 .....160 D6
Cwmgelli Dr SA5 ....160 C6
Cwmgelli Rd SA6 ....160 C6
Cwmglas Prim Sch SA1 .161 C4
Cwmgors Workshops /
  Gweithdau-cwm-gors
  SA18 ....99 D6
Cwm Gwennol SA69 ..134 C1
Cwmgwili Prim Sch
  SA14 ....97 C5
Cwm Ivor Rd SA14 ..137 F3
Cwm Ivor Terr SA1 ..160 D4
Cwm Level Rd SA4 ..160 D5
Cwm-Mwyn SA14 ...97 B8
Cwmnantffor Terr SA18 .99 E7
Cwmphil Rd SA9 ....138 F1
Cwm Prim Sch SA1 ..161 B4
Cwm Rd SA1 ....160 D1
Cwmrhydyceirw Prim Sch
  SA6 ....153 F4
Cwmrhydyceirw Rd SA6 .153 F3
Cwmtawe Bsns Pk SA8 .147 F5
Cwmtawe Coll SA8 ..147 F5
Cwmtawe Comp Sch /
  Gyfun Cwmtawe SA8 ..147 F5
Cwm Terr
  2 Llanelli SA15 ......148 C7
  Swansea / Abertawe SA1 .174 B5
Cwm The SA16 ......137 C3

Cwm-yr-Wch SA2 .... 165 B8
Cwm-ystrad Parc SA31 ..128 C2
Cwndonkin Ct SA2 ....167 A7
Cwrt Cilmeri SA6 ....154 A2
Cwrt Coed Saeson SA7 ..162 B8
Cwrt Elusendy 4 SA15 ..148 E5
Cwrt Emily SA7 ....154 F1
Cwrt Henri Cty Prim Sch
SA32 ....61 A2
Cwrt Hocys SA7 ....161 D6
Cwrt Hydd SA6 ....153 F7
Cwrt Isaf SA7 ....155 B1
Cwrt Ivor Sims SA6 ......154 A2
Cwrt Lafant SA7 ....161 E6
Cwrt Llwyn Fedwen
SA6 ....154 A1
Cwrt Llwynog SA6 ....153 F4
Cwrt Melin SA33 ....74 B5
Cwrt Merlyn SA6 ....153 F5
Cwrt Neville 8 SA15 ....148 D4
Cwrt Olwyn Ddwr SA7 ..155 A1
Cwrt Rhian SA4 ....151 C2
Cwrt Rhosyn SA7 ....161 D6
Cwrt Stanilyd SA18 ......98 B6
Cwrt Tomos SA18 ....99 C8
Cwrt Waddl 3 SA15 ......148 D4
Cwrt Woodford SA33 ....92 E5
Cwrt Y Cadno SA7 ....162 B8
Cwrt Y Castell SA4 ......156 E4
Cwrt-y-Clafdy SA10 ......162 F8
Cwrt-y-Clafdy Rd SA10 ..162 F8
Cwrt-y-Fedw SA7 ....155 B1
Cwrt Y Fedwen SA7 ......154 D1
Cwrt Y Gloch 2 SA23 ....59 A3
Cwrt-y-glyn SA14 ....78 D2
Cwrt Yr Aeron SA6 ....154 A4
Cwrt Y Waun SA8 ....147 D7
Cwt-y-barcud La SA67 ..71 D1
Cyfyng Rd SA9 ....139 A5
Cygnet Cl SA2 ....165 E6
Cyncoed Cl SA2 ....165 C8
Cynghordy Sta SA20 ......26 B3
Cynon Cl SA6 ....161 A7
Cynwal Terr SA9 ....100 C5
Cypress Ave SA3 ....172 F8
Cyril Evans Way SA6 ....153 E4
Cysgod-y-Fro SA8 ....147 D7
Cysgod-y-graig SA16 ....137 D3
Cysgod Y Llan SA15 ......148 D6

D

Dafen Inn Row SA14 ....149 C7
Dafen Rd
Llanelli, Dafen SA14 ....149 B7
Llanelli SA14 ....149 A8
Dafen Row SA15 ....148 E2
Daffodil Dr 2 SA61 ....125 A7
Daisy Pk SA73 ....131 B3
Dale Cl SA5 ....159 A4
Dale Cty Prim Sch SA62 ..84 D1
Dale Fort Field Ctr*
SA62 ....101 F4
Dale Rd SA61 ....124 D3
Dana Dr SA2 ....166 C6
Dan Danino Way SA6 ....153 E4
Dandorlan Rd SA16 ......137 E4
Daniel James Com Sch
SA5 ....160 C7
Danian Pk SA2 ....137 A3
Danlan Rd SA14 ....137 A3
Dan Lan Rd SA16 ....108 F4
Dantwyn Rd SA4 ....143 E5
Danybanc SA15 ....148 D4
Dan-y-banc 4 SA15 ....129 A5
Danybanc Rd SA15 ......95 E2
Danybryn SA33 ....39 B2
Dan Y Bryn SA65 ....122 E3
Danybryn Rd SA4 ....151 A1
Dan-y-Coed Rd SA7 ....162 C8
Danycoed Sta SA33 ......58 B5
Danycwm SA14 ....148 F8
Dan Y Dderwen 2 SA2 ..59 B6
Danygraig Clydach SA6 ..154 C8
Cwm-twrch Isaf SA9 ....138 A2
Danygraig Prim Sch
SA1 ....168 A7
Danygraig Rd SA1 ....168 B7
Dan Y Graig Rd SA8 ....147 C2
Dan Y Lan SA14 ....140 F2
Dan-y-Parc SA6 ....153 E1
Danyrallt SA14 ....148 F8
Dan Yr Allt SA4 ....158 A5
Danyrhelyg SA38 ....119 B3
Dan-yr-ogof The National
Showcaves Ctr for Wales*
SA9 ....12 A8
D'arcy Bsns Ctr SA10 ..162 D5
Dark Gate 4 SA31 ......128 F5
Dark St 6 SA61 ....125 A5
Darran Cl SA10 ....155 F1
Darran Pk SA10 ....155 F1
Darren-las 3 SA14 ......96 F6
Darren Rd SA9 ....139 B6
Darren Terr SA8 ....147 B3
Dartford Dr SA1 ....161 A3
Dartford Pl SA1 ....161 A2
Dartford Rd SA1 ....161 A3
Dartmouth Gdns SA33 ..131 C3
Dartmouth St SA73 ......131 C3
David Issac Cl SA1 ......160 D3

David St
St Dogmaels / Llandudoch
SA43 ....118 B3
Swansea / Abertawe SA5 ..160 B2
David's Way / Ffordd Dafydd
SA14 ....97 D7
David Williams Terr
SA1 ....168 C7
Davies Rd SA8 ....147 F6
Davies Row SA5 ....160 D5
Davies Sq 3 SA15 ......148 E5
Davies's St SA39 ....39 B6
Davies St 2 SA6 ....161 A8
Davis St SA6 ....160 E5
Dawlish Cl SA3 ....172 E6
Dderi Rd SA8 ....100 B5
Ddol Rd SA2 ....165 B7
Dean's Cl 2 SA61 ....125 A3
De-Breos St SA2 ....166 F5
Deeley Rd SA9 ....139 B6
Deepford La SA63 ....69 D7
Dee Pl SA6 ....154 A4
Deepslade Cl SA3 ....171 A4
Deerland Rd SA62 ....87 D5
Deer Pk Cl SA62 ....86 B5
Deer Pk La SA71 ....105 B4
Deer Pk View SA71 ......112 A5
De-La-Beche Rd SA2 ....166 D6
De-La Beche St SA1 ....174 A3
Delabeche St / Ffordd
Delabeche 17 SA15 ....148 D4
De La Beche Terr SA6 ..153 F1
Delapoer Dr SA61 ....124 E4
Delfan
Swansea / Abertawe, Llangyfelach
SA6 ....153 C2
Swansea / Abertawe, Trallwn
SA7 ....161 F5
Delfryn Capel Hendre SA18 ..97 D6
Llanelli SA14 ....149 D6
Delhi St SA1 ....174 C3
Dell The Llanelli SA15 ..148 C8
Pontlliw SA4 ....151 F6
Denant Hill SA62 ....86 C7
Denbigh Cres SA6 ....154 B5
Denham Ave SA15 ......148 A7
Denver Rd SA5 ....159 B5
Derby La SA38 ....119 D5
Deri Cl / Heol Y Deri
SA18 ....98 F8
Derlin Pk / Parc Derlin
SA18 ....97 F5
Derlwyn SA2 ....165 D8
Derlwyn Cl SA14 ....77 F1
Derwen Cl SA5 ....158 D4
Derwendeg SA32 ....77 D3
Derwen Deg SA8 ....147 D6
Derwen Fawr SA18 ......79 B1
Derwen Fawr Rd SA2 ..166 B4
Derwen Fechan SA31 ..128 D6
Derwen Gdns SA33 ......119 D6
Derwenlas SA34 ....71 D6
Derwen Rd
Llannon SA14 ....96 D7
Pontardawe SA8 ....147 D2
Ystradgynlais SA9 ......138 F1
Derwent Ave SA73 ......131 F6
Derwent St SA15 ....148 C6
Derwlas SA4 ....152 B5
Derw Rd SA8 ....147 D3
Derwydd Ave SA18 ......99 D6
Devereaux Dr SA31 ....128 E6
Devon Dr SA71 ....133 C6
Devon Pl SA3 ....173 B4
Devonshire Dr
East Williamston SA69 ..134 A1
St Florence SA70 ....106 C5
Devonshire Rd SA72 ....132 D4
Devon Terr SA1 ....167 A7
Devon View SA1 ....166 B7
Dewing Ave SA70 ....113 D6
Dewi Terr SA1 ....160 A1
Dewsbury Ct SA1 ....174 B2
Dewsland St SA73 ......131 C3
Dew St SA61 ....125 A4
Diana Rd SA19 ....130 D6
Dickslade SA3 ....173 C4
Dillwyn Ct Pontlliw SA4 ..151 F6
Swansea / Abertawe SA2 ..166 C6
Dillwyn Rd SA2 ....166 C6
Dillwyn St Llanelli SA15 ..148 D4
Swansea / Abertawe SA1 ..174 A2
Dilwyn Cl SA4 ....151 F2
Dilwyn Rd SA4 ....151 F2
Dimond St SA72 ....132 C3
Dimpath Terr SA15 ......148 E7
Dinam Rd SA1 ....161 A3
Dinas Cty Prim Sch SA42 ..12 F3
Dinas Nature Reserve*
SA20 ....7 F1
Dinas St SA6 ....160 E5
DineFwr Pk (NT)* SA19 ..130 B5
Dingat Cl SA20 ....121 C4
Dingat View SA20 ......121 C4
Dingle La SA62 ....68 C4
Dock St SA4 ....157 C8
Dolafon SA14 ....149 E3
Dolau Bran SA20 ....121 A4
Dolaucothi Goldmines (NT)*
SA19 ....23 F3
Dolau Cl SA15 ....148 E2
Dolau Fach SA15 ....148 E3
Dolau Fan Rd SA16 ....137 F4
Dolau Fawr SA15 ....148 E3
Dolau Rd SA15 ....148 E3
Dolau Tywi SA19 ....63 A5
Dolawel SA9 ....100 C7

Dolecoed Rd LD5 ....9 C1
Dolgoy Cl SA3 ....173 A7
Dolgwili Rd
Abergwili SA33 ....59 A1
Carmarthen / Caerfyrddin
SA31 ....129 C7
Dolphin Ct SA73 ....132 C5
Dolwar Fach SA14 ......149 C5
Dolwedd Llanelli SA14 ..148 F8
Llangeler SA38 ....18 C3
Y Ferwig SA43 ....3 E4
Dol Y Brenin / Kings Mead
SA48 ....120 C4
Dol-y-Coed SA2 ....165 B8
Dolycoed Ave SA16 ....137 E3
Dol-y-dderwen SA33 ....75 B2
Dol Yr Onnen SA21 ......128 D4
Donovan Reed Gdns
SA72 ....132 D3
Douglas Ct SA3 ....172 A5
Douglas James Cl SA61 ..124 D5
Douglas James Way
SA61 ....124 D5
Dove Rd SA5 ....159 E7
Downing St SA15 ....148 C4
Down Leaze SA2 ....159 D1
Downs Cl SA5 ....159 E3
Down St SA6 ....154 E7
Down The SA3 ....117 C8
Dragon Auto Ctr SA7 ..161 B7
Dredgman Hill SA61 ....124 E2
Drefach Rd SA14 ....73 E8
Dreflan SA7 ....138 F4
Dreonen 5 SA15 ....96 B6
Driftwood Cl SA62 ......85 D8
Dring St SA1 ....174 C4
Drive The
Pontardawe SA8 ....147 C3
Southgate SA3 ....171 A4
Drovers Rd SA48 ....120 C4
Druce St SA15 ....148 C3
Druids Cl SA3 ....173 A6
Druidstone Way SA4 ..152 B2
Drumau Cl SA10 ....162 F8
Drumau Pk SA10 ....162 F8
Drumau Rd
Birchgrove SA7 ....155 B1
Neath / Castell-Nedd SA7,
SA10 ....162 D8
Druslyn Rd SA3 ....172 F7
Dryslwyn Cl SA4 ....152 B2
Duffryn Rd SA4 ....151 B1
Dukefield SA4 ....164 E8
Duke St SA1 ....167 B6
Dulais Gr SA2 ....166 A5
Dulais Rd SA4 ....143 C4
Dumbarton House Ct 4
SA1 ....167 A6
Dumfries Pl SA9 ....139 E7
Duncan St SA33 ....92 F5
Dunns Cl SA33 ....173 B5
Dunns La SA33 ....173 B5
Dunns Terr SA1 ....173 B5
Dunraven Cl SA4 ....156 E4
Dunraven Rd SA2 ......166 B7
Dunsany Pk SA61 ......125 B5
Dunster Cl SA3 ....172 E6
Dunston La SA62 ....67 B5
Dunvant Jun & Inf Sch
SA2 ....165 E8
Dunvant Pl SA1 ....174 A1
Dunvant Rd Dunvant SA2 ..165 D8
Three Crosses SA2, SA4 ..158 A1
Dunvant Sq SA2 ....165 C8
Dupre Rd SA1 ....167 F8
Dwyfor SA14 ....149 D5
Dwynant
Burry Port SA16 ....137 C3
Llangyndeyrn SA15 ......95 D3
Dyfatty St SA1 ....174 B4
Dyfed Ave SA1 ....167 A8
Dyfed Cl
2 Carmarthen / Caerfyrddin
SA31 ....128 C2
Swansea / Abertawe SA1 ..166 F8
Dyfed Coll of Art / Coleg Celf
Dyfed SA31 ....128 C3
Dyfed Pembrey Ski Slope
SA16 ....108 D3
Dyfed Shires & Leisure
Farm* SA41 ....34 A8
Dyfryn SA2 ....165 B8
Dyffryn-Aur Rd SA7 ....161 E6
Dyffryn Cl SA6 ....161 A8
Dyffryn Rd
Pontardawe SA8 ....147 F4
Saron SA18 ....97 F7
Dyffryn Rd / Hoel Y Dyffryn
SA18 ....98 A7
Dylan SA14 ....149 D5
Dylan Cl SA1 ....167 F8
Dylan Rd SA2 ....165 F7
Dylan's Wlk SA33 ....92 F5
Dylan Thomas Com Sch
SA2 ....159 D2
Dylan Thomas Sq SA1 ..174 B2
Dylan Thomas Theatre*
SA1 ....174 B2
Dynevor Ave 3 SA19 ..130 D6
Dynevor Cl SA10 ....162 F8
Dynevor Pl
Neath / Castell-Nedd
SA10 ....162 D7
Swansea / Abertawe SA1 ..174 A3
Dynevor Rd SA10 ......162 F8
Dynevor Rd / Heol Dinefwr
SA18 ....99 B7
Dynevor Terr SA8 ......147 E5

Dyrus Rd SA6 ....160 E5
Dysgwylfa SA2 ....166 C6
Dyson Cl SA6 ....146 D1
Dythel Pk SA15 ....109 D6

E

Eagles Pl SA5 ....159 E6
Earl St SA1 ....160 D1
East Bank Rd SA71 ....133 C4
East Bank Way / Ffordd Glan
Y Dwyrain SA1 ....174 C3
Eastbourne Gr SA2 ....166 C7
East Burrows Rd SA1 ..174 C2
East Cliff SA3 ....171 B3
East Crossways SA8 ..147 D6
Easterfield Dr SA3 ......171 A4
Eastern Ave SA72 ......132 E3
Eastern La SA70 ....106 A3
Eastfield Cl SA1 ....159 E2
East La SA72 ....104 F6
Eastland Cl SA3 ....172 E7
Eastlands Pk SA3 ......172 E7
Eastleigh Dr SA73 ......131 D3
Eastmoor Park Cres
SA3 ....172 E7
East Perimeter Rd SA73 ..103 E7
East St SA42 ....13 E4
Eaton Cres SA1 ....167 A6
Eaton Ct SA5 ....160 D3
Eaton Rd SA1 ....160 C3
Ebenezer St
Newcastle Emlyn / Castell
Newydd Emlyn SA38 ..119 D4
Swansea / Abertawe SA1 ..174 B4
Ebens La 6 SA43 ......118 D4
Ebenzer Row SA61 ....125 A5
Eden Ave SA2 ....166 F7
Edgar Morgan Way
SA72 ....132 A3
Edge Gr SA62 ....28 F3
Edgemoor Cl SA2 ......165 B5
Edgemoor Dr SA2 ......165 B6
Edgeware Rd SA2 ......166 E7
Edison Cres SA6 ....146 D1
Edward St
Milford Haven / Aberdaugleddau
SA73 ....131 C3
9 Tenby / Dinbych-y-pysgod
SA70 ....135 E4
Eglwys Ger Yr SA33 ....93 E5
Eglwyswrw CP Sch / Ysgol
Gymunedol Eglwyswrw
SA41 ....15 B1
Egypt Ctr Mus* SA2 ..166 E5
Eiddil SA14 ....149 D6
Eiddwen Rd SA2 ....160 B4
Eigen Cres SA1 ....167 B8
Eighth Ave SA6 ....153 D5
Eileen Rd SA7 ....161 F7
Einon Ct SA4 ....151 D2
Elan Ave SA6 ....153 D1
Elba Cres SA1 ....169 C4
Elba St SA4 ....158 C6
Elder Gr SA31 ....129 B3
Elfed Rd SA1 ....167 B8
Elgin Rd SA15 ....109 A4
Elgin St SA5 ....160 B3
Elim Rd SA31 ....128 D7
Eliot Cl SA2 ....165 F8
Elizabeth Cl SA4 ......154 B4
Elizabeth Ct SA72 ....132 C1
Elkington Pk SA16 ....137 D3
Elkington Rd SA16 ....137 E3
Ellen's Rd SA10 ....162 D8
Ellis Ave SA6 ....125 A4
Elm Cl SA34 ....158 D4
Elm Cres SA4 ....152 C2
Elm Ct SA44 ....151 A3
Elm Gr Gorseinon SA4 ..151 A3
Neyland SA73 ....132 B8
Pembroke / Penfro SA71 ..133 C5
Elmgrove Rd SA13 ......172 F8
Elm Gr Rd SA17 ....136 C4
Elmhurst Cres SA1 ....174 C4
Elm La SA73 ....131 E4
Elm Pk SA62 ....68 B5
Elphin Cl SA1 ....159 E1
Elphin Gdns SA1 ......159 F1
Elphin Rd SA1 ....159 F1
Elwy Cres SA2 ....159 F1
Elwy Gdns SA2 ....159 F1
Embankment Rd SA15 ..148 F2
Emlyn Gdns SA1 ....160 B1
Emlyn Rd SA1 ....160 B1
Emlyn Sq 2 SA38 ......119 D4
Emlyn Terr SA1 ....160 E6
Emmanuel Gdns SA2 ..166 B3
Emma St / Stryd Emma 13
SA15 ....148 D4
Enfield Cl SA4 ....153 E4
Enid Ave SA6 ....153 F8
Enpynt Rd SA5 ....160 A4
Ermigate La SA71 ......111 A4
Ernald Pl SA2 ....166 F6
Erw Haf 1 LD5 ....9 D1
Erw Hydref SA9 ....139 B6
Erwlas SA14 ....149 D3
Erw Las
Fishguard & Goodwick
SA65 ....122 C4
Llannon SA14 ....96 F3
Erw Lon SA62 ....49 B2
Erw Non SA14 ....96 E2
Erw Rd SA15 ....148 C5
Erw Terr SA16 ....137 E4

Erw-wen SA37 ....34 F7
Espalone SA3 ....172 C6
Esplanade
Carmarthen / Caerfyrddin
SA31 ....129 A5
Tenby / Dinbych-y-pysgod
SA70 ....135 E4
Essex Rd SA72 ....132 D4
Essex Terr SA6 ....160 E6
E St SA71 ....103 C6
Esther's La 1 SA62 ....87 E4
Estuary Pk SA14 ....150 C7
Evans Terr SA1 ....174 A4
Evans' Terr SA15 ......148 F6
Eva Terr SA17 ....93 F5
Evelyn Rd SA10 ....162 E7
Eversley Rd SA2 ....166 D6
Ewart Pl SA5 ....160 C4
Ewenny Pl SA6 ....160 D8
Exchange Row SA14 ..149 C7
Exeter Rd SA73 ....131 F5
Eynon St SA4 ....151 D2

F

Fabian Way SA1, SA10 ..168 C7
Factory Rd Clydach SA6 ..154 D7
Pembrey & Bury Port Town
SA16 ....108 E3
Fagwr Isaf SA6 ....146 B2
Fagwr Pl SA6 ....154 A1
Fagwr Rd SA6 ....146 B2
Fairbush Cl SA62 ....68 C5
Fairfield Terr SA1 ......167 B7
Fairhaven Ct SA3 ......173 A3
Fair La SA31 ....128 F5
Fair Oakes SA61 ......124 E2
Fairsea Cl SA73 ....102 F8
Fair View SA62 ....86 E5
Fair View Cl SA7 ......161 F6
Fairview Rd SA5 ....153 C2
Fairway SA72 ....132 B1
Fairway Dr SA8 ....147 D6
Fairwood Hospl / Ysbyty
Fairwood SA2 ....165 A4
Fairwood La SA2 ......165 B5
Fairwood Rd
Dunvant SA2 ....165 C8
The Mumbles / Y Mwmbwls
SA3 ....173 A8
Fairwood Terr SA4 ....158 C6
Fairy Gr SA2 ....165 E7
Falcon Chambers 4
SA15 ....148 D4
Falcondale Dr SA48 ..120 A4
Falcon Pl SA5 ....159 E7
Falcon Rd SA61 ....124 E5
Fan Rd The SA69 ......134 C5
Faraday Rd SA6 ....146 E1
Farmers Row SA14 ....140 F1
Farm Rd SA8 ....147 B1
Faull St SA4 ....153 E1
Feidr Bentick SA42 ....13 E4
Feidr Brenin SA42 ......13 D4
Feidr Castell SA65 ....122 C2
Feidr Cefn SA65 ....12 E3
Feidr Chwech-erw
SA62 ....123 B6
Feidr Dwyli SA42 ......123 C5
Feidr Dylan SA65 ......122 C5
Feidr Fach 2 SA42 ......13 A4
Feidr Fain SA62 ....51 D6
Feidrfair SA43 ....118 D4
Feidr Fawr
Dinas Cross SA42 ......13 A4
St Dogmaels / Llandudoch
SA43 ....118 A3
Feidr Felin 1 SA42 ......13 E4
Feidr Fraich SA65 ......122 C2
Feidr Ganol SA42 ......13 D4
Feidr Gongol 6 SA65 ..122 D3
Feidr Henffordd SA43 ..118 F5
Feidr-iet SA66 ....53 A1
Feidr Las SA62 ....48 B5
Feidr Pant-y-bryn
SA62 ....122 C2
Feidr Pen-y-bont SA42 ..13 F4
Feidr Pont Eglwys SA64 ..11 D2
Feidr Treginnis SA62 ..123 A4
Feidr Y Foel 1 SA41 ....34 E4
Feilin Cl SA62 ....100 C6
Felinfoel Jun & Inf Sch
SA14 ....149 A8
Felinfoel Rd SA15 ......148 E7
Felin Fran SA7 ....154 E2
Fendrod Bsns Pk SA6 ..161 A6
Fendrod Way SA7 ......161 C7
Fenton CP Sch SA61 ..124 E4
Fenton Trad Est SA61 ..124 F4
Fermoy Ct SA5 ....159 F6
Fern Ct SA5 ....160 A5
Ferndale Dr SA4 ....157 D8
Fernhill Cl SA2 ....166 B1
Fernhill Rd SA4 ....151 A3
Fern Hill Rd SA61 ......125 A2
Fern Rise SA73 ....132 B7
Fern St SA5 ....160 B2
Ferrara Sq SA1 ....174 B2
Fern St SA31 ....128 E5
Ferryboat Cl SA6 ......161 A7
Ferry La SA72 ....133 A8
Ferry Rd
Kidwelly / Cydweli SA17 ..136 B5
Loughor SA4 ....150 C1

Ferry Rd *continued*
Pembroke Dock / Doc Penfro
SA72 . . . . .132 B1
Ferry Side SA1 . . . . .174 C2
Ferryside Sta SA17 . . . . . . .93 F5
Ferryside VCP Sch SA17 . .93 F5
Ferry Terr SA1 . . . . .125 A1
Ferry Way SA61 . . . . .13 A3
Ffairfach Sta SA19 . . . . . .130 D3
Farmers Prim Sch SA19 . . .23 D7
Fferws Rd SA18 . . . . .97 F6
Ffinant Sq 3 SA38 . . . . . .119 D4

Ffordd = road, way

Ffordd Abercastell SA62 . . .29 B5
Ffordd Abiah SA43 . . . . . .154 E8
Ffordd Afon 4 SA62 . . . . .29 B5
Ffordd Alltwen SA4 . . . . . .158 A5
Ffordd Aneurin SA15 . . . . .96 A6
Ffordd Aneurin Bevan
SA2 . . . . .166 C8
Ffordd Beck SA4 . . . . .158 B6
Ffordd Bedd Morris
Cwm Gwaun SA65 . . . . . . .32 C6
Newport / Trefdraeth SA42 . .13 D2
Ffordd Bishop / Bishop Rd
SA18 . . . . .98 B6
Ffordd Briallu SA7 . . . . . .161 D6
Ffordd Bryngwyn SA4 . . . .158 A5
Ffordd Brynheulog SA8 . .147 D5
Ffordd Butler SA4 . . . . . . .158 B6
Ffordd Cae Duke SA4 . . . .158 A8
Ffordd Caerfai SA62 . . . . .123 D4
Ffordd Cilgwyn SA62 . . . . .13 F3
Ffordd Cumbrian Way 4
SA31 . . . . .128 C4
**Ffordd Cwmaman /
Cwmamman Rd** SA18 . . .99 B8
Ffordd Cwm Tawe
Swansea / Abertawe SA7 . .160 F6
Ynysforgan SA6, SA7 . . . . .154 D5
Ffordd Cynghordy SA7 . . .161 D7
Ffordd Cynore SA5 . . . . . .159 C6
Ffordd Dafydd / David's Way
SA14 . . . . .97 D7
Ffordd Dawel SA7 . . . . . . .161 E6
**Ffordd Delabeche /
Delabeche St 12** SA15 .148 D4
Ffordd Dewi SA6 . . . . .153 B1
Ffordd Dillwyn-Llewellyn
SA4 . . . . .152 D2
Ffordd Draenen Ddu
SA3 . . . . .172 E6
Ffordd Dryden SA2 . . . . . .165 E8
Ffordd Eira SA4 . . . . .151 C2
Ffordd Ellen SA6 . . . . .146 B2
Ffordd Emlyn SA9 . . . . . . .139 B5
**Ffordd Florence / Florence
Rd 1** SA18 . . . . .98 B7
Ffordd Ger-y-Llwyn
SA4 . . . . .152 C4
Ffordd Glandwr SA9 . . . . .139 B6
**Ffordd Glan y Dwyrain / East
Bank Way** SA1 . . . . . . .174 C3
Ffordd Gwyn SA7 . . . . . . .161 D7
**Ffordd Is-Cennen / Iscennen
Rd 14** SA18 . . . . .98 B7
Ffordd Kilby SA4 . . . . .158 A8
Ffordd Lundain SA4 . . . . .161 B6
Ffordd Llyffant SA7 . . . . .162 B8
**Ffordd Maescwarrau /
Maesquarre Rd** SA18 . . .98 D6
Ffordd Melyn Mair SA7 . .161 D6
Ffordd Parc Ynysderw
SA8 . . . . .147 E4
**Ffordd Pen Twyn / Pentwyn
Rd** SA18 . . . . .98 C7
Ffordd Porth Clais
SA62 . . . . .123 A3
Ffordd Scott
Birchgrove SA7 . . . . .154 F1
Swansea / Abertawe SA2 . .162 A8
Ffordd Silkin SA8 . . . . . . .147 E5
**Ffordd Stewart / Stewart Dr
12** SA18 . . . . .98 B7
Ffordd Talbot / Talbot Rd 16
SA18 . . . . .98 B7
Ffordd Talfan SA4 . . . . . . .158 D8
Ffordd Taliesin SA2 . . . . .165 F8
Ffordd Tollborth SA7 . . . .161 D7
Ffordd Tyn-y-Coed
SA6 . . . . .155 A8
Ffordd Villers / Villers Rd
SA18 . . . . .98 B6
Ffordd Walter / Walter Rd 9
SA18 . . . . .98 C7
**Ffordd Waun Gron / Waun
Gron Rd** SA18 . . . . .98 D6
Ffordd-y-Betws / Betws Rd
SA18 . . . . .98 C6
Ffordd Y Blodau SA18 . . . .79 B1
Ffordd-y-blodau SA43 . . . .3 E3
Ffordd Y Brain SA9 . . . . . .159 F5
**Ffordd Y Brennin / Kingsway
The** SA1 . . . . .174 A3
Ffordd-y-Bryn
Birchgrove SA7 . . . . .155 B1
Swansea / Abertawe SA7 . .162 B8
Ffordd Y Cwm SA43 . . . . .118 A3
**Ffordd-y-Cyrnol / Colonel
Rd** SA18 . . . . .98 C6
**Ffordd Y Faenor / Manor Rd
15** SA18 . . . . .98 B7
Ffordd Y Felin / Mill Terr
SA18 . . . . .98 A5

**Foundry Row
3** Ammanford / Rhydaman
SA18 . . . . .98 C7
Neath / Castell-Nedd
SA10 . . . . .162 B8
Fountain Hall Terr SA31 . .128 E5
Fountain Rd SA14 . . . . .96 F3
Fountain Row 2 SA61 . . . .124 F4
Fourth Ave SA6 . . . . .153 D1
Fourth St SA71 . . . . .103 C6
Fourwinds La SA70 . . . . . .135 B3
Fox Gr SA5 . . . . .158 B8
Foxgrove SA4 . . . . .158 B8
Foxhole Dr SA3 . . . . .171 A4
Foxhole Rd SA1 . . . . .174 C4
Foyer The 1 SA1 . . . . . . .174 B3
Frampton Ct SA4 . . . . . . .150 F2
Frampton Rd SA4 . . . . . . .151 A3
Frances Rd SA69 . . . . .134 F4
Francis Rd SA6 . . . . .153 E1
Francis St
Milford Haven / Aberdaugleddau
SA73 . . . . .131 D2
Neath / Castell-Nedd SA10 .162 F7
Pontardawe SA8 . . . . .147 E4
Swansea / Abertawe SA1 . .167 A5
Francis Terr SA15 . . . . . . .128 F5
Fransham St 2 SA15 . . . .148 E6
Frederick St SA7 . . . . .161 F7
**Frederick St
8** Llanelli SA15 . . . . .148 D5
Neyland SA73 . . . . .132 B6
Swansea / Abertawe SA2 . .160 C3
Freeman St SA5 . . . . .160 C4
Freemans Way SA61 . . . . .125 A3
Freemans Wlk SA71 . . . . .133 D4
French Wlk SA5 . . . . .122 C5
Freshwater E Rd SA71 . . . .105 A2
Friars Pk SA31 . . . . .128 E4
Friars The 10 SA61 . . . . . .125 A5
Froglane SA33 . . . . .114 E4
Frogmore Ave SA2 . . . . . .166 D6
Frogmore Gdns SA33 . . . . .92 F5
Frogmore St SA33 . . . . . . .92 F5
Frondeg Terr SA15 . . . . . .148 F6
Fronhaul SA14 . . . . .141 B3
Fron Hill SA34 . . . . .71 D4
Fron Terr SA15 . . . . .148 E3
Front St
Pembroke Dock / Doc Penfro
SA72 . . . . .132 B3
Rosemarket SA73 . . . . .87 A3
F St SA71 . . . . .103 C6
Fulke St SA73 . . . . .131 D2
Fullers Row SA1 . . . . .174 A3
Fuller St SA8 . . . . .147 E5
Fulmar Cl SA3 . . . . .172 E7
Furnace Bank SA31 . . . . . .129 B6
Furnace Prim Sch SA15 . .148 B7
Furnace Rd
Burry Port SA16 . . . . .137 C2
Carmarthen / Caerfyrddin
SA31 . . . . .128 E5
Furnace Terr 3 SA15 . . . .96 B6
Furze Cres SA4 . . . . .153 D2
Furzeland Dr SA2 . . . . . . .166 B6
Furzy Bank SA31 . . . . . . .132 C1
Furzy Pk SA61 . . . . .124 D4
Fynnon Caeconna SA5 . . .159 E6

G

Gabalfa Rd SA2 . . . . .166 B5
Gables The SA4 . . . . .164 E8
Gaddarn Reach SA73 . . . . .73 D4
Gail Rise SA62 . . . . .87 D4
Gail The SA62 . . . . .87 D4
Gainer Way SA70 . . . . . . .105 E1
Gainsborough Cl SA2 . . . .166 E6
Gardde SA14 . . . . .149 E4
**Gardd Fotaneg Genedlaethol
Cymru / The National
Botanic Gdn of Wales***
SA32 . . . . .77 D5
Garden Cres SA4 . . . . .158 D8
Garden La SA20 . . . . .121 D4
Garden St SA1 . . . . .174 A2
Gardens The SA9 . . . . .139 B6
Garfield Gdns SA67 . . . . . .70 D1
Garnant Prim Sch SA18 . . .99 B8
Garnfoel SA14 . . . . .97 D7
Garngoch Hospl SA4 . . . . .158 F7
Garngoch Ind Est SA4 . . .151 E1
Garngoch Terr SA4 . . . . . .158 D8
Garn Ingli SA65 . . . . .122 D3
Garnlwyd Cl SA6 . . . . .160 C7
Garnon's Mill Rd SA31 . . . .16 B5
Garnswllt Rd SA4 . . . . .97 F1
Garn Wnda 1 SA65 . . . . .122 D3
Garode Fields SA33 . . . . .127 D4
Garreg Hollt SA14 . . . . . . .97 A8
Garreglwyd SA14 . . . . . . .108 F4
Garrod Ave SA2 . . . . .158 C2
Garth Gr Glais SA7 . . . . . .154 F6
Gwaun-Cae-Gurwen SA18 . .99 E6
Ynystawe SA6 . . . . .154 D6
Garth The SA72 . . . . .104 F6
Garth View SA6 . . . . .154 B4
Gas La SA70 . . . . .135 C4
Gatehoim Ave SA3 . . . . . .131 E4
Gate Rd
Llanfihangel Aberbythych
SA14 . . . . .78 C1
Penygroes SA14 . . . . .97 D8
Gathen Terr 11 SA15 . . . .148 D4
Gay La SA62 . . . . .84 C3

Gay's La SA72 . . . . .132 B1
Geiriol Gdns SA1 . . . . .159 E1
Geiriol Rd SA1 . . . . .159 F1
Gelert St SA1 . . . . .160 C5
Gelli Aur SA33 . . . . .58 E3
Gelli Aur / Golden Gr
SA5 . . . . .160 D6
Gellideg SA8 . . . . .147 D6
Gelli Deg
Llandovery / Llanymddyfri
SA20 . . . . .121 E4
Llanelli SA14 . . . . .149 A6
Gelliderw SA4 . . . . .147 D6
Gellifach Cres SA6 . . . . . .160 D7
Gellifawr Rd SA6 . . . . .160 D7
Gelli Gdns SA7 . . . . .162 B8
Gelliglas Rd SA6 . . . . .160 D7
Gelligron Rd SA8 . . . . . . .147 D6
Gelligwyn Rd SA6 . . . . . . .160 D7
Gelli-Gynore SA4 . . . . . . .151 F2
Gelli Hill SA66 . . . . .70 A6
Gellihyll Rd SA4 . . . . .151 F2
Gelli La SA18 . . . . .98 A5
Gellionen Rd
Clydach SA6, SA8 . . . . . . .146 F2
Pontardawe SA8 . . . . .147 B5
Gelli-Onn SA15 . . . . .148 D6
Gellionen Cl SA6 . . . . .146 E8
Gelli Rd SA14 . . . . .149 D6
Gelli St SA1 . . . . .167 B3
Gelliswick Rd SA73 . . . . . .131 A3
Gelliwen SA43 . . . . .114 E2
Gelliwriddon SA18 . . . . . . .98 A6
Gellyceiros Trad Est
SA32 . . . . .75 F3
Gelly Rd SA14 . . . . .79 A1
Gendros Ave E SA5 . . . . .160 A3
Gendros Ave W SA5 . . . . .159 F4
Gendros Cl SA5 . . . . .160 A3
Gendros Cres SA5 . . . . . .160 A3
Gendros Dr SA5 . . . . .159 F3
Gendros Prim Sch SA5 . . .159 F3
Genwen Rd SA14 . . . . . . .149 F4
George Bank SA3 . . . . . . .173 C4
George Hill 3 SA19 . . . . .130 D5
George Manning Way
SA4 . . . . .158 B4
George St
Llandeilo SA19 . . . . .130 D5
Llanelli SA15 . . . . .148 D2
Milford Haven / Aberdaugleddau
SA73 . . . . .131 C3
Neyland SA73 . . . . .132 B7
Pontardawe SA8 . . . . .147 E5
Swansea / Abertawe SA1 . .167 B6
Geotre Bellaf Rd SA2 . . . .165 C7
Gerald Rd SA61 . . . . .124 E5
Gerald St SA1 . . . . .160 D2
Gerddi Alexander SA1 . . .160 A4
Gerddi Brenhinol SA14 . . .149 B6
Gerddi Mair SA33 . . . . . . .127 D3
Gerretts Cl SA3 . . . . .172 A5
Ger-y-Capel SA33 . . . . . . .75 B3
Ger-y-Castell SA17 . . . . . .136 C4
Ger Y Coed SA15 . . . . . . .109 E4
Ger-y-Coed SA5 . . . . .95 F2
Ger Y Duad SA33 . . . . .58 A6
Ger-y-Ffrwd SA7 . . . . . . .161 D7
Ger-y-Gwendraeth
SA17 . . . . .136 C4
Ger Y Llan SA43 . . . . .16 A6
Ger-y-Llan SA32 . . . . .77 E7
Ger Y Llan Llanelli SA15 . .148 D4
Manordeilo & Salem SA19 . .62 E4
Ger-y-Maes SA14 . . . . . . .149 D5
Gerymanwydd 13 SA18 . . .98 C7
Ger Y Marbell 1 SA43 . . . .93 C7
Ger Y Mor SA15 . . . . .148 C3
Ger Y Nant
Carmarthen / Caerfyrddin
SA31 . . . . .129 B4
Llangennech SA14 . . . . . . .149 A8
Ger-y-Nant SA33 . . . . .73 E8
Ger Y Pant SA4 . . . . .143 D4
Ger-y-Parc SA6 . . . . .153 E1
Ger Yr Afon SA9 . . . . .138 A1
Ger Yr Afon SA18 . . . . .99 A8
Ger-yr-Afon SA9 . . . . .99 D6
Ger-y-Eglwys SA4 . . . . . .143 B4
Gethin Cl SA5 . . . . .160 A3
Gethin St SA1 . . . . .160 B2
Gibbas Way SA71 . . . . . . .133 E4
Gilbert Cres SA15 . . . . . . .148 D3
Gilbert Rd SA15 . . . . .148 D6
Gilbertscliffe SA3 . . . . . . .172 F4
Gilfach SA43 . . . . .152 A2
Gilfach Hill SA67 . . . . .71 C1
Gilfach Rd
Cwm-twrch Uchaf SA9 . . . .100 C6
Lampeter Velfrey SA67 . . . .71 C1
Gilgal Terr SA72 . . . . .104 A5
Gilsea Bsns Pk SA6 . . . . .161 A5
Giltar Terr SA70 . . . . .135 B2
Giltar Way SA70 . . . . .135 A1
Gilton La SA62 . . . . .85 E8
Glade The SA3 . . . . .172 F8
Glais Prim Sch SA7 . . . . .155 A6
Glais Rd SA7 . . . . .147 D1
Glamorgan St SA1 . . . . . .174 A2
Glan Aber SA16 . . . . .137 D4
Glanamman Cty Prim Sch
SA18 . . . . .99 A8
Glanamman Workshops 1
SA18 . . . . .99 A8
Glanarberth SA43 . . . . .16 C6
Glanbran Rd SA7 . . . . . . .162 A8
Glanbrydan Ave SA2 . . . .166 F6
Glan Cleddau Sch SA61 . .124 F3

Glandafen Rd SA15 . . . . . .148 A3
Glan Dulais SA2 . . . . .165 C7
Glandulas Terr SA48 . . . . .120 D5
Glandwr Cres SA1 . . . . . . .160 D4
Glanffrwd Rd SA4 . . . . . . .143 D4
Glan-ffynnon SA31 . . . . . .129 B3
Glangleddau SA62 . . . . . . .51 A5
Glanhafan SA62 . . . . .48 C3
Glan Hafan 2 SA62 . . . . . .87 E4
Glan Llwyd SA4 . . . . .143 C6
Glanllyn Rd SA7 . . . . .155 A5
Glanmor Cres SA2 . . . . . .166 F7
Glanmor Ct SA2 . . . . .166 F7
Glanmorfa SA4 . . . . .158 B5
Glan Morfa SA17 . . . . .94 A5
Glanmor Mews SA2 . . . . .166 F7
Glanmor Park Rd SA2 . . . .166 F7
Glanmor Pl 3 SA15 . . . . .148 C4
Glanmor Rd Llanelli SA15 .148 C4
Llanelli, Wern SA15 . . . . . .148 D4
Swansea / Abertawe SA2 . .166 F7
Glanmor Terr
2 Llanelli SA15 . . . . .148 C4
Pen-clawdd SA4 . . . . .156 E4
Glan Nant SA43 . . . . .16 C7
Glannant Rd
Carmarthen / Caerfyrddin
SA31 . . . . .128 E5
Pontarddulais SA4 . . . . . . .143 E5
Glannant Terr SA4 . . . . . .143 E5
Glanrhyd Prim Sch SA9 . .139 D6
Glan-Rhyd Rd
Pontardawe SA8 . . . . .147 D5
Ystradgynlais SA9 . . . . . . .139 F7
Glanrhyd Terr SA4 . . . . . .139 F7
Glan Tawe SA4 . . . . .158 C8
Glan Tawelan SA31 . . . . . .128 C4
Glantawe Pk SA9 . . . . . . .139 D7
Glantawe Row SA9 . . . . . .139 F8
**Glantawe St
2** Morriston / Treforris
SA6 . . . . .154 A1
Swansea / Abertawe SA4 . .160 A1
Glantowy SA31 . . . . .129 B7
Glantwrch SA9 . . . . .139 C7
Glan Tywi SA17 . . . . .94 A5
Glanwern SA16 . . . . .97 D8
Glan-y-Gors SA14 . . . . . . .97 D8
Glan Y Lli SA4 . . . . .157 A4
Glan-y-Mor SA3 . . . . .93 E5
Glan-y-Mor Comp Sch
SA16 . . . . .137 D3
Glanymor La SA4 . . . . . . .150 E1
Glanymor Park Dr SA4 . . .150 D1
Glanymor Rd
SA4 . . . . .150 E1
Glan-y-Mor Terr SA16 . . .137 C2
Glan yr Afon
Ammanford / Rhydaman
SA18 . . . . .98 B8
Llanelli SA15 . . . . .148 F8
Glanyrafon Cl SA4 . . . . . .152 B2
Glan-yr-Afon Gdns SA2 . .166 C6
Glanyrafon Rd SA4 . . . . . .143 D4
Glan Yr Afon Rd SA2 . . . .166 C7
Glan Yr Avon
Pantyffynnon SA18 . . . . . .139 A5
Ystalyfera SA9 . . . . .139 C5
Glan-yr-Ysgol SA9 . . . . . .139 A5
Glan-yr-Ystrad
Carmarthen / Caerfyrddin
SA31 . . . . .128 C2
Ferryside SA17 . . . . .94 C5
Glan-y-Wern Rd SA7 . . . . .161 E7
Glasbrook Pl SA5 . . . . . . .159 E5
Glasbury Rd SA6 . . . . .160 D7
Glascoed SA14 . . . . .109 E4
Glasdir SA43 . . . . .3 F3
Glasfryn Llanelli SA14 . . . .149 A7
St Clears / Sanclêr
SA33 . . . . .127 E6
Glasfryn Cl SA2 . . . . .159 E2
Glasfryn Rd
Pontarddulais SA4 . . . . . . .143 C3
St David's & the Cathedral Close
SA62 . . . . .123 D4
Glasfryn Terr SA15 . . . . . .148 E5
Glaslyn Pl SA6 . . . . .153 D1
Glasplant Terr SA38 . . . . .119 F4
Glebe La SA62 . . . . .84 C3
**Glebelands
5** Milford Haven / Aberdaugleddau
SA73 . . . . .131 A3
Glebe Rd SA4 . . . . .150 F7
Glebe The
Bishopston SA3 . . . . .172 A7
Tenby / Dinbych-y-pysgod
SA70 . . . . .135 D6
Glenalla Rd SA15 . . . . . . .148 E5
Glenfield Cl SA2 . . . . .166 A6
Glenfield Pk SA73 . . . . . . .132 F6
Glenfields Rd SA61 . . . . . .124 E2
Glengower Cl SA43 . . . . . .173 A5
Glenover Pk SA61 . . . . . . .124 D3
Glen Owen Hill SA73 . . . . .87 A1
Glen Rd
Laugharne Township SA33 . .92 F6
The Mumbles / Y Mwmbwls
SA3 . . . . .172 F6
Glenroy Ave SA1 . . . . .174 C4
Glenside Rd SA5 . . . . .159 E6
Glen The SA69 . . . . .134 F2

Glen View
Haverfordwest / Hwlffordd
SA61 ....124 E2
Tenby / Dinbych-y-pysgod
SA70 ....135 C6
Glenview Ave SA72 ....132 D3
Glenville Rd SA3 ....173 A6
Glievering St SA15 .....148 E5
Glien Rd SA31 ....128 B3
Globe Row SA14 ....149 B8
Globe St ■ SA14 ....161 A8
Gloster Row ■ SA43 ...118 D3
Gloucester Pl
Swansea / Abertawe SA1 .174 C2
The Mumbles / Y Mwmbwls
SA3 ....173 B4
Gloucester Way SA72 ..132 D3
Glyn-coch Studios* 73 A4
SA33 ....73 A4
Glyncoed Terr SA15 ....149 A5
Glyncollen Cres SA4 ...154 A3
Glyncollen Dr SA6 .....154 A3
Glyncollen Prim Sch
SA6 ....154 A4
Glyn Cres SA3 ....166 C2
Glyncnwal Rd SA9 .....100 C6
Glynderi SA31 ....129 B7
Glyn Deri SA18 ....98 F8
Glynderwen Cl SA2 ....166 B3
Glynderwen Cres SA2 ..166 B3
Glynderwen Rd SA14 ..149 D4
Glyndwr Pl SA1 ....167 A8
Glyn Hirnant SA6 ......154 A3
Glynhir Rd
Llandybie SA18 ....79 C1
Pontarddulais SA4 .....143 C4
Glyn-Llwchwr Rd SA4 ..143 C4
Glyn-Moelrt Rd SA4 ...147 C3
Glyn Moch Cotts SA18 .98 F8
Glynn Vivian Art Gall
SA1 ....174 A3
Glyn Rd / Heol Glyn
SA18 ....99 D8
Glyn Rhosyn SA4 ......151 B1
Glyn St SA1 ....160 D2
Glynteg Rd SA4 ....143 D5
Glyn-y-Mel Rd SA65 ...122 E4
Glyn Y Swistir SA14 ...140 F3
Gnoll Rd SA9 ....100 C1
Goat St
Haverfordwest / Hwlffordd
SA61 ....125 A5
■ Newport / Trefdraeth
SA42 ....13 E3
St David's / Tyddewi SA62 .123 C4
Godre Coed SA6 ....153 D2
Godre'r Fro SA8 ....147 D7
Godrergraig Prim Sch
SA9 ....100 C1
Goetre Bellaf Rd SA2 ..165 C2
Goetre Fach Rd SA2 ...165 E7
Goetre Fawr Rd SA2 ...165 D2
Goldborough Rd SA71 .103 D4
Goldcrest Ave
Haverfordwest / Hwlffordd
SA61 ....124 D5
RAF Brawdy SA62 .....49 B2
Golden Cl SA3 ....172 F7
Golden Gr / Gelli Aur
SA8 ....160 D6
Golden Hill Rd SA71 ...133 C5
Golden La SA71 ....133 C5
Golden Manor CP Sch
SA71 ....133 D5
Gollop Prep Sch The
SA20 ....121 C5
Golwg Deg SA18 ....108 F4
Golwg Hafren SA2 .....166 C4
Golwg Tywi SA31 ......129 B3
Golwg-y-Castell SA43 .118 D3
Golwg-y-Cwm SA18 ...99 D5
Golwg-y-Gan SA19 ....62 B5
Golwg Y Garn SA41 ....34 F4
Golwg Y Mor SA4 .....156 F4
Golwg Y Mor / Ocean View
SA10 ....169 C8
Golwg Y Mynydd
Craig-cefn-parc SA6 ...146 B1
Godrergraig SA9 ......100 C2
Golwg Y Mynydd SA19 .63 D7
Golwg Y Preseli ■ SA43 .16 A5
Golwg-yr-Afon SA14 ...150 B7
Golwg Yr Eglwys SA6 ..70 E6
Golwg Yr Ysgol / SA31 .77 E7
Llanarthney SA32 .....77 E7
Pontarddulais SA4 .....143 D3
Golwg-y-Tywyn SA16 ..137 D3
Golwg Yr Allt SA19 ....42 C3
Golygfor SA15 ....148 F4
Gomer Gdns SA1 ......160 A1
Gomer Rd SA1 ....159 F1
Gonhill SA3 ....172 D4
Good Hook La SA62 ...68 D3
Goodmoors La SA72 ...105 A6
Goodwick Cty Prim Sch
Fishguard & Goodwick SA64 .11 B3
Goodwick / Wdig SA64 .122 A6
Goodwick Hill
Fishguard & Goodwick SA64 .11 A3
Goodwick / Wdig SA64 .122 A6
Goodwick Ind Est SA64 .122 A6
Goole Rd SA5 ....159 D5
Goose Island SA4 .....174 B1
Goose's La SA71 ......133 C4
Goppa Rd SA4 ....143 E3

Gordon Parry Cl SA73 ...132 A7
Gordon Rd SA14 ......149 B7
Gordon Rowley Way
SA6 ....153 E4
Gordon St SA72 ....132 C3
Gordon Thomas Cl ■
SA1 ....160 C2
Goring Rd / Heol Goring
SA15 ....148 D6
Gorof Rd SA9 ....139 D8
Goronwy Rd SA2 ......159 E1
Gors Ave SA1 ....160 B1
Gorsddu Rd SA14 .....97 D8
Gorsddu Terr SA14 ....97 C8
Gorsedd SA15 ....148 F4
Gorseinon Bsns Pk SA4 .151 C1
Gorseinon Coll
Gorseinon SA4 ....151 A1
Loughor SA4 ....150 F1
Gorseinon Cty Jun Sch
SA4 ....151 B2
Gorseinon Inf Sch SA4 .151 C2
Gorseinon Rd SA4 ....151 E1
Gorse La SA1 ....167 A5
Gorse La / Heol Y Gors
SA19 ....62 B5
Gorsewood Dr SA73 ..131 A1
Gors-Fach SA14 ......149 C6
Gors Fach SA33 ......127 B5
Gors Goch Rd / Heol Gors
Goch SA18 ....99 D8
Gors La SA18 ....99 D6
Gorslwyn Terr SA18 ..99 D5
Gors Prim Sch SA4 ...159 E1
Gors Rd
Burry Port SA16 ......137 D2
Cross Hand SA14 .....96 F6
Penllergaer SA4 ......152 A3
Gorsto Rd
Gwaun-Cae-Gurwen SA18 .99 D7
Pen-Rhiw-fawr SA9 ...100 B5
Gorwydd Rd SA4 .....158 C4
Goshawk Rd SA61 ....124 E5
Goshen Pk SA10 ......162 F8
Gospel La SA62 ....123 C4
Gosport St SA33 ......92 E5
Gothic Rd SA73 ......132 A6
Gough Ave SA9 ....139 D7
Gough Rd SA9 ....139 B6
Gower Heritage Ctr*
SA3 ....170 C7
Gower Holiday Village
SA3 ....117 A6
Gower Pl SA3 ....173 A5
Gower Rd Killay SA2 ..165 D5
Swansea / Abertawe SA2 .166 C7
Gower Rise SA4 ....158 C4
Gower Terr SA4 ....156 F4
Gowerton Rd
Pen-clawdd SA4 ......157 A4
Three Crosses SA4 ...157 E1
Gowerton Sch SA4 ...158 C4
Gowerton Sta SA4 ....158 C5
Gower View Rd SA15 .148 E8
Gower View Rd SA41 .101 C6
Grafog St SA1 ....168 B7
Graham Berry Ct SA5 .160 A5
Graham St SA1 ....160 D2
Graham Terr SA10 ....162 E7
Graig Ave SA15 ....148 E4
Graigfelen Prim Sch
SA6 ....154 C8
Graig Inf Sch SA6 ....160 F8
Graiglwyd Rd SA2 ....166 E8
Graiglwyd Sq SA1 ....166 F8
Graig Newydd SA9 ...100 C2
Graigola Rd SA7 ......155 B6
Graig Pl SA1 ....174 B4
Graig Rd Glais SA7 ...155 A6
Glanaman SA18 ....99 C7
Godrergraig SA9 ......100 C2
Llandysul SA44 ....19 E3
Neath / Castell-Nedd
SA10 ....162 D7
Swansea / Abertawe SA6 .160 F7
Trebanos / Trebannws
SA8 ....147 C3
Graig St SA1 ....174 B4
Graig Terr Glais SA7 ..155 A6
Swansea / Abertawe SA1 .174 A4
Graig Twrch SA9 .....138 A1
Graig-y-Coed SA4 ....156 D4
Graig Y Darren SA9 ...139 A3
Graig-y-Dderi SA2 ....155 A6
Graigymerched SA9 ...139 A5
Graig Y Pal SA7 ......153 C6
Grampian Way SA5 ...159 E3
Grandison St ■ SA1 ..160 D1
Grand Theatre* SA1 ..174 A2
Grange Cres SA3 .....173 A7
Grange La SA3 ....173 A8
Grange Prim Sch SA3 .173 A7
Grange Rd SA3 ....173 A7
Grangwen Rd SA1 ....174 A5
Granville Rd SA1 .....148 E4
Granville Rd SA1 .....174 C4
Granville Terr SA14 ..149 C6
Grasholm SA73 ....131 E4
Grass Holm Cl SA62 ..66 E8
Grassholme Pl SA62 ..85 E8
Grassholm Gdns SA5 .159 E7
Gravel La SA72 ....132 C3
Gray Ave SA7 ....113 D6
Great Eastern Terr
SA73 ....132 B5
Great House Ct SA3 ..117 B5
Great N Rd SA73 .....131 D2

Great Western Cres
SA18 ....148 D3
Great Western Terr ■
SA15 ....148 D3
Greenacre Dr SA7 ....155 A5
Greenacres SA4 ......156 D4
Green Bank Rd SA3 ...172 F7
Green Bridge of Wales The*
SA71 ....111 A3
Green Cl
Milford Haven / Aberdaugleddau
SA73 ....131 F6
The Mumbles / Y Mwmbwls
SA2 ....166 A1
Green Cres ■ SA70 ...135 E5
Green Dragon La SA1 .174 B2
Greenfield Cl
Haverfordwest / Hwlffordd
SA61 ....125 B7
Swansea / Abertawe SA7 .161 F7
Greenfield Pl
■ Llandeilo SA19 .....130 D6
Loughor SA4 ....157 F8
Greenfield Rd / Heol
Maesglas ■ SA18 ....99 B8
Greenfield Row SA43 .118 D4
Greenfields SA1 ......142 F4
Greenfields Cl ■ SA67 .89 E6
Greenfields St SA43 ..118 D4
Greenfields Terr SA2 .166 C7
Greenfield Terr
Lampeter / Llanbedr Pont Steffan
SA48 ....120 B4
Pontyberem SA15 ....96 B6
Swansea / Abertawe,
Landore / Glandwr SA1 .160 D4
Swansea / Abertawe, Llansamlet
SA7 ....161 D8
Greenhall Pk ■ SA62 .86 E5
Green Hayes SA70 ...106 B4
Green Hill SA1 ....174 B5
Greenhill Ave SA70 ..135 D5
Greenhill Cl ■ SA31 .128 F6
Greenhill Cres SA61 .125 A1
Greenhill Pk Dr SA61 .125 A1
Greenhill Rd
Pembroke Dock / Doc Penfro
SA72 ....104 B5
Tenby / Dinbych-y-pysgod
SA70 ....135 E5
Greenhill Sch The SA70 .135 D5
Greenhill St SA1 .....174 B5
Green La Neyland SA73 .132 C5
Oil Refinery SA73 ....103 E8
Greenland Cl SA62 ..67 A6
Greenland Mdws SA43 .118 E5
Green Mdw Cl SA1 ...133 B5
Green Mdw Cl
East Williamston SA70 .106 C7
■ Marloes & St Brides
SA62 ....84 C3
Green Pk SA69 ....134 B5
Green St SA6 ....161 A8
Green The
Manorbier SA70 ......106 B1
Pembroke / Penfro SA71 .133 B5
Greenway SA62 ......87 C6
Greenway Cl SA62 ...87 C6
Greenways SA15 .....158 D3
Greenway St SA15 ...148 C6
Greenway The SA10 .162 C3
Greenwell Cl SA62 ..68 C4
Greenwood Cl SA2 ...166 C6
Greenwood Pl SA5 ...159 D6
Grenfell Ave SA4 ....151 A3
Grenfell Park Rd SA1 .167 F7
Grenfell Town SA1 ...160 F3
Grenig Rd / Heol Grenig
SA18 ....98 F8
Greville Rd SA73 .....131 D3
Greyfriars Sh Ctr SA31 .128 E4
Grey St SA1 ....160 D2
Greys Terr SA7 ......155 B1
Griffith John St SA1 ..168 C6
Griffith Jones Prim Sch /
Ysgol Gruffydd Jones
SA33 ....127 F5
Grist The SA33 ......92 F5
Groesffordd ■ SA18 ..80 E1
Groesffordd Fach ■
SA31 ....129 A6
Gron Rd SA1 ....99 D6
Grosvenor Rd SA2 ...166 F7
Grove CP Sch SA71 ..133 C4
Grove Ct SA70 ....106 B4
Grove Dr SA71 ....133 C3
Grove Farm Rd SA4 ..151 C7
Grove Hill SA31 .....133 D3
Grove Hill Pk / Parc
Bryngelli SA14 ....97 C8
Grove La SA10 ....162 E7
Groveland Leisure Pk*
SA33 ....73 A4
Grove Pk SA43 ......118 E6
Grove Pl
Swansea / Abertawe SA1 .174 A3
The Havens SA62 ....85 D7
Grove Rd Clydach SA6 .146 D1
Pontardawe SA8 .....147 F5
St Ishmael's SA62 ...85 A2
Groves Ave SA3 .....173 A8
Grove St Gorseinon SA4 .151 B3
Pembroke Dock / Doc Penfro
SA72 ....104 B5
Grove The
Carmarthen / Caerfyrddin
SA31 ....128 D5

Grove The continued
Hook SA62 ....87 D6
Kilgetty / Begelly SA68 .134 B7
The Mumbles / Y Mwmbwls
SA3 ....173 A5
Grove Way SA71 .....133 C2
Grugos Ave ■ SA15 ..96 B6
Guildford Row SA73 ..87 E3
Guildhall Rd N SA1 ..167 A5
Guildhall Rd S SA1 ...167 A5
Guildmot Ave SA61 ..125 A7
Gulliver's Cl SA3 ....173 B8
Gurnos CP Jun Sch
SA9 ....139 D8
Gurnos Rd
Gowerton / Tre-gwyr SA4 .158 B5
Ystradgynlais SA9 ...139 C7
Gwalia Cl SA4 ....151 C2
Gwalia Cres SA4 .....151 D2
Gwalia Ct Clydach SA6 .154 D7
Swansea / Abertawe SA1 .167 B5
Gwalia Terr SA4 .....151 D2
Gwaun Henllan SA18 .99 B8
Gwaun View SA65 ...122 E2
Gwbert Rd SA43 .....118 D7
Gweithdau-cwm-gors /
Cwmgors Workshops
SA18 ....99 D6
Gwelfor
■ Burry Port SA16 ...137 D2
Dunvant SA2 ....165 E8
Fishguard / Abergwaun
SA65 ....122 D3
Llanelli SA14 ....149 E4
Gwel-y-creuddyn SA48 .120 B6
Gwendraeth Pl SA1 ..161 B2
Gwendraeth Rd SA14 .96 E7
Gwenlais Rd SA4 .....151 E7
Gwent Gdns SA1 .....159 F1
Gwent Gr SA2 ....166 A1
Gwent Rd SA1 ....160 A1
Gwernant SA9 ....100 B7
Gwern Einon Rd SA2 .166 B3
Gwern Fadog Rd SA6 .154 A4
Gwernllwynchwyth Rd
Birchgrove SA7 .....154 F1
Swansea / Abertawe SA7 .161 F8
Gwernos SA6 ....154 A2
Gwili Ave SA15 ......148 C5
Gwili Pottery* SA33 ..59 A7
Gwili Rd SA13 ....149 E4
Gwili Steam Rly* SA33 .58 E4
Gwili Terr SA1 ....160 B1
Gwilliam Ct SA1 .....104 C4
Gwilym Rd SA9 ......100 B8
Gwlad-y-Gan SA66 ...153 D1
Gwrhyd Rd
Pen-Rhiw-fawr SA9 ..100 A4
Pontardawe SA8, SA9 .99 F2
Rhyd-y-fro SA8 .....147 D8
Gwscwm Pk SA16 ....137 D3
Gwscwm Rd / Heol Gwscwm
SA16 ....137 C3
Gwydr Cres SA2 .....166 F6
Gwydr Mews SA2 ....166 F6
Gwydr Rd SA2 ....150 D1
Gwydr Sq SA2 ....166 F6
Gwylfa SA14 ....149 D6
Gwylfa Rd SA1 ......159 F1
Gwylym St SA5 ......160 A2
Gwynedd Ave SA2 ...159 F1
Gwynedd Gdns SA1 ..160 A1
Gwyndaf SA32 ......76 C5
Gwynfe Rd
Dyffryn Cennen SA19 .130 F6
Loughor SA4 ....150 E3
Gwynfi St SA5 ....160 C5
Gwynfor Rd SA4 .....159 E1
Gwynfryn SA18 ......98 B7
Gwynfryn Rd SA4 ....143 C3
Gwynne Terr SA1 ....168 A8
Gwyn's Pl SA1 ......147 F3
Gwyn St SA8 ....147 E3
Gwyrddgoed SA8 ....147 E6
Gwyrosydd Jun & Inf Sch
SA5 ....160 C5
Gwysfa Rd SA6 ......154 B5
Gwyn-y-Cwm SA9 ...100 C6
Gwyther St SA72 ....132 C2
Gyfre Gdns SA31 ....129 C7
Gynol Rd SA1 ....139 D8
Gyrnosfa SA7 ....139 D8

H

Hadland Terr SA3 ....173 A6
Hael La SA3 ....171 B4
Hafan ■ SA73 ....148 D4
Hafan Glyd SA6 .....154 E8
Hafan Y Don SA2 ....165 B3
Hafan-y-morfa SA15 .148 F7
Hafnant SA1 ....161 D5
Hafod Bryan SA14 ...149 C4
Hafod Cwmin SA31 ..129 B7
Hafod Elfed SA31 ...128 E6
Hafod Pk SA1 ....160 D2
Hafod Prim Sch SA1 .160 D2
Hafod Rd SA9 ....97 F6
Hafod St SA1 ....174 B5
Hag Pl SA5 ....159 F4
Hakin CP Sch SA73 ..131 A2
Hakin Infants Sch SA73 .131 A2
Halfway Prim Sch SA14 .149 A6
Halkon Cres ■ SA67 ..70 C1

Hallbank SA3 ....173 B4
Hallbank Terr SA3 ...173 B4
Hall La SA4 ....156 D4
Hall's Nook SA73 ....87 A3
Hall St
■ Ammanford / Rhydaman
SA18 ....98 C7
Brynamman SA18 ...99 E8
Llanelli SA15 ....148 D6
Swansea / Abertawe SA1 .174 A5
Hamilton Cl SA72 ...132 B1
Hamilton Ct SA72 ...133 A8
Hamilton St
■ Fishguard / Abergwaun
SA65 ....122 D3
Swansea / Abertawe SA1 .160 D4
Hamilton Terr SA73 ..131 C2
Hammond Ave SA61 .125 A4
Hampshire Dr SA72 ..132 D4
Hangman's Cross SA3 .117 C5
Hanover Cl SA1 .....173 A6
Hanover Ct SA2 .....166 D7
Hanover La SA1 .....167 A7
Hanover St SA1 .....167 B7
Harbour Cl SA73 ....132 B6
Harbour View Rd SA1 .168 A8
Harbour Village SA64 .122 B4
Harbour Way
Milford Haven / Aberdaugleddau
SA73 ....131 A2
Pembroke Dock / Doc Penfro
SA72 ....132 C3
Harbour Winds Ct SA73 .173 A4
Harcourt St SA1 .....167 B7
Harddfan SA14 ......149 F6
Harding Cl SA4 .....158 A8
Hardingsdown La SA3 .114 E2
Harding St SA70 ....135 D5
Harebell Cl SA46 ....154 B4
Harford Ct SA62 ....166 C5
Harford Sq ■ SA48 ..120 C5
Harlech Cl SA3 .....166 B7
Harlech Cres SA2 ...166 B7
Harlech St SA18 .....99 F7
Harleyford Rd SA4 ..143 A4
Harlington Rd SA5 ..160 A2
Haroldston Cl SA61 ..125 A2
Haroldston Hill SA62 .66 D1
Harold St / Stryd Harold ■
SA18 ....98 B7
Harrier Rd SA61 .....124 C5
Harries Ave SA15 ...148 C6
Harries La SA15 .....148 C6
Harries St
Swansea / Abertawe SA1 .167 B8
Tenby / Dinbych-y-pysgod
SA70 ....135 E4
Harrington Pl SA1 ...174 B5
Harrington St SA1 ...160 D1
Harris Rd SA6 ....100 B7
Harris St SA6 ....154 D8
Harry St SA6 ....153 E1
Hartfield Cl SA2 .....166 A7
Hasguard Cross SA62 .85 C5
Hatfield Ct SA5 .....159 E5
Hatherleigh Dr SA3 ..172 E5
Haulfryn Bryn SA14 .149 F6
Carmarthen / Caerfyrddin
SA31 ....129 A3
Pontardawe SA8 ....147 E5
Haul Fryn SA7 ......155 A2
Haulwen Rd SA2 ....159 D1
Haulwen St SA15 ...148 E7
Havard Cl SA62 .....87 C6
Havard Rd SA14 ....149 A6
Havelock St SA15 ...148 E2
Haven Ct SA71 ......104 C4
Haven Dr
Milford Haven / Aberdaugleddau
SA73 ....102 A3
Pembroke Dock / Doc Penfro
SA72 ....103 A3
Haven Pk Ave SA61 ..124 D4
Haven Pk Cl SA61 ...124 D4
Haven Pk Cres SA61 .124 C4
Haven Pk Dr SA61 ...124 C4
Haven Rd SA61 .....124 D4
Haven's Head Bsns Pk
SA73 ....131 B3
Haven's Pk SA73 ....85 E2
Havenway Day Hospl
SA72 ....132 A3
Haverfordwest Castle (Ruin)
& Town Mus* SA61 ..125 A5
Haverfordwest Rd SA62 .50 F8
Haverfordwest Sta
SA61 ....125 A5
Haverfordwest Swimming
Pool SA61 ....125 A5
Haverfordwest VC Sch
SA61 ....124 F5
Haverfordwest (Withybush)
Airfield SA62 ....68 A6
Havergal Cl SA3 .....172 D4
Hawkstone Cl SA73 ..172 E7
Hawkstone Rd SA72 .132 D2
Hawthorn Ave SA4 ..166 F7
Hawthorn Rise SA61 .124 D5
Hawthorn Villas SA3 .138 F1
Hayguard La SA61 ...125 A5
Haylands La SA70 ...105 C2
Haylett Grange Sch SA62 .86 F4
Hayston Ave SA73 ...131 B2
Hayston Rd SA62 ....86 D4
Haytor Gdns SA70 ...135 D6
Hazel Bank Hill SA73 .103 F4

Hazelbeach Rd SA73 ....103 E8
Hazel Cl SA2 ....166 B6
Hazel Gr SA73 ....103 F8
Hazelmere Rd SA2 ......166 D7
Hazel Rd SA2 ....166 E7
Hazeltree Copse SA4 ...156 B2
Headland Cl SA3 ....172 A5
Headland Rd
  Bishopston SA3 ......172 A5
  Swansea / Abertawe SA1 ...167 F8
Hean Cl SA69 ....134 E4
Heaselands Pl SA2 .....165 D7
Heath Cl Johnston SA62 ..86 E6
  The Mumbles / Y Mwmbwls
  SA3 ....172 F6
Heath Ct SA3 ....172 F6
Heather Cres SA2 ......166 B6
Heatherslade Cl
  Southgate SA3 ....171 A3
  The Mumbles / Y Mwmbwls
  SA3 ....173 B4
Heatherslade Sports Pk*
  SA70 ....106 C5
Heathfield
  Gorseinon SA4 ....151 A1
  Swansea / Abertawe SA1 ...174 A3
Heathfield Ind Pk SA1 ..97 C6
Heathfield Rd SA8 .....147 F6
Heathwood Rd SA3 .....173 A8
Hebron Cl SA6 ....150 C7
Hebron Rd SA6 ....154 D7
Hedley Terr SA15 ......148 D6
Helwick Cl SA3 ....173 A5
Hendre SA2 ....165 D8
Hendre Cl SA14 ....150 A7
Hendre Cres SA14 ......150 B7
Hendrefoilan Ave SA2 ..166 B7
Hendrefoilan Cl SA2 ...166 A7
Hendrefoilan Ct SA2 ...166 B8
Hendrefoilan Dr SA2 ...166 A7
Hendrefoilan Prim Sch
  SA2 ....165 F7
Hendre-Foilan Rd SA2 ..166 B8
Hendrefoilan Student Village
  SA2 ....166 A7
Hendre Isaf SA14 ......149 D4
Hendremawr Cl SA2 ....166 C8
Hendre Owain SA2 .....166 C8
Hendre Pk SA14 ....150 A7
Hendre Rd
  Llangennech SA14 ....150 B7
  Tycroes SA18 ....97 F6
Hendre Rd / Heol Hendre
  [4] Glanaman SA18 ....99 B8
  Llanelli SA14 ....149 D4
Hendy Cl SA2 ....166 B4
Hendy Cty Prim Mixed Sch
  SA4 ....143 A4
Hendy Ind Est SA4 .....143 A4
Hendy Rd SA4 ....156 F4
Heneage Dr SA2 ....166 B1
Hen Heol Llangynnwr
  SA31 ....129 A4
Henllan Amgoed CP Sch
  SA34 ....71 E6
Henllan Ind Est SA444 ..18 E3
Henllan Sta SA444 .....18 E3
Hen Parc Ave SA2 .....165 B5
Hen Parc La SA2 ....165 C4
Henrietta St SA1 ......167 B6
Henton La SA63 ....69 D7
Heol Aaron SA9 ....139 D8
Heol Abram SA9 ......139 D8
Heol Afallon SA14 ......96 D7
Heol Afon / Afon Rd
  SA14 ....150 C8
Heol Amman SA18 .....79 F1
Heol Amman / Amman Rd
  Brynamman SA18 .....99 E8
  Glanaman SA18 ......98 F8
Heol-aneddfa [4] SA15 ..96 B6
Heol Arfryn SA31 ......128 B6
Heol Argoed / Argoed Rd
  SA18 ....98 C5
Heol Aur Llanelli SA14 ..141 C1
  Llanelli SA14 ....149 C8
Heol Awstin SA5 ....159 E5
Heol Bancyroffis SA15 ..95 D3
Heol Barcud SA7 ....162 B8
Heol Barri / Barry Rd
  SA18 ....99 D7
Heol Beca SA31 ....128 C4
Heol Bedw SA43 ....118 F5
Heol Bedwas SA7 ......155 A1
Heol Beili Glas SA14 ...141 A2
Heol Beili-glas SA20 ...44 E2
Heol Bethel SA15 ......96 C2
Heol Blaengwastod
  SA31 ....129 A3
Heol Blaenhirwaun SA14 ..96 E8
Heol Bolahaul
  Llandyfaelog SA31 ....75 F4
  Llangunnor SA31 .....129 A1
Heol Briallu SA6 ......153 F2
Heol Brithdir SA7 .....162 B8
Heol Broch SA7 ....162 B8
Heol Bronallt / Bronallt Rd
  SA14 ....143 A5
Heol Brown SA18 ......98 A5
Heol Brynamman /
  Brynamman Rd SA18 ..99 D7
Heol Bryncelyn SA14 ..149 C8
Heol Bryncyn SA7 .....155 A1
Heol Brynglas SA14 ...158 B8
Heol Bryngwili SA14 ...97 A7

Heol Brynhaul SA15 ....95 D3
Heol Bryn-Lloi / Bryn-Lloi
  Rd [5] SA18 ....99 A8
Heol Brython SA2 ......165 B8
Heol Buckley SA15 ....148 E8
Heol Cadifor SA5 ......160 B6
Heol Cadnawes SA6 ...153 F4
Heol Cae Copyn SA4 ..150 E1
Heol Cae-du SA20 .....44 E2
Heol Cae-ffynnon SA31 ..129 F7
Heol Cae-Glas SA4 ....161 F6
Heol-cae-globe SA4 ...157 F8
Heol-Cae-Gurwen SA18 ..99 D6
Heol Caegwyn SA14 ...96 D8
Heol Cae Rhosyn SA7 ..155 A1
Heol Caerllan SA4 .....154 B5
Heol Cae Tynewydd
  SA4 ....150 F1
Heol Calfin SA5 ....159 E4
Heol Callwen SA7 .....82 F3
Heol Camlan SA7 .....155 A1
Heol Capel Dewi SA15 ..129 C4
Heol Capel Ifan SA15 ..96 A5
Heol Capel Sion SA14 ..96 C8
Heol Caradog SA65 ...122 E3
Heol Cefni SA6 ....160 E8
Heol Ceirios SA18 ....79 B1
Heol Cennen SA19 ....130 D4
Heol Ceri SA5 ....158 D3
Heol Cerwyn SA65 ....122 D3
Heol Cleddau
  [3] Fishguard / Abergwaun
  SA65 ....122 D3
  Waunarlwydd SA5 ....158 D3
Heol Cledwyn SA7 ....155 A1
Heol Copperworks /
  Copperworks Rd SA15 ..148 D3
Heol Cowell / Cowell Rd
  SA18 ....99 C7
Heol Cropin SA14 .....149 C8
Heol Cross Hands / Cross
  Hands Rd SA14 ......97 B8
Heol Crwys
  Fishguard / Abergwaun
  SA65 ....122 C5
  Gorseinon SA4 ....151 B4
  Llanrhian SA62 ......29 A5
Heol Crych-gwyn SA19 ..64 E4
Heol Cwmbach SA14 ...96 D7
Heol Cwmfferws /
  Cwmfferws Rd SA18 ..97 F6
Heol Cwmmawr SA14 ..96 D8
Heol Cwper / Coopers Rd
  SA14 ....97 E5
Heol Cynan
  Fishguard / Abergwaun
  SA65 ....122 C4
  Gorseinon SA4 ....151 B4
Heol Dalycoga SA7 ....161 E6
Heol Daniel
  Cwmllynfell SA9 ......100 B7
  Llanelli SA14, SA15 ...148 F4
Heol Ddu
  Ammanford / Rhydaman
  SA18 ....98 D8
  Cross Hand SA14 .....96 D8
  Llandybie SA18 ......79 E1
  Swansea / Abertawe SA5 ...160 B7
  Trimsaran SA15 ......109 C6
  Tycroes SA18 ....97 F5
Heol Ddwr SA4 ....143 E6
Heol Derw
  Cardigan / Aberteifi SA43 ..118 F5
  Cynwyl Elfed SA33 ...58 A5
Heol Derwen
  Cross Hands SA14 ....97 C7
  SA61 ....125 A2
Heol Devi
  Fishguard / Abergwaun
  St David's / Tyddewi SA62 ..123 D5
Heol Dewi Sant SA4 ...152 A2
Heol Dinbych SA15 ....148 F4
Heol Dinefwr / Dynevor Rd
  SA18 ....99 B7
Heol Dissgwylfa [1] SA31 ..128 B6
Heol Dolfain SA6 ......153 F4
Heol Drindod SA31 ....128 C2
Heol Dulais SA7 ....155 A1
Heol Dwr SA18 ....98 E7
Heol Dyddgen SA17 ...95 E8
Heol Dyfan SA6 ....153 F3
Heol Dyfatty SA14 ....137 F2
Heol Dyfed
  Fishguard / Abergwaun
  SA65 ....122 C5
  Gorseinon SA4 ....151 B4
Heol Dyfnallt SA31 ....128 C4
Heol Dylan SA4 ....151 B4
Heol Dynys SA5 ....159 E5
Heol Dywyll SA6 ......154 C7
Heol Eglwys SA9 ......138 F1
Heol Eifion SA4 ....151 C2
Heol Eifion Wyn SA7 ..161 E6
Heol Eirlys SA6 ....153 F2
Heol Eithrim SA6 .....154 D8
Heol Elfed
  Burry Port SA16 .....137 D2
  Gorseinon SA4 ....151 B4
  Llanelli SA14 ....149 C5
  Swansea / Abertawe SA1 ...161 E6
Heol Elisabeth SA16 ..137 E3
Heol Elli SA15 ....148 F5
Heol Emrys
  Fishguard / Abergwaun
  SA65 ....122 D5

Heol Emrys continued
  Swansea / Abertawe SA5 ...160 A5
Heol Fach
  Ammanford SA18 ......97 E8
Heol Felin
  Swansea / Abertawe, Llangyfelach
  SA5 ....153 B3
  Swansea / Abertawe, Waun-Gron
  SA5 ....160 C6
Heol Fedw SA6 ....153 F3
Heol Felen
  Cwmamman SA18 .....80 B1
  Glanaman SA18 ......99 B8
Heol Felin Newydd / New
  Mill Rd SA43 ....118 F6
Heol Ffion SA14 ......151 C2
Heol Fforest / Fforest Rd
  SA4 ....143 B5
Heol Ffranc SA10 .....162 C6
Heol Ffynnon
  Llanelli SA15 ....148 F4
  Loughor SA4 ....150 E1
Heol Ffynnonau [2] SA2 ..59 A2
Heol Ficeroi / Vicarage Rd [7]
  SA18 ....99 B8
Heol Folland / Folland Rd
  SA18 ....99 B8
Heol Frank SA5 ....160 B5
Heol Gelli SA38 ....17 B4
Heol Gelli-ddu SA19 ..64 E3
Heol Gelli Fawr SA15 ..109 F7
Heol Gelligron SA44 ..20 B8
Heol Gelynen
  [3] Brecon SA18 .....80 E1
  Brynamman SA18 .....99 D8
Heol Gerrig SA5 ......160 C6
Heol Giedd
  Cwmgiedd SA9 ......138 F3
  Ystradgynlais SA9 ...138 F3
Heol Glan-gwendraeth
  SA15 ....95 A3
Heol Gianllechau SA18 ..147 E3
Heol Glan-Nant SA6 ..154 A4
Heol Glasfryn [5] SA32 ..59 A2
Heol Glasnant SA2 ...165 F7
Heol Gleien SA9 ......138 A2
Heol Glyndernwen SA8 ..147 E3
Heol Glyndwr
  Fishguard / Abergwaun
  SA65 ....122 D3
  Llangyndeyrn SA15 ..95 D4
Heol Glyn-Dyfal SA5 ..144 F4
Heol Glyn / Glyn Rd
  SA18 ....99 D8
Heol Godfrey SA18 ...98 D5
Heol Goffa SA15 ......148 E7
Heol Gollen SA43 ....118 F5
Heol Goring / Goring Rd
  SA15 ....148 D6
Heol Gors Goch / Gors Goch
  SA18 ....99 D8
Heol Graig-Felen SA6 ..154 D8
Heol Grenig / Grenig Rd
  SA18 ....99 B6
Heol Grom SA9 ....139 D8
Heol Gruffydd SA5 ....159 F5
Heol Grug SA65 ......153 E2
Heol Gwalia SA14 ....149 C5
Heol Gwanwyn SA7 ...161 F7
Heol Gwell SA5 ......160 D5
Heol Gwenallt SA41 ..96 E5
Heol Gwendraeth [2]
  SA16 ....137 D2
Heol Gwernant SA17 ..94 B2
Heol Gwernen
  Cwmrhydyceirw SA6 ..154 A3
  Swansea / Abertawe SA6 ...153 F3
Heol Gwernfelen
  Llandovery / Llanymddyfri
  SA20 ....121 F4
  Llandovery / Llanymddyfri
  Myddfai SA20 ....44 F5
Heol Gwili Gorseinon SA4 ..151 B4
  Llanelli SA14 ....149 D5
  Swansea / Abertawe SA7 ...161 E6
Heol Gwilym SA18 ....79 A2
Heol Gwscwm / Gwscwm Rd
  SA16 ....137 C3
Heol Gwyr SA15 ......148 F4
Heol Gwyrosydd SA5 ..160 B5
Heol Gwys SA9 ....100 C6
Heol Hafdy SA7 ......161 F7
Heol Hafod SA43 .....118 E4
Heol Hathren SA48 ...120 E3
Heol Haydn SA18 .....98 E7
Heol Helyg SA43 .....118 F5
Heol Hen
  Llanelli Rural SA15 ...109 F8
  Llanelli SA14 ....149 C4
Heol Hendre / Hendre Rd
  [4] Glanaman SA18 ...99 B8
  Llanelli SA14 ....149 D4
Heol Hermas SA6 .....160 B6
Heol Hir SA15 ....99 E6
Heol Hirwaun Olau SA14 ..96 E7
Heol Horeb SA15 .....140 A7
Heol Innes SA15 .....148 F4
Heol Iscoed / Iscoed Rd
  SA16 ....143 A4
Heol Islwyn SA4 ......151 B4
Heol Langdon / Langdon Rd
  Swansea / Abertawe SA1 ...167 F4
  Swansea / Abertawe SA1 ...168 A6
Heol-Las
  Ammanford / Rhydaman
  SA18 ....98 B6
  Birchgrove SA7 ......154 F2
Heol Las SA14 ....97 B8

Heol-Las Cl SA7 ......154 F1
Heol Llandeilo / Llandeilo Rd
  SA14 ....78 C1
Heol Llanelli
  Pontyates / Pont-iets SA15 ..95 E3
  Trimsaran SA17 ......109 C7
Heol Llangynnwr SA31 ..129 A4
Heol Llansaint SA17 ..94 B3
Heol Llwyd SA18 .....99 B8
Heol Llwyn Bedw SA4 ..142 F4
Heol Llwyncelyn /
  Llwyncelyn Rd SA18 ..98 F8
Heol Llwynhendy /
  Llwynhendy Rd SA14 ..149 F4
Heol Login SA31 ......129 C3
Heol Lolwen / Lotwen Rd
  SA18 ....97 D6
Heol Lucy / Lucy Rd
  SA10 ....162 D7
Heol Maesbryn SA14 ..150 F1
Heol Maes Eglwys SA6 ..153 E4
Heol Maesglas / Greenfield
  Rd [5] SA18 ....99 B8
Heol Maes / Maes Rd
  SA14 ....150 C8
Heol Maesoderwen /
  Oakfield Rd [5] SA18 ..99 B8
Heol Maespica SA9 ...138 B2
Heol Maesuchel / Highfield
  Rd SA18 ....99 C8
Heol Maes Y Cerrig
  SA4 ....150 C8
Heol Maes-y-Dre SA9 ..138 F1
Heol Maes-y-Gelynen
  SA6 ....153 F2
Heol Mafon SA39 ....20 B2
Heol Mair SA31 ......128 B6
Heol Mansant SA15 ..95 D4
Heol Mansel / Mansel St [15]
  SA15 ....148 D4
Heol Marlais
  Ammanford / Rhydaman
  SA18 ....98 B8
  Llandybie SA18 ......79 A1
Heol Meurig SA7 .....139 D8
Heol Miaren SA6 .....153 F2
Heol Morfa SA15 .....148 F3
Heol Morfa Brenin
  SA31 ....128 C2
Heol Morlais Hendy SA4 ..142 F3
Heol Morlais / Morlais Rd
  SA14 ....150 B7
Heol Mwrwg SA14 ...150 B8
Heol Myddfai SA5 ....144 F2
Heol Myrddin SA19 ..130 D3
Heol Nant Llanelli SA14 ..141 A2
  Llannon SA14 ....96 F3
Heol Nant Bran SA15 ..155 A2
Heol Nant Gelli SA5 ..160 D5
Heol Nant Gwinau / Nant
  Gwineu Rd SA18 .....99 C8
Heol Nant-y-felin SA15 ..148 F2
Heol Nant Y Glyn / Nantyglyn
  Rd SA18 ....98 F8
Heol Nazareth SA15 ..95 D3
Heol Newydd SA15 ...159 F5
Heol Newydd / New Rd
  Neath / Castell-Nedd
  SA10 ....162 C1
  Ystradowen SA9 .....100 C7
Heol Norman / Norman Rd
  [3] SA18 ....98 B7
Heol Onnen SA43 ....118 F6
Heol Palleg / Palleg Rd
  SA18 ....138 C2
Heol Panteg SA15 ....137 C3
Heol Pantycelyn [1]
  SA16 ....137 D2
Heol Pant Y Dwr SA4 ..150 F2
Heol Pantyffynnon /
  Pantyffynnon Rd SA18 ..98 B6
Heol Pant-y-Lliw SA4 ..152 A6
Heol Parc Mawr SA14 ..97 C7
Heol Penar SA5 ......160 B6
Heol Pendref SA19 ...63 D7
Heol Penfelyn SA6 ...153 F5
Heol Penlan SA64 ....11 B3
Heol Penlanffos SA31 ..129 B7
Heol Pen-nant
  Llanelli SA14 ....141 B3
  Ynysforgan SA6 .....154 A4
Heol Penprys SA14 ...149 E6
Heol Pen Storom SA19 ..130 D1
Heol Pen-Tir-Garw SA15 ..159 F6
Heol Pentre Bach SA4 ..152 C1
Heol Pentre Felen SA6 ..153 C1
Heol Pentregwenlais
  SA18 ....78 F3
Heol Pentwyn SA15 ..162 C6
Heol Pentyla SA7 ....161 F6
Heol Pen-y-Beili SA14 ..150 E1
Heol Pen Y Cae SA14 ..129 F7
Heol Penygarn / Penygarn
  Rd SA18 ....99 D7
Heol Penygroes / Penygroes
  Rd
  Ammanford SA18 ......97 F8
  Gorslas SA14 ....97 C8
Heol Pen-y-Scallen
  SA4 ....150 E1
Heol Philip SA9 ......138 D1
Heol Phillip SA18 ....147 E3
Heol Plas Isaf SA14 ..150 B7
Heol Pluguffan SA20 ..121 C4
Heol Preseli SA65 ....122 D3

Heol Rehoboth / Rehoboth
  Rd SA15 ....109 E7
Heol Rhian SA62 .....28 E4
Heol Rhos SA20 ......121 A6
Heol-Rhosybonwen
  Cefneithin SA14 .....97 A8
  Gorslas SA14 ....96 F6
Heol Rhosyn SA6 .....153 F2
Heol Rhuddos SA7 ...162 A7
Heol Rhyd SA6 ....146 B3
Heol Rhydaman /
  Ammanford Rd SA18 ..97 F6
Heol Rhyd-Ddu-Fach
  SA9 ....100 B8
Heol Roberts / Roberts Rd
  SA1 ....167 F5
Heol Rudd SA15 ......128 E6
Heol Saffrwm SA6 ...153 F2
Heol Sanne SA31 ....128 C3
Heol Santes Ann [3] SA32 ..75 F3
Heol Saron / Saron Rd
  Ammanford SA18 .....97 F8
  Capel Hendre SA18 ..97 C6
Heol Seion SA14 .....150 B7
Heol Siloh SA15 ......148 C4
Heol Smyrna SA33 ...75 B3
Heol Spurrell SA31 ...128 C6
Heol Stanllyd SA14 ..97 B7
Heol Tabernacle /
  Tabernacle Rd SA18 ..98 F8
Heol Tabernacl / Tabernacle
  Rd [2] SA18 ....99 A8
Heol Tircoed SA4 ....152 B5
Heol Tir Du
  Cwmrhydyceirw SA6 ..154 A3
  Swansea / Abertawe SA6 ...153 F3
Heol Tir Y Coed / Tirycoed
  Rd [3] SA18 ....99 A8
Heol Tir Y Coed / Woodland
  SA4 ....100 C7
Heol Tir-y-Parc / Parklands
  Rd SA18 ....98 A7
Heol Tredeg SA9 .....100 C6
Heol Treffynnon SA8 ..154 B5
Heol Trefin SA65 .....122 D5
Heol Trefor SA5 ......160 B6
Heol Trefrhiw / Trefrhiw Rd
  SA18 ....98 A6
Heol Tregroning SA15 ..148 F2
Heol Tregwyr SA17 ...94 B3
Heol-Treventy SA14 ..97 A8
Heol Troeon Bach SA4 ..97 D2
Heol Trosserch / Trosserch
  Rd / SA14 ....142 B2
Heol Trubshaw SA15 ..148 E8
Heol Twrch SA9 ......138 B1
Heol Tycroes / Tycroes Rd
  Ammanford / Rhydaman
  SA18 ....98 A5
  Tycroes SA18 ....97 F5
Heol Ty Newydd [7] SA43 ..16 A5
Heol Uchaf Yr Orsaf / Upper
  Station Rd [3] SA18 ..99 B8
Heol Valentine SA6 ..154 D8
Heol Vaughan SA16 ..137 C2
Heol Wallasey SA18 ..98 C7
Heol Waterloo / Waterloo Rd
  SA14, SA18 ....97 D7
Heol Waun Dwfn SA18 ..98 D6
Heol Waunllystir SA20 ..44 F2
Heol Waun-wen SA16 ..137 C3
Heol Waun Wen SA6 ..153 B1
Heol Waunyclun SA17 ..137 F8
Heol Wepner SA15 ...95 D3
Heol Westfa SA14 ....148 F8
Heol Will George SA5 ..158 E3
Heol Wyllt SA14 .....143 E4
Heol Y Banc SA15 ....95 F7
Heol Y Barna SA14 ..144 A3
Heol Y Bedw SA44 ...18 E3
Heol y Brenin / King's Rd
  SA1 ....174 C2
Heol-y-Bryn SA14 ....96 F6
Heol-y Bryn SA15 ....96 B6
Heol-y-Bwlch SA14 ..150 A2
Heol-y-Cae Clydach SA6 ..154 D7
  Pontarddulais SA4 ...143 E5
Heol Y Capel SA14 ...78 D3
Heol Y Celyn SA7 ....154 D1
Heol Y Cnap SA5 .....160 C6
Heol-y-Coed SA4 .....143 E5
Heol-y-Coedcae SA9 ..100 B7
Heol Y Coroni / Coronation
  Rd [15] SA18 ....99 B8
Heol Y Cwmdu SA5 ..159 F2
Heol Y Cwrt SA19 ....79 E4
Heol Y Cyw SA7 ......162 B8
Heol y Dderwen SA44 ..19 D2
Heol-y-Delyn SA21 ...128 F7
Heol-y-Deri
  Cwmgwili SA14 .....97 C5
  Cwmrhydyceirw SA6 ..154 A3
  Swansea / Abertawe SA2 ...153 F3
Heol Y Deri / Deri Rd
  SA18 ....98 F8
Heol-y-Bryn SA14 ....97 A8
Heol y Drudwen SA6 ..153 F5
Heol-y-Fagwr SA6 ....146 F1
Heol-y-Felin
  Ammanford / Rhydaman
  SA18 ....98 C6
  Burry Port SA16 .....137 E3
Heol Y Felin SA4 .....142 F5

186 Heo – Lan

Heol-y-Felin SA4 152 B2
Heol Y Felin SA15 96 A6
Heol-y-Felin SA43 3 F4
Heolyffin SA8 147 B1
Heol Y Ffinant SA38 119 D4
Heol-y-Ffowndri / Foundry Rd 5 SA18 98 C7
Heol Y Fran SA6 153 F5
Heol-y-Gaer
 Clynderwen SA66 70 F6
 Llanybyther SA40 21 D6
Heol Y Garn SA18 98 B4
Heol-y-Garreg-Las SA19 130 E6
Heol Y Garreg Wen SA3 172 E6
Heol-y-Geifr SA5 153 B2
Heol Y Gelli
 Llangadog SA19 81 A8
 Llansadwrn SA19 43 C2
Heol-y-Gelli SA4 151 F2
Heol-y-Gilfach SA44 19 E3
Heol-y-Goedlan SA9 100 B6
Heol Y Gof SA38 119 D4
Heol-y-Gog SA4 158 B5
Heol-y-Gors
 Gwaun-Cae-Gurwen SA18 99 D5
 Swansea / Abertawe SA1, SA5 160 A2
Heol Y Gors / Gorse La SA19 62 B5
Heol-y-Graig SA6 154 D7
Heol Y Graig SA14 149 E4
Heol-y-Lan SA32 75 F2
Heol-y-Llan
 Burry Port SA16 137 D2
 Llandissilio West SA66 70 F8
 Loughor SA4 157 E8
Heol y Llew Du / Black Lion Rd SA14 97 C7
Heol Y Llidiart-coch SA19 80 E8
Heol Y Lloetrach SA16 137 A2
Heol-y-Llwynan SA8 147 B1
Heol Y Maes SA40 21 E8
Heol-y-Maes SA4 143 D4
Heol Y Meinciau SA15 95 D4
Heol Y Merwydd SA44 19 B5
Heol Y Mynydd SA18 98 B3
Heol-y-Mynydd SA14 149 F6
Heol Y Mynydd SA4 151 D3
Heol Y Mynydd / Mountain Rd SA16 137 A3
Heol-y-Nant SA6 154 E8
Heol Y Nant SA4 150 F3
Heol Y Nantlais SA4 151 B4
Heol Y-neuadd SA14 96 E7
Heol-y-Neuadd 6 SA44 19 E3
Heol-y-Parc SA14 97 A8
Heol Y Parc Hendy SA4 142 F4
 Llangennech SA14 150 C7
 Pontardawe SA8 147 F3
Heol-y-Parc SA4 152 A7
Heol Y Parc SA15 96 B6
Heol Y Pentre
 Pont Henri SA15 95 E4
 Pontyberem SA15 96 B5
Heol Y Pistyll SA19 23 C7
Heol-y-Plas Fforest SA4 142 F6
 Llannon SA14 96 E3
Heol Yr Eglwys / Church Rd SA14 97 B8
Heol Yr Eithen SA6 154 A3
Heol-yr-Eos SA4 151 F2
Heol Yr Eryr
 Cwmrhydyceirw SA6 154 A5
 Swansea / Abertawe SA6 153 F5
Heol-y-Rhedyn SA6 153 E2
Heol Y Rhosfa / Rhosfa Rd SA18 80 F1
Heol Yr Wylan SA6 153 F5
Heol-yr-Ysgol
 Cefneithin SA14 97 A8
 Gorslas SA14 78 A1
Heol Yr Ysgol / School Rd
 Brynamman SA18 99 D8
 Cefn-bryn-brain SA9 100 B8
 Neath / Castell-Nedd SA10 162 C1
Heol Ysgawen SA2 166 C8
Heol Ysgol Newydd / New School Rd 15 SA18 99 B8
Heol Ysgyfarnog SA7 162 B8
Heol-y-Twyn SA4 151 F7
Heol-y-Waun SA4 143 D5
Heol Y Waun SA4 151 F7
Heol Y Waunfach SA14 149 C8
Heol Y Wawr SA31 128 B6
Heol-y-Wern
 Cardigan / Aberteifi SA43 118 F6
 Loughor SA4 157 E8
Heol-y-Wyrddol SA18 98 B8
Herberdeg Rd SA15 95 E2
Herbert St SA8 147 E4
Herbrandston Cty Prim Sch SA73 85 E3
Heritage Gate SA61 125 C7
Heritage Pk SA61 125 C8
Hermitage Gr SA61 125 C8
Hermon CP Sch SA36 35 B3
Hermons Hill SA61 125 A4
Heron Ave SA15 148 B5
Heron's Brook Leisure Pk* SA67 89 D8
Heron Way SA6 161 B8
Hewlett Rd SA15 96 B5
Hewson St SA1 167 B8
Heywood Ct SA70 135 C5
Heywood La SA70 135 D5
Hick St SA15 148 D4
Highbury Cl SA5 160 B2
Highcliffe Ct SA3 172 F4
Highfield SA4 158 A8
Highfield Pk 1 SA67 70 D1
Highfield Rd / Heol Maesuchel SA18 99 C8
Highfields Holiday Pk SA3 117 A4
Highfield Terr SA15 148 E4
Highgate La SA71 104 B3
Highgrove SA70 106 F6
Highland Cl SA10 162 F8
Highlands Ave SA61 124 F5
Highlands The SA10 162 F8
Highland Terr SA4 143 E3
Highmead Ave
 Llanelli SA15 148 E8
 The Mumbles / Y Mwmbwls SA3 172 E6
Highmead Cl SA3 172 E5
Highmead Terr SA40 21 C7
Highmoor SA1 174 B1
Highpool Cl SA3 172 E5
Highpool La SA3 172 E5
High St Abergwili SA31 129 E7
 Allt-wen SA8 147 F3
 Cardigan / Aberteifi SA43 118 D4
 Cilgerran SA43 16 A5
 Clydach SA6 154 E7
 Cross Hand SA14 96 F6
 Fishguard / Abergwaun SA65 122 C3
 Gorseinon SA4 151 C2
 Grovesend SA4 151 C6
 Haverfordwest / Hwlffordd SA61 125 A5
 Lampeter / Llanbedr Pont Steffan SA48 120 C5
 Lampeter Velfrey SA34 71 F2
 Llandovery / Llanymddyfri SA20 121 D4
 2 Llandybie SA18 79 A2
 4 Llandyssul SA44 19 E3
 Llangadog SA19 63 D7
 Llansteffan SA33 93 D5
 Narberth / Arberth SA67 70 D1
 Neath / Castell-Nedd, Pentreffynnon SA10 162 F7
 Newcastle Emlyn / Castell Newydd Emlyn SA38 119 E4
 Neyland SA73 132 B6
 Pontardawe SA8 147 E5
 Pontarddulais SA4 143 C5
 Saundersfoot SA69 134 F3
 Solva SA62 48 D3
 St Clears / Sanclêr SA33 127 D4
 St David's / Tyddewi SA62 123 C4
 St Dogmaels / Llandudoch SA43 118 A3
 Tenby / Dinbych-y-pysgod SA70 135 E5
High St Cl SA72 132 C1
High St / Prif Ffordd SA15 148 C4
High St / Stryd Fawr
 4 Glanaman SA18 99 A8
 Swansea / Abertawe SA1 174 B4
High View SA1 174 A5
High View Gdns SA2 166 B2
Hilland Dr SA3 172 B6
Hillbrook Cl SA5 158 D3
Hill Cres SA73 87 D2
Hill Crest SA3 173 B4
Hillcroft SA62 86 E5
Hillfield Villas SA17 136 A4
Hillgrove SA3 172 E4
Hill House Hospl SA2 166 D8
Hill La Camrose SA62 67 A6
 Haverfordwest / Hwlffordd SA61 125 A5
 Jeffreyston SA68 89 B1
Hill Pk SA70 135 D6
Hill Rd SA62 31 C3
Hill Rise SA69 134 C6
Hillrise Pk SA6 154 C7
Hillside Llanelli SA15 148 C7
 Loughor SA4 150 E1
Hillside Cl SA64 122 A4
Hillside Cres
 3 Goodwick / Wdig SA64 122 A4
 Swansea / Abertawe SA2 167 A7
Hillside Terr 4 SA67 89 E6
Hill St
 Goodwick / Wdig SA64 122 A6
 Gowerton / Tre-gwyr SA4 158 B5
 Haverfordwest / Hwlffordd SA61 125 A4
 Milford Haven / Aberdaugleddau SA73 131 B2
 Pembroke Dock / Doc Penfro SA72 132 B1
 Swansea / Abertawe SA1 174 A4
 The Mumbles / Y Mwmbwls SA3 173 C4
Hill Terr
 4 Fishguard / Abergwaun SA65 122 D4
 Neyland SA73 132 C6
Hilltop / Penrhiw SA14 141 A2
Hill Top Rd SA71 103 B6
Hill View SA10 169 B8
Hill View Cres SA6 160 D8
Hilton Ave SA73 131 E3
Hilton Ct Gdns* SA62 66 F6
Hodgson's Rd SA9 139 A4
Hoel Llwchwr SA18 98 B6
Hoel Y Dyffryn / Dyffryn Rd SA18 98 A7
Hoel-y-Felin
 Goodwick / Wdig SA64 122 A4
 Scleddau SA65 11 B1
Holbrook Rd 4 SA62 85 D8
Hole in the Wall 13 SA61 125 A5
Hollett Rd SA5 160 C4
Holloway SA61 125 A5
Holloway Ct SA70 135 B3
Holloway Hill SA70 135 A3
Holloway Rd SA33 92 F5
Hollybush Dr SA2 166 B8
Holly La SA73 87 D3
Holly St SA8 147 E5
Holts Field SA3 172 C5
Holyland Dr SA71 133 E5
Holyland Rd SA71 133 D4
Home Farm Way SA4 152 C2
Honddu Pl SA6 153 D1
Honeyborough Gn SA73 132 A7
Honeyborough Gr SA73 132 B7
Honeyborough Ind Est SA73 132 B8
Honeyborough Rd SA73 132 B7
Honeysuckle Dr SA6 153 D2
Hook CP Sch SA62 87 C6
Hoo St SA1 168 B7
Hop Gdn Rd SA70 105 E6
Hopkin St
 Pontardawe SA8 147 E5
 Swansea / Abertawe SA5 160 C4
Hopshill La SA69 134 C3
Horeb Rd
 Kidwelly / Cydweli SA17 136 F7
 Swansea / Abertawe SA6 153 F1
Horizon Pk SA6 161 A6
Horn's La SA61 125 A4
Horsepool Rd SA33 92 E6
Horton St SA1 174 A3
Hosea Row SA1 160 D4
Hospital Rd
 Gorseinon SA4 158 F8
 Penllergaer SA4 151 E1
Hottipass St SA65 122 D3
Hounsell Ave SA70 113 D6
Howard's Cres SA62 68 C5
Howards Way SA4 151 C3
Howarth Cl SA73 131 C4
Howells Ave 1 SA61 125 A3
Howells Cl SA71 104 C4
Howells Rd SA2 165 C8
Hoyles Cl SA70 135 B3
Hubberston VC Prim Sch SA73 131 A2
Humphrey St SA1 167 B7
Hunters Pk SA70 107 A5
Huntingdon Way SA2 166 B8
Huntington Cl SA3 173 B8
Huntington Ct SA3 173 B8
Huntsmans Cove SA3 172 E7
Hurelgy Pk SA68 134 D8
Hydfron Cl SA33 73 A1
Hywel Dda Gdns* SA34 126 D3
Hywel Rd SA61 124 D5
Hywel Way SA71 133 B3

I

Ian's Wlk SA6 154 B4
Idris Terr SA6 160 E6
Idwal Pl SA5 160 B5
Ilston SA15 148 F4
Ilston Ho 8 SA1 174 A4
Ilston Way SA3 173 A7
Imble Cl SA72 132 D1
Imble La SA72 132 D1
Imble St SA72 132 B1
Imogen Pl SA73 131 D3
Imperial Ctr SA7 161 B7
Incline The SA69 134 D4
Incline Way SA69 134 D4
India Row SA71 104 C4
Inkerman St
 Llanelli SA15 148 D5
 Swansea / Abertawe SA1 174 C3
Iorwerth St SA5 160 C2
Irfon Cres LD5 9 C1
Irfon Terr 4 LD5 9 D1
Irvine Ct SA3 173 B4
Iscennen Rd / Ffordd Is-Cennen 14 SA18 98 B7
Iscoed SA15 148 B6
Iscoed Rd / Heol Iscoed SA4 143 A4
Isfryn Burry Port SA16 137 E4
 Llangynog SA33 74 C3
Isgraig SA16 137 E4
Island Pl SA15 148 D5
Islwyn SA14 149 E5
Islwyn Rd SA1 167 B8
Ismyrddin SA31 129 E6
Is Y Bryn SA31 128 B8
Is-y-Bryniau SA9 100 B8
Is-y-Llyn SA14 78 A1
Ivey Pl SA1 174 B4
Ivy Bush Ct SA1 174 C3
Ivy Chy La SA69 134 E7

J

Jackson Dr SA73 132 C8
Jackson's Way
 Fishguard & Goodwick SA64 11 B2
 Goodwick / Wdig SA64 122 A5
James Ct SA1 161 D6
James Griffiths Rd SA18 98 D7
James John Cl 2 SA67 70 E1
James Pk SA68 134 C8
James St Gorof SA9 139 F8
 Llanelli SA15 148 E6
 Milford Haven / Aberdaugleddau SA73 131 B3
 Neyland SA73 132 B7
 Pontardawe SA8 147 D5
 Pontarddulais SA4 143 D3
Jasmine Cl SA2 166 B7
Jason Rd SA71 105 B1
Jeffreys Ct SA5 160 B5
Jenkins' Ct SA61 125 A2
Jericho Rd SA1 174 C4
Jersey Rd SA1 161 B4
Jersey St SA1 160 D1
Jersey Terr SA1 168 A7
Jesse Rd SA67 70 E1
Jessop Ct SA6 153 E4
Jim Harvard Ct 5 SA6 161 A8
Job's Well Rd SA31 128 C5
Jockey Fields SA61 125 B6
Jockey St SA1 174 B4
Jogram Ave SA71 133 C4
John Lewis St SA73 85 F1
John Morgan Cl 7 SA67 70 E1
John Penry Cres SA5 160 B6
John St
 Carmarthen / Caerfyrddin SA31 128 F5
 Llanelli SA15 148 D5
 Neyland SA73 132 B6
 Swansea / Abertawe, Cockett SA2 159 D2
 Swansea / Abertawe SA1 174 B4
 The Mumbles / Y Mwmbwls SA3 173 A4
Johnston Cty Prim Sch SA62 86 E5
Johnston Sta SA62 86 D5
Johnstown Cty Prim Sch SA31 128 C4
Joiners Rd SA4 157 D1
Jolly Rd SA18 99 C8
Jones St SA8 147 E5
Jones Terr SA1 174 A4
Jones' Terr / Teras Jones SA18 98 F8
Jordan's Cl SA73 131 F6
Jordanston Hill SA65 30 D4
Joseph Davies' Cl 6 SA1 160 C2
Jubilee Cl 1 SA62 50 F8
Jubilee Cres SA10 162 F8
Jubilee Ct SA5 159 C4
Jubilee Gdns 2 SA67 89 E6
Jubilee La SA4 158 A8
Juniper Cl SA2 166 B8
Jury La SA61 124 F5

K

Kavanagh Ct SA72 133 A8
Keats Gr
 Haverfordwest / Hwlffordd SA61 125 B3
 Swansea / Abertawe SA2 165 F7
Keepers Cl SA4 152 C2
Keep Hill End SA62 66 F6
Keeston Hill SA62 67 A6
Keeston La SA62 67 C6
Kelvin Rd SA6 146 D1
Kemble St SA2 166 F5
Kemys Way SA6 161 B7
Kendle Dr SA2 166 C8
Kenfig Pl SA1 161 A2
Kenilworth Pl SA3 173 A8
Kennington Cl SA2 165 D6
Kensington Cl 2 SA67 89 E6
Kensington Rd SA73 132 B7
Kensington St 7 SA65 122 D3
Kenystyle SA70 135 B3
Kerr's Way SA68 89 F2
Kesteven Ct SA70 105 D6
Kestrel Rd SA61 124 E5
Kew Gdns SA14 96 F6
Kidwelly Castle* SA17 136 B5
Kidwelly Ind Mus* SA17 136 E6
Kidwelly Sta SA17 136 A4
Kildare St SA5 160 C3
Kilfield Rd SA3 172 B5
Kilgetty La SA67 90 A3
Kilgetty Sports Club SA68 134 B8
Kilgetty Sta SA68 134 D8
Killan Rd SA2 165 B8
Kiln House La SA70 105 E2
Kiln Pk Rd SA67 70 E1
Kiln Rd
 Haverfordwest / Hwlffordd SA61 125 A5
 Johnston SA62 86 E6
Kilns The SA62 87 D4
Kilvey Rd SA1 174 C5
Kilvey Terr SA1 174 C4
Kimberley Cl SA2 166 D7
Kimberley Rd SA2 166 D7
King Edward Rd SA18 99 F6
King Edward's Rd SA1 167 A6
King Edward St SA34 126 C2
Kingfisher Ct SA15 149 A5
King George Ave SA15 148 E5
King George Ct SA2 166 B3
Kingrosia Pk SA6 155 A8
Kingsbridge Bsns Pk SA4 158 C8
Kingsbridge Dr SA71 133 D4
Kings Ct 8 SA67 70 D1
Kings Gdns SA72 132 B1
King's Head Rd SA5 159 F3
Kings La SA1 174 B3
Kings Mead / Dol Y Brenin SA48 120 C4
Kingsmere Cl SA62 125 C8
Kingsmoor Cl SA69 134 C7
Kings Rd Llandybie SA18 79 B2
 The Mumbles / Y Mwmbwls SA3 173 A4
King's Rd SA20 121 D4
King's Road / Heol Y Brenin SA1 174 C2
King St
 Carmarthen / Caerfyrddin SA31 128 F5
 Laugharne SA33 92 F6
 Llandeilo SA19 130 D5
 Llandyssul SA44 19 E3
 Pembroke Dock / Doc Penfro SA72 132 B3
 4 Swansea / Abertawe SA1 174 B3
Kingston Rd SA2 166 D7
Kingsway SA5 159 C4
Kingsway The / Ffordd Y Brennin SA1 174 A3
King William St SA72 132 D3
Kinley St SA1 167 F7
Kitchener Cl SA72 132 B2
Kittle Gn SA3 171 E7
Kittle Hill La SA3 171 E7
Knelston Pl SA5 159 F7
Knelston Prim Sch SA3 117 A8
Knightston Cl SA70 135 D8
Knoll Ave SA2 166 E6
Knowling Mead SA70 135 B5
Knoyle Dr SA5 160 C7
Knoyle St SA5 160 C7
Kyfts La SA3 114 E3

L

Laburnham Pl SA2 166 B6
Laburnum Gr SA61 124 E3
Lacques The SA33 92 E5
Lady Housty Ave SA3 172 E5
Lady Margaret Villas SA2 166 E7
Lady's Cross SA62 50 D2
Lady St SA17 136 B4
Lake Dr SA70 106 F5
Lakefield Cl 1 SA15 148 D4
Lakefield Pl SA15 148 C4
Lakefield Prim Sch SA15 148 C4
Lakefield Rd SA15 148 C4
Lakeside Tech Pk SA7 161 B6
Lake View Cl SA15 148 C7
Lakeview Terr SA15 148 C7
Lamack Vale SA70 135 C6
Lamb La SA2 165 E8
Lamborough Cres SA63 69 A7
Lamborough La SA62 69 C7
Lambourne Dr SA3 172 F6
Lambston Hill SA62 67 B3
Lambs Well Cl SA3 173 B4
Lammas St SA31 128 E5
Lampeter Comp Sch / Ysgol Gyfun Llanbedr Pont Steffan SA48 120 B4
Lampeter Leisure Ctr SA48 120 B4
Lamphey Cty Prim Sch SA71 105 A3
Lamphey Sta SA71 105 A3
Lampit Way SA65 122 D4
Lan Ave 1 SA6 160 F8
Lancaster Ct SA5 159 D5
Lan Coed SA1 161 D5
Landeg St SA6 160 E5
Lan Deri SA1 161 C5
Landor Ave SA2 165 F7
Lando Rd SA16 108 E4
Landor Dr SA4 150 D1
Landsdowne Ct SA5 159 D3
Landsker La SA67 70 D2
Langcliff Pk SA3 173 C3
Langdon Rd / Heol Langdon
 Swansea / Abertawe SA1 167 F7
 Swansea / Abertawe SA1 168 A6
Langer Way SA6 146 E1
Langford Rd SA62 86 E5
Langland Bay Rd SA3 172 F3
Langland Cl SA3 173 A4
Langland Court Rd SA3 172 F4
Langland Mews SA15 148 E3
Langland Rd
 Llanelli SA15 148 E3
 The Mumbles / Y Mwmbwls SA3 173 A4
Langland Terr SA2 166 E5
Langland Villas SA3 173 A4
Lan Manor SA6 160 E8
Lansdown SA3 172 F4
Lan St SA6 153 F1

Lapwing Rd SA15 148 B5
Larch Cres SA14 141 A2
Larch Rd SA73 131 E4
Lark Pl SA5 159 E7
Larkspur Cl 6 SA67 89 E6
Larkspur Dr SA3 172 E7
Latimer Ct SA5 159 E5
Latimer Rd SA19 130 E5
Lauderdale Rd SA18 99 E7
Laugharne Castle* SA33 92 F5
Laugharne Cl SA71 133 C6
Laugharne Ct SA2 166 A6
Laugharne VC Prim Sch SA33 92 E5
Laurel Dr
Ammanford / Rhydaman SA18 98 D7
Haverfordwest / Hwlffordd SA61 124 E3
Waunarlwydd SA5 158 D4
Laurel Pl SA2 166 B6
Lavinia Dr SA72 132 C1
Lawrence Terr 2 SA15 148 E5
Lawrenny St SA73 132 C6
Laws St SA72 132 C2
Layton Cl 5 LD5 9 D1
Leach Way SA70 135 D5
Le-Breos SA3 165 F1
Le-Breos Ave SA2 166 E6
Lee St SA1 167 F7
Leonardston Rd SA73 104 A8
Leonardston View SA73 132 A7
Letterston VC Sch SA62 50 E8
Leven Cl SA62 87 D6
Lewis Ave SA9 100 B8
Lewis Cres SA14 149 D5
Lewis St
Llanfihangel-ar-Arth SA44 19 E3
Pembroke Dock / Doc Penfro SA72 132 C2
Swansea / Abertawe, Sketty SA2 166 C6
Swansea / Abertawe, St Thomas SA1 167 F7
Leyshan Wlk SA3 172 E8
Leyshon Rd
Gwaun-Cae-Gurwen SA18 99 D7
Ynysmeudwy SA8 147 F6
Leys La SA62 66 E3
Libanus Rd SA4 151 C1
Libby Rd SA3 173 C3
Libby Way SA3 173 C3
Liddeston Cl SA73 131 A4
Liddeston Valley SA73 131 A4
Lighthouse Dr SA73 103 F7
Lilac Cl
Milford Haven / Aberdaugleddau SA73 131 E4
The Mumbles / Y Mwmbwls SA3 172 F8
Lilliput La SA3 173 B8
Lime Gr Killay SA2 165 D7
2 Lampeter Velfrey SA34 90 E7
Lime Gr Ave SA31 128 D6
Lime Kiln La SA3 172 B6
Limekiln Rd SA3 173 A5
Limeslade Ct SA3 173 C3
Limeslade Dr SA3 173 C3
Lime St SA4 151 C2
Lime Tree Gr 6 SA6 161 A8
Lincoln St 5 SA44 19 E3
Linden Ave SA3 173 A8
Lindsway Pk SA61 125 C7
Links Ct SA3 172 E3
Linkside SA3 172 E4
Linkside Dr SA3 171 A6
Links The SA16 137 B2
Link The SA2 166 A5
Linney Way SA73 131 E5
Lion St SA1 160 C2
Lion Way SA7 161 B7
Little Bridge St 1 SA31 128 F4
Little Castle Gr SA73 85 D2
Little Gam St SA1 174 A2
Little Wr St SA31 128 F5
Llain Delyn 4 SA33 93 C7
Llain Drigarn SA41 34 E4
Llanbed Ind Est SA48 120 C7
Llandafen Rd SA14 149 B5
Llanddowror VC Sch SA33 73 A1
Llandeilo Prim Sch / Ysgol Gynradd Llandeilo SA19 130 D6
Llandeilo Rd
Cross Hands SA14 97 B8
Cwmamman SA18 80 A1
Glanaman SA18 99 C8
Llandovery / Llanymddyfri SA20 121 B4
1 Llandybie SA18 79 A2
Llandeilo Rd / Heol Llandeilo SA14 78 C1
Llandeilo Rd Ind Est SA18 79 B3
Llandeilo Sta SA19 130 E6
Llandovery Castle (remains of)* SA20 121 D4
Llandovery Coll / Coleg Llanymddyfri SA20 121 C5
Llandovery Hospl / Ysbyty Llanymddyfri SA20 121 D5
Llandovery Sta SA20 121 C5
Llandovery Theatre SA20 121 D5
Llandybie Cty Prim Sch SA18 79 A2
Llandybie Rd SA18 98 B8
Llandybie Sta SA18 79 B2
Llandyry SA14 141 A2
Llandysul CP Sch SA44 19 E3
Llandysul Swimming Pool SA44 19 E3
Llanedi Rd Llanedi SA4 97 D1
Pontarddulais SA4 143 A7
Llanelli Ent Workshops SA15 148 F3
Llanelli Sta SA15 148 D3
Llanelli Workshops SA14 149 A3
Llanerch Cotts SA15 148 E7
Llanerch Cres SA4 151 B3
Llanerch Rd
Dunvant SA2 165 D8
Swansea / Abertawe SA1 161 B2
Llanerch Terr SA15 148 E7
Llanfaes SA9 139 F8
Llanfair Gdns SA3 173 A6
Llanfair Rd
Lampeter / Llanbedr Pont Steffan SA48 120 E5
Llandovery / Llanymddyfri SA20 121 D5
Llanfynydd VAP Sch SA32 61 A6
Llangadog CP Sch SA19 63 E7
Llangadog Rd SA17 136 E6
Llangadog Sta SA19 63 C7
Llangain CP Sch SA33 75 B2
Llangan Rd SA34 126 C3
Llangennech Jun & Inf Schs SA14 142 C1
Llangennech Sta SA14 150 C7
Llangiwg Prim Sch SA8 147 F6
Llangloffan Farmhouse Cheese Ctr* SA62 30 B3
Llangorse Rd SA5 160 B5
Llangunnor CP Sch SA31 129 A3
Llangwm SA5 159 F6
Llangwm CP Sch SA62 87 E4
Llangyfelach Prim Sch SA5 153 B2
Llangyfelach Rd SA5 160 C5
Llangyfelach St SA1 160 D1
Llangyndeyrn CP Sch SA17 76 C1
Llangynin CP Sch SA33 73 A7
Llangynog CP Sch SA33 74 C3
Llanion Cotts SA72 133 A8
Llanllienwen Cl
Swansea / Abertawe SA6 153 F4
Ynysforgan SA6 154 A4
Llanllienwen Rd
Swansea / Abertawe SA6 153 F3
Ynysforgan SA6 154 A3
Llanmiloe Cty Prim Sch SA33 92 A4
Llanmorlais Prim Sch SA4 156 B1
Llannant Rd SA4 150 F5
Llannion Pk Ind Est SA72 132 D4
Llannon Rd
Cross Hand SA14 96 F6
Llanelli Rural SA14 141 A4
Pontyberem SA15 96 B5
Llanrhian Rd SA62 28 E4
Llanrhidian Cvn Pk SA3 115 F3
Llanrhidian Prim Sch SA3 115 D2
Llanrwtyd Sta LD5 9 D1
Llansadwrn Cty Prim Sch SA19 43 C2
Llansaint CP Sch SA17 94 B3
Llansamlet Ind Est
Swansea / Abertawe SA6 160 F5
Swansea / Abertawe SA7 161 B7
Llansamlet Sta SA7 161 F8
Llansteffan Rd SA31 128 C1
Llanstephan Castle* SA33 93 E5
Llanwnen Rd SA48 120 A4
Llanwrda Prim Sch / Ysgol Gynradd Llanwrda SA19 43 D2
Llanwrda Sta SA19 43 E2
Llanybydder Cty Prim Sch SA40 21 D6
Llanychllwydog CP Sch SA65 32 C4
Llanycrwys CP Sch SA19 23 D7
Llan Y Ger 1 SA31 129 A5
Llan-yr-newydd SA4 156 F3
Llarwydden Cl SA4 152 C2
Llechyfedach SA14 96 F7
Llechyfedach CP Sch / Ysgol Gynradd Llechyfedach SA14 96 F7
Llethri Rd SA14 141 A1
Llety Rd SA14 96 F6
Llewellyn Dr SA71 133 B3
Llewellyn Rd SA4 151 F2
Llewellyn St / Stryd Llewellyn 14 SA15 148 D4
Llewelyn Circ SA1 167 B8
Llewelyn Park Dr SA6 160 E7
Llewelyn St SA2 166 C6
Llewitna Terr SA5 159 B6
Lliedi Cres SA15 148 E6
Lliw Cotts SA4 151 D6
Lliw Valley Cl / Clos Dyffrynlliw SA4 158 C6
Llon Cardi Bach 2 SA43 16 A5
Lloyd George La SA71 133 B3
Lloyd Rd SA5 160 C5
Lloyd St
17 Ammanford / Rhydaman SA18 98 B7
Pontardawe SA8 147 B2
Lloyd's Terr SA31 129 E7
Lloyd St / Stryd Lloyd SA15 148 C5
Lloyd Terr SA38 119 D6
Lluest-yr-bryn 1 SA31 128 F6
Llundain Fach SA15 140 E1
Llwyfan Cerrig Sta SA33 58 D5
Llwyn Afanc SA6 153 F5
Llwyn Arosfa SA2 166 C7
Llwyn Bedw SA5 159 D4
Llwyn Brwydrau SA7 162 A6
Llwyn Carw SA6 153 F5
Llwyncelyn
Capel Hendre SA18 97 D6
Llanelli SA15 148 E4
Mathry SA62 30 B2
Llwyn Celyn SA5 159 D4
Llwyncelyn Ave SA4 143 D4
Llwyncelyn Rd SA18 99 E6
Llwyncelyn Rd / Heol Llwyncelyn SA18 98 F8
Llwyncethin Rd SA5 160 A3
Llwyn Cl SA15 148 F5
Llwyncrwn SA15 95 E3
Llwyn-Crwn Rd SA7 161 D7
Llwyncyfarthwch SA15 149 A5
Llwynderw
Gorseinon SA4 151 B1
Three Crosses SA4 157 E1
Llwyn Derw
Pontardawe SA8 147 E4
Swansea / Abertawe SA5 159 D4
Llwynderw Cl SA2 166 B1
Llwynderw Dr SA3 173 B8
Llwyn Eithin SA5 159 D4
Llwyneryr Unit Hospl SA6 153 E2
Llwyn Helyg SA5 159 D5
Llwynhendy Jun Sch SA14 149 D5
Llwynhendy Rd / Heol Llwynhendy SA14 149 D4
Llwyn Hen Rd SA18 99 D5
Llwynifan SA14 142 B2
Llwyn Mawr Cl SA2 166 B8
Llwynmawr La SA4 157 E5
Llwyn Mawr La SA2 159 B1
Llwyn Mawr Rd
Swansea / Abertawe SA2 159 B1
Swansea / Abertawe, Ty-coch SA2 166 C8
Llwyn Meredydd SA31 129 A7
Llwyn-Nant SA18 99 D4
Llwynon SA6 146 E1
Llwyn On SA5 159 D4
Llwyn Rd SA18 99 D5
Llwyn Rhedyn SA2 166 B8
Llwynwhilwg Terr 3 SA14 148 F4
Llwyn Y Bioden SA6 153 F5
Llwyn-y-Bryn
Ammanford / Rhydaman SA18 98 B8
Neath / Castell-Nedd SA10 162 C6
Llwyn Y Gog
Cwmrhydyceirw SA6 154 A5
Swansea / Abertawe SA6 153 F5
Llwyn Y Golomen SA6 154 A5
Llwyn Y Graig SA4 151 F1
Llwyn-Y-Mor SA3 172 E4
Llwyn Yr Eos SA14 149 B6
Llwyn-Yr-Eos SA6 153 E2
Llwyn Yr Hebog SA6 154 A5
Llwyn Yr Iar SA6 154 A5
Llwyn Yr Ynys SA14 149 C4
Llygad-yr-Haul
Burry Port SA16 137 B3
Carmarthen / Caerfyrddin SA31 129 B3
Llynfa Rd SA4 157 A4
Llyn Llech Owain Ctry Pk* SA14 78 B2
Llyn Tircoed SA4 152 C5
Llyn Y Fran SA44 19 E3

Llys = court

Llys Aaron SA4 143 C4
Llys Afallon SA17 136 A5
Llys Alys SA15 148 E5
Llys Andrew SA10 162 F6
Llys Aneirin SA4 158 D8
Llys Baldwin SA4 158 B6
Llys Bethel SA14 149 C5
Llys Bronallt SA4 143 A4
Llys Brynteg SA4 151 B3
Llys Caermedi SA31 129 B6
Llys Caradog SA14 149 D5
Llys Cennech SA14 142 C1
Llys Cilsaig SA14 149 B8
Llys-Coed SA7 155 B1
Llys Derw SA38 119 B6
Llys Dewi Sant
Gorseinon SA4 151 C2
Swansea / Abertawe SA1 174 B2
Llys Dol SA6 154 A2
Llys Dur SA6 154 A2
Llys Dwyrig SA7 162 B8
Llys Eithin SA14 97 C8
Llys Elba SA4 158 B6
Llys Felin Newydd SA7 161 C6
Llys Fran SA15 148 E7
Llys Fredrick Jones SA9 139 C7
Llys Ger Y Llan SA4 143 D3
Llys Glanrafon SA8 147 E4
Llys Glan Y Mor 2 SA15 148 C3
Llys Gwalia SA4 151 D2
Llys Gwenci SA7 162 B8
Llys Gwenllian SA17 136 B5
Llys Gwernen
Cwmrhydyceirw SA6 154 A2
Swansea / Abertawe SA6 153 F2
Llysgwyn SA6 153 C2
Llys Gwynfaen SA4 150 F2
Llysgwyn Terr SA4 143 D5
Llys Hebog SA7 162 B8
Llys Hendre SA14 150 B7
Llys Holcwm SA17 93 F4
Llys Iwan 10 SA18 98 C7
Llys Jernegan 2 SA1 174 C2
Llys John Davies SA1 174 B4
Llys-Le-Breos SA3 165 F1
Llys Llanfair SA20 121 D6
Llys Llwyfen SA7 154 D1
Llys Lotwen SA18 97 E6
Llys Mair SA16 137 F2
Llys Moreia SA5 160 C6
Llysmorfa SA31 129 A4
Llys Nant Fer SA18 99 D7
Llysnewydd 4 SA15 148 C3
Llysonen Rd SA31 128 A3
Llys Onnen 2 SA64 122 A4
Llys Owen SA43 118 D4
Llys Pat Chown / Pat Chown Ct SA8 147 E4
Llys Penallt 4 SA15 148 F6
Llys Pencrug SA19 130 D6
Llys Pendderi SA14 149 F5
Llys Penpant SA6 153 C2
Llys Pentre SA5 160 D4
Llys Perl SA6 154 F8
Llys Sant Teilo SA5 153 B2
Llys Seion SA14 96 C8
Llys Tawel SA9 138 F1
Llys-Teg SA2 165 D8
Llys-uchaf
Birchgrove SA7 155 B1
Swansea / Abertawe SA7 162 B8
Llys Warner SA15 148 E7
Llys Y Brenin SA4 158 B8
Llys-y-Bryn SA7 162 B8
Llys-y-Coed
Burry Port SA16 137 A3
Loughor SA4 150 D1
Llys Y Dderwen
Llangennech SA14 150 B7
Pont Henri SA15 95 F4
Llys-y-Deri SA18 98 D7
Llys Y Drindod SA15 148 E3
Llys Y Felin
Llangennech SA14 142 B1
St Clears / Sanclêr SA33 74 B4
Llys-y-Felin SA5 160 C3
Llys-y-Ferin SA32 77 B8
Llys-y-Frân Ctry Pk* SA63 52 C4
Llys-y-Frân Visitor Ctr* SA63 52 C3
Llys Y Gof SA15 148 C4
Llys-y-graig SA10 162 F8
Llys-y-Llyfrgell 6 SA16 137 D2
Llys Y Morwr SA15 148 D4
Llys Y Nant 2 SA31 128 F6
Llys Ynyscedwyn SA9 139 D8
Llys Y Pobydd SA15 148 E5
Llys Yr Ardd
Morriston / Treforris SA6 154 A2
Swansea / Abertawe SA6 153 F2
Llys Yr Onnen SA14 149 A8
Llys Yr Orsaf 7 SA15 148 C4
Llys Yr Ysgol SA18 97 E6
Llys-y-Waun SA7 155 B1
Llythrid Ave SA2 166 E6
Lochturffin Cross SA62 29 C2
Lodge Cl The SA2 166 A7
Lodge The 4 SA1 174 A4
Login Rd SA5 159 A3
Lon Aber SA15 148 F4
Lon Alfa SA2 165 F8
Lon Bedwen SA2 166 D8
Lon Beili Glas SA18 99 D6
Lon Bele SA44 19 F7
Lon Brydwen SA4 151 B1
Lon Brynawel SA7 161 F6
Lon Bryngwyn SA2 166 E8
Lon Bryn-Mawr / Brynmawr La 9 SA18 98 B7
Lon Brynneuadd SA18 99 D7
Lon Cadog SA2 166 E7
Lon Cae Banc SA2 166 D7
Lon Cae Ffynnon 4 SA19 130 D6
Lon Camlad SA6 160 E8
Lon Caron SA2 166 E7
Lon Carreg Bica SA7 162 B8
Lon Cedwyn SA2 166 E7
Lon Ceiriog SA14 149 D5
Lon Cendy SA33 57 C2
Lon Channing 7 SA44 19 E3
Lon Claerwen SA6 160 E8
Lon Clychavr Gog SA31 129 E7
Lon Coed Bran SA2 166 E8
Lon Coed Parc SA2 166 E8
Lon Cothi SA2 159 E1
Lon Cwmgwyn SA2 166 E8
Lon Cynfor SA2 166 E7
Lon Cynlais SA2 166 D7
Lon-cywyn SA33 74 B5
Lon Dan-y-Coed SA2 166 E8
Lon Ddewi SA33 73 E7
Londeg SA8 147 D6
Lon Derw SA2 166 D8
London Rd SA72 132 D3
London Rd Ind Est SA72 132 F3
London Rd Mall The SA72 133 B8
Lon Draenen SA2 166 C7
Lon Draenog SA6 153 F5
Lon Drewen SA38 119 A7
Lon Einon SA4 151 F2
Lon Eithrym SA6 154 D8
Lon Enfys SA7 161 D6
Lone Rd SA6 146 D1
Lon Fair SA33 127 D3
Lon Fedwen 8 SA44 19 E3
Lon Ffos - Las SA17 109 B8
Long Acre SA3 172 B6
Long Acre Ct SA3 172 B6
Long Acre Gdns SA3 165 F1
Long Acre Rd SA31 128 F6
Lon Gaer SA4 151 F2
Longdown St SA43 118 B2
Lon Ger-y-Coed
Ammanford / Rhydaman SA18 98 D7
Swansea / Abertawe SA2 166 E8
Longfellow Cl 1 SA61 125 B3
Longfield
Manorbier SA70 106 A1
Tenby / Dinbych-y-pysgod SA70 135 A3
Longford Cres SA1 168 A7
Longhouse Gdns SA62 69 B5
Long La
The Havens SA62 66 E1
Walwyn's Castle SA62 85 C5
Long Mains SA71 104 C4
Long Oaks Ave SA2 166 E6
Long Oaks Ct SA2 166 E7
Long Oaks Mews SA2 166 E7
Long Ridge SA1 174 A5
Longridge Rd SA66 53 A1
Long Row Llanelli SA14 140 F1
Llanelli SA15 148 E6
Long Shepherds Dr SA3 172 D4
Long St SA42 13 E4
Longstone SA70 106 A3
Longstone La SA71 111 B3
Long View Rd SA6 153 D1
Lon Gwendraeth SA6 160 E8
Lon Gwesyn SA7 155 A1
Lon Gwynfryn SA2 166 E7
Lon Hafren
St Clears / Sanclêr SA33 127 E5
Swansea / Abertawe SA6 160 E8
Lon Heddwch
Craig-cefn-parc SA6 146 B2
Swansea / Abertawe SA7 161 E6
Lon Hir
Carmarthen / Caerfyrddin SA31 128 E6
Pontardawe SA8 147 F4
Lon Hywel SA34 126 C4
Lon Illtyd SA2 166 E7
Lon Iorwg SA2 166 C7
Lon Irfon SA2 159 E1
Lon Ithon SA6 160 E8
Lon Killan SA2 165 C8
Lonlas Ave SA10 162 C7
Lonlas Bsns Pk SA10 162 D7
Lonlas Village Workshops SA10 162 D8
Lonlas Villas SA10 162 C7
Lon Letty 3 SA44 19 E3
Lon Llwyd 1 SA18 99 B8
Lon Llysalaw SA33 127 B5
Lon Llys Havard SA18 98 C6
Lon Mafon SA2 166 D7
Lon Masarn SA2 166 C8
Lon Mefus SA2 166 D8
Lon Menai SA7 155 A1
Lon Nedd SA6 160 F8
Lon Ogwen SA7 155 A1
Lon Olchfa SA2 166 A6
Lon Penfro SA6 154 A4
Lon Penpound / Penpound La SA18 98 F8
Lon Pen-y-Coed SA2 159 D1
Lon Pen Y-coed SA2 166 E8
Lon Rhys SA19 130 C6
Lon Rhys Pritchard SA20 121 C4
Lon Sawdde SA6 160 E8
Lon Sutcliffe La SA4 158 B5
Lon Tanyrallt SA8 147 E3
Lon Teify SA2 159 E1
Lon Tir-y-Dail / Tir-y-Dail La 11 SA18 98 B7
Lon Towy SA2 159 D1
Lon Tyr Haul SA7 161 F6
Lon Wesley 9 SA44 19 E3
Lon Y Bedydd / Baptist La 13 SA18 98 B7
Lon-y-Coed SA8 147 D6
Lon Y Dderwen
Llanelli Rural SA15 140 E1
Llanelli SA15 148 E8
Lon Y Deri SA33 93 D7
Lon Y Derwydd SA18 99 C8

Lon-y-Felin SA18 ....98 B5
Lon-y-Gruglas SA18 ....98 A6
Lon Y Maes SA14 ......149 B6
Lon Y Parc / Park La
  SA18 ....99 D8
Lon Y Plas SA31 ....128 C2
Lon Yr Eglwys SA14 ...141 A2
Lon Yr Ysgol SA14 ....75 F2
Lon-Yr-Ysgol SA14 ....149 A7
Lon Yr Ysgol SA14 ....150 C7
Lon-y-Wern SA8 ....147 F3
Lord Nelson Ho SA1 ...174 B4
Lords Mdw View SA71 ..133 D4
Lota Pk Rd SA65 ....122 C3
Lotwen Rd / Heol Lotwen
  SA18 ....97 D6
Loughor Castle* SA4 ..157 D8
Loughor Comn SA4 .....151 B2
Loughor Rd SA4 ....158 B8
Loveston Cty Prim Sch
  SA68 ....89 A4
Lower Banwell St **6**
  SA6 ....160 F8
Lower Colbren Rd SA18 ..99 D6
Lower Cross Rd SA15 ..148 F5
Lower Dell The **1** SA48 ..15 A5
Lower Frog St SA70 ...135 E4
Lower La SA48 ....105 C8
Lower Lamphey Rd
  SA71 ....133 D3
Lower Mwldan **3** SA43 ..118 D3
Lower New Hos SA9 ....138 A1
Lower Pantteg SA9 ....139 A4
Lower Pk Rd SA70 .....135 D5
Lower Quay Rd SA62 ....87 D6
Lower Rd SA20 ....121 C3
Lower Row SA71 ....133 C6
Lower Station Rd **10**
  SA18 ....99 B8
Lower St Mary's St **8**
  SA42 ....13 E4
Lower Thornton SA73 ..131 C7
Lower Trostre Rd SA15 ..148 F3
Lower Wern Rd SA9 ....139 B6
Lowless CI SA71 ....133 C2
Lucas Rd SA7 ....155 A5
Lucy Rd / Heol Lucy
  SA10 ....162 D7
Lucy Walters CI SA73 ..87 A3
Lundy CI SA17 ....131 E5
Lundy Dr SA3 ....172 F7
Lundy View SA71 ......105 A1
Lunnon CI SA3 ....170 F8
Luton Terr **4** SA15 ...148 C2
Lydbrook Ct **2** SA1 ..160 C2
Lydford Ave SA1 ......174 C4
Lynden SA9 ....138 D1
Lyndhurst Ave SA68 ..106 C8
Lynne Brianne Visitor Ctr*
  SA20 ....8 A3
Lynn St SA1 ....160 B2
Lynsdale Rd SA1 ......160 C4
Lynton Bungalow SA16 ..137 F5
Lynton Ct SA3 ....172 E6
Lyric Ct SA8 ....147 E4
Lyserry La SA71 ....111 D4

M

Mabon CI SA4 ....150 F3
Machynys Rd SA15 ....148 E1
Mackworth Ct **3** SA1 ..174 C3
Mackworth Terr SA1 ...174 C3
McRitchie PI SA5 .....159 F3
Madoc PI SA1 ....174 A2
Madoc St SA1 ....174 A2
Maen-dedwydd Rd SA42 ..51 C6
Maengwyn SA1 ....100 B1
Maengwynne SA15 ....140 B1
Maenol Glasfryn SA14 ..150 B7
Maenor Helyg
  Burry Port SA16 .....137 A3
  Pembrey & Burry Port Town
  SA16 ....108 F3
Maerdy Rd SA18 ....98 B5
Maes-Ar-Ddafen Rd
  SA14 ....149 C4
Maes Awel **1** SA65 ...30 F5
Maes Awelon SA32 .....61 A2
Maes Briallu SA7 .....161 F7
Maes Brynglas **6** SA3 ..59 A3
Maes Cader SA3 ....39 B6
Maescanner Rd SA14 ..149 B7
Maescelyn SA19 ....42 C3
Maes Collen SA6 ......153 F3
Maes Conwy SA14 ....149 B6
Maescynog SA9 ....138 F1
Maes Dafydd SA4 .....158 B8
Maesderi Hendy SA4 ...142 F4
  4 Llandyfaelog SA32 ...75 F3
Maes-Deri SA1 ....161 D5
Maes Derwen SA4 .....97 C7
Maes Derwenydda SA9 ..39 B7
Maes Dewi
  Carmarthen / Caerfyrddin
  SA31 ....128 B5
  St David's / Tyddewi SA62 ..123 D5
Maesdolau SA32 ....75 F2
Maesdygwil SA62 .....123 D4
Maesegryn SA35 ....35 E3
Maes Elwyn John SA68 ..89 C3
Maes Ernin SA62 ......29 F5

Maes Ewan SA62 ....48 C3
Maes Gareth Edwards
  SA18 ....99 D7
Maesglas
  Cardigan / Aberteifi SA43 ..118 E5
  Llandovery / Llanymddyfri
  SA20 ....121 D5
  Penygroes SA14 ....97 D7
  Pontyates / Pont-iets SA15 ..95 D4
Maes Glas SA4 ....151 B1
Maes Glasnant
  Llandyfaelog SA31 .....75 F4
  Llangunnor SA31 ......76 A4
Maesglas Rd SA5 .....160 B3
Maes Golau SA15 .....148 F8
Maesgrenig SA18 ....98 F8
Maesgriffith SA33 .....93 E5
Maesgrug SA14 ....11 B3
Maesgwyn SA15 ....95 D4
Maesgwyn Dr SA4 ....143 C4
Maesgwynne Rd SA65 ..122 C3
Maes Hafren SA41 .....34 F5
Maes-henffordd SA43 ..118 F3
Maeshyfryd SA43 .....118 A4
Maes Hywel SA17 .....95 C5
Maes Ingli **3** SA42 ....13 E4
Maes-Lan SA7 ....161 F6
Maeslan SA48 ....100 C5
Maesllawddog **1** SA43 ..16 A5
Maes-llewelyn **2** SA31 ..129 A6
Maes Llewelyn SA18 ...98 F8
Maes Lliedi SA15 ......148 F8
Maesllwyn SA18 ....98 F8
Maes Maddock SA4 ...151 B1
Maes Margam / Margam PI
  SA15 ....148 E4
Maes Marlog SA18 ....119 E4
Maes Meigan SA41 ....34 F5
Maes Meillion SA7 ....161 F7
Maes Morfa **7** SA42 ....13 E4
Maesmynach SA43 ....118 B3
Maesolbri **2** SA33 .....93 C7
Maes Penrhyn SA14 ..149 B6
Maespiode SA18 ....79 A2
Maesquarre Rd / Ffordd
  Maescwarau SA18 ....98 D6
Maes Rd / Heol Maes
  SA14 ....150 C8
Maes Sant Teilo SA5 ..153 B2
Maes St SA1 ....167 F7
Maes Teg SA4 ....143 D5
Maesteg St SA1 ......174 C4
Maestir SA15 ....148 F7
Maestir Rd SA48 .....120 A5
Maes Tomos SA17 ....109 B8
Maestref SA15 ....148 F8
Maes Ty Cwrdd / Meadow Ct
  SA14 ....149 D4
Maes Ty Gwyn SA14 ..142 C1
Maeswerdd SA15 .....148 F8
Maesybedol SA18 .....99 B8
Maes-y-berllan
  Ammanford / Rhydaman
  SA18 ....98 C6
  Llangyndeyrn SA17 ....95 C8
Maesybont SA18 ......98 F8
Maesybont CP Sch SA14 ..78 B3
Maesybryn SA15 ......70 F8
Maes Y Bryn SA33 ....127 F7
Maes-y-Bryn SA6 ......153 F2
Maes-y-Capel SA16 ...137 B3
Maes Y Celyn SA4 ....157 D1
Maes-y-Cnwce **1** SA42 ..13 E4
Maesycoed
  Ammanford / Rhydaman
  SA18 ....98 D7
  Cardigan / Aberteifi SA43 ..118 E6
Maes-y-Coed
  Gorseinon SA4 ....158 B8
  Llanelli SA15 ....148 B6
  Swansea / Abertawe SA6 ..153 F2
Maesycoed Rd
  Godrergraig SA8 ....100 B1
  Lampeter / Llanbedr Pont Steffan
  SA48 ....120 B6
Maes-y-Coleg SA20 ..121 C5
Maesycwm SA9 ....138 F1
Maes-y-Dail SA18 .....98 A7
Maes-y-darren SA9 ...139 C6
Maesydderwen
  Beulah SA38 ....17 B4
  Llangennech SA14 ...142 D1
  Ystradgynlais SA9 .....139 E7
Maes-y-Dderwen
  Bronwydd SA33 ....58 E3
  Carmarthen / Caerfyrddin
  SA31 ....128 D4
  Swansea / Abertawe, Llangyfelach
  SA6 ....153 B2
  Swansea / Abertawe,
  Llwynbrwydrau SA7 ...162 A6
Maesydderwen Comp Sch
  SA9 ....139 E7
Maes Y Dderwen Gdns
  SA9 ....139 E7
Maesyderi SA15 ......148 B6
Maes Y Deri SA18 .....99 E8
Maes-y-Deri
  Gowerton / Tre-gwyr SA4 ..158 A5
  Lampeter / Llanbedr Pont Steffan
  SA48 ....120 B6
Maes Y Deri SA7 .....154 D1
Maes-y-Dre SA62 .....123 D4
Maesydre Ind Est LD5 ...9 D1
Maes Y Farchnad **2**
  SA19 ....130 E6
Maes Y Fedwen SA6 ..153 F3

Maesyfelin
  Lampeter / Llanbedr Pont Steffan
  SA48 ....120 C6
  Pontyberem SA15 .....96 A6
Maes Y Felin SA5 .....159 D5
Maesyffynnon
  Dinas Cross SA42 ......13 A3
  Ferryside SA17 ....93 F5
  Trimsaran SA17 ......109 B7
Maes Y Ffynnon SA14 ..96 F3
Maes Y Forwen SA62 ..48 C3
Maes Y Frenni SA14 ...34 F4
Maes Y Fron **13** SA18 ..99 B8
Maesyglyn SA18 ....99 D8
Maes-y-Glyn SA18 ....99 D8
Maes Y Gollen SA22 ..166 B6
Maesygors SA4 ....97 C8
Maes Y Gors SA15 ....148 D4
Maes Y Gruffydd Rd
  SA2 ....166 A3
Maes Y Gwernen CI
  SA15 ....153 E4
Maes Y Gwernen Dr
  SA15 ....153 E4
Maes-y-Gwernen Rd
  SA6 ....153 F4
Maes-y-Hedydd SA12 ..123 D4
Maes Y Mynach SA62 ..123 D4
Maes Y Neuadd **5** SA43 ..16 A5
Maes Y Parc
  Kidwelly / Cydweli SA17 ..136 B3
  Swansea / Abertawe SA5 ..159 D5
Maes-yr-Awel SA16 ...108 C4
Maes Yr Awel SA7 ....161 F7
Maes-yr-Efail
  Dunvant SA2 ....165 D8
  Gorseinon SA4 ....151 B1
Maes Yr Efail SA14 ...150 F7
Maes Yr Eglwys SA62 ..48 C3
Maes-yr-Eglwys SA17 ..94 B3
Maes-yr-Eithin SA7 ...155 B1
Maesyrhaf
  Cardigan / Aberteifi SA43 ..118 E4
  Cross Hands SA14 .....97 B3
  Llanelli Rural SA15 ...109 E4
  Llanelli SA15 ....148 F7
Maes-yr-Haf SA18 .....98 A7
Maes-yr-Haf SA14 ....156 E4
Maes-yr-Haf SA7 .....161 F6
Maesyrhaf PI SA4 ....151 A1
Maes-yr-Helyg SA18 ...79 B1
Maesyrhendre SA18 ...99 B8
Maesyrodyn SA44 .....20 B8
Maes-yr-Onnen SA6 ..153 F4
Maes Yr Orsaf **4** SA43 ..16 A5
Maes Yr Ysgol
  3 Abergwili SA32 ......59 A3
  1 Templeton SA67 ....89 E7
Maes Y Wennol SA31 ..128 B5
Maes-y-Wern SA17 ....95 D1
Maes Y Wern SA18 ....98 F8
Magdalen St SA1 .....124 F2
Maidens Gr SA18 ......79 A2
Main Rd SA73 ....132 B2
Main St
  Fishguard / Abergwaun
  SA65 ....122 D4
  Llangwm SA62 ....87 D4
  Pembroke / Penfro SA71 ..133 C4
  Solva SA62 ....48 E3
Mainwaring Terr SA1 ..160 D2
Major St SA5 ....160 C2
Maliphant St SA1 .....160 E1
Malt Hall SA3 ....115 D3
Malvern Terr SA2 .....166 F5
Manchester Sq SA73 ..131 C3
Mandinam Pk SA4 ....166 A7
Mannesmann CI SA7 ..161 C7
Manorbier Castle*
  SA70 ....113 C6
Manorbier Sta SA70 ..113 D5
Manorbier Voluntary CP Sch
  SA70 ....105 F2
Manor Cres
  Carmarthen / Caerfyrddin
  SA31 ....128 A3
  Manorbier SA70 ......105 F1
Manor Ct SA5 ....160 C3
Manor Daf Gdns SA33 ..127 E2
Manordeifi C in W VC Sch
  SA37 ....16 E2
Manor House Wildlife Pk*
  SA70 ....106 B5
Manorowen Walled Gdn*
  SA65 ....11 B1
Manor Par SA4 ....122 A5
Manor Rd SA5 ....160 C3
Manor Rd / Ffordd Y Faenor
  15 SA18 ....98 B7
Manor Way
  Carmarthen / Caerfyrddin
  SA31 ....128 A3
  Goodwick / Wdig SA64 ..122 A5
Mansel Ct SA4 ....158 B5
Mansel Dr SA3 ....172 C6
Manselfield Rd SA3 ...172 C6
Mansel Rd SA1 ....161 B4
Mansel St
  Burry Port SA16 .....137 D3
  6 Carmarthen / Caerfyrddin
  SA31 ....128 A3
  Gowerton / Tre-gwyr SA4 ..158 B5
  Pembroke / Penfro SA71 ..133 C4
  Swansea / Abertawe SA1 ..174 A3
Mansel St / Heol Mansel **15**
  SA15 ....148 D4

Manselton Prim Sch
  SA5 ....160 C3
Manselton Rd SA5 ....160 B3
Mansfield St SA73 ....131 D2
Maple Ave SA61 ......124 C3
Maple CI SA4 ....151 A3
Maple Cres
  Carmarthen / Caerfyrddin
  SA31 ....128 C5
  Swansea / Abertawe SA2 ..166 E7
Maple Dr SA5 ....158 D4
Maple Gr SA2 ....166 B6
Mapletree CI SA6 ....153 D1
Marble Hall CI SA73 ..131 D4
Marblehall Rd SA73 ..148 E5
Marble Hall Rd SA73 ..131 D3
Marchgate Paddock **1**
  SA65 ....122 D4
Mardy Trad Est SA4 ..158 C8
Margam Ave SA15 ....148 E4
Margam PI / Maes Margam
  SA15 ....148 E4
Margaret Rd **3** SA18 ..79 A1
Margaret St / Stryd Marged
  6 SA18 ....99 B8
Margarets Way SA71 ..133 E3
Margaret Terr SA1 ...168 A7
Marine Dr SA71 ......103 C6
Marine Rd SA7 ....85 C8
Mariners Sq SA1 .....148 D5
Mariner St SA1 ......174 B4
Mariners The SA1 ....148 C3
Mariners Way SA73 ..131 F5
Marine St SA1 ....148 C3
Marine Wlk **4** SA1 ..174 A1
Maritime Ind Pk SA72 ..132 C4
Market La
  Cardigan / Aberteifi SA43 ..118 E4
  Laugharne SA33 ....92 F5
Market Mews **4** SA4 ..160 F8
Market Sq
  Llandovery / Llanymddyfri
  SA20 ....121 D4
  Narberth / Arberth
  SA67 ....70 D1
Market St
  Haverfordwest / Hwlffordd
  SA61 ....125 A5
  1 Lampeter / Llanbedr
  Pont Steffan SA48 ...120 C5
  Laugharne SA33 ....92 F5
  2 Llandeilo SA19 ...130 D5
  Llanelli SA15 ....148 D5
  13 Narberth / Arberth
  SA67 ....70 D1
  4 Newport / Trefdraeth
  SA42 ....13 E4
  Pembroke Dock / Doc Penfro
  SA72 ....132 B2
  8 Swansea / Abertawe
  SA1 ....161 A8
  Whitland / Hendy-Gwyn
  SA34 ....126 D3
Marlais PS SA14 ......78 D4
Marlborough Rd
  Gorseinon SA4 ....158 B8
  Swansea / Abertawe SA2 ..166 F6
Marloes Ct SA5 ......159 F6
Marsden St **5** SA1 ..160 C2
Marshal Rd SA71 .....133 A5
Marshlands SA39 .....39 B6
Marsh Rd
  Pendine / Pentywyn SA33 ..91 E3
  Tenby / Dinbych-y-pysgod
  SA70 ....135 C5
Marsh St SA15 ....148 D4
Martell St SA1 ....159 E3
Martin Rd SA15 ......148 D5
Martletwy Cross SA67 ..88 D6
Mary Immaculate RC Sch
  SA6 ....124 F3
Mary St SA4 ....96 D8
Mary Twill La SA3 ....172 E4
Masefield Dr SA61 ...125 B4
Masefield Way SA2 ..166 E6
Mathry Hill SA62 ......29 F4
Mathry Voluntary Controlled
  Sch SA62 ....29 F4
Matthew St SA1 ......174 B4
Maxime Ct SA2 ....166 D6
Mayals Ave SA2 .....166 A1
Mayals Gn
  The Mumbles / Y Mwmbwls
  SA3 ....165 F1
  The Mumbles / Y Mwmbwls
  SA3 ....172 F8
Mayals Prim Sch SA3 ..173 A8
Mayals Rd
  The Mumbles / Y Mwmbwls
  SA3 ....166 A1
  The Mumbles / Y Mwmbwls
  SA3 ....172 F8
Mayfield Dr SA70 ....135 D6
Mayfield Rd SA73 ....132 B7
Mayfield Terr SA1 ...160 B3
Mayflower CI SA2 ....166 B6
Mayford La SA17 ......95 C1
Mayhill Gdns SA1 ...160 B1
Mayhill Rd SA1 ....160 B1
Maytree Ave SA3 ....172 F7

Maytree CI Loughor SA4 ..150 F2
  Swansea / Abertawe SA4 ..160 D8
Meadow Bank SA71 ..111 C6
Meadowcroft SA3 ....171 A5
Meadow Croft CI SA5 ..158 E4
Meadow Ct / Maes Ty Cwrdd
  SA14 ....149 D4
Meadow Pk SA14 .....132 F6
Meadow Pk SA3 ......172 F6
Meadow Rd SA10 ....105 E2
Meadow Rise
  Swansea / Abertawe, Cockett
  SA1 ....159 E2
  Swansea / Abertawe,
  Lower Sketty SA2 ....166 C4
Meadows Rd
  Cross Hands SA14 .....97 B7
  Cross Hands SA14 .....97 C6
Meadow St SA1 ......159 F2
Meadows The
  East Williamston SA69 ..134 B6
  Fishguard & Goodwick SA64 ..11 B2
Meadows The / Y Waun
  SA10 ....162 E7
Meadow View
  Dunvant SA2 ....165 C3
  Haverfordwest / Hwlffordd
  SA61 ....125 A6
  Swansea / Abertawe SA7 ..162 A6
Meadow Wlk **1** SA61 ..125 C7
Meads CI SA73 ....131 C4
Meads Ind Sch The
  SA73 ....131 D3
Meads Sports & Leisure Ctr
  The SA73 ....131 C4
Meads The SA62 ......87 D6
Mead The SA3 ....165 D8
Medway Workshops
  SA43 ....151 F1
Megan CI SA4 ....151 C3
Megan St SA5 ....160 A2
Meidrim CP Sch SA33 ..73 E7
Meidrim Rd SA33 ....127 F7
Meinciau Rd SA17 ...136 C4
Melcorn Dr SA3 ......172 E5
Melin-y-Coed SA14 ..118 E6
Melin Y Dre SA43 ....118 D5
Melrose CI SA6 ......161 B7
Melville St SA1 ......132 B2
Melville Terr SA72 ..132 A2
Memorial Sq SA16 ...137 E2
Mendip CI SA5 ....159 D3
Merchant's Pk SA71 ..133 B4
Merlin Cres SA1 .....166 F8
Merlin's Ave SA61 ...124 F2
Merlins Ct SA70 .....135 E5
Merlins Gdns **1** SA70 ..135 E5
Merlin's Hill SA31 ...124 F3
Merlin's Hill Ctr* SA32 ..76 C8
Merlin St SA1 ....128 E5
Merrion Cross SA71 ..111 B5
Methodist La SA62 ....68 C5
Meyler Cres SA73 ...131 D4
Meyrick Owen Way
  SA7 ....132 B3
Meyrick St SA72 .....132 C2
Michael's Field SA2 ..173 C3
Middlecroft La SA3 ..171 F7
Middlekilns Rd SA73 ..85 D2
Middle Mwldan SA43 ..118 D3
Middle Rd SA1 ....159 F4
Middle Row **3** SA71 ..133 C6
Middle St SA3 ....87 A3
Middleton St SA1 ....167 F7
Middle Walls La SA70 ..135 B3
Midland Ct SA1 ......174 C3
Midland La SA62 ......50 E8
Midland Rd SA7 .....161 D7
Midland Rd SA7 .....161 D7
Midland Terr SA9 ...139 D8
Miers St SA1 ....174 C3
Milborough Ct SA9 ..139 B7
Milborough Rd SA4 ..139 B7
Mile End CI SA5 .....159 F3
Miles La SA3 ....172 C6
Miles Rd SA5 ....160 C2
Miles St SA15 ....148 C7
Milford Comn Coll SA73 ..131 B2
Milford Haven Jun Sch
  SA73 ....131 D3
Milford Haven Mus*
  SA73 ....131 C2
Milford Haven Sec Sch
  SA73 ....131 B5
Milford Haven Sta SA73 ..131 B3
Milford Rd
  Haverfordwest / Hwlffordd
  SA61 ....124 F4
  Tiers Cross SA62 ......86 D4
Milford St SA69 ......134 F3
Milford Way SA5 ....159 F6
Military Rd SA73 .....132 B3
Millands CI SA3 .....172 D5
Millard Pk SA62 ......123 D4
Mill Back SA71 ......104 B4
Millbank Rd SA31 ...125 B5
Millbrook Cres **4** SA31 ..128 C5
Millbrook Rd SA5 ...160 D5
Millennium Coastal Park*
  SA15 ....149 B1
Millennium Coast Pk
  SA14 ....156 C8
Millennium Coast Pk Visitor
  Ctr* SA15 ....148 B4
Miller's Ct SA5 ......159 F6

Millfield Cl
Pentlepoir SA69 . . . . 134 A5
Swansea / Abertawe SA2 . . 166 B5
Millfield Rd SA14 . . . . . . 140 F1
Mill Hill SA67 . . . . 88 A6
Mill La
Haverfordwest / Hwlffordd
SA61 . . . . 124 F2
Llanelli SA15 . . . . 148 D6
Llanrhidian SA3 . . . . 115 D3
Narberth / Arberth SA67 . . . 70 D1
Newport / Trefdraeth SA42 . . 13 E3
The Mumbles / Y Mwmbwls
SA3 . . . . 166 B2
Millmoor Way SA62 . . . . . . 66 D1
Mill Pill SA33 . . . . 92 E3
Mill Pond Rd SA67 . . . . 70 D1
Mill Rd SA61 . . . . 125 B5
Mill Row SA8 . . . . 147 F4
Mills Dr SA73 . . . . 132 B8
Mill St
Carmarthen / Caerfyrddin
SA31 . . . . 128 E4
Gorseinon SA4 . . . . 151 C2
Gowerton / Tre-gwyr SA4 . . 158 B5
Lampeter / Llanbedr Pont Steffan
SA48 . . . . 120 C5
Llangwm SA62 . . . . 87 D4
Newcastle Emlyn / Castell
Newydd Emlyn SA38 . . . . . 119 F4
Pen-clawdd SA4 . . . . 156 F4
St Dogmaels / Llandudoch
SA43 . . . . 118 B3
Mill Terr / Ffordd Y Felin
SA18 . . . . 98 A5
Millway La SA68 . . . . 88 E1
Millwood Ct 3 SA1 . . . . . 160 C2
Millwood St SA5 . . . . 160 C3
Milton Cl SA61 . . . . 125 B4
Milton Cres SA73 . . . . 131 E2
Milton Mdws SA70 . . . . . . 105 C6
Milton Terr
Pembroke Dock / Doc Penfro
SA72 . . . . 132 C2
Swansea / Abertawe SA1 . 174 A4
Milward Cl 5 SA61 . . . . . 124 F5
Mincing La SA15 . . . . 148 D5
Minster Cl SA6 . . . . 161 B7
Minster Ct SA6 . . . . 161 B7
Min Y Dre 1 SA38 . . . . . . 119 D4
Minyffordd SA9 . . . . 139 B6
Min-y-Graig SA15 . . . . 96 B7
Min-y-Llan SA62 . . . . 50 E8
Min Y Mor SA15 . . . . 148 C5
Minyrafon SA9 . . . . 139 B5
Minyrafon Rd SA6 . . . . . . 146 D1
Mirador Cres SA2 . . . . 167 A6
Misty Hills Cl SA4 . . . . . . 157 C1
Mitre La SA62 . . . . 123 C4
Mixen Cl SA3 . . . . 172 F5
Model C in W Sch SA31 . 128 D5
Molleston Cross SA67 . . . . 89 C7
Mona Cl SA6 . . . . 161 A6
Monger St 1 SA1 . . . . . . 160 D1
Monksford St SA17 . . . . . 136 C4
Monksland Rd SA3 . . . . . 117 A6
Monkton SA71 . . . . 133 A4
Monkton Priory CP Sch
SA71 . . . . 133 A5
Monmouth Ho 8 SA1 . . . . 174 C2
Monmouth Pl SA6 . . . . . . 154 A5
Monnow Cl SA73 . . . . 86 D2
Montana Pl SA1 . . . . 160 D3
Monterey St SA5 . . . . 160 C3
Montgomery Cl SA71 . . . 133 A4
Monton Terr SA1 . . . . 168 A7
Montpellier Terr SA1 . . . . 167 B7
Monument Hill SA31 . . . . 128 C4
Moorfield Ave SA63 . . . . . . 69 A7
Moorfield Rd 5 SA67 . . . . 70 D1
Moorings The SA43 . . . . . 118 A5
Moor La SA3 . . . . 114 C2
Moorland Ave SA3 . . . . . . 172 E6
Moorland Rd SA62 . . . . 87 A6
Moorside Rd SA3 . . . . 172 F7
Moorview Cl SA5 . . . . 159 F4
Moorview Rd SA5 . . . . 159 F4
Morawel SA1 . . . . 161 D5
Mor-Awel Llanelli SA14 . . . 149 C5
Llanrhian SA62 . . . . 28 F3
Morfa CP Jun Mix Sch
SA15 . . . . 148 F3
Morfa Inf Sch SA15 . . . . . 148 E2
Morfa La
Carmarthen / Caerfyrddin
SA31 . . . . 128 E5
Kidwelly / Cydweli SA17 . . . 136 B4
Morfa Las SA65 . . . . 122 D3
Morfa Maen SA17 . . . . 136 B3
Morfa Rd SA1 . . . . 174 B4
Morfydd St SA6 . . . . 160 F8
Morgan Cl SA4 . . . . 151 F2
Morgan St
3 Cardigan / Aberteifi
SA43 . . . . 118 D4
Carmarthen / Caerfyrddin
SA31 . . . . 128 E5
Pontardawe SA8 . . . . 147 C2
Swansea / Abertawe SA1 . 160 D2
Morgans Way 2 SA67 . . . . 90 C2
Moriah Rd SA5 . . . . 160 C6
Morlais Rd SA5 . . . . 160 B5
Morlais Rd / Heol Morlais
SA14 . . . . 150 B7
Morlan Terr SA16 . . . . 137 F2
Morley St SA31 . . . . 128 E5
Morris La SA1 . . . . 174 C3
Morris St 7 SA6 . . . . 161 A8
Morris Terr SA5 . . . . 159 B6
Morriston Comp Sch
SA6 . . . . 153 F4
Morriston Hospl SA6 . . . . 153 E5
Morriston North Ind Est
Llansamlet SA6 . . . . 154 B1
Swansea / Abertawe SA6 . 161 C8
Morriston Pl SA18 . . . . 99 E6
Morriston Prim Sch / Ysgol
Gynradd Treforys SA6 . . 161 A8
Morriston South Ind Est
SA6 . . . . 161 A7
Mostyn Ave SA31 . . . . 129 C7
Mountain La SA67 . . . . 89 C8
Mountain Rd
Craig-cefn-parc SA6 . . . . . 146 C1
Cwmamman SA18 . . . . 80 A1
Llandybie SA18 . . . . 79 E1
Quarter Bach SA18 . . . . 80 E1
Mountain Rd / Heol Y
Mynydd SA16 . . . . 137 A3
Mount Airey Cty Prim Sch
SA61 . . . . 125 A3
Mountbatten Ct SA5 . . . . 159 E5
Mount Cres
Penllergaer SA4 . . . . 151 F2
Swansea / Abertawe SA6 . 153 D2
Mount Hill Rise SA31 . . . 129 A3
Mount La SA62 . . . . 67 C3
Mount Vernon SA67 . . . . . . 89 A7
Mount Pleasant
Gowerton / Tre-gwyr SA4 . . 158 B4
Swansea / Abertawe SA1 . 174 A3
Mount Pleasant Bldgs 2
SA15 . . . . 148 D6
Mount Pleasant Ct
SA10 . . . . 162 E7
Mount Pleasant Dr SA1 . 174 A3
Mount Pleasant Way
SA73 . . . . 131 E4
Mount Sch The SA73 . . . . 131 F3
Mount Sion La SA71 . . . . 110 F5
Mount St
Gowerton / Tre-gwyr SA4 . . 158 B5
Swansea / Abertawe SA6 . 153 E1
Mount The
7 Carmarthen / Caerfyrddin
SA31 . . . . 128 F5
Gowerton / Tre-gwyr SA4 . . 158 B5
Mount Wlk SA48 . . . . 120 B5
Moylgrove Cty Prim Sch
SA43 . . . . 14 E7
Muirfield Dr SA3 . . . . 165 F1
Mulberry Ave SA3 . . . . . . 172 F8
Mulgrave Way SA2 . . . . . 166 A1
Mumbles Bay Ct SA2 . . . . 166 B1
Mumbles Head Pk SA16 . 137 B4
Mumbles Pier* SA3 . . . . . 173 E3
Mumbles Rd
Swansea / Abertawe SA2 . 166 D3
The Mumbles / Y Mwmbwls
SA3 . . . . 173 C4
West Cross SA3 . . . . 173 A7
Munro Ct SA72 . . . . 133 A8
Murrayfield Cl SA5 . . . . . 159 D3
Murray Rd SA73 . . . . 131 E2
Murray St SA15 . . . . 148 D5
Murton La SA3 . . . . 172 D5
Museum of Speed*
SA33 . . . . 91 E3
Musselwick Rd SA62 . . . . . 84 F1
Mwtshwr SA43 . . . . 118 B3
Mydam La SA4 . . . . 151 A2
Myddynfych SA18 . . . . 98 B8
Mylett's Hill SA71 . . . . . . 133 D7
Mynyddbach SA18 . . . . 97 F5
Mynydd Garnllwyd Rd
SA6 . . . . 160 D8
Mynydd Gelli Wastad Rd
Clydach SA6 . . . . 154 B6
Swansea / Abertawe SA6 . . 153 E5
Mynydd Mawr Woodland
Pk* SA14 . . . . 96 F7
Mynydd-Newydd Rd
SA5 . . . . 160 A7
Myrddin CP Sch SA31 . . . 128 E6
Myrddin Cres SA31 . . . . . 128 F6
Myrddin Gdns SA1 . . . . . . 161 B3
Myrddin Rd SA1 . . . . 161 B3
Myrtle Gr SA2 . . . . 166 E7
Myrtle Hill
Carmarthen / Caerfyrddin
SA31 . . . . 128 F2
Llanelli Rural SA15 . . . . . . 109 F3
Pen-clawdd SA4 . . . . 156 E3
Pontarddulais SA4 . . . . . . 143 C5
Pont Henri SA15 . . . . 95 F4
Myrtle Hill Ret Area
SA31 . . . . 128 E2
Myrtle Rd SA4 . . . . 158 D8
Myrtle Terr Llanelli SA15 . . 148 E5
The Mumbles / Y Mwmbwls
SA3 . . . . 173 B4
Mysydd Rd SA1 . . . . 160 D4
Mysydd Terr SA1 . . . . 160 D3

N

Nant Arw SA18 . . . . 97 D6
Nant Cadle SA5 . . . . 159 E6
Nant-fach SA14 . . . . 141 B2
Nant Fach SA66 . . . . 53 C2
Nant Glas SA4 . . . . 152 C5
Nant Gwineu Rd SA18 . . . . 80 C1
Nant Gwineu Rd / Heol Nant
Gwinau SA18 . . . . 99 C8
Nantlais
Ammanford / Rhydaman
SA18 . . . . 98 B8
Cefn-bryn-brain SA9 . . . . . 100 B8
Nantong Way SA1 . . . . . . 160 F4
Nantucket Ave 3 SA73 . . 131 C3
Nantwen SA14 . . . . 149 F4
Nant Y Berllan SA43 . . . . 118 A5
Nantybryn SA14 . . . . 149 A7
Nantybwla SA31 . . . . 128 A7
Nant-y-Ci Rd SA18 . . . . . . 97 F7
Nant-y-Coy Mill* SA62 . . . 51 A4
Nant-y-Cwm Steiner Sch /
Ysgol Rudolf Steiner
Nant-y-Cwm SA66 . . . . . . 53 D3
Nant-y-Dderwen SA18 . . . 97 F7
Nant Y Dderwen SA14 . . . . 96 D8
Nantydd Terr SA14 . . . . . . 149 C5
Nantyffin SA32 . . . . 77 D2
Nantyffin N SA7 . . . . 161 D7
Nantyffin Rd
Pontarddulais SA4 . . . . 143 D3
Swansea / Abertawe SA7 . 161 C7
Nantyffin S SA7 . . . . 161 C6
Nantyglyn Rd SA18 . . . . . . 79 F1
Nantyglyn Rd / Heol Nant Y
Glyn SA18 . . . . 98 F8
Nant-y-Gro Llanelli SA14 . 149 C6
Llangennech SA14 . . . . 142 B1
Nantygroes CP Sch SA18 . 78 E4
Nant-yr-Arian SA31 . . . . 128 D5
Nant Yr Eglwys SA62 . . . . . 51 F4
Nant-yr-Ynys SA33 . . . . . . 58 E8
Napier Gdns SA43 . . . . . . 118 E4
Napier St SA43 . . . . 118 D4
Narberth CP Sch SA67 . . . 70 D1
Narberth Mus Bookshop*
SA67 . . . . 70 E1
Narberth Rd
Tenby / Dinbych-y-pysgod
SA70 . . . . 135 C7
Uzmaston & Boulston
SA61 . . . . 125 D5
Narberth Sta SA67 . . . . . . 70 F1
Nash Ave SA31 . . . . 129 B7
Nathan St SA15 . . . . 148 C3
National Botanic Gdn of
Wales The / Gardd Fotaneg
Genedlaethol Cymru*
SA32 . . . . 77 D5
National Coracle Ctr*
SA38 . . . . 17 B4
National Wetlands Centre
Wales* SA14 . . . . 149 C2
National Woollen Mus*
SA44 . . . . 18 E2
Neath Rd
Morriston / Treforris SA6 . . 154 A2
Swansea / Abertawe, Plasmarl
SA1, SA6 . . . . 160 E5
Swansea / Abertawe, Tircanol
SA6 . . . . 154 A2
Ystradgynlais SA9 . . . . 139 F6
Nell's La SA42 . . . . 14 C5
Nelson Ave SA73 . . . . 131 B2
Nelson St
Pembroke Dock / Doc Penfro
SA72 . . . . 104 B5
Swansea / Abertawe SA1 . 174 A2
Nelson Terr SA15 . . . . 148 C4
Netherwood Sch SA69 . . . 134 E5
Netpool Rd SA43 . . . . 118 C4
Neuadd Rd SA18 . . . . 99 C8
Nevills Cl SA4 . . . . 158 C6
Nevill St SA15 . . . . 148 C4
Newbridge Rd SA33 . . . . . . 92 F5
Newcastle Emlyn Castle
(rems of)* SA38 . . . . . . 119 E5
Newcastle Emlyn Ind Est
SA38 . . . . 119 E5
New Ceidrim Rd 14 SA18 . 99 B8
New Cross Bldgs 1
SA6 . . . . 154 A1
New Cut Rd SA1 . . . . 174 B4
New Dock Rd SA15 . . . . . 148 D3
New Dock St SA15 . . . . . . 148 D2
Newell Hill SA70 . . . . 135 D5
Newell Rd SA10 . . . . 162 E8
Newgale Cl SA5 . . . . 159 F7
Newgale Hill SA62 . . . . 49 B1
New Hill SA64 . . . . 122 B6
New Inn Prim Sch / Ysgol
Gynradd New Inn SA39 . . 39 E8
New Mill Rd SA2 . . . . 166 A6
New Mill Rd / Heol Felin
Newydd SA43 . . . . 118 F6
Newnham Cres SA2 . . . . . 166 E7
New Orchard St SA1 . . . . 174 B4
New Oxford Bldgs SA1 . . 174 A2
New Park Holiday Pk
SA3 . . . . 117 A4
Newport Bsns Pk SA42 . . . 13 E4
Newport Castle* SA42 . . . 13 E3
Newport Rd 2 SA65 . . . . . 122 E4
New Quarr Rd SA5 . . . . . . 160 C5
New Rd
Ammanford / Rhydaman
SA18 . . . . 98 B6
Birchgrove SA7 . . . . 154 F1
Brecon SA18 . . . . 80 E1
Crofty SA4 . . . . 156 B3
Freystrop SA62 . . . . 87 B6
Goodwick / Wdig SA64 . . . 122 A5
Grovesend SA4 . . . . 151 C6
Gwaun-Cae-Gurwen SA18 . . 99 E7
Haverfordwest / Hwlffordd
SA61 . . . . 125 B4
Kilgetty / Begelly SA68 . . . 134 B8
New Rd *continued*
Llandeilo SA19 . . . . 130 D5
Llandovery / Llanymddyfri
SA20 . . . . 121 C5
1 Llandysul SA44 . . . . 19 E3
Llanelli, Mount Pleasant
SA15 . . . . 148 C6
Llanelli, Penceiliogi SA14 . . 149 B6
Neath / Castell-Nedd SA10 . 162 F7
Newcastle Emlyn / Castell
Newydd Emlyn SA38 . . . . . 119 C5
Pontarddulais SA4 . . . . 143 B4
Pontyberem SA15 . . . . 96 B6
Swansea / Abertawe SA2 . 159 D1
Swansea / Abertawe, Tre-boeth
SA5 . . . . 160 C6
Trebanos / Trebannws
SA8 . . . . 147 B2
New Rd / Heol Newydd
Neath / Castell-Nedd
SA10 . . . . 162 C1
Ystradowen SA9 . . . . 100 C7
New School Rd / Heol Ysgol
Newydd 15 SA18 . . . . 99 B8
Newslade 8 SA1 . . . . 174 A4
New St Burry Port SA16 . . . 137 F2
Kidwelly / Cydweli SA17 . . . 136 B4
Lampeter / Llanbedr Pont Steffan
SA48 . . . . 120 C4
Llanelli SA15 . . . . 148 E2
Solva SA62 . . . . 48 D3
St David's / Tyddewi SA62 . 123 D5
Swansea / Abertawe SA1 . 174 B4
Ystalyfera SA9 . . . . 139 A4
Newton La SA68 . . . . 88 C2
Newton Prim Sch SA3 . . . 172 E5
Newton Rd Clydach SA6 . . 146 D1
Llanstadwell SA73 . . . . 103 F7
Oystermouth SA3 . . . . 172 F5
The Mumbles / Y Mwmbwls
SA3 . . . . 173 A5
Newton St SA1 . . . . 174 A2
Newton Terr SA68 . . . . 89 F2
Newtown SA18 . . . . 98 A7
Newtown Cl SA18 . . . . 98 A7
Newtown Rd
Ammanford / Rhydaman
SA18 . . . . 98 A7
Hook SA62 . . . . 87 C5
New Villas SA3 . . . . 173 B4
New Way SA71 . . . . 133 C5
New Well La SA3 . . . . 172 F5
New Wells Rd SA73 . . . . . . 87 D3
New Zealand St SA15 . . . 148 C6
Neyland Athletic Club
SA73 . . . . 132 B7
Neyland CP Sch SA73 . . . 132 B7
Neyland Dr SA5 . . . . 159 F7
Neyland Hill SA73 . . . . . . 132 B6
Neyland Hts SA73 . . . . . . 132 B7
Neyland Inf Sch SA73 . . . 132 B6
Neyland Rd SA73 . . . . 131 F6
Neyland Terr SA73 . . . . . . 132 B5
Neyland Vale SA73 . . . . . . 132 A7
Nicander Par SA1 . . . . 167 B8
Nicander Pl SA1 . . . . 167 B8
Nicholas Ct SA4 . . . . 151 C3
Nicholas Rd SA7 . . . . 155 A6
Nicholl Ct SA3 . . . . 173 C3
Nicholls Rd SA71 . . . . 133 E3
Nicholl St SA1 . . . . 167 B6
Nightingale Ct SA15 . . . . 149 A5
Ninth Ave SA6 . . . . 153 D2
Nixon Terr SA6 . . . . 154 A1
Noddfa Dewi SA62 . . . . . . 123 D5
Nolton Ct SA5 . . . . 159 F6
Norfolk St SA1 . . . . 167 B7
Norgans Hill SA71 . . . . . . 133 A3
Norgan's Terr SA71 . . . . . 133 B4
Normandy Rd SA1 . . . . . . 160 E3
Norman Rd / Heol Norman
3 SA18 . . . . 98 B7
Northampton La SA1 . . . . 174 A3
North Bank SA19 . . . . 130 D5
North Cl SA69 . . . . 134 D4
North Cottage Dr SA4 . . . 151 B1
North Cres SA61 . . . . 125 A6
North Ct SA61 . . . . 124 D5
North Dock Bsns Workshops
SA15 . . . . 148 B4
North End SA62 . . . . 29 A5
Northeron SA3 . . . . 172 F8
Northfield Rd SA67 . . . . . . 70 D1
Northgate St SA71 . . . . . . 133 B5
North Hall Est SA62 . . . . . 85 A2
North Hill Rd SA1 . . . . 174 A4
North Hills La SA3 . . . . . . 170 C6
North La
Castlemartin SA71 . . . . 111 B6
Marloes & St Brides SA62 . . . 84 C3
Northlands Pk SA3 . . . . . 172 A7
North Lodge Cl SA4 . . . . . 152 B3
North Par SA31 . . . . 129 A5
North Rd
Cardigan / Aberteifi SA43 . 118 D4
Lampeter / Llanbedr Pont Steffan
SA48 . . . . 120 C6
Loughor SA4 . . . . 150 F1
Whitland / Hendy-Gwyn
SA34 . . . . 126 C4
North St
Haverfordwest / Hwlffordd
SA61 . . . . 125 A5
Pembroke Dock / Doc Penfro
SA72 . . . . 132 B1
North Terr SA14 . . . . 149 B7
Northway SA3 . . . . 172 B7
Northway Ct SA3 . . . . 172 A7
Norton SA70 . . . . 135 E5
Norton Ave SA3 . . . . 173 A6
Norton Dr SA3 . . . . 171 A6
Norton La SA3 . . . . 171 B7
Norton Rd
Penygroes SA14 . . . . 97 D8
The Mumbles / Y Mwmbwls
SA3 . . . . 173 A6
Norwood Gdns* SA39 . . . . 21 A3
Nottage Mews SA3 . . . . . . 172 E4
Nottage Rd SA3 . . . . 172 E4
Notts Gdns SA2 . . . . 166 F7
Nubian Ave SA61 . . . . 124 D4
Nubian Cres SA73 . . . . . . 131 B2
Nun St SA62 . . . . 123 C5
Nurseries The SA15 . . . . . 109 F3
Nursery Cl 8 SA34 . . . . 90 E7
Nurses Cnr SA4 . . . . 156 F4
Nythfa SA4 . . . . 152 C5

O

Oakdene SA2 . . . . 165 D7
Oak Dr SA5 . . . . 158 D4
Oakfield Dr SA68 . . . . 134 D8
Oakfield Rd SA8 . . . . 147 E5
Oakfield Rd / Heol
Maesoderwen 5 SA18 . . . 99 B8
Oakfield St SA4 . . . . 143 C4
Oakfield Terr 7 SA18 . . . . 98 C7
Oakford Pl SA5 . . . . 159 D6
Oak Hill Pk SA10 . . . . 162 E8
Oakland Cl SA7 . . . . 155 A5
Oakland Rd SA3 . . . . 173 A4
Oaklands Llanelli SA14 . . . 141 A2
The Mumbles / Y Mwmbwls
SA3 . . . . 172 F6
Oaklands Cl / Clos-y-derwen
SA14 . . . . 97 B8
Oaklands Ct SA2 . . . . 166 A1
Oaklands Rd SA4 . . . . 152 A6
Oaklands Terr
Swansea / Abertawe SA1 . . 167 B7
Wiston SA62 . . . . 69 B4
Oakleigh House Sch
SA2 . . . . 166 F7
Oakleigh Rd SA4 . . . . 150 F2
Oak Rd SA72 . . . . 132 B1
Oak Ridge SA2 . . . . 166 A6
Oakridge Acres SA70 . . . . 135 B5
Oak St SA4 . . . . 158 D8
Oak Tree Ave SA2 . . . . . . 166 C6
Oak Tree Cl SA3 . . . . 172 E6
Oak Tree Cl / Clos Y
Dderwen SA18 . . . . 98 D7
Oak Way SA4 . . . . 152 C2
Oakwood Ave SA6 . . . . . . 153 D1
Oakwood Cl SA8 . . . . 147 A1
Oakwood Dr Clydach SA8 . 147 A1
Gowerton / Tre-gwyr SA4 . . 158 D4
Oakwood Gr SA61 . . . . . . 125 A6
Oakwood Leisure Pk*
SA67 . . . . 88 F7
Oakwood Rd SA2 . . . . 166 F6
Oakwood Rise SA8 . . . . . . 147 A1
Oberon Gr SA73 . . . . 131 F5
Observatory Ave SA73 . . . 131 A2
Ocean Cres 6 SA1 . . . . . . 174 B1
Ocean View SA2 . . . . 166 B3
Ocean View / Golwg Y Mor
SA10 . . . . 169 C8
Ocean Way SA72 . . . . 103 F5
Ochr-y-Waun Rd SA9 . . . 100 B7
Oddfellows' St SA9 . . . . . 138 F2
Odo St SA1 . . . . 160 D2
Ogmore Rd SA1 . . . . 161 A2
Olchfa Cl SA2 . . . . 166 A6
Olchfa La SA2 . . . . 166 A7
Olchfa Sch SA2 . . . . 166 A6
Old Amroth Rd SA67 . . . . . 90 D4
Old Bridge SA61 . . . . 125 A5
Old Castle Rd
Cardigan / Aberteifi SA43 . 118 B4
Llanelli SA15 . . . . 148 C5
Old Conduit The SA71 . . . 133 A4
Old Farm Ct SA7 . . . . 161 F6
Old Graig St SA38 . . . . . . 119 C5
Old Hakin Rd SA61 . . . . . . 124 E2
Old Keg Yd The 9 SA67 . . . 70 D1
Old Kittle Rd SA3 . . . . 171 F7
Old Llangyfelach Rd
SA4 . . . . 152 B3
Old Llansteffan Rd
SA31 . . . . 128 D3
Old Lodge SA15 . . . . 148 D4
Old Newport Rd 1
SA65 . . . . 122 E4
Old Oak La SA31 . . . . 129 A6
Old Priory Rd SA31 . . . . . 129 A5
Old Rd
Ammanford / Rhydaman
SA18 . . . . 98 B8
Llanelli SA15 . . . . 148 D6
Llansteffan SA33 . . . . 93 D5
Neath / Castell-Nedd SA10 . 162 F7
Old Road Prim Sch
SA15 . . . . 148 D6
Old Sch Rd SA33 . . . . 93 E6
Old Sta Rd 5 SA31 . . . . . . 129 A5
Old Tenby Rd SA33 . . . . . 127 C3
Old Tramway SA16 . . . . . . 137 E2
Oldway SA3 . . . . 172 A6
Old Wern Rd SA9 . . . . 139 B6
Olive Rd SA3 . . . . 172 F8

Olive St SA15 ......148 F3
Orange Way SA71 ......133 B4
Orchard Bldgs 3 SA71 ..133 D4
Orchard Cl
 Burry Port SA16 ......137 C3
 Porteynon SA3 ......117 A4
Orchard Ct SA1 ......174 B4
Orchard Dr SA4 ......152 D1
Orchard Gr SA4 ......152 A2
Orchard Pk SA33 ......92 E5
Orchard Row 2 SA62 ..87 E4
Orchard St
 2 Carmarthen / Caerfyrddin
 SA31 ......128 F5
 Llandovery / Llanymddyfri
 SA20 ......121 D4
 Pontardawe SA8 ......147 E5
 Swansea / Abertawe SA1 ..174 B3
Orchard Terr SA4 ......115 F4
Orchard The SA3 ......172 F5
Orchid Ct SA3 ......172 E6
Orielton CP Sch SA71 ..104 A3
Orielton Field Ctr*
 SA71 ......104 A2
Orielton Terr SA72 ......104 A6
Ormes Rd SA10 ......162 E8
Ormsby Terr SA4 ......168 A7
Orpheus Rd SA6 ......154 B4
Orton La SA63 ......69 A7
Osborn Cl SA73 ......132 C7
Osborne Pl SA4 ......156 B2
Osborne Terr SA2 ......166 E5
Osborn Pk SA73 ......132 C6
Osprey Cl SA3 ......172 E7
Osprey Dr 5 SA61 ......124 E5
Osterley St SA1 ......168 A7
Ostrey Bank SA33 ......127 D4
Overdale SA61 ......124 E3
Overland Cl SA3 ......173 A4
Overland Rd SA1 ......173 A4
Overton Cl 6 SA1 ......174 A4
Owenfforddd SA42 ......123 C4
Owen's La SA9 ......100 C2
Owen St SA71 ......133 B4
Owls Lodge La SA3 ......165 F1
Oxford Street / Stryd
 Rhydychen SA1 ......174 A2
Oxwich Castle* SA3 ......117 D5
Oxwich Ct SA6 ......161 A7
Oxwich Leisure Pk SA3 ..117 D5
Oxwich Nature Reserve*
 SA3 ......117 E5
Oystermouth Castle*
 SA3 ......173 A5
Oystermouth Prim Sch
 SA3 ......173 A5
Oystermouth Rd SA1 ..174 A1
Ozanam Ct SA5 ......159 F6

P

Paddock La SA70 ......105 D5
Paddock St SA15 ......148 D4
Paddock The
 Tenby / Dinbych-y-pysgod
 SA70 ......135 B3
 The Mumbles / Y Mwmbwls
 SA3 ......173 A8
Page La SA1 ......167 B6
Page St SA1 ......167 B7
Palace Ave SA15 ......148 E5
Pale Rd SA10 ......162 F6
Palleg Rd / Heol Palleg
 SA9 ......138 C2
Palmerston Rd SA61 ..124 D3
Palmyra Ct SA3 ......173 A6
Pant Bryn Isaf SA14 ..149 D5
Panteg Rd SA62 ......48 D3
Pantglas
 Carmarthen / Caerfyrddin
 SA31 ......129 C8
 Gorseinon SA4 ......151 B1
Pantgwyn SA2 ......166 C6
Pantiago Rd SA4 ......143 D4
Pant Lasau Rd SA5, SA6 ..153 C4
Pant St SA1 ......168 B7
Panteg SA9 ......139 A4
Pant-Teg SA15 ......148 F8
Pant-y-Blawd Rd
 Llansamlet SA6 ......154 D1
 Swansea / Abertawe, Llansamlet
 SA7 ......161 A8
 Swansea / Abertawe SA6 ..161 A8
Pant-y-Blodau SA6 ....153 B2
Pantyblodau Rd SA18 ..97 F8
Pant Y Brwyn SA9 ......100 C7
Pantycelyn SA4 ......151 B1
Panty Celyn SA65 ......122 C5
Pant Y Celyn Rd SA1 ..166 F8
Pant-y-dwr SA4 ......157 D1
Pant Y Fedwen
 1 Abergwili SA32 ......59 A3
 Gwaun-Cae-Gurwen SA18 ..99 B6
Pant-y-Felin Rd SA4 ..143 D6
Pantyffynnon Rd / Heol
 Pantyffynnon
 Pantyffynnon SA18 ......98 B6
 Pantyffynnon SA18 ......98 B6
Pantyffynnon Terr SA9 ..139 A4
Pantyffynon Rd SA4 ..139 F8
Pantygwydr Rd SA2 ..166 F6
Pant-y-Pistyll SA8 ......147 C3
Pant Yr Helys SA5 ....159 B6

Pant-yr-Odyn SA2 ......159 C1
Pant-yr-Ychain SA64 ..122 A6
Pant-y-Sais SA10 ......162 C1
Parade Rd 3 SA31 ......129 A5
Parade The
 Carmarthen / Caerfyrddin
 SA31 ......129 A5
 Pembroke / Penfro SA71 ..133 B4
Paradise Cotts SA14 ..149 D4
Paradise Row SA71 ....133 B5
Paradise View SA1 ....167 A8
Paragon 2 SA7 ......170 D4
Parc Andrew SA10 ....162 F6
Parc Ave
 Swansea / Abertawe SA6 ..160 F6
 Swansea / Abertawe SA6 ..160 F7
Parc Bagnall SA31 ....128 E6
Parc Berwig SA14 ......149 F2
Parc Bryn SA10 ......162 E5
Parc Bryngelli / Grove Hill
 Pk SA14 ......97 C8
Parc Brynmawr
 Llanelli SA15 ......140 E1
 Llanelli SA15 ......148 E8
Parc Bryn Rhos SA18 ..99 A8
Parc Busnes Canolog /
 Central Bsns Pk SA2 ..154 C2
Parc Busnes Glan yr Afon /
 Riverside Bsns Pk SA6 ..154 B1
Parc Bwtrimawr SA18 ..98 C6
Parc Cawdor SA19 ....130 D3
Parc Cilddewi SA31 ....128 B3
Parc Ddiwydiannol Betws /
 Betws Ind Pk SA18 ....98 C7
Parc Derlin / Derlin Pk
 SA18 ......97 F5
Parc Frenni SA7 ......34 F7
Parc Gitto SA14 ......149 D4
Parc Glanffrwd 12 SA18 ..99 B8
Parc Glan Yr Afon 2
 SA18 ......99 B8
Parc Glas SA18 ......162 F6
Parcgweydd Hill SA43 ..16 F6
Parc-gwyn SA31 ......128 C8
Parc Hendy Cres SA4 ..156 F3
Parc-Henry La SA18 ....98 B8
Parc Heol Ddu SA15 ..109 D6
Parc Howard Ave SA15 ..148 D7
Parc Howard Mus*
 SA15 ......148 D7
Parc Landwr / Benson Way
 SA6 ......161 A6
Parc Le Breos Burial
 Chamber* SA3 ......170 D8
Parcmaen St SA31 ....128 E5
Parc Mansant SA15 ....95 D4
Parc Mawr SA14 ......152 B2
Parc Menter SA14 ......97 C7
Parc Morlais SA14 ....142 C1
Parc Newydd SA14 ....77 F1
Parc Noi SA43 ......118 A4
Parc Onen SA10 ......162 E6
Parc Pant Glas SA19 ..130 E7
Parc Pendre SA17 ......136 B3
Parc Penrhiw SA18 ....98 C5
Parc Pensarn Ret Pk
 SA31 ......128 F2
Parc Rd SA6 ......160 F6
Parc Richard SA14 ....149 E4
Parc Roberts 2 SA67 ..70 D1
Parc Sandringham /
 Sandringham Pk SA6,
 SA7 ......154 C1
Parc Teifi SA43 ......118 F4
Parc Teifi Bsns Pk SA43 ..118 F4
Parc Terr SA6 ......160 F7
Parc Thomas SA31 ....128 F6
Parc Trostre SA14 ....149 A4
Parc Tyisha SA16 ......137 F3
Parc Wern SA10 ......162 F6
Parc Wern Rd SA2 ....166 E7
Parc Y Delyn
 Carmarthen / Caerfyrddin
 SA31 ......128 F6
 3 Llansteffan SA33 ....93 C7
Parc-y-Delyn SA6 ....153 B1
Parc-y-Deri SA10 ......162 E6
Parc-y-Duc Terr SA6 ..160 F7
Parc Y Felin SA48 ....120 D6
Parc Y Ffordd SA31 ..128 A4
Parc-y-Gwenyn SA17 ..136 B3
Parc Y Llan SA18 ......79 A2
Parc-y-Minos St SA14 ..137 E2
Parcymynach 6 SA15 ..96 B6
Parc Yr Efail SA41 ....14 C2
Parc Yr Eglwys 1 SA42 ..13 A4
Parc Yr Eos SA36 ......35 B2
Parc-yr-Helig Rd
 Birchgrove SA7 ......155 B1
 Swansea / Abertawe SA7 ..162 B8
Parcyrhun SA18 ......98 B6
Parc Yr Odyn SA31 ....128 A3
Parc Yr Onen SA31 ....129 A6
Parc-yr-Ynn SA44 ......19 E4
Parc S Ynwt SA41 ......94 B3
Parc S Ynwt 3 SA65 ..122 D3
Park Ave
 Capel Hendre SA18 ....97 C6
 Cardigan / Aberteifi SA43 ..118 E5
 Kilgetty / Begelly SA68 ..134 D8
 Neath / Castell-Nedd
 SA10 ......162 C7
 The Mumbles / Y Mwmbwls
 SA3 ......173 B4
Park Cl Gorseinon SA4 ..151 B2
 Pontardulais SA4 ......143 C3
 Swansea / Abertawe, Bon-y-maen
 SA1 ......161 B3

Park Cl continued
 Swansea / Abertawe, Cae-mawr
 SA6 ......153 E1
Park Cor Rd SA61 ....124 B4
Park Cres Llanelli SA15 ..148 C5
 Neath / Castell-Nedd
 SA10 ......162 C7
Park Dr
 Neath / Castell-Nedd
 SA10 ......162 C7
 Swansea / Abertawe SA6 ..153 E1
Parkes St SA16 ......137 E2
Park Eynon 6 SA15 ....148 D5
Park Hall SA1 ......129 A6
Parkhill Rd SA5 ......160 C5
Parkhill Terr SA5 ......160 C5
Park Howard Rd SA18 ..99 D6
Park La
 Dyffryn Cennen SA18 ....78 F6
 Llangennech SA14 ....150 C8
 Pembroke Dock / Doc Penfro
 SA72 ......132 C2
Park La / Lon Y Parc
 SA18 ......99 D8
Parkland Prim Sch SA2 ..166 B6
Parklands SA70 ......106 A4
Parklands Ct
 Ammanford / Rhydaman
 SA18 ......98 A6
 Swansea / Abertawe SA2 ..166 B6
Parklands Rd / Heol
 Tir-y-Parc SA18 ......98 A7
Parklands View SA2 ..166 B5
Park Mill Rd SA18 ......98 A7
Park Pl
 Swansea / Abertawe SA2 ..166 E5
 Tenby / Dinbych-y-pysgod
 SA70 ......135 D4
Park Rd Clydach SA6 ..154 E8
 Gorseinon SA4 ......151 B2
 Gowerton / Tre-gwyr SA4 ..158 C4
 Haverfordwest / Hwlffordd
 SA61 ......125 B6
 Pen-clawdd SA4 ......156 E4
 Southgate SA3 ......171 A5
 Tenby / Dinbych-y-pysgod
 SA70 ......135 D4
 Ynystawe SA6 ......154 C4
Park St
 Fishguard / Abergwaun
 SA65 ......122 D3
 Llanelli SA15 ......148 D5
 Pembroke Dock / Doc Penfro
 SA72 ......132 C2
 Swansea / Abertawe SA1 ..174 A3
 The Mumbles / Y Mwmbwls
 SA3 ......173 B5
 Whitland / Hendy-Gwyn
 SA34 ......126 C3
Park St / Stryd Y Parc
 Brynamman SA18 ......99 D8
 Ammanford / Rhydaman
 SA18 ......98 C6
Park Terr
 Burry Port SA16 ......137 D3
 Pontardulais SA4 ......143 D2
 Swansea / Abertawe SA1 ..160 C1
 10 Tenby / Dinbych-y-pysgod
 SA70 ......135 E4
Park The SA2 ......166 A7
Park View
 Lamphey SA71 ......105 A3
 Llanelli SA14 ......140 F1
 Loughor SA4 ......157 D8
Park View Cres SA17 ..132 C2
Park View Dr SA17 ....136 A4
Park View Terr SA2 ..166 D6
Parkview Terr / Trem Y Parc
 SA15 ......148 C5
Park Way SA2 ......166 B6
Parkway Cl SA62 ......68 B4
Parkwood SA4 ......158 C4
Parrog Rd SA42 ......13 A4
Parrog The SA64 ......122 B5
Parry Rd SA6 ......153 E1
Parsonage La SA68 ....134 A8
Parsons Gn SA70 ......106 B4
Paskeston Rd SA70 ..105 C6
Pastoral Way SA2 ....166 B8
Patagonia Wlk 3 SA1 ..167 A6
Pat Cornick Ct / Llys Pat
 Chown SA8 ......147 E4
Paterchurch SA72 ....133 B8
Paviland Pl SA5 ......159 F5
Paxton Dr SA1 ......174 A1
Paxton St SA1 ......174 A2
Paxton's Twr (NT)*
 SA32 ......77 F6
Paynter St SA71 ......133 C4
Pearl St SA6 ......154 F8
Pebbles The SA62 ....123 C4
Pedrog Terr SA1 ......160 B1
Peggys La 4 SA61 ....124 E5
Pegler St SA5 ......160 C3
Pelcomb Hill SA62 ....128 C8
Pelcomb Villas SA62 ..67 D5
Pelican St SA9 ......138 F2
Pell St SA1 ......174 A3
Pemberton Ave 4
 SA16 ......137 D2
Pemberton Pk SA14 ..149 C6
Pemberton St SA14 ..148 D4
Pembrey & Burry Port Sta
 SA16 ......137 E2

Pembry Ctry Pk*
 SA16 ......108 D3
Pembrey Properties Ind Est
 SA16 ......108 E3
Pembrey Rd
 Kidwelly / Cydweli SA17 ..136 B2
 Llanelli SA15 ......148 C6
Pembrey Village CP Sch
 SA16 ......137 A2
Pembroke Bldgs 5
 SA1 ......174 C2
Pembroke Castle (remains
 of)* SA71 ......133 B5
Pembroke Dock Com Sch
 SA72 ......132 D2
Pembroke Dock Sta
 SA72 ......132 D2
Pembroke Leisure Ctr
 SA72 ......133 A7
Pembroke Pl 1 SA1 ..174 C2
Pembroke St
 Freystrop SA62 ......87 A6
 Haverfordwest / Hwlffordd
 SA61 ......124 F2
 Pembroke Dock / Doc Penfro
 SA72 ......132 C2
Pembroke Sch SA72 ..133 A6
Pembrokeshire Candle Ctr*
 SA3 ......33 A7
Pembrokeshire Coll / Coleg
 Sir Benfro SA61 ......124 C3
Pembrokeshire Cty
 Showground* SA62 ....68 A5
Pembrokeshire Motor Mus*
 SA62 ......67 A6
Pembroke St
 Pembroke Dock / Doc Penfro
 SA72 ......132 B2
 Swansea / Abertawe SA5 ..160 B2
Pembroke Sta SA71 ....133 D4
Penallt 1 SA2 ......165 E8
Penallt Rd SA15 ......148 F6
Penallt Terr SA15 ....148 E8
Penally Hts SA70 ......135 A2
Penally Pottery* SA70 ..135 B2
Penally Rd SA70 ......135 E4
Penally Sta SA70 ......135 B2
Penally VC Sch SA70 ..135 B3
Penbanc SA65 ......122 C3
Penblewin SA67 ......70 E3
Penbryn SA48 ......120 C6
Penbryn Ave SA15 ....128 D5
Penbryn Rd SA10 ....162 F7
Penbryn Terr SA2 ....166 F5
Pen-Cae-Crwn Rd SA4 ..151 A3
Pencaerfenni Ct SA4 ..156 B3
Pencaerfenni La SA4 ..156 B3
Pencaerfenni Pk SA4 ..156 B3
Pencae Terr SA15 ....148 F5
Pen-Cefn-Arda Rd SA4 ..151 B4
Penclawdd Prim Sch
 SA4 ......156 E4
Penclawdd Rd SA4 ..157 C5
Pencoed SA2 ......165 E8
Pen Coed Isaf Rd SA14 ..150 D4
Pencoed Rd SA16 ....137 E3
Pencwmdu SA8 ......100 A1
Pendarren SA8 ......100 B1
Pedderi Rd Bynea SA14 ..150 A4
 Llanelli SA14 ......149 F5
Penderry Rd SA5 ......160 B4
Pendine Hill SA33 ....91 D3
Pendre SA43 ......118 D4
Penffordd CP Sch SA63 ..53 E1
Penfilia Rd SA5 ......160 C4
Penfilia Terr 3 SA5 ....160 C4
Pengelli Prim Sch SA41 ..151 C6
Pengorof Ct SA1 ......166 A2
Pengors Rd SA5 ......153 B2
Pengry Rd SA4 ......160 C8
Pengwern Rd SA6 ....160 C8
Peniel Green Rd SA7 ..162 A8
Peniel Rd SA5 ......160 C8
Pen Isa Coed SA1 ....167 F7
Penlan SA14 ......160 A6
Penlan Cres SA2 ......166 F7
Penlan Fach SA5 ......160 B4
Penlanffos Heol SA31 ..129 B3
Penlanffos Rd SA31 ..129 B4
Penlan Gr SA5 ......160 B5
Penlan Rd
 Carmarthen / Caerfyrddin
 SA31 ......128 F7
 Loughor SA4 ......150 F1
 Neath / Castell-Nedd
 SA10 ......160 D6
 Swansea / Abertawe SA5 ..160 C6
Penlan Village SA38 ....17 A4
Penllech SA15 ......109 C3
Penlan-uchaf Farm Gdns*
 SA65 ......32 D6
Penllergaer Bsns Pk
 SA4 ......152 D3
Penllergaer Forest Walks*
 SA4 ......152 D4
Penllergaer Prim Sch
 SA4 ......152 A2
Penllwyngwyn Farm Dr
 SA14 ......149 F6
Penllwyngwyn Rd SA14 ..150 A6
Pen-Llwyn-March Rd
 SA65 ......160 A3

Penllwynhodyn Rd
 SA14 ......149 F4
Penmachno SA6 ......153 D1
Penmaen Burrows Burial
 Chamber* SA3 ......170 C5
Penmaen Terr SA1 ....167 B7
Penmynydd SA4 ......151 B1
Penmynydd Rd SA5 ..160 B5
Pen-nant SA14 ......141 B2
Pennar CP Schools
 SA72 ......132 A1
Pennard Dr SA3 ......171 A6
Pennard Prim Sch SA3 ..171 A5
Pennard Rd
 Bishopston SA3 ......171 E7
 Southgate SA3 ......171 B5
Pennard St SA5 ......160 C3
Pennine Cl SA5 ......159 E3
Penn's Cl SA61 ......124 D3
Pen Parc SA14 ......96 E6
Penplas Rd
 Swansea / Abertawe, Cadle
 SA5 ......159 F7
 Swansea / Abertawe SA5 ..160 A7
Penpound La / Lon
 Penpound SA18 ......98 F8
Penprys Rd
 Llanelli, Bryn SA14 ....149 E7
 Llanelli Burial SA14 ....141 E1
 Llanelli SA14 ......149 E8
Pen Rhiw SA62 ......123 B6
Penrhiw / Hilltop SA14 ..141 A2
Penrhiwiau SA18 ......147 E3
Penrhiw Rd SA6 ......153 D2
Penrhos SA4 ......151 A1
Penrhos Cottage* SA66 ..53 D4
Penrhos Pl SA5 ......159 F4
Penrhyn Ave SA5 ....160 B4
Penrhyn Ct SA6 ......154 A3
Penrice Ct
 Swansea / Abertawe,
 Graig Trewyddfa SA6 ....161 A6
 1 Swansea / Abertawe,
 Mount Pleasant SA1 ....174 A4
Penrice Forest Wlks*
 SA3 ......117 C7
Penrice St SA6 ......153 F1
Penryce Ct SA1 ......174 B2
Penry Pl SA15 ......148 E5
Penry Point SA3 ......87 C3
Pensarn Rd SA31 ......160 B5
Pensalwent
 Neath Abbey SA10 ....155 F1
 Neath / Castell-Nedd SA10 ..162 F8
Penslade SA5 ......122 D4
Pentewan Cl SA6 ....160 B5
Pentip Church in Wales Prim
 Sch SA15 ......148 C6
Pentland Cl SA5 ......159 D4
Pentle Dr SA69 ......133 B6
Pentlepoir CP Sch SA69 ..134 B6
Pentood Ind Est SA43 ..118 E3
Pentre Banadl SA2 ....165 E2
Pentrechwyth Prim Sch
 SA1 ......161 A3
Pentrechwyth Rd SA1 ..160 F2
Pentre-Chwyth Rd SA1 ..161 A3
Pentre-Dwr Rd SA1 ..161 E5
Pentrefelin St SA31 ..128 E5
Pentregethin Rd SA5 ..159 F5
Pentreguinea Rd SA1 ..174 C4
Pentrehafod Comp Sch
 SA1 ......160 D3
Pentre Hedyn SA38 ..119 D6
Pentremalwed Rd SA6 ..160 F7
Pentre Mawr Rd SA1 ..160 D2
Pentremeurig Rd SA31 ..128 A4
Pentrepoeth Jun & Inf Schs
 SA6 ......154 A1
Pentrepoeth Rd
 Llanelli SA15 ......148 D8
 Swansea / Abertawe SA6 ..153 F2
Pentrepoeth School Rd
 Morriston / Treforris SA6 ..154 A1
 St Clears / Sanclêr
 SA33 ......127 C4
Pentre-Treharne Hill
 SA1 ......160 D4
Pentre-Treharne Rd
 SA1 ......160 D4
Pentwyn 1 SA15 ....148 D8
Pentwyn Rd SA14 ....157 F1
Pentwyn Rd SA19 ....139 B7
Pentwyn Rd / Ffordd Pen
 Twyn SA18 ......98 C7
Pentyla SA10 ......162 F7
Pentyla Rd SA2 ......166 E8
Penuel Cl SA4 ......151 A1
Penuel St SA15 ......129 A5
Pen Wallis SA65 ......122 D2
Penybanc
 Carmarthen / Caerfyrddin
 SA31 ......129 B7
 Llangunnor SA31 ......129 B3
Penybanc La SA14 ....151 A4
Pen-y-banc Rd SA18 ..98 A6
Penybedd Rd SA16 ..108 E6
Pen-y-Bigyn SA15 ....148 E4
Penybryn Llanelli SA14 ..141 A2
 Llanelli SA14 ......149 E6
 Pontyberem SA15 ......95 F7
Pen-y-Bryn
 Cwmllynfell SA9 ......100 B7
 Fishguard / Abergwaun
 SA65 ......122 C3

Pen-y-Bryn continued
Pen-y-Bryn, Nedd /
Castell-Nedd, Pen-yr-Heol
SA10 .... 162 E6
Penybryn Ave SA15 ....137 E3
Pen-y-Bryn Cl SA4 ....152 E3
Pen-y-bryn Cvn Site
SA14 .... 149 E2
Penybryn Rd SA4 ....151 B2
Penybryn Senior Secl Sch
SA4 .... 160 D7
Pen Y Cae SA31 ....128 A3
Pen-y-Cae La SA4 ....150 E2
Pen Y Cwm SA2 ....159 D2
Pen-y-Dre SA4 ....158 B4
Penydre Rd SA6 ....146 F1
Penyfai La SA15 ....148 B8
Pen-y-Fai La SA15 ....140 B1
Pen-y-Fan SA7 ....161 F6
Penyfan Rd SA15 ....148 F4
Pen-y-Ffordd SA33 ....127 F8
Pen-y-Fro SA4 ....148 E3
Pen-y-Fro SA2 ....158 B1
Pen-y-Fro Cl SA2 ....158 B1
Pen Y fro Prim Sch SA2 ...165 B8
Pen-y-gaer Cotts SA14 ....149 A8
Penygaer Rd SA14, SA15
SA14 .... 148 F7
Penygaer Rd SA14, SA15 ..148 F6
Pen-y-Garn
St David's & the Cathedral Close
SA62 .... 123 C4
Swansea / Abertawe SA1 ..161 A3
Penygarn Rd / Heol
Penygarn SA18 ....97 F5
Penygraig SA8 ....89 E6
Penygraig Rd SA14 ....149 E4
Pen-y-Graig Rd
Pontardawe SA8 ....147 F3
Swansea / Abertawe SA1 ..167 B8
Ystradowen SA9 ....100 C7
Penygroes Prim Sch
SA14 .... 97 D8
Penygroes Rd / Heol
Penygroes
Ammanford SA14 ....97 F8
Gorslas SA14 ....97 C8
Pen-y-Heol SA10 ....162 D4
Pen Y Maes SA6 ....153 C2
Pen Y Maes SA6 ....153 C2
Penymorfa SA31 ....129 A3
Pen-y-Morfa SA15 ....148 E3
Pen Y Morfa SA4 ....157 A4
Penymorfa La SA31 ....129 A3
Pen-y-Mor Rd SA5 ....160 C5
Pen Y Pwll SA4 ....143 D2
Penyraber SA62 ....48 D3
Pen-yr-Alley Ave SA10 ...162 E6
Penyrallt SA18 ....99 D7
Pen-yr-Allt SA9 ....139 B8
Pen-yr-Grug SA14 ....139 A8
Pen-yr-Heol SA10 ....162 E5
Penyrheol Com Sch
SA4 .... 151 B3
Penyrheol Dr SA15 ....148 E8
Pen-yr-Heol Dr SA2 ......166 B7
Penyrheol Rd SA4 ....151 A4
Pen-y-Rhiw
Cardigan / Aberteifi SA43 .....2 F2
Pen-Rhiw-fawr SA9 ....100 A5
St Dogmaels / Llandudoch
SA43 .... 118 A4
Pen-y-Yrfa SA31 ....153 D1
Penywarc Rd SA15 ....148 F5
Penywern Llanelli SA15 ...148 A7
Ystalyfera SA9 ....139 A7
Penywern Rd SA9 ....139 A6
Pen-y-Wern Rd SA6 ......154 E8
Pen-y-Wern Terr SA1 .....160 D4
Peregrine Cl 1 SA61 ....124 E5
Peris Rd SA1 ....160 A5
Perrot Ave SA1 ....125 A5
Perrots Rd SA1 ....125 A5
Peter Cash Ho SA1 ....167 A5
Peter's Finger La SA67 ...89 D7
Peter's La SA62 ....123 C4
Peter St SA1 ....160 C1
Peter Terr SA1 ....160 C1
Peterwell Terr SA48 .....120 B5
Pheasant Rd SA4 ....147 B2
Pheonix Pk Rugby & Soccer
Gd SA14 ....122 B5
Philadelphia Ct 4 SA61 .161 A8
Philadelphia La SA1 .....160 D2
Phillips Ave SA73 ....131 D4
Phillips La SA72 ....132 B3
Philip's La SA71 ....104 F5
Phillips Par SA1 ....167 B6
Phillip St SA1 ....160 C1
Phoenix Bowl & Seal Hospl*
SA73 .... 131 B2
Phoenix Bsns Pk SA7 ....161 B7
Phoenix Ctr SA7 ....161 C7
Phoenix Way
Penllergaer SA4 ....151 F1
Swansea / Abertawe SA7 .161 B6
Phyllis St SA5 ....160 A2
Pibwrlwyd La SA31 ....128 F1
Picket Mead Rd SA3 .....172 E5
Picton Arc SA1 ....174 A2
Picton Castle* SA62 ......88 A8
Picton Castle Gdns*
SA62 .... 87 F8
Picton Cl
Milford Haven / Aberdaugleddau
SA73 .... 131 A2
 3 Templeton SA67 ....89 E6

Picton Ct SA31 ....128 D5
Picton La
Lampeter / Llanbedr Pont Steffan
SA48 .... 120 C4
Swansea / Abertawe SA1 .174 A2
Picton Pl
Carmarthen / Caerfyrddin
SA31 .... 128 D5
 1 Haverfordwest / Hwlffordd
SA61 .... 125 B5
 2 Narberth / Arberth
SA67 .... 70 D1
Pembroke Dock / Doc Penfro
SA72 .... 132 C1
Picton Rd
Milford Haven / Aberdaugleddau
SA73 .... 131 A2
Neath / Castell-Nedd SA10 .162 F7
Neyland SA73 ....132 B5
Tenby / Dinbych-y-pysgod
SA70 .... 135 E4
Picton Terr
Carmarthen / Caerfyrddin
SA31 .... 128 D4
Swansea / Abertawe SA1 .174 A4
Tenby / Dinbych-y-pysgod
SA70 .... 135 E4
Pier Hill SA70 ....135 F5
Pier Rd
Milford Haven / Aberdaugleddau
SA73 .... 131 A2
Pembroke Dock / Doc Penfro
SA72 .... 132 C3
Pier St SA1 ....174 C2
Pigsfoot La SA62 ....123 C4
Pilgrim's Way SA62 ....66 E8
Pill La SA73 ....131 D2
Pill Parks Way 5 SA62 ..87 F4
Pill Rd Hook SA62 ....87 D6
Swansea / Abertawe SA1
SA73 .... 131 E3
Pilot St SA43 ....118 A4
Pineacre Cl SA2 ....166 C6
Pine Cres SA6 ....153 E2
Pine Tree Cl / Clos Y
Binwydd SA14 ....137 F3
Pinetree Ct SA2 ....166 C6
Pineway SA5 ....160 C6
Pinewood Cl SA6 ....153 D2
Pinewood / Coed Y Pin
SA18 .... 98 D8
Pinewood Ct SA14 ....149 D6
Pinewood Rd SA2 ....166 E4
Pinkney St SA1 ....174 C3
Pitch La SA67 ....89 D7
Pit St SA62 ....123 B4
Pittsburgh Ct SA5 ....159 F7
Plaistow* SA1 ....174 B3
Plas Cadwgan SA4 ....152 C2
Plas-Cadwgan Rd SA4 ....154 C5
Plas Croeso SA4 ....151 B1
Plas Gwernfadog Dr
SA6 .... 154 A5
Plasgwyn SA4 ....143 D4
Plas-Gwyn Rd SA14 ......97 D8
Plas Hos SA4 ....151 C6
Plas Ioan SA31 ....128 C2
Plasycoed SA9 ....138 F2
Plas Y Coed Ave SA4 ....160 F8
Plas Y Coed Rd SA4 .....160 F8
Plas Y Ddol 4 SA31 ....128 C2
Plas-y-Fforest
 1 Fforest SA4 ....142 F6
Penllergaer SA4 ....152 C2
Plas-y-Fron SA65 ....122 E3
Plas-y-Gamil Rd SA64 ...122 A5
Players Ave SA6 ....154 D8
Players Ind Est SA6 .....154 D6
Pleasant Cl SA4 ....150 F3
Pleasant Rd SA4 ....151 E2
Pleasant Row
 5 Llanelli SA15 ....148 E5
Swansea / Abertawe SA5 .160 C5
Pleasant St
Swansea / Abertawe, Clun-Du
SA6 .... 153 F1
 2 Swansea / Abertawe,
Mount Pleasant SA1 .....174 B3
Pleasant View
Hundleton SA71 ....103 B3
Llanelli SA15 ....148 F8
Trimsaran SA17 ....109 C7
Pleasant View Terr
Swansea / Abertawe,
Mount Pleasant SA1 .....174 A4
 1 Swansea / Abertawe, Penfilia
SA5 .... 160 C4
Plough Rd SA1 ....160 D3
Plover Cl SA5 ....160 C6
Plum Tree Dr SA62 ......67 D7
Plunch La SA3 ....173 C3
Plymouth St SA1 ....174 B3
Pobbles Cl SA3 ....171 A4
Pocketts Wharf 1 SA1 .174 C2
Pointfields Cres
SA73 .... 131 B1
Point La SA72 ....104 E6
Point Rd SA62 ....85 C7
Point St SA73 ....131 B2

Pond Mdw SA73 ....131 F5
Pondside SA31 ....128 C4
Pond St 2 SA31 ....128 E5
Pontamman Rd SA18 .....98 D7
Pontardawe Ind Est
SA8 .... 147 F5
Pontardawe Rd
Clydach SA6 ....155 A8
Pontardawe SA8 ....99 D3
Pontarddulais Prim Sch
SA4 .... 143 D3
Pontarddulais Comp Sch
SA4 .... 143 D5
Pontarddulais Ind Est
SA4 .... 143 C6
Pontarddulais Junction
SA4 .... 143 B5
Pontarddulais Rd
Cross Hands SA14 ....97 B6
Gorseinon SA4 ....151 C3
Llangennech SA14 ....142 E2
Swansea / Abertawe SA5 .159 C6
Tycroes SA18 ....97 E5
Pontarddulais Workshops
SA4 .... 143 C6
Pont Aur SA9 ....139 E7
Pont-ceri SA38 ....119 B7
Pontfaen SA32 ....77 C3
Pontfaen Rd
Cwm Gwaun SA65 ....32 B4
Lampeter / Llanbedr Pont Steffan
SA48 .... 120 B5
Ponthenry Ind Est SA15 .95 F3
Pontiets CP Sch SA15 ...95 A5
Pontlliw Prim Sch SA4 ..152 A4
Pontyberem CP Sch
SA15 .... 96 A6
Pontybrenin Prim Sch /
Ysgol Gynradd Y Sir
Pontybrenin SA4 ....151 B1
Pont-y-Cleifion SA43 ....118 C4
Pont-y-Cob Rd
Gowerton SA4 ....157 F5
Gowerton / Tre-gwyr SA4 .158 A6
Pont-y-Glasdwr 4 SA1 .160 D1
Pont-y-Shoot SA6 ....160 D5
Poplar Cl
Cross Hands SA14 ....97 B7
Swansea / Abertawe SA2 .166 A4
Poplar Ct SA14 ....148 C5
Poppy Dr SA73 ....132 B7
Popton Rd SA71 ....103 B5
Portfield SA61 ....124 E4
Portfield Ave SA61 ......124 F4
Portfield Specl Sch
SA61 .... 124 E4
Porth St SA38 ....119 C4
Porth Y Plas SA31 ....128 C3
Porth Y Waun SA4 ....158 A6
Portia Terr SA1 ....174 A4
Portland Sq SA62 ....48 D3
Portland St SA1 ....174 A3
Portmead Ave SA5 ......159 E7
Portmead Prim Sch
SA5 .... 159 F5
Port Talbot Pl SA5 ......159 E5
Port Tennant Rd SA1 ....168 A7
Portway SA3 ....172 A7
Port Way SA17 ....109 F5
Post-gwyn SA35 ....36 C3
Pothouse Rd SA1 ....128 E4
Pottery Pl SA15 ....148 D5
Pottery St / Stryd Y
Crochendy 7 SA15 .....148 D5
Pound The SA72 ....104 F6
Powell Cl SA71 ....133 C5
Powell St SA1 ....174 B4
Powys Ave SA1 ....167 A8
Powys Gdns SA1 ....166 F8
Poyer's Ave SA71 ....133 B4
Poyers Gr SA71 ....89 E6
Poyston Cl 3 SA61 .....124 F5
Precelly Cres SA64 ......122 A6
Prendergast
Haverfordwest / Hwlffordd
SA61 .... 125 B6
Solva SA62 ....48 D4
Prendergast Cty Prim Jun
Sch SA61 ....125 B6
Prendergast Infants Sch /
Ysgol Fabanod Prendergast
SA61 .... 125 C6
Prendergast St SA15 ....148 E4
Prescelly Ho SA1 ....160 A5
Prescelly Pk 6 SA61 ....125 B7
Prescelly Pl SA73 ....131 C3
Prescelly Rd 7 SA61 ...124 F5
Preseli Mohair Ctr*
SA66 .... 34 C1
Preseli Venture Activity Ctr*
SA62 .... 16 C7
Preseli View SA41 ....19 D2
Presely View SA2 ....132 B2
Presswylfa Ho SA15 .....148 D3
Preswylfa Row 5 SA15 .148 D3
Prettyman Dr SA10 .....162 D3
Prif Ffordd / High St
SA15 .... 148 C4
Prifysgol Cymru Abertawe /
Univ of Wales Swansea
SA2 .... 166 D4
Prifysgol Cymru Llanbedr
Pont Steffan / Univ of
Wales Lampeter SA48 ....120 D5
Prifysgol Cymru / Univ of
Wales SA31 ....75 E4

Primrose Cl SA73 ....132 B7
Primrose Ct SA5 ....160 A5
Primrose Dr SA2 ....125 A7
Primrose Hill
Carmarthen / Caerfyrddin
SA31 .... 129 A3
Swansea / Abertawe SA1 .167 B7
Primrose La SA15 ....147 D5
Primrose Row SA8 ....147 D5
Primrose St SA1 ....167 B7
Prince of Wales Cl SA73 .87 C2
Prince Of Wales Rd
SA1 .... 160 D7
Prince Philip Hospl The
SA14 .... 149 B7
Princess Cl SA15 ....148 C5
Princess of Wales Ct
SA1 .... 161 C5
Princess Royal Way
SA61 .... 125 A4
Princess St
Gorseinon SA4 ....151 B2
Llanelli SA15 ....148 C5
Princess St SA72 ....132 B2
Princess Way SA1 ....174 B2
Priors Cres SA3 ....165 B8
Priors Town SA3 ....114 C2
Priors Way SA3 ....165 B8
Priory Ave SA61 ....125 A3
Priory Cl SA31 ....129 B6
Priory Day Hospl SA31 ..128 D3
Priory Lodge Dr SA73 ...131 C3
Priory Lodge Est SA73 ..131 C3
Priory Rd SA73 ....131 C3
Priory St
 7 Cardigan / Aberteifi
SA43 .... 118 D4
Carmarthen / Caerfyrddin
SA31 .... 129 A5
Kidwelly / Cydweli SA17 .136 C4
Milford Haven / Aberdaugleddau
SA73 .... 131 C2
Priory St / Stryd Y Prior
SA17 .... 136 C5
Prioryville SA73 ....131 D3
Promenade SA73 ....174 A3
Promenade Cl SA73 .....132 B6
Promenade Terr SA3 ....132 A6
Promenade Terr SA3 ....173 B4
Promenade The
Llanstadwell SA73 ....132 A5
Pen-clawdd SA4 ....156 C4
Swansea / Abertawe SA2 .166 E4
The Mumbles / Y Mwmbwls
SA3 .... 173 B8
Prospect Pl
Cwmllynfell SA9 ....100 B7
Llanelli SA15 ....148 D6
Pembroke Dock / Doc Penfro
SA72 .... 132 C2
Swansea / Abertawe SA2 .166 C7
Ystalyfera SA9 ....139 B6
Prosper Cl SA31 ....129 A6
Prosser Cl SA31 ....129 A6
Providence La SA3 ......172 A7
Pryce St SA15 ....148 C6
Pryderi Foopath SA1 ....167 B8
Prydwen Rd SA5 ....159 B4
Puffin Way 3 SA62 .....85 D8
Pumporth SA43 ....16 A6
Puncheston Cty Prim Sch
SA62 .... 51 F8
Pwll CP Sch SA15 ....109 E4
Pwlldu La SA3 ....171 F4
Pwllhai SA43 ....118 D4
Pwll Melyn SA62 ....48 C3
Pwll Rd Burry Port SA16 .137 F3
Pembrey & Burry Port Town
SA16 .... 109 D4
Pwll St
Castlemartin SA71 ....103 C1
Swansea / Abertawe SA1 .160 D4
Pwll-y-Domen Rd SA5 ...160 B3
Pwll-yr-Hwyaid SA5 ....159 E6
Pyle Cl SA3 ....172 A5
Pyle Rd SA3 ....172 A5
Pyntws Terr 2 SA15 ...148 F4
Pyst Gwynion SA35 .....36 A4

Quadrant Sh Ctr The
SA1 .... 174 A2
Quadrant The SA2 ....166 E6
Quarr Dr SA2 ....166 D7
Quarr Rd Clydach SA6 ...154 D7
Pontardawe SA8 ....147 E5
Quarry La SA2 ....51 A6
Quarrypark La SA63 ....52 A2
Quarry Pk SA67 ....90 B5
Quarry Rd 8 SA31 .....99 D7
Quarry Rd 8 Brecon SA18 .80 E1
Swansea / Abertawe SA5 .160 D5
Quarry St SA1 ....174 B4
Quay Par SA1 ....174 C3
Quay Rd
Goodwick / Wdig SA64 ...122 A6
Kidwelly / Cydweli SA17 .136 A3
Quay St
Cardigan / Aberteifi SA43 .118 D3
Carmarthen / Caerfyrddin
SA31 .... 128 F4
Fishguard & Goodwick
SA61 .... 122 C4
Haverfordwest / Hwlffordd
SA61 .... 125 B4

Quay St continued
Llandeilo SA19 ....130 D5
Quay St / Stryd Y Cei 2
SA31 .... 98 C7
Quay The SA31 ....128 F4
Quay W SA1 ....174 B3
Queen Elizabeth Ave
SA73 .... 132 B6
Queen Elizabeth Cambria
Comp Sch SA31 ....128 D2
Queen Elizabeth Maridunum
Comp Sch SA31 ....128 D2
Queen Mary's Wlk / Rhodfa'r
Frenhines Mary SA15 ....148 C4
Queen's Ave SA41 ....151 B1
Queen's Ct 6 SA67 ......70 D1
Queen's Ditch 6 SA61 .124 F5
Queens Par SA70 ....135 D4
Queens Rd SA2 ....166 D6
Queen's Rd
Neath / Castell-Nedd SA10 .162 F7
The Mumbles / Y Mwmbwls
SA3 .... 173 A5
Queen's Sq 14 SA61 ....125 A5
Queen St
 6 Carmarthen / Caerfyrddin
SA31 .... 128 F5
Llandovery / Llanymddyfri
SA20 .... 121 D4
Pembroke Dock / Doc Penfro
SA72 .... 132 C3
Queen's Terr 6 SA43 ...118 C4
Queensway
Haverfordwest / Hwlffordd
SA61 .... 125 B5
Llandovery / Llanymddyfri
SA20 .... 121 C4
Swansea / Abertawe SA5 .159 D4
Queen Victoria Rd SA15 .148 C4
Quickwell Hill SA62 .....123 C5

R

Raby St / Stryd Raby
SA15 .... 148 C6
Rackhill Ct 2 SA61 ....124 F5
Radford La SA5 ....105 C6
Radnor Dr SA6 ....154 B4
Radnor Ho 9 SA1 ......174 C2
Radyr Ave SA1 ....165 F2
Ragged Staff SA69 .....134 E2
Raglan Rd SA2 ....166 C7
Railway Cotts SA6 ......153 F3
Railway Pl SA14 ....96 E6
Railway Pl / Ffordd Y Wagen
 8 SA15 ....148 C4
Railway Terr
Cwmllynfell SA9 ....100 B7
Ffairfach SA19 ....130 D4
Gorseinon SA4 ....151 C1
Neyland SA73 ....132 C6
Swansea / Abertawe SA5 .159 E3
Railway Terr / Rhes Yr Orsaf
 9 SA15 ....148 C4
Rainbow Bsns Ctr SA7 .161 B6
Raleigh Cl SA2 ....166 C6
Ralph St SA15 ....148 D5
Ralph Terr SA15 ....148 C6
Ramsay Gdns SA62 .....123 B4
Ramsay Rd SA6 ....146 E1
Ramsden Ct SA1 ....104 C4
Ramsden Rd SA1 ....154 C7
Ramsey Dr
Milford Haven / Aberdaugleddau
SA73 .... 131 D4
Swansea / Abertawe SA5 .153 D1
Ramsey Pl SA62 ....159 E7
Randell Sq SA16 ....137 A3
Rath The SA73 ....131 D2
Ravenhill Rd SA5 ....159 F4
Raven Ind Est SA18 .....99 B8
Ravensfield SA4 ....165 F2
Ravens Wlk SA3 ....172 F6
Rawlings Rd SA18 ....79 A2
Recorder St SA1 ....174 A2
Rectory Ave SA73 ......131 A3
Rectory Cl
Letterston SA62 ....50 E8
 3 Llangwm SA62 ....87 F4
Loughor SA4 ....150 F1
Rectory Ct 3 SA70 .....135 C5
Rectory Rd
Llangwm SA62 ....87 E4
Trecwn SA62 ....31 B4
Redford Hill SA71 ......103 F2
Redhill Pk SA61 ....125 A7
Redstone Cross SA67 ...70 D3
Redstone Rd SA67 ......70 F2
Redwood Ct SA5 ....160 A5
Redwood Rd SA4 ....172 F7
Refinery Rd SA71 ....103 B5
Regalia Terr SA15 ......148 E5
Regency Ho 4 SA1 ....174 A3
Reginald Cl SA41 ....104 A3
Reginald St SA1 ....168 A7
Rehoboth Rd / Heol
Rehoboth SA15 ....109 E7
Reigit La SA3 ....172 C6
Rembrandt Ct SA2 .....166 E4
Reservoir Rd
Carmarthen / Caerfyrddin
SA31 .... 129 C5
Rhoscrowther SA71 ....103 C5
Retreat Rd SA70 ....135 B3

Rhandir SA14 . . . . .149 E4
Rhandirfelin SA15 . . . . .140 E1
Rhandir Terr SA14 . . . . .142 B1
Rhandir Wen **6** SA39 . . . . . .39 B6
Rheidol Ave SA6 . . . . .160 C8
Rheidol Ct SA6 . . . . .160 C8
Rhes Gwaith Tyn SA15 . . . . .148 F2
Rhestr Fawr SA9 . . . . .138 F2
Rhes Yr Orsaf / Railway Terr
6 SA15 . . . . .148 C4
Rhianfa Gdns SA1 . . . . .167 A7
Rhianfa La SA1 . . . . .167 A7
Rhiw Babell SA31 . . . . .128 F3
Rhiwderyn
  Birchgrove SA7 . . . . .155 B1
  Swansea / Abertawe SA7 . . .162 B8
Rhiw-dol-Badau **8** SA43 .16 A5
Rhiwfawr Rd SA9 . . . . .138 A1
Rhiw Felen SA41 . . . . .33 B8
Rhiwlas SA2 . . . . .165 E8
Rhiw Peter SA42 . . . . .33 A7
Rhiw'r Cyrph SA19 . . . . .24 A2
Rhiw Rd SA9 . . . . .100 C5
Rhiw Rhydings SA20 . . . . .121 F2
Rhiw Ydw SA15 . . . . .44 C1
Rhodfa Bryn-Mawr /
  Brynmawr Ave **6** SA18 . . .98 B7
Rhodfa Bryn Rhos SA18 . . . . .99 A8
Rhodfa Deg SA43 . . . . .15 E5
Rhodfa Fadog
  Cwmrhydyceirw SA6 . . . . . . .154 A4
  Swansea / Abertawe SA6 . . .153 F4
Rhodfa Frank SA18 . . . . .98 B7
Rhodfa Llwyneithin
  SA15 . . . . .148 D7
Rhodfa'r Brain SA15 . . . . .159 E5
Rhodfar Capel SA16 . . . . .137 B3
Rhodfa'r Dryw
  Cwmrhydyceirw SA6 . . . . . . .154 A5
  Swansea / Abertawe SA6 . . .153 F5
Rhodfa'r Eos
  Cwmrhydyceirw SA6 . . . . . . .154 A5
  Swansea / Abertawe SA6 . . .153 F5
Rhodfa'r Ffenhimes Mary /
  Queen Mary's Wlk
  SA15 . . . . .148 E4
Rhodfar Gwendraeth
  SA17 . . . . .136 D5
Rhodfa'r Wennol SA6 . . . . . . .154 A5
Rhodfa'r Wiwer / Squirrel
  Wlk SA4 . . . . .143 A5
Rhondda St SA1 . . . . .167 B7
Rhoose Ferry Rd SA73 . . . . . . .87 E1
Rhos Cotts SA10 . . . . .139 F3
Rhosdeg SA19 . . . . .130 F8
Rhosfa Rd SA18 . . . . .80 F1
Rhosfa Rd / Heol Y Rhosfa
  SA18 .80 F1
Rhoslan **1** SA14 . . . . .96 F6
Rhos Las SA31 . . . . .129 A3
Rhosmaen St SA19 . . . . .130 E6
Rhos Rd SA5 . . . . .159 F4
Rhossili Visitor Ctr*
  SA3 .116 B6
Rhos-y-Dre SA43 . . . . .118 E4
Rhyddings Park Rd SA2 . . . . .166 F6
Rhyddings Terr SA2 . . . . .166 F6
Rhyddwen Pl SA6 . . . . .146 B1
Rhyddwen Rd
  Craig-cefn-parc SA6 . . . . . . .146 B1
  Swansea / Abertawe SA6 . . .145 F1
Rhydlanfair SA48 . . . . .4 F7
Rhydwen SA9 . . . . .139 E6
Rhyd Wen SA18 . . . . .100 A8
Rhyd-y-Coed SA7 . . . . .162 A8
Rhyd-y-Defaid Dr SA2 . . . . . .166 B5
Rhyd-y-Felin SA7 . . . . .161 F5
Rhyd Y Fenni SA4 . . . . .156 B3
Rhydyffynnon SA15 . . . . .95 E3
Rhyd Y Fro SA19 . . . . .63 D7
Rhyd-y-fro Prim Sch
  SA8 .147 D8
Rhyd-y-Glyn SA7 . . . . .161 F6
Rhyd-y-Gors SA32 . . . . .127 E5
Rhyd-y-Pandy Rd SA6 . . . . . . .153 E7
Rhyd Y Polan SA4 . . . . .151 B1
Rhydyrafon SA15 . . . . .148 F7
Rhyd-yr-Helyg SA2 . . . . .166 B5
Rhys Prichard Sch / Ysgol
  Rhys Prichard SA20 . . . . . . .121 D5
Rice St SA15 . . . . .148 E4
Rice Street SA18 . . . . .98 C6
Rice St / Stryd Rice
  SA18 .98 C6
Richard John Rd SA73 . . . . . . .131 D3
Richardson Rd SA1 . . . . .167 B6
Richardson St
  Pontardawe SA8 . . . . .147 C3
  Swansea / Abertawe SA1 . . .167 B6
Richard's Pl SA1 . . . . .174 B3
Richard St
  10 Llanelli SA15 . . . . .148 D5
  Swansea / Abertawe SA5 . . .160 C2
Richmond Cres SA61 . . . . .124 F4
Richmond Ct SA1 . . . . .167 A7
Richmond Mews **1**
  SA1 .167 A6
Richmond Pk SA2 . . . . .150 F1
Richmond Pk CP Sch / Ysgol
  Gynradd Parc Waundew
  SA31 . . . . .129 A6
Richmond Rd
  Loughor SA4 . . . . .150 F1
  Pembroke Dock / Doc Penfro
  SA72 . . . . .132 C4

Richmond Rd continued
  Swansea / Abertawe SA2 . .167 A7
Richmond Terr
  Carmarthen / Caerfyrddin
  SA31 . . . . .129 A6
  Llanelli SA15 . . . . .148 C4
  Swansea / Abertawe SA2 . .166 F7
Richmond Villas SA1 . . . . .167 A7
Richmond Way SA5 . . . . .159 E5
Ridge Acre SA2 . . . . .166 C4
Ridge The SA2 . . . . .166 C4
Ridgeway
  Cardigan / Aberteifi SA43 .118 D2
  Killay SA2 . . . . .165 D6
  Llanelli SA14 . . . . .141 A2
Ridgeway La SA2 . . . . .104 F7
Ridgeway The
  Cardigan / Aberteifi SA43 .118 D2
  Lamphey SA70 . . . . .105 D3
  Penally SA70 . . . . .135 A3
  Saundersfoot SA69 . . . . .134 D4
  St Florence SA70 . . . . .106 B4
Ridgewood Pk SA15 . . . . .149 A5
Ridley Way SA3 . . . . .172 A6
Rifleman's Row SA1 . . . . .160 F2
Riga Ave SA14 . . . . .132 B6
Rise The SA6 . . . . .125 B5
Ritec Row SA70 . . . . .135 B3
River Hill SA43 . . . . .118 A4
Riverdale Rd SA14 . . . . .172 E6
Riverside SA4 . . . . .156 B2
Riverside Arc **11** SA1 . . . . .125 A5
Riverside SA73 . . . . .132 B6
Riverside Bsns Pk / Parc
  Busnes Glan yr Afon
  SA6 .154 B1
Riverside Cvn Pk SA6 . . . . . . .154 B3
Riverside Ind Pk SA14 . . . . . . .150 C8
Riverside Quay Sh Ctr
  SA61 . . . . .125 A6
Riverside View SA62 . . . . .125 E3
River Terr SA4 . . . . .143 A4
Riverview SA14 . . . . .143 A5
River View
  Hundleton SA71 . . . . .104 B3
  Llangain SA62 . . . . .87 E3
Robert Davies Ct SA4 . . . . . . .112 A1
Robert Owen Gdns SA1 . . . . .168 B8
Roberts Rd / Heol Roberts
  SA1 .167 F5
Robert St
  Milford Haven / Aberdaugleddau
  SA73 . . . . .131 D2
  Swansea / Abertawe SA1 . . .167 F5
Robeston Cross SA73 . . . . .85 F4
Robin Rd SA5 . . . . .159 E7
Robins La SA13 . . . . .115 C1
Robinson St SA15 . . . . .148 D5
Roch Com Prim Sch
  SA62 . . . . .66 E8
Roche Castle (rems of)*
  SA53 .92 E5
Roch Hill SA62 . . . . .49 E1
Rock Chwyth Rd SA8 . . . . .147 F3
Rockhill SA3 . . . . .173 B4
Rock La SA3 . . . . .117 B4
Rockland Terr SA1 . . . . .160 C1
Rock Mill Woollen & Water
  Mill* SA44 . . . . .20 B5
Rock St SA14 . . . . .24 A2
Rock Terr
  Pembroke / Penfro SA71 . . . .133 C4
  Swansea / Abertawe SA6 . . .153 F1
Rocky Pk SA71 . . . . .133 B5
Rodfa Glyndwr SA31 . . . . .129 A7
Rodney St SA1 . . . . .167 B5
Roebuck Cl SA73 . . . . .131 F5
Roger Beck Way SA2 . . . . .166 E6
Roger St SA5 . . . . .160 B7
Roland Ave SA15 . . . . .148 C7
Roman Bridge Cl SA3 . . . . . . .166 B7
Roman Ct SA3 . . . . .166 B7
Roman Rd SA31 . . . . .129 A3
Romilly Cres SA73 . . . . .131 B3
Roperwright Cl SA4 . . . . .158 B5
Ropewalk SA65 . . . . .122 C4
Ropewalk Rd SA15 . . . . .148 F2
Ropewalk Terr SA71 . . . . .133 D4
Rope Wlk The SA72 . . . . .131 B2
Ropeyard Cl SA65 . . . . .122 C3
Rose Ave SA11 . . . . .125 A2
Roseberry Terr SA6 . . . . .160 E5
Rose Cotts SA4 . . . . .115 F5
Rose Hill SA1 . . . . .167 A7
Rosehill Terr SA1 . . . . .167 B7
Roseland Rd SA5 . . . . .158 F4
Roseland Terr SA1 . . . . .167 F7
Rosemary Cl SA2 . . . . .159 B1
Rosemary Ct SA6 . . . . .153 F1
Rosemary La
  Amroth SA67 . . . . .90 B4
  Carew SA68 . . . . .105 C8
  Haverfordwest / Hwlffordd
  SA61 . . . . .125 A4
Rosemoor Nature Reserve*
  SA62 .85 D8
Rosemount Gdns SA70 . . . . . .135 D5
Rosewarne Cl SA4 . . . . .158 F3
Rosewood Way SA5 . . . . .159 F5
Rosser's Field SA3 . . . . .173 C3
Rotary Way SA11 . . . . .125 A4
Rotherslade Rd SA3 . . . . .172 F4
Rowan Ave SA2 . . . . .166 C4
Rowan Cl Gorseinon SA4 . . . .151 A4
  Killay SA2 . . . . .165 D5
Rowland's Way SA71 . . . . .133 C3
Royal Oak Rd SA2 . . . . .166 B3

Rufus Lewis Ave SA4 . . . . .151 A3
Ruggles Terr SA4 . . . . .153 D1
Rumsey Dr SA73 . . . . .132 B7
Runnymede SA2 . . . . .166 E7
Rural Way SA2 . . . . .166 B8
Rushacre La SA67 . . . . .70 D2
Rushwind Cl SA1 . . . . .172 E6
Rushwind Mews SA1 . . . . .172 E6
Russell St Llanelli SA15 . . . . .148 D5
  Swansea / Abertawe SA1 . . .167 B6
Russell Terr SA31 . . . . .128 D6
Rustic Cl SA2 . . . . .166 B8
Ruther Pk SA61 . . . . .124 C4
Ryelands La SA68 . . . . .134 D8
Ryelands Way SA68 . . . . .89 F2
Ryw Blodyn SA2 . . . . .161 D6

S

Saddler St SA1 . . . . .160 D4
Sageston CP Sch SA70 . . . . . . .105 B6
St Aidans Va Sch SA62 . . . . . . .69 B5
St Aiden Dr SA2 . . . . .165 D6
St Alban's Rd SA2 . . . . .166 F5
St Andrews Cl SA2 . . . . .165 E1
St Andrews Rd **8** SA31 . . .128 F4
St Andrew's Rd SA72 . . . . .132 D2
St Anne's Ave **2** SA32 . . .75 F3
St Anne's Cl SA31 . . . . .173 A3
St Anne's Dr
  Milford Haven / Aberdaugleddau
  SA73 . . . . .131 B2
  St Mary out Liberty SA70 . . .106 F6
St Annes Pl SA73 . . . . .131 B2
St Anne's Rd SA73 . . . . .131 B2
St Ann's Cres SA71 . . . . .133 B5
St Anthony's Way SA62 . . . . . .124 F3
St Brides Cl SA4 . . . . .143 D4
St Bride's La SA69 . . . . .134 F2
St Brides Rd SA62 . . . . .85 C7
St Brides View SA62 . . . . .48 C2
St Bride's View SA62 . . . . .66 E8
St Brides Way SA73 . . . . .131 D5
St Catherines Cl SA67 . . . . . . .90 A7
St Catherine St SA31 . . . . .128 E5
St Catwg Wlk SA2 . . . . .166 A7
St Cenydd Rd SA5 . . . . .159 F6
St Christopher Dr SA2 . . . . . . .165 D6
St Clears Bsns Pk / Parc
  Busnes Sanclêr SA33 . . . . . .127 D4
St Clears Leisure Ctr
  SA33 . . . . .127 E5
St Clears Pl SA5 . . . . .160 B7
St Clears Rd SA31 . . . . .128 B4
St Clements Pk SA62 . . . . .87 A6
St Clement's Rd SA73 . . . . . . .132 B5
St Daniel's Dr SA71 . . . . .133 C3
St Daniel's Hill SA71 . . . . .133 B3
St David Dr SA2 . . . . .165 D6
St David's Ave
  Carmarthen / Caerfyrddin
  SA31 . . . . .128 E5
  Whitland / Hendy-Gwyn
  SA34 . . . . .126 C3
St David's Cath SA62 . . . . .123 C4
St David's Cl Hendy SA4 . . . . .143 B4
St David's Cl
  Llanelli SA15 . . . . .148 C3
  Loughor SA4 . . . . .143 D4
  Tenby / Dinbych-y-pysgod
  SA70 . . . . .135 C5
St David's Cty Sec Sch /
  Ysgol Dewi Sant SA62 . . . . .123 C5
St David's Est SA46 . . . . .101 D8
St Davids Hospl SA31 . . . . . . .128 C5
St David's Pl
  Goodwick / Wdig SA64 . . . .122 A5
  2 Swansea / Abertawe
  SA1 .174 B2
St Davids RC Prim Sch
  SA3 .173 A6
St David's Rd SA18 . . . . .99 E7
St David's Rd
  Camrose SA62 . . . . .124 D6
  Letterston SA62 . . . . .30 D1
  Milford Haven / Aberdaugleddau
  SA73 . . . . .131 C3
  Pembroke / Penfro SA71 . . . .133 A4
  Swansea / Abertawe SA6 . . .161 B8
  Ystalyfera SA9 . . . . .139 C6
St David's Sh Ctr SA1 . . . . . . .174 B2
St David's Sq SA1 . . . . .174 B2
St Davids St SA15 . . . . .115 C1
St Dogmans SA71 . . . . .103 B5
St Dogmaels Rd SA43 . . . . . . .118 C3
St Donat's Ave SA2 . . . . .166 B7
St Elli Sh Ctr SA15 . . . . .148 D5
St Elmo Ave SA1 . . . . .174 C4
St Faith's SA71 . . . . .105 A3
St Florence Cheese & Maze*
  SA70 . . . . .106 B4
St Florence Par **1**
  SA70 . . . . .135 E4
St Florence VC Sch
  SA70 . . . . .106 A4
St Francis RC Prim Sch
  SA73 . . . . .131 D4
St George SA15 . . . . .148 C4
St George's Ave SA34 . . . . . . .126 C1
St George's Ct SA70 . . . . .135 E4
St George's Terr SA3 . . . . .115 C1
St Giles Ct SA62 . . . . .50 E8
St Govans Pl SA5 . . . . .160 B8
St Govans Sh Ctr SA72 . . . . . .132 C3
St Helen's Ave SA1 . . . . .167 A5
St Helen's Cres SA1 . . . . .167 A5
St Helens Prim Sch SA1 . . . . .167 B6

St Helen's Rd SA1 . . . . .167 B6
St Helens Rugby & Cricket
  Gd SA2 . . . . .166 F5
St Hilary Dr SA2 . . . . .165 D7
St Illtyd Rise SA16 . . . . .137 B3
St Illtyd's Cres SA1 . . . . .168 A7
St Illtyd's RC Prim Sch
  SA1 .161 A3
St Ishmaels CP Sch
  SA62 .85 A2
St James Cl SA61 . . . . .125 A2
St James Ct SA1 . . . . .167 A6
St James Gdns SA1 . . . . .167 A6
St James's Cres SA1 . . . . .167 A6
St James's Ct SA1 . . . . .70 E1
St John Lloyd RC Comp Sch /
  Ysgol Gyfun Gatholig Sant
  Ioan Llwyd SA14 . . . . .149 B6
St Johns Ct SA6 . . . . .154 B1
St John's Hill SA70 . . . . .135 D5
St John's Ho SA1 . . . . .160 D2
St John's St SA34 . . . . .126 C3
St Joseph's Ct SA15 . . . . .148 E5
St Joseph's RC Inf Sch
  SA1 .160 D2
St Joseph's RC Jun Sch
  SA1 .160 D1
St Joseph's RC Prim Sch
  SA6 .155 A7
St Judes Cl SA6 . . . . .160 C7
St Julian's St SA70 . . . . .135 E4
St Katherines Ct SA1 . . . . .161 D6
St Lawrence Rd SA73 . . . . .131 B3
St Lawrence Cl SA73 . . . . .131 B3
St Lawrence Ct SA5 . . . . .160 B7
St Lawrence Hill SA73 . . . . . . .131 B3
St Leger Cres SA1 . . . . .167 F7
St Leonards SA62 . . . . .168 A3
St Leonards Ave SA62 . . . . . . .48 C5
St Leonard's Pk SA73 . . . . .87 A3
St Lukes Ct SA1 . . . . .167 A6
St Margaret's Ave SA10 . . . . .169 C8
St Margaret's Cl SA61 . . . . . . .125 A2
St Margaret's Ct SA15 . . . . . . .148 B7
St Margaret's Way SA7 . . . . . . .85 E2
St Marks C in W Sch
  SA61 . . . . .125 A2
St Marks Cl SA61 . . . . .125 A2
St Martin's Pk SA61 . . . . .125 A2
St Martin's Rd SA71 . . . . .133 A4
St Marys Cath Prim Sch
  SA1 .132 C1
St Mary's Pl SA68 . . . . .134 D8
St Mary's RC Prim Sch
  SA1 .149 B6
St Mary's Rd SA31 . . . . .128 D5
St Mary's Rd SA72 . . . . .132 D2
St Mary's Rise SA16 . . . . .137 F2
St Mary's Sq SA1 . . . . .174 B2
St Mary St
  Cardigan / Aberteifi SA43 .118 D3
  Swansea / Abertawe SA1 . . .174 B2
St Matthews Ct SA1 . . . . .174 B4
St Michael's Ave SA4 . . . . .143 B4
St Michael's Rd SA71 . . . . .133 C4
St Michael's Sch SA14 . . . . . . .149 E6
St Nicholas Cl SA3 . . . . .158 E3
St Nicholas Cres
  Pembroke / Penfro SA71 . . . .133 B5
  Tenby / Dinbych-y-pysgod
  SA70 . . . . .135 B3
St Nicholas Ct SA72 . . . . .165 F6
St Nicholas La **8** SA70 . . .135 E4
St Nicholas Sq **13** SA1 . . .174 C2
St Non's Ave SA31 . . . . .128 D5
St Non's Cl SA62 . . . . .123 C4
St Oswalds VA Sch SA48 . . . .101 B8
St Patrick's Rd SA72 . . . . .132 D2
St Paul's Terr SA1 . . . . .158 D8
St Peter's Ave SA15 . . . . .159 D3
St Peter's Cl SA31 . . . . .129 A5
St Peters Rd **8** SA72 . . . . . .85 D2
St Peter's Rd
  Milford Haven / Aberdaugleddau
  SA73 . . . . .131 C3
  Pembroke Dock / Doc Penfro
  SA72 . . . . .132 D2
  The Mumbles / Y Mwmbwls
  SA3 .172 E5
St Peter's St **8** SA31 . . . . .128 F5
St Peters Terr **11** SA15 . . .148 C4
St Peter's Terr SA2 . . . . .159 E2
St Petrox Cl **3** SA71 . . . . . .133 A4
St Rhidian Dr SA2 . . . . .165 D7
St Rhidian Rd SA5 . . . . .159 F6
St Teilo's Ct SA3 . . . . .171 F6
St Teilo's RC Prim Sch
  SA70 . . . . .135 C5
St Teilo's Rd SA72 . . . . .132 D2
St Teilo St SA4 . . . . .143 C4
St Thomas Ave SA61 . . . . .125 A2
St Thomas Gn SA61 . . . . .125 A3
St Thomas Prim Sch
  SA1 .174 C4
St Thomas St **8** SA48 . . . .120 C5
St Twynnell's Cl **2**
  SA71 . . . . .133 C3

St Tygwydd's Sch SA43 . . . . .16 E6
St Vincent Cres **3** SA1 . . .174 B1
Salem Rd Llanelli SA15 . . . . .148 F8
  St Clears / Sanclêr
  SA33 . . . . .127 C4
  Swansea / Abertawe SA6 . . .160 D5
Salisbury Cl SA3 . . . . .117 A6
Saltern Ind Est SA70 . . . . .135 D4
Salthouse Cl SA4 . . . . .156 A3
Salubrious Pass SA1 . . . . .174 B2
Salubrious Pl SA1 . . . . .174 B2
Samlet Rd SA7 . . . . .161 C8
Samlet Sh Ctr SA7 . . . . .161 C8
Samuel Cres SA5 . . . . .160 A3
Samuels Rd SA9 . . . . .100 B7
Sanderling Cl **8** SA1 . . . . .124 E5
Sandfield Rd SA16 . . . . .137 E2
Sandhurst Rd SA31 . . . . .131 D2
Sandpiper Rd SA15 . . . . .148 B6
Sandringham Cl SA4 . . . . .158 B8
Sandringham Pk SA2 . . . . .154 C1
Sandringham Pk / Parc
  Sandringham SA6, SA7 . . . .154 C1
  Sandy Hill Rd SA69 . . . . . . .134 D2
Sandyke Rd SA62 . . . . .85 D8
Sandy La SA3 . . . . .171 A6
Sandy Rd Llanelli SA15 . . . . . .109 F3
  Llanelli SA15 . . . . .148 A6
Sardis Cl SA5 . . . . .158 E3
Sarlou Cl SA3 . . . . .173 C3
Sarlou Ct SA2 . . . . .166 F6
Sarn Helen SA19 . . . . .23 E6
Saron Cl SA4 . . . . .150 F3
Saron Rd Bynea SA14 . . . . . . .149 F4
  Llangeler SA44 . . . . .19 B1
Saron Rd / Heol Saron
  Ammanford SA18 . . . . .97 F6
  Capel Hendre SA18 . . . . .97 E6
Saundersfoot CP Sch
  SA69 . . . . .134 F4
Saundersfoot Sta SA69 . .134 C4
Saunders Rd SA2 . . . . .105 E6
Saunders Way SA2 . . . . .166 B5
Sawdern Rd SA71 . . . . .103 B6
Sawel Ct SA4 . . . . .143 A4
Sawel Terr SA4 . . . . .143 A4
Scandinavia Hts SA69 . . . . . . .134 E2
Scarrowcaant La SA61 . . . . . . .124 E3
School Gdns SA72 . . . . .132 B1
School La
  Llandovery / Llanymddyfri
  SA20 . . . . .121 D5
  Penally SA70 . . . . .135 B3
  Pontardawe SA8 . . . . .147 E5
  Tycroes SA18 . . . . .97 F5
School Rd Glais SA7 . . . . .155 A6
  Llanelli SA15 . . . . .109 E4
  Llanelli SA15 . . . . .148 F2
  Ystalyfera SA9 . . . . .139 B6
  Ystradgynlais SA9 . . . . .139 D8
School Rd / Heol Yr Ysgol
  Brynamman SA18 . . . . .99 D8
  Cefn-bryn-brain SA9 . . . . . . .100 B8
  Neath / Castell-Nedd
  SA10 . . . . .162 C1
Scolton Manor Ctry Pk*
  SA62 .68 D8
Scotchwell La SA61 . . . . .125 C6
Scotchwell View SA61 . . . . . . .125 B6
Scotchwell Wlk **3** SA61 .125 B5
Scotsborough View
  SA70 . . . . .135 C6
Scoveston Rd SA73 . . . . .86 E2
Scurlock Dr SA73 . . . . .132 B8
Sealands Dr SA3 . . . . .173 C3
Seascape SA70 . . . . .135 D6
Seaside Cres **4** SA15 . . . .148 C4
Sea View SA4 . . . . .156 E4
Sea View Com Prim Sch /
  Ysgol Golwg-y-Mor
  SA1 .174 A4
Seaview Cres SA64 . . . . .122 A5
Seaview Terr SA1 . . . . .161 C2
Sea View Terr SA1 . . . . .174 A4
Sebastopol St SA1 . . . . .167 F7
Second Ave SA6 . . . . .160 C8
Second St SA71 . . . . .103 B5
Seion Hill SA44 . . . . .19 B3
Senny Pl SA4 . . . . .154 A5
Sentence Gdns **5** SA67 . . .89 E6
Serecold Ave SA10 . . . . .162 D6
Serpentine Rd SA70 . . . . .135 C5
Settlands Hill SA62 . . . . .85 C8
Severn Rd SA6 . . . . .160 D8
Shakespeare Ave SA3 . . . . .131 D3
Shakespeare Cl SA61 . . . . .125 A3
Shands Rd SA18 . . . . .98 B8
Sharpsburgh Rl SA1 . . . . .160 D3
Shaw St SA4 . . . . .158 B5
Shearwater Cl SA3 . . . . .172 F6
Sheepwalk Rd SA66 . . . . .70 A8
Sheffield Dr SA3 . . . . .131 F5
Shelley Rd SA61 . . . . .125 A3
Shelley Way SA62 . . . . .67 F6
Shepherd's Rd SA6 . . . . .160 E6
Shepherd's Terr SA4 . . . . .151 A3
Sherborne Wlk SA1 . . . . .166 A1
Sherringham Dr SA3 . . . . .172 F5
Shingrig SA13 . . . . .118 B3
Shipman's La SA61 . . . . .125 A4
Shirburn Cl SA71 . . . . .102 D5
Shire Horse Ctr* SA9 . . . . .82 E3
Shoals Hook La SA61 . . . . .125 B7
Shopper's Wlk SA1 . . . . .174 A2
Short St Clydach SA6 . . . . .146 D1
  Swansea / Abertawe SA1 . . .174 A4
Shoulder of Mutton **2**
  SA71 . . . . .133 C5

Shropshire Rd SA72 . . . . .132 D4
Shute La SA67 . . . . .89 F8
Siding Terr SA10 . . . . .162 D7
Sidney Webb Cl SA73 . . . . .132 B6
Siemens Way SA7 . . . . .161 A5
Signal View SA61 . . . . .124 F7
Silent World Aquarium*
SA70 . . . . .135 E6
Siloh Cres SA1 . . . . .160 D4
Siloh Rd SA1 . . . . .160 D4
Silver Cl SA3 . . . . .172 F7
Silverhurst SA1 . . . . .173 B3
Silverstream SA1 . . . . .131 A3
Silverstream Cres SA73 . .131 A3
Silverstream Dr SA73 . . . .131 A3
Silver Terr SA16 . . . . .137 E2
Singleton Botanical Gdns*
SA2 . . . . .166 D6
Singleton Hospl SA2 . . . . .166 D4
Singleton St SA1 . . . . .174 A2
Sir Thomas Picton Sch
SA61 . . . . .125 B5
Siskin Cl SA61 . . . . .124 E5
Six Pit Junction Sta*
SA7 . . . . .161 C6
Sixth La SA71 . . . . .104 F4
Sketty Ave SA2 . . . . .166 D6
Sketty La SA2 . . . . .166 D4
Sketty Park Cl SA2 . . . . . . .166 C6
Sketty Park Dr SA2 . . . . . . .166 B6
Sketty Park Rd SA2 . . . . . . .166 C6
Sketty Prim Sch SA2 . . . . . .166 C7
Sketty Rd SA2 . . . . .166 E6
Skewen Sta SA10 . . . . .162 E7
Skinners La 8 SA61 . . . . . .125 A5
Skinner St SA1 . . . . .160 C1
Skomer Dr SA73 . . . . .131 D4
Skomer Marine Nature
Reserve* SA62 . . . . .83 D5
Skomer Pl SA5 . . . . .159 D7
Slade Gdns SA2 . . . . .172 F6
Slade Hall 6 SA1 . . . . .174 A4
Slade La SA62 . . . . .124 E7
Slade Pk SA3 . . . . .125 D4
Slade Rd SA3 . . . . .172 F5
Sladeway SA65 . . . . .122 D4
Slate St
Swansea / Abertawe SA6 . .160 F8
Swansea / Abertawe SA6 . .161 A8
Slaughter House La 2
SA73 . . . . .131 C3
Slip Hill SA73 . . . . .131 D2
Slippery Back SA70 . . . . . . .135 D8
Smithfield Rd SA8 . . . . .147 E5
Smith's Rd SA7 . . . . .155 A2
Smyrna St SA6 . . . . .160 E5
Smyth St SA65 . . . . .122 D3
Snady Hill Pk SA69 . . . . . . .134 D2
Snowdon Dr SA5 . . . . .159 D3
Snowdon Rd SA16 . . . . .137 E2
Snowdon Cl 3 SA61 . . . . . .124 E4
Snowdrop La SA61 . . . . .124 F4
Soar Terr SA9 . . . . .139 E6
Soar Cl SA4 . . . . .150 F7
Soar Rd SA14 . . . . .149 E4
Soar Terr SA61 . . . . .124 F5
Solva City Prim Sch SA62 .48 C3
Solva Rd SA6 . . . . .160 C8
Solva Woollen Mill*
SA62 . . . . .48 D4
Somerset Pl SA1 . . . . .174 C2
Somerset Rd SA3 . . . . .173 A4
Somerville Ct SA2 . . . . .166 E7
Southall Ave SA10 . . . . .162 E6
Southampton Row
SA72 . . . . .132 A2
South Cl SA3 . . . . .172 A6
South Cliff St SA4 . . . . .135 E4
South Ct SA61 . . . . .124 D5
Southdown Cl SA71 . . . . . . .133 C2
Southdown SA3 . . . . .173 C4
Southerndown Ave SA3 . .165 F1
Southgate Pk SA62 . . . . . . .51 C1
Southgate Rd SA3 . . . . .171 A4
South Hook Rd SA73 . . . . . .102 F3
Southlands
Pembroke / Penfro SA71 . .133 C3
Tenby / Dinbych-y-pysgod
SA70 . . . . .135 D6
Southlands Dr SA3 . . . . .172 F6
South Mdws SA71 . . . . .133 D3
South Mews SA71 . . . . .133 B4
South Par SA70 . . . . .135 E4
South Pembrokeshire Hospl
SA72 . . . . .132 A4
South Prospect SA1 . . . . . .174 B3
South Rd SA71 . . . . .133 B4
South Row SA68 . . . . .88 F1
South St SA62 . . . . .101 C4
South Terr SA1 . . . . .133 A4
South View SA4 . . . . .151 D2
Southward La SA3 . . . . .172 F4
Spencer Cl SA70 . . . . .105 E1
Spencer St SA5 . . . . .160 C4
Spencer Terr SA9 . . . . .139 D8
Spenser Way SA61 . . . . . . .125 B4
Sperricomb La SA7 . . . . . . .135 D7
Spien Rd SA14 . . . . .97 D7
Spike's La SA71 . . . . .131 B2
Spilman St SA31 . . . . .128 F5
Spinney The SA2 . . . . .166 A6
Spionkop Rd SA14 . . . . .154 C6
Spittal VC Sch SA62 . . . . . .51 C2
Sportsway SA73 . . . . .132 B6
Spowart Ave SA15 . . . . .148 C6
Springbourne Cl SA4 . . . . .158 D3

Springburn Cl 1 SA67 . . . .90 A2
Springfield SA3 . . . . .117 B4
Springfield Ave
Neyland SA73 . . . . .132 B7
Upper Killay SA2 . . . . .165 B5
Springfield Cl
Gowerton / Tre-gwyr SA4 . .158 B5
2 Haverfordwest / Hwlffordd
SA62 . . . . .125 B7
Neyland SA73 . . . . .132 B7
Springfield Pk SA67 . . . . . . .70 E2
Springfield Rd
Carmarthen / Caerfyrddin
SA31 . . . . .128 F6
Neath / Castell-Nedd SA10 .162 F7
Pembroke Dock / Doc Penfro
SA72 . . . . .132 D1
Springfields SA15 . . . . .148 F2
Springfield St SA4 . . . . .153 F1
Springfield Terr SA16 . . . . .137 E2
Spring Gdns
Gorseinon SA4 . . . . .151 D1
Letterston SA62 . . . . .50 F8
Narberth / Arberth SA67 . . .70 D1
Whitland / Hendy-Gwyn
SA34 . . . . .126 D3
Spring Gdns Ind Est
SA34 . . . . .126 F3
Spring Gdns La 1 SA1 . . . .125 A5
Spring Gdns N SA10 . . . . . .162 F7
Spring Gdns S SA10 . . . . . .162 F7
Spring Terr SA1 . . . . .167 B6
Sprinkle La SA62 . . . . .87 D5
Spruce Way SA4 . . . . .152 C2
Square The SA65 . . . . .122 D3
Squire Ct SA1 . . . . .174 B2
Squirrel Wlk / Rhodfa'r
Wiwer SA4 . . . . .143 A5
Stackpole Rd SA71 . . . . . . .112 C6
Stackpole VC Sch SA71 . . .112 A6
Stadwen Rd SA7 . . . . .161 E7
Stafford Comm SA4 . . . . . . .158 D7
Stafford St SA15 . . . . .148 D3
Stambridge La SA70 . . . . . .105 C5
Stammers Gdn* SA69 . . . .134 E3
Stammers La SA69 . . . . . . .134 E2
Stammers Rd SA69 . . . . . . .134 E3
Stanley Pl SA1 . . . . .174 A3
Stanley Rd
6 Llanelli SA15 . . . . .148 D3
Neath / Castell-Nedd SA10 .162 F7
Stanley St
Gwaun-Cae-Gurwen SA18 . .99 D6
Llanelli SA15 . . . . .148 D2
The Mumbles / Y Mwmbwls
SA3 . . . . .173 A5
Stanley Terr SA1 . . . . .174 A3
Stapleton Pl 2 SA6 . . . . . .160 F8
Starbuck Rd SA73 . . . . .131 C3
Station App
Carmarthen / Caerfyrddin
SA31 . . . . .128 F4
Narberth / Arberth SA67 . . .70 E1
Station Ct SA1 . . . . .174 B4
Station Hill
Goodwick / Wdig SA64 . . .122 B6
St Clears / Sanclêr
SA33 . . . . .127 E7
Station Rd Brecon SA18 . . .80 E1
Brynamman SA18 . . . . .99 E8
Burry Port SA16 . . . . .137 E2
Bynea SA14 . . . . .150 A3
Cardigan / Aberteifi SA43 . .118 D3
Crymych SA41 . . . . .34 F4
Glais SA7 . . . . .155 A6
Gowerton / Tre-gwyr SA4 . .158 C5
Grovesend SA4 . . . . .151 D6
Kidwelly / Cydweli SA17 . . .138 A4
Kilgetty / Begelly SA68 . . .134 D8
Letterston SA62 . . . . .50 F8
Llandeilo SA19 . . . . .130 E6
Llandyssul SA44 . . . . .19 E3
Llanelli SA15 . . . . .148 D4
Llanfihangel-ar-Arth SA39 . .39 B7
Llangadog SA19 . . . . .63 D7
Llangennech SA14 . . . . . . .150 C4
Llanwrda SA19 . . . . .156 C2
Llanwrtyd Wells LD5 . . . . . .9 D1
Loughor SA4 . . . . .157 C8
Narberth / Arberth SA67 . . .70 E1
Neath / Castell-Nedd
SA10 . . . . .162 E7
Newcastle Emlyn / Castell
Newydd Emlyn SA38 . . . . .119 E4
Newcastle Emlyn / Castell
Newydd Emlyn SA38 . . . . .132 C6
Pembroke / Penfro SA71 . .133 D4
Pen-clawdd SA4 . . . . .156 F4
Pentlepoir SA69 . . . . .134 C7
Pontarddulais SA4 . . . . . . .143 B5
Pontyberem SA15 . . . . .96 B6
St Clears / Sanclêr
SA33 . . . . .127 E7
Swansea / Abertawe, Cockett
SA5 . . . . .159 E3
Swansea / Abertawe,
Landore / Glandwr SA1 . . .160 D4
Swansea / Abertawe, Trallwn
SA7 . . . . .161 E7
Tenby / Dinbych-y-pysgod
SA70 . . . . .135 D4
Whitland / Hendy-Gwyn
SA34 . . . . .126 C2
Ystradgynlais SA9 . . . . . . .139 B8
Station Rd / Ffordd-yr-Orsaf
5 SA18 . . . . .98 B7

Station Terr
Lampeter / Llanbedr Pont Steffan
SA48 . . . . .120 C5
Newcastle Emlyn / Castell
Newydd Emlyn SA38 . . . . .119 E4
Pen-clawdd SA4 . . . . .156 F4
Stebonheath Prim Sch /
Ysgol Gynradd Stebonheath
SA15 . . . . .148 F5
Stebonheath Terr SA15 . . .148 F5
Steele Ave SA31 . . . . .128 D5
Stembridge Ave SA5 . . . . . .159 D5
Stepaside CP Sch SA68 . . .134 D8
Stepaside Craft Village*
SA67 . . . . .90 A2
Stephen's Gn La SA70 . . . .105 C4
Stephen's La SA62 . . . . .123 C4
Stephenson Rd SA7 . . . . . . .165 F6
Stephen St 1 SA73 . . . . . . .131 C3
Stephens Way SA31 . . . . . . .128 F3
Stephens Way Ret Pk
SA31 . . . . .128 F4
Stepney La SA2 . . . . .159 D1
Stepney Pl SA15 . . . . .148 D5
Stepney Prec 4 SA15 . . . .148 D5
Stepney St
Burry Port SA16 . . . . .137 E3
Glanaman SA18 . . . . .99 C8
Llandeilo SA19 . . . . .130 E6
Llanelli SA15 . . . . .109 F3
Swansea / Abertawe SA2 . .159 D1
Waunarlwydd SA5 . . . . . . .158 E3
Sterry Rd SA15 . . . . .158 B5
Stewart Dr / Ffordd Stewart
12 SA18 . . . . .98 B7
Stewart Hall SA2 . . . . .166 D6
Stewart St SA15 . . . . .148 C6
Steynton Rd SA73 . . . . .131 D3
Stockwell Rd SA72 . . . . .132 C4
Stokes Ave SA61 . . . . .125 B6
Stone Cl SA73 . . . . .131 D4
Stone St SA20 . . . . .121 D5
Stoneway Rd SA33 . . . . .92 E5
Stradey Cl 3 SA15 . . . . . . .148 C4
Stradey Hill SA15 . . . . .109 F4
Stradey Park Ave SA15 . . .148 C6
Stradey Rd SA15 . . . . .148 C7
Strand
Cardigan / Aberteifi SA43 . .118 D3
Swansea / Abertawe SA1 . .174 B4
Swansea / Abertawe SA1 . .174 B4
Strand Row SA1 . . . . .174 B3
Strand The
Laugharne Township SA33 . .92 F5
Saundersfoot SA69 . . . . . . .134 F4
Stranraer Ave SA72 . . . . . . .132 A1
Stranraer La SA72 . . . . .132 A1
Stranraer Rd SA72 . . . . .132 A1
Stratford Rd SA73 . . . . .131 C3
Strawberry Gdns SA70 . . . .135 B8
Strawberry Hill SA62 . . . . . .85 C7
Strawberry La SA70 . . . . . . .135 B2
Strawberry Pl SA6 . . . . .153 F1
Strongbow Wlk SA71 . . . . . .133 B6
Stryd Arthur / Arthur St
SA18 . . . . .98 B8
Stryd Cannon / Cannon St
SA18 . . . . .99 D8
Stryd Chapman / Chapman
St SA15 . . . . .148 D6
Stryd Emma / Emma St 13
SA15 . . . . .148 D4
Stryd Fawr / High St
4 Glanaman SA18 . . . . . . .99 A8
Swansea / Abertawe SA1 . .174 B4
Stryd Fawr / High Street
SA18 . . . . .98 C7
Stryd Harold / Harold St 4
SA18 . . . . .98 B7
Stryd Llewellyn / Llewellyn
St 14 SA15 . . . . .148 D4
Stryd Lloyd / Lloyd St
SA15 . . . . .148 C5
Stryd Marged / Margaret St
SA18 . . . . .98 C7
Stryd Raby / Raby St
SA18 . . . . .98 C6
Stryd Rhydychen / Oxford St
SA1 . . . . .174 A2
Stryd Rice / Rice St
SA18 . . . . .98 C6
Stryd Y Cei / Quay St 2
SA18 . . . . .98 C7
Stryd-y-Coleg / College St
SA18 . . . . .98 B7
Stryd Y Crochendy / Pottery
St 7 SA15 . . . . .148 D5
Stryd-y-Gwynt / Wind St
SA18 . . . . .98 B7
Stryd Y Parc / Park St
Brynamman SA18 . . . . .99 E6
Ammanford / Rhydaman
SA18 . . . . .98 B8
Stryd Y Prior / Priory St
SA17 . . . . .136 C5
Stryd-yr-Eglwys / Church St
6 SA18 . . . . .98 B7
Studio Pottery* SA62 . . . . .48 D8
Style Pk SA61 . . . . .125 C5
Sugar Loaf Sta SA19 . . . . . .26 F6
Summercliffe Chalet Pk
SA3 . . . . .172 D4
Summer Hill 2 SA62 . . . . .50 F8
Summerhill Cl SA62 . . . . . . .66 F6

Summerhill La SA70 . . . . . .105 D3
Summerhill Pk 8 SA62 . . . .90 C2
Summerland La SA3 . . . . . .172 E5
Summerland Pk SA2 . . . . . .165 B5
Summer Pl SA7 . . . . .161 F7
Summers Villas SA2 . . . . . .165 B5
Sunderland Ave SA72 . . . . .132 B2
Sunningdale Ave SA3 . . . . .165 F1
Sunningdale Dr SA4 . . . . . .151 B4
Sunninghill Terr SA15 . . . .148 E6
Sunnybank Cl SA3 . . . . .172 F8
Sunny Hill SA15 . . . . .148 D6
Sunnyland Cres SA10 . . . . .162 F8
Sunnymead Cl SA1 . . . . . . .159 E2
Sunny Rd SA15 . . . . .148 D6
Sunny View SA19 . . . . .63 C7
Sussex Rd SA10 . . . . .137 F3
Sutton St SA70 . . . . .135 E4
Swallow Dale SA69 . . . . . . .134 E2
Swan Cl SA2 . . . . .165 E6
Swanfield SA9 . . . . .139 C7
Swanfield Pl 1 SA15 . . . . .148 D6
Swan La SA9 . . . . .139 C7
Swansea Castle* SA1 . . . . .174 B3
Swansea Coll / Coleg
Abertawe (Tycoch Campus)
SA2 . . . . .166 D7
Swansea Coll of Art
SA1 . . . . .174 B3
Swansea Ent Pk SA7 . . . . . .161 B7
Swansea Inst / Athrofa
Abertawe (Townhill
Campus) SA2 . . . . .166 F8
Swansea Inst (Mount
Pleasant Campus) SA1 .174 A3
Swansea Maritime &
Industrial Mus* SA1 . . . .174 B2
Swansea Mus* SA1 . . . . . .174 B2
Swansea Rd
Gorseinon SA4 . . . . .158 E7
Llanelli, Box SA15 . . . . . . .148 F6
Llanelli, Marble Hall SA15 . .148 E6
Penllergaer SA4 . . . . .152 B2
Pontardawe SA8 . . . . .147 C2
Pontlliw SA4 . . . . .152 B7
Swansea / Abertawe, Cadle
SA5 . . . . .159 C2
Swansea / Abertawe, Llangyfelach
SA5 . . . . .160 A6
Waunarlwydd SA5 . . . . . . .158 E4
Swansea Sta SA1 . . . . .174 B4
Swansea Vale Rly*
SA7 . . . . .161 B3
Swansea West Ind Pk
SA5 . . . . .159 C4
Swansquare 10 SA61 . . . .125 A5
Swan St SA1 . . . . .174 B4
Swan Wlk SA15 . . . . .148 B5
Sway Rd SA6 . . . . .154 A1
Sweet Briar La SA3 . . . . . . .173 A8
Swiss Valley SA14 . . . . .149 A2
Swiss Valley Prim Sch
SA14 . . . . .141 A2
Swn-y-gwent Day Hosp
SA18 . . . . .98 B7
Swn-y-Nant SA9 . . . . .138 B2
Swn Yr Afon SA9 . . . . .126 B8
Swn yr Eos SA9 . . . . .139 E2
Sybil St SA6 . . . . .154 E7
Sycamore Cl
Milford Haven / Aberdaugleddau
SA73 . . . . .131 E4
Swansea / Abertawe SA2 . .166 A7
Sycamore Rd SA14 . . . . . . .159 F8
Sycamore St
Newcastle Emlyn / Castell
Newydd Emlyn SA38 . . . . .119 D5
Pembroke Dock / Doc Penfro
SA72 . . . . .132 B1
Sycamore Way SA31 . . . . . .128 C5
Sydney Rees Way SA15 . . .125 B6
Sydney St SA5 . . . . .160 C4
Sylen Rd SA15 . . . . .96 B5
Sylvan Way SA2 . . . . .165 E6
Sylvia Terr SA5 . . . . .160 C4
Symmons St SA1 . . . . .160 C1

Tabernacle La 3 SA67 . . .70 E1
Tabernacle Rd / Heol
Tabernacl 2 SA18 . . . . . .99 A8
Tabernacle Rd / Heol
Tabernacle SA18 . . . . .98 F8
Tabernacle St
Neath / Castell-Nedd SA10 .162 F7
Swansea / Abertawe SA1 . .160 D3
Tabernacle Terr 3
SA31 . . . . .128 F6
Tabor Terr SA14 . . . . .149 E6
Tai Gwalia SA9 . . . . .100 C5
Tair Ffynnon 1 SA34 . . . . .90 C7
Tairgwaith Prim Sch
SA18 . . . . .99 E6
Talbot Gn SA4 . . . . .158 C5
Talbot Rd / Ffordd Talbot 10
SA18 . . . . .98 B8
Talbot St
Gowerton / Tre-gwyr SA4 . .158 B5
Llanelli SA15 . . . . .148 D4
Talfan Rd SA1 . . . . .161 B3
Taliesin Ct SA48 . . . . .120 C7
Taliesin Pl SA41 . . . . .150 E1
Taliesyn Rd SA1 . . . . .161 B4
Talley CP Sch SA19 . . . . . . .42 D3
Talley Rd SA5 . . . . .160 B5

Tall Trees Cl 2 SA62 . . . . .86 E5
Tal-y-bont Hill SA67 . . . . . .70 B4
Talyclun SA14 . . . . .142 E2
Tal Y Coed SA4 . . . . .142 F3
Talycopa Prim Sch SA7 . . .161 F7
Talywern SA14 . . . . .150 B7
Tan Bank SA61 . . . . .125 B6
Tanerdy SA31 . . . . .129 B6
Tank Farm Rd SA10 . . . . . .162 C3
Tanner's La
Lampeter Velfrey SA67 . . . .90 A6
Templeton SA67 . . . . .89 E6
Tanyard La SA18 . . . . .119 D4
Tan-y-Bryn SA16 . . . . .137 C2
Tan Y Bryn SA44 . . . . .19 C2
Tan-y-bryn Terr SA14 . . . . .156 F4
Tanycoed Rd SA6 . . . . .146 F1
Tanydarren SA8 . . . . .100 B1
Tan y fan SA18 . . . . .97 E6
Tan-y-Farteg SA9 . . . . .139 C7
Tan-y-Gelli SA18 . . . . .99 B8
Tanygraig Rd SA14 . . . . . . .149 E4
Tan Y Lan SA18 . . . . .79 B1
Tan-y-Lan Terr SA6 . . . . . . .160 F8
Tan-y-Lon SA15 . . . . .146 D1
Tan Y Marian Rd SA1 . . . . .167 B8
Tanyrallt SA18 . . . . .118 A3
Tanyrhodyn SA15 . . . . .140 F1
Tanywern La SA9 . . . . .139 B7
Taplow Terr SA1 . . . . .160 F2
Targate Rd SA62 . . . . .87 A5
Tasker Milward Sch / Ysgol
Tasker Milward SA61 . . . .124 E4
Taskers La SA62 . . . . .66 E1
Tavernspite CP Sch SA34 . .90 F7
Tavistock Cl SA2 . . . . .166 E7
Tavistock Rd SA2 . . . . .166 D7
Tawe Ave SA1 . . . . .160 E2
Tawe Bsns Village SA6 . . .161 A5
Tawelan SA32 . . . . .77 B8
Tawelfan Tircoed SA4 . . . . .152 C5
Ystradgynlais SA9 . . . . . . .138 F4
Tawel Fan SA14 . . . . .149 A6
Tawe Pk SA9 . . . . .139 F7
Tawe St SA6 . . . . .154 E7
Tawe Rd SA1 . . . . .161 E8
Tawe St SA6 . . . . .161 A8
Tawe Terr SA8 . . . . .147 E4
Tawe View Cres SA6 . . . . . .153 F1
Technium Bsns Pk SA1 . . .174 C3
Tegfan
Swansea / Abertawe SA7 . .161 F5
Tircoed SA4 . . . . .152 C5
Teg Fan SA10 . . . . .162 E6
Tegfynydd SA14 . . . . .141 A2
Tegid Rd SA4 . . . . .174 A5
Teglan Pk SA18 . . . . .97 F5
Teglyn SA67 . . . . .70 C2
Teifi Marshes Nature
Reserve* SA43 . . . . .118 F3
Teifi Terr SA14 . . . . .120 C4
Teifi Valley Bsns Pk
SA38 . . . . .119 F4
Teilo Cres SA1 . . . . .167 B8
Telyn Aur SA6 . . . . .153 E2
Temperance La SA4 . . . . . . .138 F1
Templebar Rd SA44 . . . . . . .134 A6
Temple St Llanelli SA15 . . .148 E5
Swansea / Abertawe SA1 . .174 B3
Templeton Cty Prim Sch
SA67 . . . . .89 E7
Templeton Way SA15 . . . . .159 F7
Tenby Cottage Hospl
SA70 . . . . .135 D4
Tenby CP Sch SA70 . . . . . .135 C5
Tenby Ct SA71 . . . . .104 C4
Tenby Leisure Ctr SA70 . . .135 B5
Tenby Mus & Art Gall*
SA70 . . . . .135 E4
Tenby Rd
Cardigan / Aberteifi SA43 . .118 E2
St Clears / Sanclêr
SA33 . . . . .127 D4
Tenby Sta SA70 . . . . .135 D5
Tennyson Way SA2 . . . . . . .165 F8
Tenth Ave SA6 . . . . .153 D2
Teras Brynteg / Bryn-Teg
Terr 13 SA18 . . . . .98 B7
Teras Caersalem /
Caersalem Terr 2
SA15 . . . . .148 C5
Teras Jones / Jones' Terr
SA18 . . . . .98 F8
Teras Parc Bigyn / Bigyn
Park Terr SA15 . . . . .148 E4
Teras Tyisha / Tyisha Terr
SA15 . . . . .148 E8
Teras Waterloo / Waterloo
Terr SA18 . . . . .97 D6
Teras Yr Arced / Arcade Terr
11 SA18 . . . . .99 B8
Terrace Rd SA1 . . . . .167 B7
Tŷ Coed Road Prim Sch
SA1 . . . . .167 B7
Theatre Mwldan SA43 . . . .118 D4
Third Ave SA6 . . . . .153 D1
Third La SA71 . . . . .133 E4
Third St SA71 . . . . .103 C5
Thistleboon Cvn Site
SA3 . . . . .173 C4

Thistleboon Dr SA3 . . . . . . .173 C4
Thistleboon Gdns SA3 . . .173 B3
Thistleboon Rd SA3 . . . . . .173 B4
Thomas Ave SA15 . . . . .95 C4
Thomas Evans Ho SA1 . .159 F1
Thomas Parry Way
SA61 . . . . .124 F6
Thomas Row SA1 . . . . .174 B4
Thomas St
  Llandeilo SA19 . . . . .130 E6
  Llanelli SA15 . . . . .148 D6
  Pembroke / Penfro SA71 . .133 B4
  Pontardawe SA8 . . . . .147 E5
  Swansea / Abertawe SA1 .174 C3
Thomas Terr
  Llandeilo SA19 . . . . .130 E6
  Swansea / Abertawe SA6 .160 E6
Thompson Ct SA4 . . . . .158 D8
Thornberry Gdns SA67 . . . .90 A5
Thornhill Rd SA14 . . . . .97 C6
Thornton Bsns Pk SA73 .131 D5
Thornton Ind Trading Est
SA73 .131 D6
Thornton Rd SA73 . . . . . . .131 D6
Three Cliffs Dr SA3 . . . . . .171 A6
Three Ships Ct SA1 . . . . . .173 C3
Thurston La
  Burton SA73 . . . . .132 E8
  Rosemarket SA73 . . . . .87 B3
Tichbourne St SA4 . . . . . . .173 B4
Tirbach Rd SA9 . . . . .139 C7
Tir Becca SA14 . . . . .96 E6
Tir Capel SA14 . . . . .149 A6
Tir Dafydd SA15 . . . . .95 D4
Tirdeunaw Cl SA5 . . . . .160 C7
Tir Einon SA14 . . . . .149 C4
Tirforgan SA14 . . . . .149 A7
Tirgof SA14 . . . . .150 B8
Tir John North Rd SA1 . .168 C8
Tir Llan SA32 . . . . .77 E2
Tirmynydd SA4 . . . . .151 B1
Tirmynydd Rd SA2, SA4 . .164 D8
Tir Newydd SA14 . . . . .149 D4
Tir-owen SA33 . . . . .127 C5
Tirpenry St SA6 . . . . .154 A1
Tirprys SA18 . . . . .98 A5
Tir Treharn ⊕ SA42 . . . . . . .13 E4
Tirwaun
  Burry Port SA16 . . . . .137 C2
  Cross Hands SA14 . . . . .97 B7
Tirycoed Rd / Heol Tir Y
  Coed ⊕ SA18 . . . . .99 A8
Tir-y-Dail La / Lon
  Tir-y-Dail ⊕ SA18 . . . . .98 B7
Tirynys SA15 . . . . .148 F8
Tir Yr Hen Ysgol SA14 . .149 F3
Tir Ysgawen SA31 . . . . . . .129 B3
Tir Ysgol SA15 . . . . .148 D6
Tlysfan ⊕ SA65 . . . . .122 D3
Toft Pl SA15 . . . . .148 E6
Tom Williams Ct SA1 . . .174 B4
Tontine St SA1 . . . . .174 B4
Tor Ho SA3 . . . . .173 A4
Tori-gwddwg Hill SA62 . . .68 D5
Tor La ② SA70 . . . . .135 F4
Torrington Rd SA5 . . . . . .160 A3
Tor View SA3 . . . . .170 D6
Tower Ct
  Swansea / Abertawe, Llansamlet
  SA6 . . . . .161 B8
  Swansea / Abertawe SA1 .166 F8
Tower Gdns SA1 . . . . .159 F1
Tower Hill
  Fishguard / Abergwaun
  SA65 .122 C4
  ④ Haverfordwest / Hwlffordd
  SA61 .125 A5
Tower View ② SA62 . . . . . .84 C3
Town Hall La SA62 . . . . . .123 D5
Townhill Com Prim Sch
SA1 . . . . .167 A8
Townhill Gdns SA2 . . . . . .166 F8
Townhill Rd SA2 . . . . .167 A8
Towy Ave SA20 . . . . .121 C5
Towy Cl ⊕ SA31 . . . . .128 C2
Towy-side ⊕ SA31 . . . . . . .128 F4
Traeth Ffordd
  Llanelli SA15 . . . . .148 B4
  Llanelli SA15 . . . . .148 C4
Trafalgar Pl SA2 . . . . .166 F5
Trafalgar Rd
  Haverfordwest / Hwlffordd
  SA61 .124 E4
  Milford Haven / Aberdaugleddau
  SA73 .131 C3
  ⑥ Tenby / Dinbych-y-pysgod
  SA70 .135 E4
Trafalgar Terr
  Neyland SA73 . . . . .132 B5
  The Havens SA62 . . . . .85 D8
Trallwm Rd SA14 . . . . .149 D5
Trallwn Pl SA2 . . . . .161 E6
Trallwn Prim Sch / Ysgol
  Gynradd Trallwn SA7 . .161 E7
Trallwn Rd SA7 . . . . .161 E6
Trawler Rd SA1 . . . . .174 B1
Trawsffordd SA9 . . . . .139 C7
Trebuan SA15 . . . . .140 E1
Tre Cynon SA48 . . . . .4 F3
Tredafydd VC Sch SA65 . . .30 E4
Tredegar Rd SA4 . . . . .151 C1
Tree-tops SA14 . . . . .141 A2
Trefasser Cross SA64 . . . .10 D2
Trefloyne La SA70 . . . . . . .135 C1
Treforis SA18 . . . . .98 C6

Trefrhiw Rd / Heol Trefrhiw
SA18 . . . . .98 A6
Tregarne Cl SA6 . . . . .153 F4
Tregelles Ct
  Cwmrhydyceirw SA6 . . . . . .154 A4
  Swansea / Abertawe SA6 . .153 F3
Tre-gendeg Rd SA66 . . . . . .53 B1
Tregoyls Wood Nature
  Reserve* SA19 . . . . .79 D8
Tregroes Cty Prim Sch /
  Ysgol Gynradd Tregroes
  SA44 . . . . .19 D7
Tregwyr Inf Sch SA4 . . . .158 B5
Tregwyr Jun Sch SA4 . . .158 B5
Treharne Rd SA6 . . . . .153 F1
Treherbert St SA48 . . . . . .120 E3
Trenewydck St SA72 . . . . .132 D3
Tremoilet VCP Sch / Ysgol
  Gynradd Wr Tremoilet
  SA33 . . . . .91 D4
Trem-y-Bedol ⊕ SA31 . . .129 A6
Trem Y Ddol SA38 . . . . . . .119 B6
Trem-y-Dref ② SA31 . . . .128 E6
Trem Y Môr
  Fishguard & Goodwick
  SA65 .122 C4
  Llanmorlais SA4 . . . . .156 B2
Trem-y-Mynydd SA16 . . .137 D3
Trem Y Parc / Parkview Terr
  SA15 .148 C6
Trem Y Teifi SA44 . . . . .19 E3
Tre-nel SA16 . . . . .108 E4
Treoven Rd SA72 . . . . .132 B1
Tre Uchaf Prim Sch
  SA4 . . . . .150 F1
Trevaughan Cl SA61 . . . . .125 A4
Trevaughan Gdns SA34 . .126 C2
Trevaughan Lodge Rd
  SA61 .125 B4
Trevaughan Rd SA31 . . . .128 D7
Trewarren Cl SA62 . . . . . . .85 A2
Trewarren Dr SA62 . . . . . . .85 A2
Trewarren Rd SA62 . . . . . .85 A2
Trewen Rd
  Birchgrove SA7 . . . . .155 A1
  Swansea / Abertawe SA7 . .162 A8
Trewent Hill SA71 . . . . . . .105 A1
Trewyddfa Comm SA6 . . .160 F6
Trewyddfa Gdns SA6 . . . .160 E6
Trewyddfa Rd SA6 . . . . . . .160 E6
Trewyddfa Terr SA6 . . . . . .160 E6
Trilwm SA17 . . . . .109 C3
Trimsaran CP Sch SA15 . .109 C7
Trimsaran Rd SA15 . . . . . .109 C6
Trinity Cl
  Pontardulais SA4 . . . . .143 C3
  The Mumbles / Mwmbwls
  SA3 . . . . .173 A5
Trinity Coll / Coleg Y
  Drindod SA31 . . . . .128 C5
Trinity Ct ② SA1 . . . . .174 A3
Trinity La SA1 . . . . .156 D4
Trinity Pl Neyland SA73 . .132 B6
  Pontardulais SA4 . . . . .143 C3
  Swansea / Abertawe SA1 . .174 B3
Trinity Rd Llanelli SA15 . .148 E3
  Pembroke Dock / Doc Penfro
  SA72 .132 D2
Trinity St SA4 . . . . .151 C1
Trinity Terr Llanelli SA15 .148 D3
  Neyland SA73 . . . . .132 F6
Trippis Rd SA67 . . . . .70 B7
Troed Y Bryn SA14 . . . . . . .96 F6
Troed-y-Bryn SA40 . . . . . . .21 E6
Troed Y Rhiw
  ⑪ Goodwick / Wdig SA64 .122 A4
  Pencaer SA64 . . . . .11 B2
Troed-y-Rhiw SA7 . . . . . . .161 F6
Troed-y-Rhiw Rd SA14 . . . .71 E2
Troedyrynys SA33 . . . . .58 F3
Troserch Rd / Heol
  Trosserch SA14 . . . . .142 B2
Trostre Ind Pk SA14 . . . . .149 A3
Trostre Rd
  Llanelli SA14, SA15 . . . . . .148 F3
  Llanelli SA15 . . . . .148 F4
Tro Tircoed SA4 . . . . .152 C4
Tudno Pl SA5 . . . . .160 A5
Tudor Cl SA71 . . . . .133 C3
Tudor Ct Bishopston SA3 . .172 A6
  Llandeilo SA4 . . . . .97 D1
Tudor Gdns SA61 . . . . .125 A4
Tudor Merchants House (NT)
  The* SA70 . . . . .135 F4
Tudor Pl SA42 . . . . .86 B5
Tudor Rd SA5 . . . . .160 B5
Tudor St SA9 . . . . .139 E7
Tudor Way
  Bishopston SA3 . . . . .172 B7
  Haverfordwest / Hwlffordd
  SA70 .135 C5
Tunnel Rd SA15 . . . . .148 E5
Twll La SA67 . . . . .70 F1
Twopenny Hay Cl ⊕
  SA71 .133 D4
Twyn Bedw Rd SA6 . . . . . .154 D7
Twyniago SA4 . . . . .143 D4
Twyn Teg SA2 . . . . .165 E8
Twynrefail Pl SA18 . . . . . . .99 D6
Twyn-yr-Ysgol SA9 . . . . . .139 B7

Ty = house

Ty Beddoe SA1 . . . . .168 B7
Ty Caitlin ⑤ SA1 . . . . .174 A3

Ty Canol National Nature
  Reserve* SA41 . . . . .33 C8
Ty-coch Maisonettes
  SA2 . . . . .166 D7
Tycoch Rd SA2 . . . . .166 D7
Tycroes Rd / Heol Tycroes
  Ammanford / Rhydaman
  SA18 . . . . .98 A5
  Tycroes SA18 . . . . .97 F5
Ty Cydwel ⑩ SA15 . . . . . .148 D4
Ty Dewi Sant SA5 . . . . . . .159 E3
Ty-Draw Cres SA1 . . . . . . .161 B2
Ty-Draw Pl SA1 . . . . .161 B2
Ty-Draw Rd SA1 . . . . .161 C2
Ty Elizabeth ⑥ SA15 . . . .148 D4
Ty Fforest ③ SA6 . . . . .154 A1
Ty Florence Asher SA6 . .146 E1
Ty Gwyn SA4 . . . . .158 C5
Tygwyn Rd SA6 . . . . .154 E7
Ty Hermon SA6 . . . . .160 E5
Ty Horeb SA6 . . . . .153 F1
Ty Howard ⑦ SA15 . . . . . .148 D4
Tyisha Rd Llanelli SA15 . .148 E4
  Llannon SA14 . . . . .96 C3
Tyisha Terr / Teras Tyisha
  SA15 .148 E8
Tyle Catherine SA15 . . . . .109 E3
Tyle Glas SA18 . . . . .99 C7
Tyle Teg
  Burry Port SA16 . . . . .137 F3
  Clydach SA6 . . . . .154 C7
Ty-mawr SA4 . . . . .147 E4
Tymawr St SA1 . . . . .167 B6
Ty Meriel ⑧ SA15 . . . . . . .148 D4
Ty-myrtwydd SA4 . . . . . . .157 E8
Tynewydd Terr SA14 . . . . . .97 B8
Ty'n-y-Bonau Rd SA4 . . . .143 C5
Tyn-y-Cae SA4 . . . . .147 F3
Ty-n-y-Cae Rd SA1 . . . . . .161 D7
Ty'n-y-Pant Rd SA8 . . . . . .147 C5
Tyn-y-Waun Rd SA4 . . . . .161 C6
Ty'r Felin SA5 . . . . .159 F6
Ty'r Fran SA1 . . . . .155 A2
Ty'rfran Ave SA1 . . . . .148 E2
Ty Rhiannon SA2 . . . . .166 E5
Tyrisha Ave SA4 . . . . .151 C6
Tyrisha Ct SA4 . . . . .151 C6
Ty'r Maes SA15 . . . . .159 F6
Tyrwaun SA15 . . . . .109 D4
Ty Sivertsen SA1 . . . . .167 B6
Ty Stafford ⑨ SA15 . . . . .148 D4
Tywi Ave SA20 . . . . .121 C5

U

Ullswater Cres SA6 . . . . . .160 E7
Underhill La SA3 . . . . .117 B4
Under Par Rd SA31 . . . . . .129 A5
Under the Hills SA61 . . . .124 E2
Union Bldgs SA15 . . . . . . .148 D7
Union Hill SA61 . . . . .125 B4
Union St
  ⑪ Ammanford / Rhydaman
  SA18 . . . . .98 C7
  Swansea / Abertawe SA1 . .174 A2
United Counties
  Showground* SA31 . . . . . . .75 A5
University of Wales Lampeter
  / Prifysgol Cymru Llanbedr
  Pont Steffan SA48 . . . . . .120 D5
University of Wales /
  Prifysgol Cymru SA31 . . .75 A4
Univ of Wales Swansea /
  Prifysgol Cymru Abertawe
  SA2 . . . . .166 D4
Uplands
  Gowerton / Tre-gwyr SA4 .158 B5
  Gwaun-Cae-Gurwen SA18 . .99 D5
Uplands Cres SA2 . . . . . . .166 F6
Uplands Rd SA8 . . . . .147 D4
Uplands Terr
  Swansea / Abertawe,
  Graig Trewyddfa SA6 . . . . .160 F8
  Swansea / Abertawe, Uplands
  SA2 . . . . .166 F6
Upper Banks Sta* SA1 . . .161 A4
Upper Church Pk SA3 . . .173 B4
Upper Colbren Rd SA18 . . .99 D6
Upper Cross Rd SA15 . . . .148 F5
Upper Fforest Way
  Llansamlet SA6 . . . . .154 B1
  Swansea / Abertawe SA6 . .161 B8
Upper Frog St SA70 . . . . . .135 E5
Upper Gendros Cres
  SA5 . . . . .160 A3
Upper Heathfield Rd
  SA8 . . . . .147 E6
Upper Hill St SA73 . . . . . . .131 B2
Upper Inkerman St ⑨
  SA15 .148 D5
Upper King's Head Rd
  SA5 . . . . .159 F4
Upper La SA68 . . . . .105 D7
Upper Lamphey Rd
  SA71 .133 E4
Upper Mill SA15 . . . . .148 E6
Upper Mill Rd SA4 . . . . . . .143 D4
Upper Mkt St SA1 . . . . . . .125 A4
Upper Mwldan ④ SA43 . .118 D4
Upper Park St SA15 . . . . .148 D5
Upper Pk Rd SA70 . . . . . . .135 E4
Upper Robinson St ⊕
  SA15 .148 D5
Upper Row SA71 . . . . .133 C6
Upper Station Rd / Heol
  Uchaf Yr Orsaf ⑨ SA18 . .99 B8

Upper St Mary's St ⑤
  SA42 . . . . .13 E4
Upper Strand SA1 . . . . . . .174 B5
Upper Terr SA42 . . . . .50 F8
Upper Thornton SA73 . . . .131 C7
Upper William St ⑪
  SA15 .148 E5
Upper W St SA42 . . . . .133 E4
Upton Castle* SA72 . . . . . .105 B7
Upton Castle Gdns*
  SA72 .105 A7
Upton Terr SA1 . . . . .168 A7
Usk Pl SA6 . . . . .154 A5
Uwch Gwendraeth ③
  SA14 . . . . .96 E8
Uzmaston Rd SA61 . . . . . .125 C4

V

Vale Ct SA1 . . . . .160 E3
Valence Wlk ⑪ SA71 . . . .133 C6
Vale Of Wern Terr SA1 . .168 B7
Vale Rd Burton SA73 . . . . . .87 D2
  Llanstadwell SA73 . . . . . . .131 E2
Valley Cl SA69 . . . . .134 A4
Valley Rd
  Llawhaden SA67 . . . . .70 C1
  Pentlepoir SA69 . . . . .134 C4
Valley View SA2 . . . . .166 B5
Valley Way SA4 . . . . .161 A6
Vanderhoot Way SA69 . . .134 A4
Vanewood Ct SA3 . . . . .173 C3
Vardre Rd SA6 . . . . .154 E8
Varteg Rd SA9 . . . . .139 B5
Vaughan Pl SA4 . . . . .150 E1
Vaughan St SA15 . . . . .148 D5
Vauxhall Rd SA1 . . . . .148 D5
Vawers Cl SA61 . . . . .124 F5
Vaynor Rd SA73 . . . . .131 D3
Velfrey Rd SA37 . . . . .126 B1
Venables Cl SA1 . . . . .159 D2
Vennaway La SA3 . . . . .171 D7
Venns Cl SA61 . . . . .124 E4
Vensland SA3 . . . . .172 A6
Verandah St SA1 . . . . .174 A3
Vera Rd SA6 . . . . .154 E8
Vergam Terr SA65 . . . . . . .122 C4
Verig St SA5 . . . . .160 C3
Vernon Cl SA4 . . . . .152 A5
Vernon St SA1 . . . . .160 D1
Veron St SA1 . . . . .174 B5
Versil Terr SA1 . . . . .157 F8
Vetch Cl SA71 . . . . .133 C4
Vetch Field (Swansea City
  Fball Gd) SA1 . . . . .174 A2
Vicarage Cl SA17 . . . . .93 F5
Vicarage Dr SA8 . . . . .147 F6
Vicarage Field SA71 . . . . .133 D4
Vicarage Fields SA70 . . . .105 F1
Vicarage La
  Kidwelly / Cydweli SA17 . .136 B3
  Swansea / Abertawe SA5 . .160 A2
Vicarage Rd
  Llangadog SA19 . . . . .63 D7
  Swansea / Abertawe SA6 . .160 E8
Vicarage Rd / Heol Ficeroi ⑦
  SA18 . . . . .99 B8
Vicarage Terr SA1 . . . . . . .174 C3
Vicary Cres SA73 . . . . .131 E2
Vicary St SA73 . . . . .131 E2
Victoria Ave
  Fishguard / Abergwaun
  SA65 .122 C4
  Swansea / Abertawe SA1 . .167 A5
  The Mumbles / Mwmbwls
  SA3 . . . . .173 A5
Victoria Cres SA20 . . . . . .121 D5
Victoria Ct SA3 . . . . .172 D4
Victoria Pl SA61 . . . . .125 C5
Victoria Quay SA1 . . . . . . .174 B2
Victoria Rd
  Gowerton / Tre-gwyr SA4 .158 B7
  Llanwrtyd Wells LD5 . . . . . .9 C1
  Milford Haven / Aberdaugleddau
  SA73 .131 C3
  Pembroke Dock / Doc Penfro
  SA72 .132 A2
  Pen-clawdd SA4 . . . . .156 E3
  Pont Henri SA15 . . . . .95 E4
  Swansea / Abertawe SA1 . .167 A5
  Waunarlwydd SA5 . . . . . . .158 C2
Victoria Row SA4 . . . . .156 E4
Victoria St
  Laugharne SA33 . . . . .92 F5
  Llandovery / Llanymddyfri
  SA20 .121 D5
  Swansea / Abertawe SA2 . .166 F7
  Tenby / Dinbych-y-pysgod
  SA70 .135 E4
Victoria Terr
  Lampeter / Llanbedr Pont Steffan
  SA48 .120 C4
  Swansea / Abertawe SA1 . .167 A5
Vicwr Rd SA6 . . . . .154 D7
Viking Way SA1 . . . . .161 D6
Village La SA3 . . . . .173 B4
Villas Eynon SA67 . . . . .90 B5
Villa Terr SA1 . . . . .160 C5
Villiers Rd / Ffordd Villiers
  SA18 . . . . .98 B6
Villiers St SA1 . . . . .167 A6
Villiers St SA1 . . . . .160 D1
Vincent St SA1 . . . . .167 B6
Vine Rd SA62 . . . . .86 E5
Vine Row SA9 . . . . .139 A6
Vineyard Vale SA69 . . . . . .134 B4

Vivian Ct SA2 . . . . .166 D7
Vivian Dr SA73 . . . . .131 B2
Vivian Ho SA3 . . . . .166 B2
Vivian Mans SA2 . . . . .166 D7
Vivian Rd SA2 . . . . .166 D7
Vivians Row SA1 . . . . .153 D4
Vivian St SA1 . . . . .160 D2
Voylart Cl SA2 . . . . .165 C8
Voylart Rd SA2 . . . . .165 C8

W

Wade Ave SA9 . . . . .139 B6
Waldhof Ct SA5 . . . . .159 E7
Wallace Rd SA1 . . . . .167 F7
Wallaston Cross SA71 . . . .103 D4
Wallis St SA65 . . . . .122 C4
Wallsfield La ④ SA70 . . . .135 E5
Walnut Cl SA3 . . . . .172 E7
Walter Rd SA1 . . . . .167 B6
Walter Rd / Ffordd Walter ⑨
  SA18 . . . . .98 C7
Walter's Ave SA61 . . . . . . .125 A2
Walter's Cres SA3 . . . . .173 A5
Walters La SA3 . . . . .114 C2
Walters Rd
  Cwmllynfell SA9 . . . . .100 B7
  Llangadog SA19 . . . . .63 D7
  Llansamlet SA7 . . . . .154 E1
  Swansea / Abertawe SA7 . .161 D8
Walter's Rd SA15 . . . . .148 E4
Walters Row SA2 . . . . .165 C8
Walters St SA5 . . . . .160 C3
Waltham Cl SA6 . . . . .160 D7
Walton Hill SA62 . . . . .85 C7
Walton Rd SA62 . . . . .85 D8
Warborough Cl SA15 . . . .148 C2
Warborough Rd SA15 . . . .148 C2
Warlow's Mdw SA70 . . . . .105 F1
Warren Cl SA71 . . . . .148 E7
Warren St SA70 . . . . .135 E5
Warrior Way
  Milford Haven / Aberdaugleddau
  SA73 .131 F5
  Pembroke Dock / Doc Penfro
  SA72 .132 E3
Warwick Pl SA3 . . . . .173 A8
Warwick Rd
  Milford Haven / Aberdaugleddau
  SA73 .131 D2
  Swansea / Abertawe SA2 . .166 B4
Washington St SA1 . . . . . .160 D3
Water La
  Llanstadwell SA73 . . . . .87 A2
  Llansteffan SA33 . . . . .93 E5
  Swansea / Abertawe SA1 . .174 C4
Waterloo Ind Est SA72 . . .132 E3
Waterloo Pl SA1 . . . . .166 F5
Waterloo Rd
  Milford Haven / Aberdaugleddau
  SA73 .131 A3
  Pembroke Dock / Doc Penfro
  SA72 .132 D4
Waterloo Rd / Heol Waterloo
  SA14, SA18 . . . . .97 D7
Waterloo St
  Llandovery / Llanymddyfri
  SA20 .121 D4
  Llanelli SA15 . . . . .148 D4
Waterloo Terr SA31 . . . . .128 F5
Waterloo Terr / Teras
  Waterloo SA18 . . . . .97 D6
Water St
  Carmarthen / Caerfyrddin
  SA31 .128 C5
  Ferryside SA17 . . . . .93 F5
  Gwaun-Cae-Gurwen SA18 . .99 D6
  Kidwelly / Cydweli SA17 . .136 B5
  ⑪ Laugharne SA33 . . . . . . .92 E5
  Llandovery / Llanymddyfri
  SA20 .121 C4
  Llanelli SA15 . . . . .148 D6
  ⑪ Narberth / Arberth
  SA67 . . . . .70 D1
Newcastle Emlyn / Castell
  Newydd Emlyn SA38 . . . . .119 D4
  Neyland SA73 . . . . .132 B7
  Pontarddulais SA4 . . . . . . .143 B4
  Pontardulais SA4 . . . . .143 C4
Waterston Rd SA73 . . . . . .103 F8
Waterwynch La SA70 . . . .135 E7
Watery La SA71 . . . . .133 A3
Watkin St SA1 . . . . .174 A4
Waunarlwydd Prim Sch
  SA5 . . . . .158 D3
Waunarlwydd Rd SA2,
  SA5 . . . . .159 D2
Waun Burgess SA31 . . . . .128 C5
Waun Cl SA4 . . . . .157 F8
Waun Deri SA16 . . . . .137 B3
Waun Dr SA6 . . . . .154 D8
Wauneos Rd SA15 . . . . . . .109 F4
Waunfarlais Rd
  Ammanford / Rhydaman
  SA18 . . . . .98 A8
  Llandybie SA18 . . . . .79 B1
Waunfawr SA18 . . . . .98 A7
Waun Giach SA43 . . . . .16 B7
Waun Gron SA8 . . . . .147 D6
Waun-Gron Cl SA5 . . . . . .160 C6
Waungron Rd SA6 . . . . . . .154 D8
Waun-Gron Rd SA5 . . . . . .160 C6
Waun Gron Rd / Ffordd
  Waun Gron SA18 . . . . .98 A8
Waunhafog Rd SA18 . . . . . .98 A8
Waunhwyad La ⑪ SA18 . . .80 A1
Waun Isaf SA62 . . . . .123 A4
Waunlanyrafon SA15 . . . .148 D5

Waun Las SA65 ....30 F5
Waunleision SA1 ....99 D7
Waun Penlan SA8 ......147 D7
Waun Rd Llanelli SA15 ...148 E7
Loughor SA4 ....157 F8
Morriston / Treforris SA6 ..154 A2
Swansea / Abertawe SA6 ..153 F2
Waun Sidan SA16 ......108 F4
Waun Wen SA4 ....147 D7
Waun Wen Prim Sch
SA1 ....160 C2
Waun-Wen Rd SA1 .....174 A5
Waun Terr SA11 ....160 C1
Waun Y Felin SA4 ......157 A4
Waun-y-Pistyll SA5 .....160 A3
Wavell Cres SA73 ......133 A8
Waverley Dr SA3 ....173 A5
Waverley St SA6 ....154 D7
Waverly Cl SA6 ....154 E8
Waverly Pk SA6 ....154 F8
Wda Ind Est SA16 .....137 F2
Weavers Ho 7 SA1 .....174 C2
Weavers Mill SA1 ......160 C4
Webbons Way SA1 .....159 F2
Weig Fach La SA5 ......159 D3
Weig Gdns SA5 ....160 A4
Weig La SA5 ....159 F3
Weig Rd SA5 ....159 F3
Welcome La SA1 ....174 B3
Wellfield SA3 ....171 F6
Well Field SA2 ....165 E8
Wellfield Cl SA4 ....151 B1
Wellfield Rd SA31 ......128 F6
Wellhead La SA62 ......87 E4
Well Hill SA71 ....133 C4
Wellington Gdns SA73 ..131 B2
Wellington Rd SA73 ....131 B2
Wellington St
Pembroke Dock / Doc Penfro
SA72 ....132 B2
Swansea / Abertawe SA1 .174 A2
Well La SA61 ....125 B7
Wellpark SA3 ....114 C2
Well Rd SA73 ....103 E8
Well St SA44 ....19 E4
Welsh Bird of Prey Ctr*
SA43 ....16 D5
Welsh Mus of Public Road
Transport* SA1 ......161 A4
Welsh Rd SA62 ....66 C6
Welsh Wildlife Ctr The*
SA43 ....118 F2
Wembley Gdns SA33 ...127 E4
Wembley Way SA9 .....139 A6
Wentworth Cres SA3 ...165 E1
Weobley Castle* SA3 ..115 B3
Weobley Ct SA5 ....159 F6
Wern Cres SA10 ....162 E5
Wern-ddu Rd SA18 ....79 D1
Wern-Ddu Rd / Ffordd
Wern-Ddu SA18 ......98 D8
Wern Fawr Rd SA1 ....148 B1
Wernolau Rd SA18 .....98 D7
Wern Rd Glanaman SA18 .99 B8
Goodwick / Wdig SA64 ..122 A5
Llanelli SA15 ....148 E5
Llanmorlais SA4 ....156 C1
Neath / Castell-Nedd
SA10 ....162 E7
Swansea / Abertawe SA1 .160 D4
Ystalyfera SA9 ....139 B6
Wern Terr
Ammanford / Rhydaman
SA18 ....98 D6
Swansea / Abertawe SA1 .168 C7
Wernwood Rd SA9 .....139 B6
Wesley Cl 1 SA67 .....90 B2
Wesley Ct SA2 ....92 B3
Wesley Rd 3 SA3 ......31 B3
Wesley Rd SA62 ....85 C7
Westaway Dr SA73 ....131 A2
Westaway Pk SA73 ....87 A3
Westbourne Gr SA2 ...166 C7
Westbourne Pl SA3 ....173 B4
Westbourne Rd SA2 ...166 C7
Westbury Bglws SA15 ..148 E3
Westbury La SA1 ......167 A6
Westbury St
Llanelli SA15 ....148 E3
Swansea / Abertawe SA1 .167 A6
Westcliff SA3 ....173 C3
West Cliff SA3 ....171 A3
Westcliff Mews SA3 ....173 C3
Westcross Ave SA3 ....173 A4
Westcross La SA3 .....172 F7
West Crossways SA8 ...147 D6
West Ct SA61 ....124 D5
Westdale Rd SA5 ......159 D7
West End Llanelli SA15 .148 C6
Pen-clawdd SA4 ....156 D4
Western Cl SA3 ....173 A4
Western La SA3 ....173 A4
Western Rd Clydach SA6 .154 C6
Pontardawe SA8 ......147 D4
Western St SA1 ....167 B6
Western Terr SA1 .....160 D3
Western Way SA72 ....132 C3
Westerton Ct SA67 ....90 B5
Westfa SA1 ....141 A1
Westfa Rd SA2 ....166 F7
Westfield Ct SA70 ....105 E6
Westfield Dr
Milford Haven / Aberdaugleddau
SA73 ....131 E4
Neyland SA73 ....132 B8
Westfield Pill Nature
Reserve* SA73 ....87 B1
Westfield Rd

Saundersfoot SA69 .....134 E3
Westfield Rd continued
Waunarlwydd SA1 .....158 D4
Westgate Hill SA71 ....133 B5
West Gr La SA71 ......104 A4
Westgrove Ct SA4 .....151 B4
Westhaven SA72 ......104 F6
West Hill SA73 ....105 A3
Westhill Ave SA73 .....131 D4
West Hill Cres SA17 ...136 A4
West Hook Rd SA62 ...87 C6
West La Camrose SA62 .67 A6
Castlemartin SA71 .....111 A6
Cosheston SA72 ....133 F8
Llanstadwell SA73 .....89 C7
Neyland SA73 ....132 A7
Nolton & Roch SA62 ...66 D5
Templeton SA67 ....89 C7
West La Cl SA62 ......67 B6
Westland Ave SA3 ....172 C7
Westland Cl SA4 ......150 E1
Westmead SA33 ......92 A3
Westlan La SA67 ......88 B5
West Perimeter Rd
SA73 ....103 D8
Westport Ave SA2 ....166 A2
West St
Fishguard / Abergwaun
SA65 ....122 D4
Gorseinon SA4 ....151 B1
Newport / Trefdraeth SA42 .13 D3
Pembroke / Penfro SA71 .133 B4
Rosemarket SA73 .....87 A3
Whitland / Hendy-Gwyn
SA34 ....126 C3
West Wales Arts Ctr*
SA65 ....122 D4
West Wales Eco Ctr*
SA73 ....13 D2
West Wales General Hosp
SA31 ....129 D7
Westward Cl SA2 .....166 A1
West Way / Ffordd Y
Gorllewin SA1 ....174 A2
Westwinds SA3 ....172 E3
Westwood Cl SA5 .....158 E3
Wheatfield Terr SA1 ...174 A5
Wheatsheaf Dr SA6 ...154 A4
Wheeler's Way
Manorbier SA70 ....113 D6
4 Pembroke / Penfro
SA71 ....133 C3
White City Rd SA5 ....159 D4
Whiteford Bay L Pk
SA3 ....114 C4
Whiteford Rd SA5 .....159 F6
Whitegates SA2 ......166 A1
White Gr SA3 ....172 E2
Whitehall Ave SA71 ...133 B6
Whitehall Dr SA7 .....133 B6
White Lion St 8 SA70 ..135 E5
Whites Farm Way SA72 .132 A3
Whiteshell Dr SA3 .....172 E4
White St SA1 ....167 B7
Whitestone Ave SA3 ..172 A5
Whitestone Cl SA3 ....172 F8
Whitestone La SA3 ....172 E5
Whitestone Prim Sch
SA3 ....172 E7
Whitestone Rd SA3 ...172 A5
Whitethorn Cl SA5 ....159 F5
Whitethorn Pl SA2 ....166 B6
White Walls SA1 ......174 B2
Whitland Abbey* SA34 .126 C6
Whitland Cl SA5 ......159 F6
Whitland Sta SA34 ...126 C2
Whitley Rd SA4 ....150 F1
Whitlow SA69 ....134 E4
Whittington Terr SA4 ..151 D2
Wilks Row SA1 ....174 A4
William Bowen Cl SA4 .158 A5
William Ct SA1 ....174 A2
William Dennis Ave
SA4 ....158 A8
Williams Ct SA1 ......70 C2
Williamson St SA71 ...133 B4
Williams Row 2 SA43 .118 D4
Williams St SA4 ......143 C4
William St
Cardigan / Aberteifi SA43 .118 D4
Pontardawe SA8 ......147 B1
Swansea / Abertawe SA1 .174 A2
The Mumbles / Y Mwmbwls
SA3 ....173 A5
Williams Terr 2 SA43 ..118 E4
Williams' Terr SA16 ...137 E3
Williston La SA3 ......173 A4
Willow Bank SA4 .....158 D3
Willowbrook Gdns SA5 .165 F1
Willows Pl SA1 ....174 A3
Willows The SA15 ....148 C2
Wilson Mdw 2 SA62 ..85 D8
Wimble Wood Cl SA3 .173 A7
Wimmerfield Ave SA2 .165 E7
Wimmerfield Cl SA2 ..165 E7
Wimmerfield Cres SA2 .165 E7
Wimmerfield Dr SA2 ..165 F7
Winch Cres SA61 .....125 A4
Winch La SA61 ....125 A4
Winch Wen Ind Est SA1 .161 C6
Windermere Rd SA6 ..160 E7
Windmill La SA1 ......103 E1
Windmill Terr SA1 ....174 C4

Wind Rd SA9 ....139 D7
Windsor Ct 3 SA1 ....174 A3
Windsor Pl SA1 ......173 B5
Windsor Rd
Pembroke / Penfro SA71 .133 C5
Stackpole SA71 ....111 E3
Windsor St SA2 ......166 F7
Windsor Terr SA4 ....151 D2
Windsor Way SA61 ...125 B4
Wind St
Llanfihangel-ar-Arth SA44 .19 E3
Swansea / Abertawe SA1 .174 B2
Wind St / Stryd-y-Gwynt
SA18 ....98 B7
Windyhall SA65 ......122 C5
Windy Ridge SA70 ...106 A1
Winifred Rd SA10 ....162 F7
Winston St SA1 ......174 A4
Wiston St 2 SA61 ....133 C6
Withybush General Hosp
SA61 ....125 B7
Withybush Rd
Haverfordwest / Hwlffordd
SA62 ....125 B8
Withybush SA62 ......68 B5
Withybush Trad Est SA62 .68 A5
Withy Pk SA3 ....173 A4
Wogan Rd 1 SA71 ...133 C5
Wogan St SA33 ......127 D3
Wogan Terr SA69 ....134 F3
Woodbine Cl SA71 ...133 C5
Woodbine Terr SA71 .133 B5
Woodbine Way SA73 ..85 F1
Woodbrook Terr SA16 .137 F2
Woodcote Dr SA3 ....173 B6
Woodcote SA2 ....165 D6
Woodcote Gn SA4 ...151 C7
Woodend Rd SA15 ...148 E6
Woodfield Ave
Kilgetty / Begelli SA68 ...89 F2
Llandybie SA18 ....79 A2
Pontlliw SA4 ....152 A5
Woodfield Gr SA72 ...104 F7
Woodfield Rd SA18 ...79 A1
Woodfield St SA6 ....160 F8
Woodfield Terr SA18 ..98 D7
Woodford La SA67 ...70 B2
Woodford Rd SA5 ....159 E7
Wood Hill SA62 ......66 C8
Woodholm Cl SA62 ...68 B4
Woodland Av SA3 ....132 B8
Woodland Cl
Llanddowror SA33 ....92 A3
Neath / Castell-Nedd
SA10 ....162 F7
Woodland Cres SA3 ..131 E3
Woodland Ct SA2 ....166 A6
Woodland Dr SA3 ....131 E3
Woodland Pk
Llanstadwell SA73 ....132 A6
Ynystawe SA6 ....154 B5
Woodland Rd SA10 ...162 E8
Woodland Rd / Heol Tir Y
Coed SA9 ....100 C5
Woodlands SA3 ......158 C5
Woodlands Ave SA4 ..154 F8
Woodlands Bsns Pk
SA9 ....139 D7
Woodlands Pk
Ammanford / Rhydaman
SA18 ....98 C6
Haverfordwest / Hwlffordd
SA61 ....124 F2
Nolton & Roch SA62 ...67 A8
Woodlands Rd SA4 ...150 F1
Woodland St SA8 ....147 F5
Woodlands Terr
Cross Hands SA14 ....97 B7
Swansea / Abertawe SA2 .165 E6
Woodlands View 1 SA4 .158 D4
Woodmans Terr SA9 ..139 B6
Woodside Ave
Pembroke / Penfro SA71 .133 B5
Swansea / Abertawe SA2 .165 E6
Woodside Cl
Bishopston SA3 ......172 A5
Swansea / Abertawe SA2 .165 E6
Woodside Cres SA6 ..154 C8
Wood's Row SA31 ...128 F5
Woodview SA4 ....158 D4
Woodview Pl SA5 ....159 E6
Woodville Rd SA3 ....173 A4
Woodville St SA4 ....143 C5
Woollacott Dr SA3 ...172 D5
Woollacott Mews SA3 .172 C7
Worcester Ct SA1 ....161 C7
Worcester Dr SA1 ....161 C7
Worcester Pl SA1 ....174 B3
Worcester Rd SA3 ...173 B4
Wordsworth Ave SA61 .125 A3
Wordsworth St SA1 ..124 A4
Works Rd SA8 ....147 F5
Wrench Cl 1 SA71 ...133 C3
Wychtree St SA6 ....161 A7
Wychwood Cl SA3 ...173 A6
Wy Cli SA1 ....161 B3
Wyndham Cl SA4 ....143 C4
Wyndham Ct SA6 ....161 C8
Wyndham St SA4 ....143 C4
Wyngarth SA1 ....161 D5
Wynter Ct SA4 ....160 C6

Yalton SA3 ....172 F7
Y
Y Bannen / Banwen Pl
SA18 ....99 D8
Y Berllan Dunvant SA2 .165 D7
Swansea / Abertawe SA6 .153 C2
Ystradgynlais SA9 ....139 C3
Y Bwthyn Llanelli SA15 .148 E4
Maenclochog SA66 ...53 A8
Y Clos Cwmllynfell SA9 .100 B7
Llanelli SA15 ....149 A5
Y Crofft SA17 ....94 B3
Y Cyswllt SA4 ....152 C5
Y Dderwen Maes SA42 .12 F3
Y Ddwyberth SA16 ...137 E3
Y Derwydd SA16 .....137 D2
Ydgol Gruffydd Jones /
Griffith Jones Prim Sch
SA33 ....127 F5
Y Dolau SA3 ....153 C2
Y Drim SA15 ....95 F3
Yevtree Cl SA3 ......172 F8
Y-fan SA14 ....149 C5
Y Felin Mill* SA43 ...118 B3
Y Fron Cefneithin SA14 .97 A8
Llanelli SA15 ....140 F1
Y Gaer SA14 ....149 A8
Y Garn SA41 ....152 A2
Y Garreg Llwyd SA4 ..97 D2
Y Gefnen SA7 ....161 F6
Y Gerddi Gdn Suburbs
SA17 ....109 C7
Y Gilfach SA9 ....139 B7
Y Gilwern SA9 ....139 B6
Y Glyn Cefneithin SA14 .97 A8
Y Goedlan SA9 ......165 D7
Y Gorlan SA9 ....100 C6
Y Gorlan SA42 ......165 C2
Y Gorsedd 7 SA18 ..98 B7
Y Gribin SA3 ....48 D3
Y Gwernydd SA7 ....154 F6
Y Llan SA14 ....141 A2
Y Llanerch SA4 .....152 A7
Y Llwyn SA15 ....149 A5
Y Llwyn SA14 ....153 C2
Yniscedwyn Rd SA9 ..139 C3
Ynisderw Rd SA8 ....147 E4
Ynysallan Rd SA6 ...154 B4
Ynyscedwyn Ind Est
SA9 ....139 B8
Ynys-Cedwyn Lodge
SA9 ....139 D7
Ynys Ct SA6 ....161 B7
Ynys Dawel SA62 ...48 C3
Ynysderw Ho SA8 ...147 E4
Ynys-Las SA14 ......149 C5
Ynys Newydd Rd SA2,
SA7 ....154 E7
Ynystawe Prim Sch SA6 .154 C3
Ynyswen SA14 ......149 A8
Ynyswerdd SA4 .....152 B2
Ynys Y Cwm Rd SA15 .148 C7
Ynysydarren Rd SA9 ..139 B6
Ynys-y-gwial SA9 ...138 F5
Ynys-y-Mond Rd
Glais SA7 ....155 B7
Pontardawe SA8 .....147 E2
Ynys Y Plant SA3 ...173 A7
York Ct SA1 ....174 B2
Yorke Cl SA73 ......131 C2
Yorke St SA73 ......131 C2
York St SA1 ....174 B2
Yr Allt SA14 ....142 B1
Yr Aran SA2 ....158 D1
Yr Elain SA2 ....165 D8
Yr Hafod Cefneithin SA14 .97 A8
Swansea / Abertawe SA6 .153 F2
Y Rhodfa SA16 ......137 F3
Yr-rhos SA43 ....118 F5
Y Rhos SA15 ....148 F7
Y Rhos SA14 ....13 A3

Ysgol Cwmbach SA34 ...56 A4
Ysgol Cynlais Prim Sch
SA9 ....138 F2
Ysgol Cynwyl Elfed SA33 .58 A6
Ysgol Dewi Sant / St David's
Cty Sec Sch SA62 ....123 E5
Ysgol Dolafon LD5 ....9 C1
Ysgol Drefach SA14 ...96 E8
Ysgol Dyffryn Taf SA34 .126 C3
Ysgol Esgob Gore / Bishop
Gore Sch SA2 ....166 C6
Ysgol Fabanod Prendergast /
Prendergast Infants Sch
SA61 ....125 C6
Ysgol Glandwr SA34 ..55 A7
Ysgol Golwg-y-Mor / Sea
View Com Prim Sch
SA1 ....174 A3
Ysgol Grynradd Parcyrhun
SA18 ....98 B6
Ysgol Gyfun Bryn Tawe
SA5 ....160 A6
Ysgol Gyfun Cwmtawe /
Cwmtawe Comp Sch
SA8 ....147 E3
Ysgol Gyfun Dyffryn Teifi
SA44 ....19 C3
Ysgol Gyfun Emlyn
SA38 ....37 E3
Ysgol Gyfun Gatholig Sant
Ioan Llwyd / St John Lloyd
RC Comp Sch SA14 ...149 B6
Ysgol Gyfun Gwyr SA4 .158 C5
Ysgol Gyfun Llanbedr Pont
Steffan / Lampeter Comp
Sch SA48 ....120 B4
Ysgol Gyfun Maes Yr Yrfa
SA14 ....97 A8
Ysgol Gyfun Pantycelyn
SA20 ....121 C5
Ysgol Gyfun Tre-gib
SA19 ....139 C6
Ysgol Gyfun Ystalyfera
SA9 ....139 C6
Ysgol Gyfun Y Strade
SA15 ....148 A6
Ysgol Gymraeg Brynsierfel
SA14 ....149 D5
Ysgol Gymraeg Cwmtwrch
SA9 ....138 F1
Ysgol Gymraeg Dewi Sant
SA14 ....148 F7
Ysgol Gymraeg Gwenllian
SA17 ....109 C7
Ysgol Gymraeg Pontybrenin
SA4 ....158 C5
Ysgol Gymraeg Teilo Sant
SA19 ....130 C6
Ysgol Gymraeg Ynysgedwyn
SA9 ....139 C3
Ysgol Gymraeg Y Wern
SA9 ....139 B6
Ysgol Gymunedol Eglwyswrw
/ Eglwyswrw CP Sch
SA41 ....15 B1
Ysgol Gynradd Alltwalis /
Alltwalis Prim Sch SA32 .39 B2
Ysgol Gynradd Bethlehem
SA19 ....63 B4
Ysgol Gynradd Blaenau
SA19 ....97 F8
Ysgol Gynradd Brynsaron /
Brynsaron Prim Sch
SA44 ....38 B7
Ysgol Gynradd Bynea /
Bynea Prim Sch SA14 .149 F3
Ysgol Gynradd Crymlyn /
Crymlyn Prim Sch
SA10 ....162 C12
Ysgol Gynradd Ffairfach
SA19 ....130 C4
Ysgol Gynradd Gorslas
SA14 ....97 B8
Ysgol Gynradd Gymraeg
Bryniago SA4 ....143 D2
Ysgol Gynradd Gymraeg
Bryn-y-mor SA2 .....166 C5
Ysgol Gynradd Gymraeg
Draddodiadol Rhiwfawr
SA9 ....100 B5
Ysgol Gynradd Gymraeg
Draddodiadol Trebannws
SA8 ....147 C2
Ysgol Gynradd Gymraeg
Draddodiadol Cwmllynfell
SA9 ....100 B7
Ysgol Gynradd Gymraeg
Draddodiadol Cwmgors
SA18 ....99 D5
Ysgol Gynradd Gymraeg
Draddodiadol Glyn SA18 .99 D8
Ysgol Gynradd Gymraeg
Felindre SA5 ....144 F2
Ysgol Gynradd Gymraeg
Garnswllt SA18 .....98 B3
Ysgol Gynradd Gymraeg
Gellionnen SA6 .....154 E8
Ysgol Gynradd Gymraeg
Gwaun Cae Gurwen
SA18 ....99 D7
Ysgol Gynradd Gymraeg
Llwynderw SA2 .....166 C6
Ysgol Gynradd Gymraeg
Lonlas SA7 ....161 D8

Ysgol Gynradd Gymraeg
  Pontardawe SA8 ...... **147** E6
Ysgol Gynradd Gymraeg Y
  Login Fach SA5 .... **158** F3
Ysgol Gynradd Llandeilo /
  Llandeilo Prim Sch
  SA19 .... **130** D6
Ysgol Gynradd Llanedi
  SA4 .... **97** D2
Ysgol Gynradd Llanwrda /
  Llanwrda Prim Sch
  SA19 .... **43** D2
Ysgol Gynradd Llechryd
  SA43 .... **16** C6
Ysgol Gynradd Llechyfedach
  / Llechyfedach CP Sch
  SA14 .... **96** F7
Ysgol Gynradd
  Mynyddygarreg SA17 ..**136** F7
Ysgol Gynradd New Inn /
  New Inn Prim Sch SA39 .**39** E8
Ysgol Gynradd Parc
  Waundew / Richmond Pk
  CP Sch SA31 .... **129** A6

Ysgol Gynradd Saron
  SA18 .... **97** E6
Ysgol Gynradd Stebonheath
  / Stebonheath Prim Sch
  SA15 .... **148** F5
Ysgol Gynradd Trallwn /
  Trallwn Prim Sch SA7 ..**161** E7
Ysgol Gynradd Treforys /
  Morriston Prim Sch
  SA6 .... **161** A8
Ysgol Gynradd Tregroes /
  Tregroes Cty Prim Sch
  SA44 .... **19** D7
Ysgol Gynradd Trewen
  SA38 .... **119** A8
Ysgol Gynradd Tycroes
  SA18 .... **97** F5
Ysgol Gynradd Wr Tremoilet
  / Tremoilet VCP Sch
  SA33 .... **91** D4
Ysgol Gynradd y Crwys /
  Crwys Prim Sch SA4 ...**157** E1
Ysgol Gynradd Y Sir
  Pontybrenin / Pontybrenin
  Prim Sch SA4 .... **151** B1
Ysgol Gynradd Ystradowen
  SA9 .... **100** C7

Ysgol Gynrad Llandudoch
  SA43 .... **118** B4
Ysgol Hafodwenog SA33 ..**36** C1
Ysgol Hayscastle SA62 ...**50** B5
Ysgol Heol Goffa SA15 ..**148** E7
Ysgol Llanarthne SA32 ...**77** D7
Ysgol Llanboidy SA34 ...**55** C2
Ysgol Llanddarog SA32 ...**77** B3
Ysgol Llanfihangel-ar-arth
  SA39 .... **20** C2
Ysgol Llanllwni SA39 ....**20** F2
Ysgol Llanoni SA14 ......**96** F3
Ysgol Llanpumsaint SA33 .**58** F8
Ysgol Llansawel SA19 ....**42** B7
Ysgol Llansteffan SA33 ..**93** E5
Ysgol Llanwenog SA40 ...**21** A8
Ysgol Maenclochog
  SA66 .... **53** B6
Ysgol Myddfai SA20 .....**44** D1
Ysgol Mynyddcerrig
  SA15 .... **96** B8
Ysgol Nantgaredig SA32 ..**77** A8
Ysgol Penboyr SA44 .....**18** E1
Ysgol Peniel SA32 ....**59** A3
Ysgol Ponthenri SA15 ....**95** E4
Ysgol Pum Heol SA15 ...**109** F8

Ysgol Rhydcymerau
  SA19 .... **22** C2
Ysgol Rhydygors SA31 ..**128** C1
Ysgol Rhys Prichard / Rhys
  Prichard Sch SA20 .....**121** D5
Ysgol Rudolf Steiner
  Nant-y-cwm / Nant-y-cwm
  Steiner Sch SA66 ...... **53** D3
Ysgol St SA1 ....**168** B7
Ysgol Tasker Milward /
  Tasker Milward Sch
  SA61 ....**124** E4
Ysgol Trapp SA19 ....**79** E5
Ysgol Tymbl SA14 ....**96** E7
Ysgol Wirfoddol Abergwili
  SA31 ....**129** F7
Ysgol Wirfoddol Babanod /
  Tenby VC Inf Sch
  SA70 ....**135** D5
Ysgol Y Babanod SA14 ..**149** A8
Ysgol Y Dderwen SA31 ..**128** E6
Ysgol Y Ddwylan SA38 ..**119** D5
Ysgol Y Ferwig SA43 .....**3** C5
Ysgol Y Gwendraeth
  SA14 .... **96** E7
Ysgol Y Preseli SA41 ....**34** F4
Ysgol Yr Ynys SA14 ....**149** C4

Ysgubor Fach St SA1 ...**160** C2
Yspitty Rd SA14 ....**150** B3
Ystrad Cl **3** SA31 ....**128** C2
Ystrad Dr SA31 ....**128** D2
Ystrad Einon SA4 ....**151** B1
Ystradgynlais Workshops
  SA9 ....**139** E8
Ystrad Rd SA5 ....**159** B4
Ystwyth Pl SA6 ....**153** D1
Y Talar SA31 ....**129** A3
Y Waun SA14 ....**149** C6
Y Waun Fach SA6 ......**153** B2
Y Waun / Meadows The
  SA10 ....**162** E7
Y-Wern SA6 ....**153** B2

Z

Zammit Cres SA15 ......**149** A5
Zion Row SA15 ....**148** E6
Zion St **1** LD5 ....**9** C1
Zoar Rd SA9 ....**139** B6
Zouch St SA5 ....**160** C3